Communicating in Groups

Communicating in Groups

Building Relationships for Group Effectiveness

Third Edition

JOANN KEYTON
University of Kansas

New York ● Oxford
OXFORD UNIVERSITY PRESS
2006

Oxford University Press, Inc., publishes works that further Oxford University's
objective of excellence in research, scholarship, and education.

Oxford New York
Auckland Cape Town Dar es Salaam Hong Kong Karachi
Kuala Lumpur Madrid Melbourne Mexico City Nairobi
New Delhi Shanghai Taipei Toronto

With offices in
Argentina Austria Brazil Chile Czech Republic France Greece
Guatemala Hungary Italy Japan Poland Portugal Singapore
South Korea Switzerland Thailand Turkey Ukraine Vietnam

Copyright © 2006 by Oxford University Press, Inc.

Published by Oxford University Press, Inc.
198 Madison Avenue, New York, New York 10016
http://www.oup.com

Oxford is a registered trademark of Oxford University Press

Library of Congress Cataloging-in-Publication Data

Keyton, Joann.
    Communicating in groups: building relationships for group effectiveness / Joann
Keyton. – 3rd rev. ed.
        p.   cm.
    Previously published: New York : McGraw-Hill, c2002.
    Includes bibliographical references and index.
    ISBN 13: 978-0-19-51843-6 (alk. paper)
    ISBN 0-19-518343-6 (alk. paper)
        1. Communication in small groups.   2. Group decision making.   I. Title.

HM736.K49 2005
302.3'4 – dc22   2005047278

Printing number: 9 8 7 6 5 4 3 2 1

Printed in the United States of America
on acid-free paper

Brief Contents

Contents

5 Building Group Communication Competence 99

8 Assessing Decision Processes and Implementing Decisions 176

9 Managing Conflict in Groups 195

10 Providing Leadership in Groups 219

11   Managing Group Meetings   241

12   Making Observations and Giving Feedback   265

Preface

In order to understand what it means to communicate successfully in groups, students must develop both a foundation of communication skills and an understanding of the key elements critical to achieving group success. I wrote this book to provide a framework for learning these necessary skills in a way that emphasizes the uniqueness of each group and each individual within the group. Successful group communication starts with strong relationships. This text emphasizes the necessary skills in building and maintaining these relationships in order to make decisions and complete group tasks and activities—that is the essence of group work.

When we look at the dynamics of group communication, it is easy to see why it can be a challenging topic to teach. Experience in groups is what students need, yet this takes time. Until they get this experience, it is up to the teacher to provide them with the conceptual foundation and introduce them to the skills necessary for understanding and implementing successful group communication. This text will help with these teaching challenges.

I had three main goals in writing this text:

- **Accuracy** This book is the result of many years of facilitating, researching, and teaching group communication. It is important to teach our students skills that are based in research from both the field of communication and other related disciplines. This book places a clear emphasis on teaching skills first but also ensures that those skills are based on rigorous and current research.

- **Simulation of the group experience** To describe and explain group communication concepts, this book uses realistic examples to help students get inside what group work is really like. In addition to examples, I have provided dialogues of interacting groups so students can *watch* the group process unfold. Both types of examples will help students distinguish between effective and ineffective group communication practices, as well as help them identify the practices they wish to adopt to improve their group interaction.

- **A structured approach** I have defined group communication in terms of five key elements that can be used to evaluate group effectiveness. These elements—group size, interdependence of group members, group identity, group goals, and group structure—are introduced in Chapter 1 and integrated throughout the book in the boxed feature *Putting the Pieces*

Together. This framework allows students to place new information and skills development into a larger context.

Approach

The title of this book, *Communicating in Groups: Building Relationships for Group Effectiveness*, speaks to two fundamental components of group interaction: building relationships and group performance. In this text, students will discover the unique dynamics of group communication, the essential skills that lead to success, and the group roles, tasks, and processes that pave the way for effective group work. By examining groups from each of these viewpoints, students come to understand the dynamic capacity of each group and learn to treat each group as a unique communication opportunity. To be competent in group communication, as this text emphasizes, students must learn to identify each group situation as unique, assess what skills are needed, and effectively apply the appropriate skills and procedures. In essence, the goal of this text is to provide a toolbox from which students can draw in any group situation—whether planning a function with a social club on campus or participating in a task-oriented group project in an academic or business context. To start this process, students must first become aware of their own communication in groups and the ways in which it can be improved to enhance group dynamics. The emphasis here is on critical thinking, skills assessment, and practice.

Features

This book contains a number of features to enhance student learning:

- *Putting the Pieces Together* **boxes** The five core elements in defining a group are used as a structure for evaluating group effectiveness. The five elements are group size, interdependence of members, group identity, group goals, and group structure. These elements are introduced in Chapter 1 and integrated in every chapter as a special feature so that students become more aware of how communication inhibits or facilitates group success.
- **Skills grounded in a solid research base** The best advice for communicating in groups is drawn from group research and theory, which has identified the most effective processes and results for group interaction. Thus the skills presented and suggested in the text are research based. For example, Chapter 1 uses the characteristics of bona fide groups to situate a group within its larger context. Chapter 4 introduces the influence of participation, time, diversity, and technology on task activity, information drawn from current research in small group communication. Functional theory is used as a framework in Chapter 7 to evaluate decision-making procedures. And situational leadership is used in Chapter 10 to help

students identify and compare leadership styles and choose the most effective style for a particular group situation.

- **Extensive use of realistic examples** In addition to describing what is happening in groups through the use of extensive examples, this text provides transcripts of group dialogues so students can see the communication process unfold. Group dialogues also provide an opportunity to suggest and test different communication approaches. Using the dialogue examples in this way can help students analyze how the group's conversation might have proceeded differently if alternative communication strategies were employed.

- **A wide range of group types** The text speaks to students' experiences by providing information about a wide variety of groups, including family and social groups, work teams and high-performance task groups, civic and community groups, and discussion and decision-making groups. Whether students' experiences are with groups that are formal or informal, personal or professional, task oriented or relationally oriented, they need communication skills to build and maintain relationships that support effective problem solving and decision making.

- **Two types of pedagogical boxes emphasizing skills development**
  - *Mastering Groups Skills*: This boxed feature provides students with the opportunity to use an assessment technique to determine the influence of their own communication style on the eventual success or failure of the group. This feature is designed to help students understand their stake in and responsibility for group effectiveness.
  - *Skill Builder*: Integrated throughout the text, these boxes give students an opportunity to test, develop, and practice their group communication skills through exercises and activities.

- **Other in-text learning aids**
  - Group skills previews: At the beginning of each chapter, there is an overview for students about which skills they will be learning and practicing in the chapter.
  - End-of-chapter summaries and discussion questions and exercises.
  - Glossary.
  - Extensive list of references for further study.

Revision Highlights

This third edition has a number of revisions to benefit students:

- **Updated research** The literature has been thoroughly updated, drawing upon recent communication and interdisciplinary group theory and research.

- **Focus on relational and task dimensions of groups** The text emphasizes that all groups—decision-making and social—have both relational and task dimensions, and their members communicate both relational and task messages. A new section has been added to Chapter 2 to introduce both types of messages to students.

- **Diversity** Material from the second edition chapter on gender and cultural diversity has been blended into each chapter where appropriate to emphasize the need for students to consider the multiple ways in which diversity influences group interaction.

- **Communication structures** Chapter 3 includes discussion of the way in which communication networks, conversational coherence, group member roles, and group norms provide structure for groups.

- **Group tasks and activities** The coverage of group tasks in Chapter 4 has been simplified and expanded to demonstrate the ways in which groups accomplish a variety of task and relational activities. This chapter has also been revised to include the influences of the degree of participation, time, diversity, and technology on group activities.

- **Communication competence** Chapter 5 has been reframed to include the characteristics of the ideal group member.

- **Decision making** Chapter 7 has been revised to include summaries of the task as well as, relational, and procedural skills required for decision-making activity. Chapter 8 has been revised to include material on information bias.

- *Putting It All Together* A short section has been added after Chapter 12 to provide two cases studies, so students can test their ideas about the ways relationship building, decision making, conflict management, and leadership are simultaneously at play in group interaction.

Organization

To provide a foundation, Chapters 1–5 describe basic communication concepts as they apply to groups or teams. By increasing their abilities to effectively send and receive messages—which, in turn, create the group's structure—students accomplish the first step in achieving more effective group participation. Chapters 6–10 address building relationships, decision making, problem solving, conflict management, and leadership—both as interaction opportunities and interaction problems that are a regular and dynamic aspect of group interaction. Increasing students' skills in these areas will help them maximize their group interaction efforts.

Despite the extensive research on group interaction, there is no blueprint for group success. What works in one group situation may fail in another. Thus Chapters 11–12 cover meeting management, facilitation skills, and techniques for providing feedback to the group. Whether in the role of leader or member, students should be able to facilitate their group's interaction to help the group stay or get back on track. Armed with specific principles, procedures, and feedback techniques, students can make more informed choices about how to help their group.

Instructors' Resources

To assist in teaching with this text, I have updated the *Instructor's Manual.* This manual includes the teaching philosophy that was a foundation for this book, syllabus examples for the group communication course, methods of obtaining feedback from students about the course and their learning experiences and expectations, chapter-by-chapter teaching resources and exercises, a chapter-by-chapter test bank with both objective and essay questions, and suggestions for term-long group projects.

The companion website (www.oup.com/us/keyton) has additional information for both instructors and students. Instructors can access PowerPoint presentations and the *Instructor's Manual*, review recent contributions to group communication literature, and find links to other resources for teaching the course. The student section contains individual chapter objectives, practice tests, flashcards, and a glossary review. Students will also find links to groups portrayed in the media, as well as to the type of groups in which they regularly participate. The website is regularly updated with new features and content.

Acknowledgments

Perhaps you find it odd that a book about group communication is written by a single author. I can simply tell you that's not the case. Four groups supported me and helped me see this book through to completion. My first "group" of supporters never came together face to face; they existed as a group only in my head. Nonetheless, this group provided the foundation for how I think and feel about group communication. Paying off a debt is difficult. But I would like to think that I've done so partially by completing this book. Many ideas presented in this book originated in my classroom experiences with Steven C. Rhodes, Western Michigan University, and Victor D. Wall, then of The Ohio State University. I owe my love of groups to these two men. Before Steve and Vic, however, two others generously mentored me: my high school journalism teacher, Ron Clemons, who initiated the spark of learning and writing; and my boss at the Federal Reserve Bank of Kansas City, Nick Santoro, who recognized my analytical ability and provided me with opportunities well beyond my level of education and experience. Thank you. Although these men have never had a face-to-face conversation, they have met many times as a virtual group in my head, providing me with guidance through some difficult writing days.

As with the previous editions, thanks also to my life helpers faye smith and Jeff Solomon. Their friendship, support, and encouragement are most meaningful.

Third, I was fortunate enough to have a group of excellent reviewers for the previous editions who pointed out problems, identified difficulties with examples, and so on. I applaud the following scholars for helping me: Carolyn M. Anderson, University of Akron; Dale E. Brashers, University of Illinois; John O. Burtis, Kansas State University; Elizabeth M. Goering, Indiana University–Purdue University Indianapolis; Michael E. Holmes, University of Utah; Michele H. Jackson, Florida State University; Bohn D. Lattin, University of Portland; Michael E. Mayer, Arizona State University; Mary B. McPherson, Boise State University; Renée A. Meyers, University of Wisconsin, Milwaukee; Marshall Scott Poole, Texas A&M University; Barbara Eakins Reed, Wright State University; and Matthew W. Seeger, Wayne State University. Reviewers who assisted with this third edition include Laurie Arliss, Ithaca College; Marybeth Callison, University of Georgia; Randy Hirokawa, University of Iowa; Virginia Kidd, University of Minnesota; M. Sean Limon, Illinois State University; Vanessa Sandoval, Chandler-Gilbert Community College; Kristi Schaller, University of Hawaii at Manoa; Lyn M. Van Swal, Northwestern University; Nick Trujillo, California State University; and Clay Warren, George Washington University.

And thanks to Sally for reminding me of the simple pleasures in life. We both miss Maggie.

Communicating in Groups

1

The Basics of Group Communication

GROUP SKILLS PREVIEW

In this chapter, you will learn to do the following:

- Name the characteristics essential for defining a group
- Describe the ways in which a group is interdependent with its context
- Recognize the ways in which members socially construct the group through their interactions
- Develop an understanding for thinking about a group as a process
- Explain ways in which group communication is complex and messy
- Explain why both task and relational communication are required in group interactions

As you embark on the study of group communication by reading this book and taking this course, you are entering both familiar and uncharted territory. The focus of your study will be familiar because you have been a member of many groups—groups of people with whom you live and play; with whom you work, or whom you manage or supervise; and with whom you celebrate life. Yet each group is a puzzle waiting to be solved.

Your Experience with Groups

You have always belonged to groups. You have lived and played in groups—your family, your classmates, sports teams, clubs, church groups. You have worked in groups, and you have socialized in groups. Some of your groups have focused on decision making and problem solving; others have focused on social activities or entertainment. Some of your memories may be positive: the committee that had fun decorating for the dance, or the ecology club that earned recognition for cleaning up trails in the park. Other groups may have been more negative: the family event that ended with everyone frustrated and angry, or the civics classroom group that couldn't present its project because certain members didn't do their part.

Regardless of how you evaluated the outcomes, in each group or team, members created relationships and interdependencies among themselves to accomplish some task or activity. This book examines groups in the broadest terms, looking at how members use communication to address relational issues in groups and teams, for example, creating relationships among members, developing and maintaining cohesiveness among members, and managing conflict. This book also looks at how members use communication to address task issues in groups and teams, for example, leading groups, facilitating decision making, and implementing decisions. The book is designed to help you reflect upon your previous group experiences and reconsider some of your attitudes and ideas. It will also help you improve existing group skills and develop new ones.

One group is never exactly like another. You can't predict other group members' behavior, nor can you control how other members will react to you. Thus, as a member of a group, you are always entering uncharted territory. Regardless of the many factors that may be the same from one group to the next, just one significant difference creates a new and unique group experience.

For example, consider a group of coworkers who effectively solve problems on the job and decide to get together for a relaxed dinner at one member's home. When everyone arrives, the team's leader takes over, organizing and directing the group's social activities. She may think she's merely doing her part, but the other group members are both offended and astonished that she feels a need to manage the group in this social setting. Back at work, the harmony of the group is now disrupted as previously effective task and social roles are confused. Or consider some neighbors who walk their dogs together every morning and who then form a book club. They now have to decide when and where to meet and how to select a book every month. Their previously harmonious interactions are disrupted by conflicting expectations, desires, tastes, and styles. An obvious solution may seem to be not to mix task and social groups. But in our complex society, we often find that relationships developed in one context extend to other settings; thus people in one part of our lives may show up as group members somewhere else.

You cannot avoid groups. Regardless of your experiences with and feelings about groups, it is unlikely that you will be able to avoid participating in them. In fact, our society is increasingly reliant on groups. Although individuality is emphasized in U.S. culture, we are expected to interact in groups as part of the social fabric of families and other living arrangements. The effective interaction of groups is the foundation of our government at the local, state, and federal level. Group structures are often the basis of the organizations on which we depend for economic survival, as well as for our goods and services. As you progress through organizational hierarchies, you'll both participate in and manage groups. In fact, the more professional responsibility you have, the less you will work on your own and the more you will interact with or manage groups or teams. You will also participate in groups in your community as a member of a parent-teacher organization, the leader of a community choir, or as a board member of a nonprofit organization.

The objective of this book is to help you understand the groups or teams of which you are a member or for which you are responsible. By being able to analyze group activities, the interactions among members, and the environment in which a group operates, you will discover what's unique about a particular group and what are the most effective ways to participate in the group and help it accomplish its activities.

Figure 1.1 You may be good at some aspects of group communication but poor at others.

As Figure 1.1 illustrates, you may have certain kinds of group interaction knowledge and skills but be deficient in others. Several features in this book can help you improve your repertoire of group skills. To help you become more sensitive to the many factors that inhibit or facilitate group interaction, the book contains many *Mastering Group Skills* boxes that focus your attention on a specific group issue and gauge the effectiveness of your group experiences. Also interspersed throughout the book are brief stopping points called *Putting the Pieces Together* to help you quickly identify group problems that occur when five basic group principles are violated. (In this chapter, these group principles are introduced in the box "Laying Out the Pieces of the Puzzle.") As you encounter new material, you will see how it relates to these five basic group issues. In addition, *Skill Builder* exercises identify a critical group skill and provide some suggestions for building or developing that skill. At the end of each chapter is a set of questions to guide your reflections about your group experiences.

Groups are like individuals—no two are alike. The better equipped you are to analyze what is happening in and around the group, the more successful and satisfying your group experiences will be. To guide you through your investigation of group communication, this book is organized into four parts.

The first part—Chapters 1–5—describes basic communication concepts as they apply to groups or teams. By increasing your ability to send and receive messages effectively and to help a group develop its structure, you will have accomplished the first step to achieving more effective group participation. These chapters also explore the variety of tasks and activities that individuals engage in for both task and relational groups. Although it may seem obvious that group members must know what their task is and how to accomplish it, group members frequently assume they know what the group is supposed to do without getting verbal consensus or commitment from other group members. Learning to assess the group's task or activity will help you decide which interactive processes will be most productive for your group.

The second part of the book—Chapters 6–10—focuses on the communication processes among group members when they are building relationships, solving problems, making and implementing decisions, managing conflicts, and leading groups. Whether a group is task-oriented or relationally oriented, all groups must effectively manage these simultaneous processes.

Despite all the research on group interaction, there is no blueprint for group success. What works in one group situation fails in another. Moreover, what works at one point in time may not work later as relationships among group members mature or the group takes on different tasks or activities. Thus the third part of the book—Chapters 11 and 12—covers meeting management and facilitation skills, and discusses techniques for providing feedback to the group. Whether or not you are the leader of a group, if you recognize group interaction patterns and know how to help a group stay or get back on track, you will be a valuable group member. Thus it is important that you learn to analyze the group task, environment, members, and interaction. Armed with more than just a gut feeling, you will make better choices about which group skills to use.

There are no magic formulas for group interaction or set procedures that work in each group setting. Each group is different, so your approach to each group must differ as well. This book is a guide for your exploration of groups, based on theory and research studies. Theories from a range of disciplines including communication, counseling, management, psychology, and sociology provide frameworks that both describe and explain group interaction. From these theoretical foundations, we can identify the skills needed for effective and successful group interaction. By developing your group communication skills, you will be able to develop practical and viable solutions to the group interaction problems you encounter.

What Is a Group?

Through your experiences, you probably already have your own definition of a group. However, you may have overlooked a few of the critical elements that differentiate group communication from other communication contexts. So, although you may have great familiarity with groups, you may not be sure about the defining characteristics of a group. Are two people having dinner together a group? What about five people waiting for a bus on a street corner? or 50,000 fans in a football stadium? And what about your favorite chat room on the internet? How exactly is a group differentiated from other forms or contexts of interaction?

Characteristics for Defining a Group

Five characteristics are central to the definition of groups: group size, interdependence of members, group identity, group goal, and group structure. In addition to defining what a group is, these characteristics are a good place to start in understanding how members of a group interact effectively. These characteristics can help you isolate group interaction problems and understand why they develop. As you read in more detail about each of the characteristics, you will come to understand why a **group** is defined as three or more people who work together interdependently on an agreed-upon activity or goal. They identify themselves as members of the group, and they develop structure and roles, based on norms and rules, as they interact and work toward their goal.

Group Size One of the primary characteristics of a group is **group size**. The minimum number of members in a group is three; the maximum number depends on the other characteristics, discussed shortly. Early in the study of group interaction, many researchers examined **dyadic interaction**, or interaction between two people (a dyad). In the communication discipline, this form of interaction is labeled as interpersonal interaction.

The interaction of three people differs significantly from the interaction of two, because the introduction of the third person sets up the opportunity to form coalitions. As an example, **coalition formation** occurs when one member takes sides with another against a third member of the group. This type of 2-to-1 subgrouping creates an imbalance of power, one that can only occur when at least three group members are present. A coalition creates interaction dynamics that cannot occur with two people. Of course, once a group expands beyond three members, different types of coalitions can occur. Three members can contest the ideas of one member who refuses to be persuaded, or a group can break into multiple subgroups or coalitions, each promoting its own view.

Introducing a third group member also allows hidden communication to take place. These hidden interactions are often attempts to build alliances, which underscores the role of relationship building as groups work on tasks. For example, let's say that Nancy and Michelle meet on their way to a meeting; Jeff is waiting for them in the conference room. Nancy takes this opportunity to brief Michelle on the background of the project and to give her evaluation of her previous interactions with Jeff. Jeff does not have access to this hidden interaction, but Nancy's musings to Michelle will certainly affect the interaction among these group members. In this case, there was no strategic attempt to manipulate Jeff, but Nancy and Michelle's interaction still affected the group. Naturally, the larger the group, the more these hidden interactions are likely to occur.

The size of a group has an impact not only on how members interact with one another but also on how roles are assumed (or assigned) within the group and how interactions are regulated. On the one hand, it may be more difficult for members of larger groups to decide who takes what role because many members may have the skills necessary for various roles. Also, larger groups typically have more difficulty in scheduling time to interact. On the other hand, members of smaller groups may find that no one in the group possesses a critical skill or certain knowledge essential to the group's activity. You may be thinking that smaller groups are preferable because fewer interaction problems arise, but artificially limiting the size of the group forces more responsibility on each member. Thus group size is more appropriately fixed by the group's task or activity.

However, research has demonstrated that increased size can produce diminishing returns. In other words, bigger isn't always better (Bettenhausen, 1991; Hare, 1982; Wheelan & McKeage, 1993). Although the addition of group members can expand the pool of skills and talents from which to choose, it can also increase problems with coordination and motivation. There is a point at which groups become too large and members become dissatisfied, feel less group cohesion, and perceive less identification with the group. Why? The larger the group, the fewer opportunities each member has to talk, and as group size increases, what the group can achieve decreases because of the logistical problems in coordinating so many people. Thus increased group size affects group productivity because members have less opportunity to participate. Because of their size, large groups require more attention to group norms and group roles. Even more problematic is the fact that group members are more likely to accept the illusion that someone else is responsible for accomplishing the group's task and so fail to do their own part. As a result, there are greater demands on group leadership in large groups. But large groups can be effective—if the goal is clearly identified for all group members, if members share a consensus about the goal, and if they recognize and fulfill their roles.

Clearly, groups need to be the appropriate size to effectively complete the task or activity before them. Three members may be too few for a complex task or goal. When there are too few members and there is too much work to do, group members are likely to become frustrated, and even angry, about the task and toward the group. Relationships also are affected by group size. Twenty members are probably too many to deliberate on a problem and make recommendations in one written report. When group members feel as if they are not needed to produce the group's outcome, or if their individual efforts are not recognized, they become apathetic and feel distant from the group. This form of detachment is known as **social loafing** (Comer, 1995). Thus **social loafers** are group members who do not perform to their maximum level of potential contribution. Rather, they use the other group members as a shield they can hide behind and still reap the same benefits as other group members who work to make the group a success. The opportunity for social loafing increases as the size of the group increases.

While some groups and teams (juries, sports teams) have specific size limits or standards, other groups (work groups) can be designed with size in mind. For decision-making groups and other types of groups with well-defined tasks, research suggests that the optimum group size is five. Members of five-person groups generally are more satisfied with the experience and believe that they have adequate opportunities to talk in the group. Having too few members may make members feel pressured into talking; having too many members decreases the opportunity to participate. An odd number of members is also preferred for decision-making groups to avoid a deadlock. However, that standard is regularly challenged. It wouldn't make sense to have a five-member top management team if all of an organization's vice-presidents were not part of it. Likewise, it wouldn't make sense to restrict a support group to five members if others wanted to join and participate.

You can probably see that, although we identify the minimum number of members of a group, the maximum number depends on the other four characteristics. Rather than limiting group membership to some arbitrary number, we need to consider issues such as group goals, task complexity, and interaction opportunities to identify the appropriate number of group members.

Interdependence of Members   A second critical characteristic of a group is the interdependence of group members. **Interdependence** means that both group and individual outcomes are influenced by what other group members do (Brewer, 1995). Members must rely on and cooperate with one another to complete the group activity, because they are attempting to accomplish something that would be difficult or impossible for one individual to achieve. Through their interdependence, group members mutually influence one another.

For example, members of a softball team are a group. It's impossible to play effectively without a catcher, pitcher, and shortstop. Each member of the softball team fills a specific role that functions interdependently with those of other players. Moreover, how well one player fulfills his or her role affects how another player responds and fulfills his or her role. Even if the team has one outstanding hitter, the team will not win very often without members who specialize in defense. Not only do these team members have to fulfill their specialized roles and depend on one another, but they have to communicate with one another. It is not enough to identify the necessary roles and to assign members to them; individuals in these roles have to be actively engaged and interacting with one another.

As another example, consider a project team at a computer company that has been given the task of developing a new software program. This task can be seen as a **superordinate goal**—that is, a task or goal that is so complex, difficult, or time-consuming that it is beyond the capacity of one person. The team, however, brings together several people with a variety of strengths and skills. Team members are interdependent as they share ideas in the early stages of the project; later they can test various ideas with one another before engaging expensive resources. Such interdependence is likely to save their organization time, energy, effort, and money; it is also likely to create a better software program.

The communication within groups also illustrates the interdependence of group members. Let's look at a student group concerned about course and faculty evaluations. Jennetta asks the group to think of ways to improve the evaluation process. Her question prompts group members to respond with ideas that she writes on the board. When they finish, Jerome comments about one trend he sees in the list. Sara asks him to elaborate. As Jerome and Sara continue their conversation, Jennetta circles the ideas they are talking about and links them together while she gives affirming nods to indicate that they should continue. Pamela, who said very little during the idea generation process, now says, "But the ideas you are circling are ones we as students can do little about. What about working

Normally, when we think of groups, we think of formal work teams like those in organizations that make decisions and solve problems (top). Likewise, sports teams are groups that play together, usually under the direction of a group leader—the coach (bottom).

through student government to develop an independent evaluation process that could be published in the student newspaper? Student government set up its own book co-op in spite of opposition from the administration." Jennetta, Jerome, and Sara turn to Pamela expectantly. Their silence encourages Pamela to continue talking: "What I'm saying is that the ideas on the board are attempts to fix a system that is not under our control. So, why not develop an independent system that students control?" Jerome replies enthusiastically, "Great idea, Pam. . . . Do you mind if I call you Pam?"

Notice how the verbal and nonverbal messages in this group depend on one another to make sense. Jennetta first invites members' participation, and they all generate ideas. The list they generate motivates Jerome to make an analytical comment, which is further encouraged by Sara's question. Although Pamela initially says little, her action has an impact on other group members' communication by giving Jerome and Sara more opportunities to talk. Jennetta's nonverbal messages further contribute to Pamela's silence as she acknowledges Jerome and Sara, and not Pamela. Pamela's interjection into the conversation startles the others, and their conversation stops. Her acute observation reminds them that she has not been ignoring what's going on; rather, her assessment helps them see that they may be wasting their time.

In this example, the communication itself was interdependent. One statement can only make sense when it is placed before and after other strings of the conversation. Each individual in the group is influenced by what others say (and don't say). The group's success depends on the extent to which the verbal and nonverbal messages make sense together.

Group Identity   A third defining characteristic for a group is group identity. Group members must know and act as if they are members of this particular group. In essence, **group identity** means that individuals identify themselves with other group members and the group goal. Group identity is fully achieved when members behave as a group, believe they belong to a group, and come to like the group—both its members and its tasks (Henry, Arrow, & Carini, 1999). Without this type of identification, group focus and interdependence will weaken.

Unfortunately, many times people are identified as a group when they have little or no expectation that group interaction will occur. Such gatherings or collections of people are more appropriately called **groupings**. Throughout our lives, we are constantly identified by the groupings people assign to us. For example, I live in Kansas, I am female, and I have a Dalmatian. But these identifiers do not put me in groups where I interact and interdependently work on tasks and activities with other Kansans, women, or Dalmatian owners. These categories make it easier to identify who I am, but alone they do not create the opportunities for me to interact with others. At the same time, individuals may join particular groups because they want to be identified as members of the group (for example, a fraternity, sorority, or community chorus). But doing so will not result in group interaction opportunities unless the individuals are motivated to talk to others.

Remember that, just because individuals have some reason to be together or some surface connection seems to exist among them, group interaction may not occur. Simply being identified with others who share similar characteristics doesn't create a sense of groupness. However, when group members identify with one another and the group's goal, they adopt the norms and values of the group, increasing group members' motivations and abilities to work together effectively.

Group Goal Identity, then, is a necessary but not sufficient characteristic for a group. We also need a fourth characteristic: group goal. A **group goal** is an agreed-upon task or activity that the group is to complete or accomplish. This goal may be long term and process-oriented (such as a family functioning as a social and economic unit), or it may be short term with specific boundaries and parameters (for example, a church group holding a car wash to raise money). Regardless of the duration or type of goal, group members must agree on the group's goal to be effective (Larson & LaFasto, 1989). That does not mean that all group members have to like the goal, but it does mean that there is clarity on what the goal is and that it is perceived by members as being worthwhile.

Having a group goal gives the group direction and provides members with motivation for completing their tasks. A group's goal should be cooperative. This means that, as one member moves toward goal attainment, so do other group members. A group goal is cooperative when it integrates the self-interests of all group members. Groups that are having trouble have often lost sight of their goals—sometimes because of distractions and other times because of external forces (such as other people or a change in deadline or objectives). Groups that cannot identify why they exist and what they are trying to achieve are doomed to failure.

For example, as a student in the class for which you are reading this textbook, your goal is probably to get a good grade. But getting a good grade is your individual goal, not a group goal. Each student in the class may have the same goal, but it is not a shared, consensual goal that motivates interaction and activity. If it were, everything you did in preparation for class would be designed to help you, as well as other students, achieve the *good grade* goal. Thus agreement on a common goal among individuals, not similarity in individual goals, defines individuals as members of the same group. Group goals create cooperation whereas individual goals often create competition.

Group Structure The final defining characteristic of a group is its structure. Whether informal (a group of friends) or formal (a parent-teacher organization), some type of structure must develop. **Group structure** tends to develop along with, or to emerge from, group rules and **norms**—patterns of behavior that others come to expect and rely on. For example, Pat, Emily, Donna, and Greg meet for social activities every Friday night. If the group does not set plans for the next week, Pat takes it upon himself to call everyone to get suggestions. No one has appointed him to this role; he does it naturally in reaction to the other group members' lack of initiative. Pat has assumed the role of the group's social organizer, and the group has come to depend on him to play that role. His role playing has created a certain structure in the group, and that structure has become a norm.

In more formal settings, a group may elect someone to record what happens in the meetings as a way of tracking the group's progress and keeping an account of details. Again, the person taking on the recorder or secretary role is providing structure for the group, as well as behaving in a normative pattern. Thus both the recorder's actions and the record of the meeting provide structure for the group. Anytime a group member takes on a formal or informal role, group structure is created. Likewise, any discussion or outcome that provides direction for the group is considered group structure. Suppose your family decides to visit Disneyland on vacation. That decision creates structure for your future family discussions because now your interactions will center around the logistics of traveling to California and planning your vacation.

To be viable, groups must have some form of structure, but the structure does not have to remain constant throughout the life of the group. Much of a group's structure is provided by the **group roles**, or the functions group members assume through their interactions, and roles are not necessarily fixed. Formal roles—those filled through appointment, assignment, or election—are likely to be more permanent. Informal roles—functions that emerge spontaneously from the group's interaction (such as the group member who eases tension in the

Some families interact as groups, making decisions about weekend activities, planning vacations and holiday activities, and celebrating significant achievements of family members.

Laying Out the Pieces of the Puzzle

The five characteristics that define groups—group size, interdependence, group identity, group goal, and group structure—can provide a foundation for analyzing the effectiveness of a group. The following exercise will lead you through this analysis.

The Group and Its Interaction

Like most students assigned a group project, Gayle, Rebecca, Sean, Jim, and Sonya wait too long to begin work on their assignment. Now, pressed for time, each member has other obligations and, quite frankly, more pressing interests and motivations. Still, the group has to produce what the professor expected in order to receive 20 percent of their course grade. Meeting once to get organized, Rebecca, Sean, Jim, and Sonya each assume responsibility for one area of the project, and Gayle agrees to take responsibility for integrating these parts. The group gives itself 2 weeks before reconvening to turn in finished materials to Gayle, who will pull it all together before its oral presentation to the class. Due to the members' late start, there will be only a few days between the group's second meeting and the oral presentation, putting extreme pressure on Gayle to integrate the project's parts and get it back to the other members so they can perform effectively during the presentation. These members are juniors and seniors, and they have done this type of group project many times in the past. They know they can pull it off.

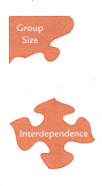

This group has five members. Deciding to separate responsibilities into four distinct parts and one integration role makes sense if there are four major parts of the topic or project to be researched. Or does it? What other factors might come into play? Does it make sense to have one person be responsible for integrating the results of the others' work?

The group decides to break up the task into distinct parts. This seems reasonable given their tight deadline. Or does it? As Sean completes his research, his findings might impact the research of others. What other interdependence issues might arise? Think about the lack of interdependence in coordinating the research and then forcing interdependence in the oral presentation. Is the class project a superordinate group goal? What supports your argument?

group)—will change as the talents of group members become apparent or are needed by others.

To summarize: We have defined a group as three or more people who work together interdependently on an agreed-upon activity or goal. They identify themselves as members of the group, and they develop structure and roles, based on norms and rules, as they interact and work toward their goal.

Due to the defining characteristics of groups, each group takes on a life of its own. Each is unique. What we as individuals bring to group interactions is a unique compilation of all our past group experiences, good and bad (McCanne, 1977). Your set of expectations resembles no one else's set of expectations, and members of the same group bring different expectations to the same group experience. As a result, we live in a world of constant ebb and flow of group interactions in our personal, social, and professional lives that overlap and affect one another.

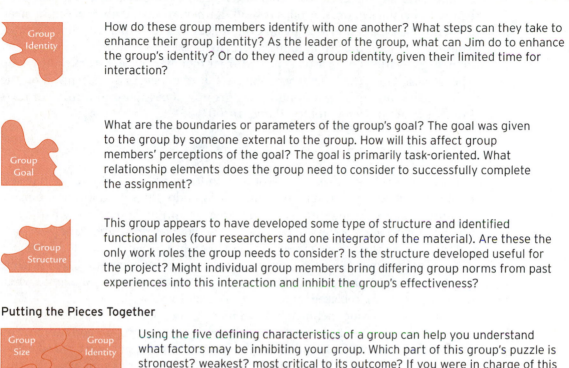

Group Identity How do these group members identify with one another? What steps can they take to enhance their group identity? As the leader of the group, what can Jim do to enhance the group's identity? Or do they need a group identity, given their limited time for interaction?

Group Goal What are the boundaries or parameters of the group's goal? The goal was given to the group by someone external to the group. How will this affect group members' perceptions of the goal? The goal is primarily task-oriented. What relationship elements does the group need to consider to successfully complete the assignment?

Group Structure This group appears to have developed some type of structure and identified functional roles (four researchers and one integrator of the material). Are these the only work roles the group needs to consider? Is the structure developed useful for the project? Might individual group members bring differing group norms from past experiences into this interaction and inhibit the group's effectiveness?

Putting the Pieces Together

Using the five defining characteristics of a group can help you understand what factors may be inhibiting your group. Which part of this group's puzzle is strongest? weakest? most critical to its outcome? If you were in charge of this group, which element would you work on first? Knowing, for example, that identity is weak in your group, you might want to suggest that group members spend some time getting to know one another before beginning work on the task. Or, if the group goal is not clear and agreed upon by everyone, it will be helpful to spend a few minutes talking specifically about what the group is trying to accomplish. When one or several of the defining characteristics are weak or missing, the sense of groupness may be too fragile for the individuals to function effectively as a group.

It is to our benefit to understand these interactions and influence them. Not only are our groups charged with completing tasks and activities: they also provide us with opportunities to develop and maintain relationships, to learn about ourselves, and to enhance our personal and professional skills. And all of this is accomplished through communication. "Laying Out the Pieces of the Puzzle" illustrates how the five elements that define groups can help you determine whether a group is effective.

A Group's Connection to Its Context

The five characteristics essential to defining a group do not, however, help us understand a group within its context. The **bona fide group perspective** illuminates the relationship of the group to its context or environment. For any group, members are not snatched from somewhere, leaving their ideas about groups or their memberships in other groups behind. Rather, group members are influenced by their existing and previous group experiences and the other members in these groups, the role of the group in members' lives, the way in which groups are set up by organizations or institutions, and what members expect from their group experiences. Thus, the bona fide group perspective focuses our attention on the reciprocities among group boundaries, group process, and multiple contexts (Putnam & Stohl, 1996; Stohl & Putnam, 2003).

Permeable and Fluid Boundaries

This perspective recognizes that group boundaries are generally stable but also permeable. In reality, a group's membership is seldom fixed. Additions are made to family groups through marriage, divorce, adoption, and death. Changes in organizational teams occur when employees leave the organization and new ones are hired. Even though we expect jury membership to remain stable, alternates are frequently required to step in when other jurors must be excused. Thus, while we often think of group membership as being static, it can be dynamic when group members are replaced, exchanged, added, or removed.

Thinking of group membership and its resulting boundaries in this way, it is easy to understand that groups are socially constructed through communication (Frey & Sunwolf, 2005). Let's look at two examples. First, juries are the size they are because legal authorities debated the issues and made recommendations that became state and federal law. However, being named to a jury isn't the defining feature. Rather, it's the interactions among jury members that moves them from being *a* jury to being *this* jury. In essence, the jury as a group emerges through the interactions of people assigned to that role and function. When these jury members reflect upon and describe their experiences to others, they will point to specific interactions and specific relationships among jury members that caused them to agree that that defendant was guilty. In a second example, family members may agree that Sandra is a member of the family even though she is not related to any member. Rather, she was your mother's best friend who now lives on her own. Your family includes her as a member, inviting her to all family functions because they appreciate Sandra's thoughtfulness and helpfulness during your mother's illness. To signify her relationship to your family, you've taken to calling her *Aunt* Sandra. Communication between your family members and Sandra established a connection that encouraged your family to identify Sandra as a part of it and encouraged Sandra to think of herself as a member of your family. Thus, group membership is perceived to be stable when you can identify who is in and who is not a member of the group. These identifications are made based upon who is communicating with whom and to what degree that interaction results in individuals identifying as being members of a particular group. That is, individuals negotiate their identity with a group as their interactions construct the group. Still, membership can change or be altered, permanently or temporarily.

A Group's Interdependence with Its Context

Despite identifying with any particular group, members participate in other groups. As a result, groups can interact with and influence one another. For example, if you are a member of many groups at work, you're likely to pass information from one group to another. Information gained in one group is taken—sometimes intentionally, sometimes unintentionally—to another group.

From the bona fide group perspective, a group is not a distinct entity with an environment that separates it from all other groups. Rather, groups are located within a fluid social context. The group is continually influenced by the environment in which it completes its tasks and by the social ties members have with other groups. The concepts of connectivity and embeddedness further explain how a group interacts with its larger social environment.

Connectivity is the degree to which several groups share overlapping tasks or goals. The more tightly coupled the groups, the more likely that change in one group will alter activities in others. For example, organizations are composed of many groups. A policy change developed and recommended by the human resources team is likely to affect the supervisory team. Although the groups have unique and specific goals, both groups function to meet the ultimate goal of producing the organization's products. When change occurs in one group, it is likely to affect the group to which it is most tightly connected.

Connectivity increases in complexity when individuals participate in multiple groups. For instance, as a student taking several classes in your major, it is likely that during any one term you are a member of several classroom groups. Although each group has unique membership and a goal specific to its particular course, you probably use the information learned in one group in another. This information transfer is possible due to group members' multiple group membership. Although information transfer is often viewed as a positive characteristic, it can be a negative when information learned in one group is used to the detriment of another. For example, Bryce is not thrilled to find himself in another group with Katerina. In their statistics group, Katerina comes unprepared and seldom contributes anything meaningful. When Bryce learns that both he and Katerina have been assigned to the same group in their persuasive campaigns class, he immediately tells other group members about Katerina's substandard performance.

Another factor that contributes to complexity is embeddedness. **Embeddedness** reflects the centrality of the group to its larger organizational structure. A group's position within the informal power structure or formal hierarchical structure affects its ability to obtain information and retain resources. Its position with respect to its environment also determines its degree of impact on the larger organization. For example, the student government group of your university is more deeply embedded within your university than any other student club or organization. Members of the student government have direct access to university officials; in fact, university officials may look to your student government as a primary source of student feedback and input. In contrast, a club such as Lambda Pi Eta (the communication students' honors organization) is affiliated with both the university and its national organization. To both the university and the national organization, the club is merely one student organization that competes with other organizations for attention and resources. Thus its level of embeddedness in either the university or the national organization is shallower. In the university system, the student government group deals with issues more relevant to the university than the local Lambda Pi Eta chapter. In the Lambda Pi Eta system, this one chapter is not likely to have more influence than any other local chapter.

When a group is characterized by high connectivity and high embeddedness, its boundaries are fluid. Information flows easily into and out of the group, making connections with other groups possible. Actually, it is the placement of a group within its environmental context that contributes to the challenges, conflicts, and stresses group members are likely to face (Lammers & Krikorian, 1997). The more connected and the more embedded the group, the more pressures and influences it faces. When a group becomes highly embedded and connected, it may be difficult to clearly identify the group's membership.

For example, think about your biology study group. You and four classmates meet every Thursday night to prepare for Friday's biology test. But your interactions with other group members are not limited to your Thursday night meetings. After biology class on Tuesday, you talk in the hallway about a problem that involves the use of a specific lab instrument. No one in the group is sure how to use the instrument. But another student, Tommy, overhears your conversation and offers to help. Because he is your instructor's lab assistant, Tommy is a reliable source of information. As the conversation about the lab instrument continues, Assaundra invites Tommy to join this Thursday night's study group. Getting nonverbal agreement from the group, Tommy says he will be there. Depending on how well the group interacts with Tommy, he may become a regular member, and not simply a visitor. Suppose group members come to like Tommy and value his contributions to the group, but by midsemester your own involvement with the group is growing problematic. In fact, each Thursday night you struggle to decide whether to meet with the group or to play in a basketball league with your fraternity. So, although Tommy regularly joins the group, your own attendance comes to depend on when basketball games are scheduled.

To clarify the concepts of flux and ambiguous boundaries, let's continue with the example. By the end of the semester, only two of the initial group members are left. Tommy comes regularly now. You seldom study with the group, but you could use an extra night of study before the final. You join the group for this last session, but you arrive late. To your amazement, almost half of the class is there, sitting in small subgroups going over different parts of the test material. Who is in this group? Who is not? What boundary separates this group from its environment?

Time and Space of Group Interaction

A part of a group's relationship to its context is the time and space of its interactions. Groups can have considerable histories or be of limited duration. While it is easy to think of groups that have short histories (for example, an emergency task force assigned to provide services for homeless persons during an extremely cold winter) and long histories (for example, a book club that was established by sorority sisters in college who continue to meet once a month for more than 20 years), not all group histories are this simplistic. For example, in my town, elections for city commissioners are held every 2 years, with three of the five commission seats up for reelection. If we measured the history of the city commission as a group, its duration would be 2 years. However, the two commissioners who receive the most votes are elected for 4-year terms, while the commissioner receiving the least votes is elected for only 2 years. Thus, some commissioners can have considerably more experience in the group than others. This effect becomes particularly pronounced when a commissioner wins reelection many times. As another example, think of the board of directors of your local United Way. This group has considerable influence in your community, making decisions about how money is raised and how nonprofit organizations are funded. Yet any individual board member serves only a 3-year term. In this case, the influence of the institution or organization enhances the credibility and visibility of the board members. Thus, group member influence can be enhanced by the organization sponsoring the group (Lammers & Krikorian, 1997).

Another influence of context on groups is the frequency and duration of its tasks and activities (Lammers & Krikorian, 1997). One breast cancer support group, whose members are over 65, has met every Monday night for 1 hour since 1989, while another group for younger women with breast cancer was established in 1999 and meets only once a month, but for 2 hours each meeting. The older women in the first group rely upon the companionship and social support of the group's members, as many are widowed. Their weekly meetings are highly social, with conversation turning to talk about vacations and grandchildren, not just methods of coping with their illness. The younger women, many of whom have children, meet less regularly but for a longer time so they can invite guest speakers to keep informed of the latest advances in breast cancer treatment and in order to minimize the need for babysitters. Thus, frequency, or how often a group meets, and duration, how long a group meets, depends on the context of the group, the needs of members, and the task or activity the group undertakes. In turn, the length of time group members interact and the time between those interactions will influence group member relationships and how group members construct their interactions to connect the meetings together.

Space is also a contextual influence on group interaction. An interdisciplinary medical team at a geriatric oncology center engaged in two different types of conversation in the same work setting (Ellingson, 2003). In their formal, patient-centered conversations, team members requested information and shared impressions of patients. In this case, the presence of patients in examination rooms and the requirements of their tasks necessitated task-oriented messages. But when there was time between patients, conversations were used to build relationships among team members by talking about outside interests, such as families and vacations. Team members also bonded by complaining about their work schedules, the overbooking of patients, and the behavior of other clinic staff. Both the task-oriented and relationship building conversations occurred in the same location—in the hallway and work space separate from the examination rooms. Although the space was the same, the presence of a patient in an examination room created a different perception of the context, and, as a result, required a different type of communication among team members.

Looking at groups from the bona fide group perspective, we are reminded that groups have permeable and fluid boundaries, are interdependent with their context, and are influenced by the time and space of their interactions. Most importantly, these characteristics exist because individuals construct any group and their identity in it through their interactions. If we were members of only one group at a time, then life would be simple and we could focus our attention on that group. But we are members of multiple groups, requiring that we negotiate multiple identities and manage many interaction relationships simultaneously.

As a result, individuals, as group members, can experience conflict because their multiple group memberships create conflicting group identities. Or individuals may experience different interaction patterns or interaction roles when new members join an existing group. Moreover, the entrance and interaction of a new or temporary member can even cause group membership to change. Because individuals are members of multiple groups, an individual can serve as an implicit or explicit boundary spanner, taking information from one group to another, with the potential of creating communication exchanges between or among groups. When relationships between or among groups become established through interaction they must coordinate or negotiate their actions and, at the same time, negotiate how they are different from one another. Thus, a member's sense of identity with a group, or sense of belonging, can shift, depending on the fluidity and permeability of the group's boundaries, the way in which the group is interdependent with its context, and the way in which group members use time and space to create a context for its interactions (Waldeck, Shepard, Teitelbaum, Farrar, & Seibold, 2002).

Interdependence of Task and Relational Dimensions

At this point, it should be obvious that a group is really a process. A group is not defined by its number of members, its effectiveness, or its type of task or activity. Although it is convenient to use the label *the group*, doing so masks the interactions between and among group members that create roles and relationships among group members that allow them to accomplish their mutual goal or activity—and that process is both complex and messy. For example, group members need to meet together in order to construct role relationships and generate group identity, but most groups seldom have all members meeting together for all interactions. Likewise, in any group or team, there are likely to be multiple goals at multiple levels—group, subgroup, and individual. Finally, all group interactions are not likely to be friendly or produce positive outcomes.

Despite our best efforts, groups are not always effective, fun, or productive. When a difficulty occurs, it is often a signal that a core group characteristic—

group size, interdependence of members, group identity, group goal, or group structure—is deficient, at risk, missing, or out of balance for that group's task or activity. That is, the group's size is too large or too small; group identity is too weak or too strong; interdependence of members is too loose or too strong; agreement and enactment of the group goal is under- or overemphasized; or the group structure is too rigid or too loose. Moreover, groups are not objects in containers. As the bona fide group perspective demonstrates, a group's relationship to its context is fluid and complex, which can create challenges for group members to address and resolve.

Part of this challenge is to balance the **task dimension**, or what a group does, with its **relational dimension**, or the social and emotional interactions of group members from which roles and relationships emerge. All groups have both task and relational dimensions. Groups with a strong task focus must also pay attention to the relationships that develop among group members, and even groups that are primarily social or relational have some task to perform. In these types of groups, the task may be as simple as members being there for one another, or it may be more specific, such as providing a place for members to explore their feelings. Regardless of a group's primary focus, both task and social dimensions are present, and they are inseparably interdependent (Fisher, 1971).

This two-dimensional aspect of groups is important because a group that concentrates solely on work without attending to its members' social or relational needs becomes boring and ineffective. Likewise, a group that focuses solely on having a good time can become tiresome if that social interaction does not lead to new information or provide opportunities to perform meaningful activities. The most effective groups are those that keep each of these dimensions in balance relative to their purposes and the needs of their members.

Satisfying Task and Relational Dimensions

Some groups form deliberately; others emerge from spontaneous interaction. When groups form deliberately (for example, work groups), someone decides that a collection of individuals should accomplish a purpose or goal. Most problem-solving or decision-making groups (such as city councils) and social action groups (for instance, Mothers Against Drunk Driving) are examples of deliberately formed groups—it would be impossible for fewer people to accomplish their goals.

Other groups form spontaneously. Generally, individuals come together in these groups because of the satisfaction they expect to gain from associating with one another. A group of friends at work is a good example of a spontaneous group. In these cases, group membership is by mutual consent—each member wants to be in the group, and each is accepted as a group member. Typically, these groups form when individuals communicate frequently and voluntarily with one another. Thus group membership is based on attraction.

If a group is deliberately formed, group member selection is key to its success. For example, a group of activists (such as the National Organization for

Women) needs members with the technical skills of recruiting new volunteers and seeking and obtaining funding. Members also need the relational skills of motivating members to continue to work on behalf of the organization and the ability to create a supportive environment for members. The challenge is to find the appropriate balance between the two sets of skills. The balance will vary depending on the type of group and its activities and goals.

A group deliberately formed for a short period of intense work on a complex project may prefer members with a balance favoring technical skills over relational skills. For example, the technical skills of a team of doctors, nurses, and medical technicians delivering sextuplets are more important to the success of the group's task than team members' interpersonal relations. The team works together for a very short time and then disbands. Roles and responsibilities within the team are highly defined, which helps the team work effectively in the absence of well-developed personal relationships.

In contrast, a team that expects to stay together for a long period may initially favor a balance toward personal and relational skills. This is because, over time, group members can help one another increase their technical proficiency if the relationships among group members are well developed. Let's say that a project team with members representing different operations of a food manufacturer is assigned to develop prototypes for new market initiatives. With representatives from manufacturing, marketing, quality control, and food sourcing, the new product development team has 6 months to develop at least four products for consumer testing. If members possess the ability to work well with one another, they can also rely on one another to help fill in the technical expertise they may lack as individuals.

For instance, Jerry, the representative from manufacturing, knows very little about marketing. Initially, he relies heavily on Shanita's marketing expertise. Jerry asks Shanita lots of questions, requests marketing reports to read, and talks with her over lunch about marketing initiatives that have worked for other products. As the team works on product development, Jerry learns enough about marketing from Shanita to give informed opinions and ask appropriate questions. This process is enhanced because Jerry finds it easy to approach Shanita, and Shanita appreciates Jerry's willingness to learn about marketing.

Most spontaneously formed groups favor relational over task skills. Because group membership is based primarily on individuals' personal attraction to one another, relational skills are more important. If group members cannot get along and form a cohesive group, attraction will decrease, and members will leave the group voluntarily. This does not mean that task skills are not important—merely that relational skills are more primary.

For example, Rea's golf foursome started over lunch when the four women discovered their common hesitance to take golf lessons. The decision first to take lessons together and then to practice together one day a week was a natural outgrowth of the women liking one another; forming the group was not based on anyone's technical skill in golf. As the group completes its lessons and starts to play on the golf course, members become confident enough to give one another friendly advice about selecting clubs, teeing up, and reading greens. However, if one member consistently gives poor advice or advice that detracts from another's ability to achieve par, this member's technical skill or motivation will come into question and may even disturb the relational balance of the group.

Simply put, group members will find it necessary to talk to one another to accomplish their task or activity. However, groups cannot accomplish their objectives only through task-related communication. Even if members try to constrain their messages to task issues, they are delivering implicit messages about relational issues in the group. A group is a social context, and social influence will occur whenever members are communicating. In whatever way the task and relational dimensions are balanced, the messages sent create the climate within which group members accomplish their tasks and activities (Keyton, 1999b).

Summary

Group communication is something that is both familiar to you and a bit confusing. You have always belonged to groups, so you have already developed attitudes and habits associated with working in groups. Although you may have lumped all of your group experiences together, each group is a unique experience. One group is never exactly like another. By analyzing group activities, engaging in reflection after group interaction, and assessing the environment in which groups operate, you will gain a better understanding of group interaction and optimize your group skills.

A group is defined as three or more individuals who identify themselves as a group and who can identify the activity of the group. Five characteristics define groups: group size, interdependence of members, group identity, group goal, and group structure. Using these defining characteristics as avenues of analysis can help us understand the uniqueness of each group and the complexity of group interaction.

The bona fide group perspective illuminates the relationship of the group to its context or environment. The perspective recognizes that group boundaries are generally stable, but also permeable and fluid when group members are replaced, exchanged, added, or removed. As a result, as group members communicate with one another they socially construct or negotiate the group's boundaries. This perspective also acknowledges that a group is not a distinct entity within an environment, but is connected to or embedded in other groups in a fluid social context. Finally, this perspective highlights the ways in which groups are influenced by the time and space of their interactions.

Obviously, it's more accurate to talk about a group as a process rather than defining a group by its number of members, its effectiveness, or its type of task or activity. The group interaction process is both complex and messy. Part of the challenge is to balance a group's task dimension, or what a group does, with its relational dimension, or the social and emotional interactions of group members from which roles and relationships emerge. All groups have both task and relational dimensions that should be balanced, based on the group's purpose and the needs of its members. Groups cannot accomplish their objectives only through task-related communication. A group is a social context, and social influence and messages about relational issues will occur whenever members are communicating.

Discussion Questions and Exercises

1. Think of a group to which you belonged in the past. Analyze it according to the five characteristics for defining groups.

2. Reflect on one of your childhood groups. Compare that experience with one of your adult group experiences. What has changed? What is similar? What do you believe accounts for the differences and similarities?

3. Think of some past classroom group projects. What characteristics made them interesting? What characteristics made them unbearable?

4. When groups are large, some members may think that their individual contributions won't be noticed and, as a result, decrease their level of activity in the group. When circumstances dictate that a group have many members, what strategies can group members use to control this type of social loafing?

5. Think back to a group to which you belonged that was primarily task-oriented. In what ways, or to what degree, did permeable and fluid boundaries, the group's interdependence with its context, or the time and space in which the group interacted influence the group's effectiveness or success? Do the same analysis for a group that was primarily relationally oriented. What are the similarities and differences in your assessments?

6. Review the table of contents for this book. Thinking about your current level of group skills, develop three lists: (a) group skills and knowledge that you have now, (b) group skills and knowledge that you'd like to learn, and (c) group skills and knowledge that you've mastered and could share with others.

2 Your Communication in Groups

GROUP SKILLS PREVIEW

In this chapter, you will learn to do the following:

- Use verbal symbols to clearly express yourself about group tasks and activities
- Use nonverbal symbols to build positive group relationships
- Explain how verbal and nonverbal symbols work together to form a complete message system
- Identify listening pitfalls and employ strategies to overcome them
- Provide examples of task communication appropriate for a group's task or activity
- Use relational communication to create connections with other group members
- Describe the interdependence of task and relational messages

Many disciplines study group process (for example, anthropology, counseling, management, psychology, and sociology), but communication researchers and consultants have a unique perspective on groups. Group process relies on interaction—both the verbal and nonverbal communication among members of the group. In some contexts, communication may also include written and electronic channels (such as with brainstorming or computer technology). Most researchers believe that communication is the medium through which individuals form a group because communication creates and sustains interdependency among group members. Groups cease to exist when interdependency and group identity are threatened by a lack of communication.

The study of groups originated in the field of social psychology, so many of the early studies examined individual behavior in groups. Later, social psychologists focused on the entirety of the group process, but they examined the perceptions of group members rather than group members' communication behavior. Researchers in counseling and management also study groups, but they are restricted in the types and contexts of groups they study. Anthropologists study groups in relation to their role in society or their impact on culture. Thus viewing group interaction from a communication perspective is a distinct and unique approach.

Communication scholars interested in groups traditionally have focused on task groups or decision-making groups, but any type of group can be studied from the communication perspective. A counseling group that provides support for those grieving the loss of a loved one is quite different from a committee planning a golf tournament as a community fundraiser. Some groups focus on relationships; others focus on tasks. But for each group to exist, communication must occur. What results from or is achieved in a group is a function of what is communicated (or not communicated) in that particular group environment and situation. Thus communication is central to what it means to be a member of a group.

Verbal Communication

Words are the lifeblood of group interaction. Even when we communicate nonverbally, we translate those behaviors into words (thoughts, impressions) as we construct meaning for the behaviors. Verbal communication, or what we say, can hold a group together or drive a wedge among members, hindering the accomplishment of goals. Because words are abstract and can act as symbols for different referents, meanings are not centrally located within words themselves. Rather, meaning is derived by the communicators (both sender and receiver) based on the communication context, previous experiences with the words, previous experiences with the other person, and even previous experiences with the task. Meaning is perceptually based and so is not predictable. For example, think of the word *group*. Before you encountered this book, you likely had a different definition of group than the one presented here.

Words and Meanings

Because verbal communication relies on language and because you have more receivers (and more potential errors) in group settings, you must choose your words carefully to communicate clearly. To be effective communicators, you should choose words that are specific and **concrete** in meaning rather than abstract. **Abstract** words paint broad generalizations whereas concrete words help the sender and receiver agree upon what was said. For example, in a group setting, "be on time" may mean that members will come when they think the meeting starts. In contrast, "the meeting starts at 2 P.M." is more precise and will generate questions about the starting time if group members have different ideas about when the meeting starts.

SKILL BUILDER

What Did You Say?

In your next group meeting, challenge yourself to use more concrete than abstract words or clichés. Each time you use an abstract word or phrase, immediately provide a more detailed description or explanation. For example, instead of simply saying "Sounds good," add "I agree with the plan you proposed" immediately after. Practice this skill in at least three meetings. Eventually, you will begin to automatically edit your verbal messages before you talk.

Moreover, some words or phrases can be specific and unique to the group because the group develops meaning for its own use. For example, "the report" to one specific group might mean no less than a 20-page detailed recommendation with an executive summary. Group members will come to use the shorthand "the report" to refer to this detail. Unless all group members mutually understand these details, the verbal message about "the report" is meaningless. See "What Did You Say?" for tips on how to avoid clichés and other abstractions.

Patterns of Language

Verbal messages can direct ("Let's have a moment of silence, please"), structure ("Harriet, you give your report first, then Rashad will talk about the budget"), or dominate ("Shut up!") the communication system within the group. When other group members respond to these direct verbal requests, interdependence is created among members, which can be observed in the pattern of language used in that group.

Naturally, the patterns of verbal messages that emerge and the relationships that follow differ among various types of groups (Ellis, 1979). For example, decision-making groups can develop messages that indicate symmetry, or equality, among members. When group members perceive themselves as equal to other group members, the discussion is more likely to reflect a spirit of inquiry and participation. But decision-making groups can also experience competitive messages as members compete for leadership and other group management roles. And members of support groups send different types of verbal messages. In this context, messages are almost exclusively symmetrical, providing a foundation for members to share their feelings.

To illustrate, examine the following two conversations:

Golf Fund-raising Committee

TYLER: Okay, let's get rolling.

NAOMI: I'd like to hear about what corporate sponsors we've got lined up.

TYLER: I think it would move us along quicker to see which golf courses are willing to donate green fees.

NAOMI: But I have to leave the meeting early, and I want to let everyone know about the sponsors.

Grief Support Group

DEBBIE: It's been a really hard week. I'm glad you're all here tonight.

KARL: Me, too. At least here, I can let all of the emotion just be, without having to explain myself.

AVERI: Do you want to begin, Debbie?

Notice how the verbal communication functions differently in these two conversations. In the first, communication directs and structures the activities of the group as Tyler and Naomi compete with each other about what should be first on the agenda. If this pattern of competitive messages continues, their relationship in the group will likely suffer. Certainly, their messages to each other will have to demonstrate more equality if they are to communicate effectively. In the second conversation, communication is less directive and more focused on building relationships. No one member is trying to dominate the group or its activity. Averi's comment to Debbie suggests structure for the group, but the request has a completely different tone than Naomi's.

Impact of Verbal Activity

Some group members talk more; some talk less. However, because it is difficult to hear more than one person talking at a time, it is important to note the person who does the most talking in a group. Differing amounts of **vocal activity**, or the amount of time a member talks in a group, can create different perceptions of group members (Daly, McCroskey, & Richmond, 1977). In general, group members are perceived as being credible and influential as they increase their level of vocal activity. However, if a group member talks too much or consumes all of the talking time in a group, perceptions of credibility decline and influence turns from positive to negative.

Vocal activity in a group is also noticed when there is silence—when no group member is talking. In a conversation between two people, we expect one person to talk until finished, and then the other person takes over. In a group, things are a bit more complicated. Often, there is no obvious way to decide who has the next talking turn. When silence occurs, two members may compete to talk next. This is not to say that the competition to talk is negative—members may be enthusiastic about joining the conversation.

Improving Verbal Communication Skills

Given the symbolic nature of communication and the number of interaction partners in groups, miscommunication can occur easily. Several techniques can help you be sensitive to misunderstandings that result from the verbal messages you send. Some group members may hesitate to ask questions or to seek clarification, so be sure to watch for nonverbal messages that indicate group members' need for further information. A member who has a puzzled look or who leans in as if to hear better likely did not receive your verbal message clearly. But also be sensitive to more subtle cues. A group member who is afraid to confront you directly might use the verbal strategy of changing the subject. Or group members might simply avert their gaze and act as if they are bored. Monitoring others' verbal and nonverbal messages can help you identify those instances in which your messages are not clear.

Another way to improve your verbal communication skills is to carefully consider the words you choose. Avoid words that can evoke strong emotions from other group members or that have negative connotations. For instance, labeling someone as a "flunky," "radical," or "do-gooder" can cause other group members to stop listening. Even said in a joking manner, words with strong emotional content distract from your verbal messages.

Linking your verbal messages to others' comments is another way to improve your verbal skills in a group. Linking shows that you are listening and are contributing to the group. Comments like "Another way of planning for the project is to . . ." and "I agree that students' evaluations of professors are important, but I wonder what professors think of them" indicate that you are focused on the group's task.

Finally, monitor how much you're talking in the group. Is your vocal activity equal to the quality of your contribution? Are you talking simply to hear yourself talk? Are you repeating the same message over and over? Your verbal messages will be better received by other group members if what you're saying is effectively presented and important to the group. Now consider the opposite scenario —you're hardly talking in the group. Your participation is minimal, and when you do speak, it's only to say "yes" and "okay." If this verbal pattern describes you, you need to enhance your group participation by elaborating on your comments. If you have trouble being assertive in a group, write some notes for yourself before the meeting. These can help you feel more confident and participate more.

Nonverbal Communication

Meaning can also be derived from how words are said or how behaviors are used to replace or substitute for verbal messages. This is known as **nonverbal communication**. Nonverbal communication occurs in many forms: through the tone and sound of your voice, your facial expressions and other body gestures, and your use of space, touch, time, and objects. Even when you are not talking in a group, you are communicating nonverbally. Sometimes you do so purposely— for example, looking at your watch and tapping at it to draw attention to the few minutes the group has left. Other times you are unaware of the nonverbal signals you are sending—for example, continuously lacing and unlacing your fingers or closing your eyes when your least favorite person is mentioned. Even when you do not mean to, you are sending powerful signals that others will interpret. Nonverbal communication can be described in terms of both its type and its functions in group interaction (Ketrow, 1999).

Types of Nonverbal Communication

One type of nonverbal communication, **vocalics**, or vocal characteristics, accompanies everything we say. Meaning can be derived from how we use our voices while we talk. Vocalics include inflection (upward as in asking a question, downward as in making a statement), tone (monotone, excited), accent (southern, eastern

Even though you may be unaware of your own nonverbal communication in a group, you are interpreting other members' nonverbal behaviors.

seaboard), rate (fast, slow), pitch (deep, nasal), volume (fast, slow), number of vocal interrupters ("aaaahhh," "well," "uh"), and quality of voice indicators (clear, scared).

Subtle (and not so subtle) cues—like irony and sarcasm—about intensity and emotion are given through vocalics. Dominant and high-status group members speak rapidly and use a loud and sure tone of voice whereas more submissive members use a passive tone and a slow rate of speech. Friendliness toward other group members can be demonstrated by warm voice qualities whereas unfriendliness comes through in irritable and sarcastic tones.

Facial expressions and other body movements such as gestures, posture, and eye behavior are referred to as **kinesics**. Gestures and body movements are often associated with leadership displays in groups. Eye contact is particularly important in group settings because it regulates who will talk next. When group members are willing to talk, they are more likely to look at the current speaker or at the leader or facilitator, signaling their intention to communicate. In contrast, members who want to avoid speaking might look away or down at their laps. Group members often use facial expressions to demonstrate their approval or disapproval of the topic being discussed or the person making the presentation.

Proxemics, or the use of space, is particularly important in group interactions because where group members sit relative to one another affects the flow of the conversation. Generally, group members who are dominant tend to position themselves more centrally in the group's space. This is why group leaders often sit at the end of a conference table. Members who want to participate more position themselves where they are visible to more group members and more likely to be included in the flow of the conversation. Members who want to participate less are more likely to find a seating position that removes them from the flow of the conversation or from direct eye contact with other group members.

Haptics, or touch, is the use of nonverbal cues that demonstrate perceptions of warmth and liking. Group members can touch one another on the hands, shoulders, and arms to demonstrate their affiliation with one another. Handshakes are a common nonverbal cue used at the beginning and end of meetings.

The use of time, or **chronemics**, is also important in group interaction. How much members talk, or how much time they let elapse before responding to other group members contributes to perceptions of leadership and influence. Likewise, showing up at a meeting on time or being habitually late nonverbally communicates information to other group members.

Group membership and identity is often expressed through **artifacts**, or the use of clothing, jewelry, and other accessories. For instance, a group member who wants to demonstrate her affiliation with a sorority can wear a sweatshirt monogrammed with the sorority's insignia. Artifacts can also provide cues for starting conversations, especially when group members are unfamiliar with one another.

Of course, nonverbal communication does not occur as a single cue. Rather, multiple nonverbal communication cues occur simultaneously, from all group members. Thus group members must learn to decode multiple nonverbal cues that can serve many different functions.

Multiple Meanings of Nonverbal Communication

Like verbal communication, nonverbal communication is highly symbolic, so precise meanings are sometimes difficult to determine. For example, you may like wearing black because it's your favorite color, but another group member may think you are sad. Similarly, if you always have a smile on your face, others may perceive you as happy-go-lucky. But you may simply have been taught as a child to be pleasant to everyone, to smile and nod your head while listening to others. In such cases, these behaviors are automatic and are performed unconsciously. However, others in the group may attribute a specific meaning to such nonverbal actions.

Reading nonverbal cues from others is both a conscious and an unconscious activity. It is conscious when we are looking to attribute meaning to words and then develop attitudes toward others based upon those meanings. But many other attributions are made unconsciously. Our perceptual abilities to select and pick up nonverbal cues affect what we hear and how we perceive others. Alternately, we are often unaware of the nonverbal cues that we display. Because many nonverbal cues are physiologically based (for example, your face reddens when you are nervous, or you shuffle your feet while sitting because your knee hurts), many receivers believe that nonverbal messages are more credible or believable than verbal messages. Thus knowing what nonverbal cues you display and how others read them is important to your success as a group member.

To a large extent, our use of nonverbal communication and our interpretations of others' nonverbal behavior is culture-bound. As children, we learn many nonverbal practices by watching others and gauging how they respond to our own nonverbal messages. As you take this class, you already have participated in hundreds of groups, and these culturally bound experiences have formed your expectations for the use of nonverbal behavior. You have learned how to use nonverbal communication to indicate your willingness to join groups and talk with others, to leave groups or avoid interaction with others, and to protect your

Cracking the Nonverbal Code

In one of your next group experiences, plan to do the following: During the interaction, concentrate on the nonverbal messages that other group members use or display. Afterward, ask yourself these questions: Did any of the nonverbal messages displayed cause you to evaluate group members positively or negatively? If so, how did the nonverbal messages in those two categories differ? What attributions did you make about the people displaying these nonverbal messages? Finally, how did you respond to their nonverbal messages—positively, negatively, or neutrally?

individuality in groups (Cathcart & Cathcart, 1996). Thus groups with culturally diverse members may have some difficulty making sense of nonverbal communication. If someone says something you do not understand, you are likely to ask for clarification. But if someone gestures or makes a facial expression you do not understand, you are more likely to develop an interpretation without checking with the other person. See "Cracking the Nonverbal Code" for some practice in recognizing nonverbal communication.

Functions of Nonverbal Communication

Nonverbal communication can help group members structure and manage their interaction, manage their identities with the group, and convey relationship information including messages expressing dominance, power, and leadership, and warmth, liking, and affection. Nonverbal cues provide key information about the relational interests of group members. These effects are more likely to converge and be expressed by all group members in situations where more intense emotions (e.g., cheerful enthusiasm, hostile irritability) rather than less intense emotions (e.g., serene warmth, depressed sluggishness) are displayed (Bartel & Saavedra, 2000). Thus nonverbal communication can become an emotional contagion that consciously and unconsciously further influences group member behavior (Barsade, 2002).

Even when they are not aware of it, group members use nonverbal messages for some communication functions that are important in group settings. Nonverbal communication indicates intensity and emotion, regulates who will talk (turn taking, initiation and termination of conversations), reveals comfort levels, symbolizes community, helps to develop or clarify relationships (dominance, power, intimacy), and influences others. Nonverbal communication can also provide cues about other group members' culture, race, gender, and personality. In short, nonverbal communication is the primary means by which we develop and manage impressions.

In group settings, some nonverbal behaviors, such as physical distance, posture, and touch, change relatively little once the group has settled into its interaction setting and created norms for the use of such behavior. Other nonverbal behaviors, however, such as facial expressions, body movements, and the use of silence, are powerful indicators about the dynamic process occurring within the group (Argyle & Kendon, 1967). Nonverbal cues are particularly good at revealing deception, especially when there are mixed messages. What you say is controllable; the nonverbal cues you provide are often more spontaneous. When these two channels of communication do not match or reinforce each other, group members will suspect that you are attempting to deceive them (Burgoon, 1980, 1985).

Nonverbal cues are also powerful indicators about the quality of a group's interaction and the status of group members. For instance, once a week, Gloria, Marcia, Linda, and Anika meet over breakfast to discuss common issues they face as nontraditional students returning to undergraduate life. Although their conversations generally focus on school topics, the primary purpose of these get-togethers is the mutual support group members provide. It is easy to tell when it has been a bad week for one of the women. The conversation starts slowly but then builds to such an intensity level that others in the restaurant turn to look at what is going on. The women's voices get louder, and the pace of the conversation quickens—emphasizing their interest in the topic of conversation—as they all complain about Wednesday's midterm. Those who overhear and witness their conversation can tell that, even with all of the complaining, these women are best friends: Hugs are routinely given, bodies are hunched over the table toward one another, one woman leans across the table to playfully poke at another. Even if you could not hear exactly what the women were saying, you could make interpretations about their conversation based on the displayed nonverbal dynamics. Thus their nonverbal communication serves specific functions within their group even as it provides information to outside observers.

Nonverbal messages can be used to signal that you are uncomfortable. Perhaps the group is talking about an issue that you find too personal, but you are not willing to state your objection overtly. To communicate your level of comfort, you could withdraw from the group and fall silent. You could also decrease eye contact with other group members and physically draw your body inward. If the topic is making your very uncomfortable, your face may even redden. These nonverbal messages let other group members know that you uncomfortable in the group.

Nonverbal messages can also be used to establish or clarify relationships between group members. For example, suppose Hillary shifts her eyes from the speaker to Sam. As she does this, she widens her eyes, arches her eyebrows, and smiles slightly. This seemingly innocuous behavior may be the first signal that a coalition is forming between Hillary and Sam. If Sam returns her glance with a smile or a wink, these nonverbal signals indicate a shift in their relationship from merely colleagues in a group to something more significant.

When group members use more direct eye contact and more face-to-face body orientation, it indicates that greater intimacy is developing within the group. These nonverbal behaviors suggest two things: (a) that members are developing greater positive regard for one another and (b) that they have a greater desire to affiliate with one another (Mabry, 1989a). Generally, as group members interact over time and in multiple sessions, their nonverbal behaviors give cues to the relationships that are developing among them.

Physical appearance, vocalics, and the use of time are especially important in influencing others in groups. The image you present of yourself often influences how others receive what you say. For instance, if you come to group meetings dressed comfortably but neatly and speak confidently, group members will likely pay attention and remember what you say. They will see you as a credible source of information. But if you disregard standards of dress or cleanliness, you may unknowingly create an impression that what you say cannot be taken seriously. Finally, group members often pay specific attention to how other group members use time. Group members who habitually arrive late may create the impression that they cannot be trusted with important group business or activities, or that the group, its members, or its activity are unimportant to them.

Proxemics, or group members' uses of space, also serve important functions in group settings. How group members are seated affects the flow of inter-action within the group. Members who are most centrally located and who have visual access to others are likely to participate more in the group's interaction. Frequently in decision-making meetings, members sit around a rectangular table. If someone takes the end chair, members typically look to that person to initiate the discussion and to identify who talks next. Because it is difficult to see others on the same side of the table, members are more likely to talk to those sitting across from them or to those sitting next to them. If possible, hold meetings at a round table so all members can see one another and communicate directly.

If given a choice about where to sit, group members who have developed relationships outside the group structure will usually sit next to one another. When this happens, detrimental side conversations are more likely to occur. If group members do not know one another, they are more likely to first develop a relationship with the person sitting next to them.

Verbal and Nonverbal Communication as a System

Verbal and nonverbal communication are intertwined. However, the two mess-age systems are not always in agreement. Research has demonstrated that when receiving inconsistent messages—messages in which the verbal and nonverbal components do not agree—receivers are more likely to believe the nonverbal message. When inconsistent messages are sent, receivers respond in one of three ways (Leathers, 1979). They acknowledge to you that they cannot determine the meaning of the inconsistent message, giving you a second chance to get your message across. Or they become more diligent and pay more attention to you, thinking that they must have missed something. Or they withdraw from the interaction when they cannot clarify the inconsistency.

You probably do not want to send messages in which the verbal and non-verbal components do not match. However, this happens frequently in groups.

For example, at times group members may feel pressured to commit verbally to something they know they cannot deliver. Although their verbal message indicates agreement, their tones of voice reveal that they are unsure about their commitment. Inconsistent messages also occur when group members do not think they can provide honest criticism or feedback to other group members. To the extent that you can deliver clear verbal and nonverbal messages in your group's interaction, your participation in the group will be more favorably received.

Improving Nonverbal Communication Skills

Improving nonverbal communication skills is more difficult than improving verbal communication skills because we're less conscious of the nonverbal messages we send. Thus the first step is to identify what nonverbal messages you send and how they influence the group's interaction. One way to do this is to ask a group member you trust to observe you during a group meeting. This person can help you identify those nonverbal messages that contribute to the group and those that detract from it.

Another way to learn more about how your nonverbal messages influence the group is to watch how others respond to you. Suppose you want to ask a question and look toward the group member speaking to get his attention, but he ignores you. What other nonverbal message could you use to establish your talking turn? It's easy to assume that the other group member is being rude or impolite, but maybe your nonverbal cue wasn't strong enough to signal that you wanted to talk. Perhaps you need to make your nonverbal message more direct and forceful. You could lean forward in your chair and open your mouth in preparation to speak while directing your gaze at the speaker. Or you could add a short verbal message, such as "Tom?" to your lean and gaze.

You can also improve your nonverbal communication skills by observing and analyzing the effectiveness of other group members. Select a group member whom you admire, and pay careful attention to the type of nonverbal cues he or she uses. Try to identify how those cues functioned during the meeting. You are likely to identify a skill that you can incorporate into your communication repertoire.

The Listening Process

When we think about how we communicate in groups, we often forget that, in addition to verbal and nonverbal messages, listening is a major part of the communication process. Because we focus so much energy on what we say and how we say it, we often overlook our listening skills. In the group context, listening is important because we spend far more time listening than talking. In fact, personnel managers asked to rate group communication skills identified listening effectively as most important (Hawkins & Fillion, 1999).

Unfortunately, most listening research focuses on listening to one other person in instructional, public, or relational (dyadic) contexts. Although these findings

Contrary to what most people believe, you spend much more time listening than talking in groups.

certainly can tell us something about listening, they do not address the complexities the group context imposes on the listening process. Group interactions are more complex than dyadic interactions because group conversations frequently include competing side conversations or multiple speakers striving to gain other group members' attention. But the basic principles of listening identified from these other contexts can help you become a better listener in groups.

Why is listening so important in groups? There are several reasons. First, speakers don't often realize that other group members are not listening and so continue to talk, assuming that they are listening. As a result, listening errors go undetected. This is particularly problematic because there are multiple group members in the listening role. Some members may even fake listening, believing that the presence of other group members will cover for their lack of attention. In comparison to dyadic interaction, there is less social pressure to listen in groups, and as a result, ineffective listening goes unnoticed (Watson, 1996). Second, group settings can lend themselves to extraneous interaction, which gives some group members the license to take a break from listening. Some group members might even try to work on other activities when they should be listening. Third, listening errors can occur when listeners interpret the message differently from the sender of the message. The problem is compounded in groups—three listeners can mean that three different interpretations exist, four listeners can result in four different interpretations, and so on. Fourth, listeners have a more difficult job in group interactions because it is difficult to attend to the many points of view being presented. It is easier to concentrate on one person speaking or on one idea at a time.

Listening Pitfalls

Poor listening can be a major obstacle to group participation (Gastil, 1993). One of the most frequently occurring listening pitfalls involves prejudging the speaker or her or his content. What evidence of prejudging can you find in this example?

MELISSA: (to Ken) I can't find Ricky. (Ricky comes in late to the meeting.) Ricky, where were you?

RICKY: Just went to do some business for the group.

KEN: Right, Ricky . . . You? Business?

RICKY: You know, I had to cash some checks at the bank.

KEN: Please don't tell me you're in charge of our finances!

MELISSA: I asked Ricky to open an account for us.

KEN: Yeah, what kind of account is that? What are *you* doing with our money?

The more heterogeneous the group, the more likely it is that group members will express a variety of ideas or opinions. Although these differences can benefit groups, you can only negotiate these differences if you allow yourself to hear what others say. If you prejudge others because their views are different, ignore views that differ from your own, or reinterpret what was said to fit your own ideas, you have generated your own listening barriers. Not only have you failed to hear what was said, but you have arbitrarily created a barrier to establishing positive relationships with those members.

Another listening pitfall involves rehearsing a response. This happens in two ways. First, it occurs when you convince yourself that you know exactly what another group member will say, and so rehearse your response before you get to the group meeting. Thus you are armed with a response to something you have not even heard! The second way this pitfall occurs is when you rehearse a response while another group member is speaking. In doing so, you may miss important aspects of the speaker's comments that come later in his or her speaking turn. This pitfall usually revolves around your overly selective attention to flaws in the argument or to irrelevant factors. That is, you hear something that catches your attention—often because you are looking for something negative —and then focus on creating a response rather than hearing the other group member out.

In groups in which members are brought together because they have specialized knowledge or represent different interests, effective listening becomes even more important. Group members representing different departments, factions, or interests bring with them a unique perspective or frame for listening. Such a frame may make it difficult for them to hear or understand what other group members are trying to say. In other words, they are using **selective listening**.

Let's examine how easily selective listening operates in the following group. Several individuals have been appointed to an advisory group whose task is to recommend ways to improve a city park and playground facility. The mayor requested that the group include a member of the city's planning department, a member of the city's park commission, three residents from the area of the park site, and a social worker with knowledge about gang violence. Because each individual is a part of this group due to his or her special interest in or knowledge of the group's task, it is going to be difficult for them to avoid selective listening. When selective listening occurs, group members not only do not hear other points of view but also tend to interpret what was said according to their personal expectations:

> PARK COMMISSION REPRESENTATIVE: It looks like we all agree that this park needs to be kept in better physical shape than we have been doing. Now, let's talk about what type of activities we want this park to support.
>
> RESIDENT WITH YOUNG CHILD: I think we should have plenty of playground equipment . . . slides, swings, that kind of thing.
>
> RESIDENT WITH OLDER CHILD: Tim, my son, really likes to play softball with his friends, and I like him to be close to home. So I suggest we have a ball diamond.
>
> RESIDENT WITH YOUNG CHILD: Okay, but I don't want the bigger kids hitting balls into the area where the smaller kids are playing.
>
> ELDERLY RESIDENT WITH NO GRANDCHILDREN: Parks are for us, too. Just because we're senior citizens you want to leave us out!
>
> PARK COMMISSION REPRESENTATIVE: No one's trying to leave you out—we don't want to leave anyone out. Have you been to Elmway Park? Plenty of senior citizen activities there. If you'd like, I could introduce you to the activities coordinator.
>
> ELDERLY RESIDENT: Thank you, I'd like that.
>
> SOCIAL WORKER: I thought we were discussing park activities.
>
> PLANNING DEPT. REPRESENTATIVE: We are; what are your ideas?
>
> SOCIAL WORKER: Well, I'm most concerned about gangs and gang violence. I certainly don't want to see the neighborhoods around the park deteriorate because we create a space for illegal drug activity.

Notice how, when the park commission representative asks about park activities, each member of the advisory board hears something a little different. One resident is concerned that her child have a play area close to home. Another is more concerned about how the activities of different age groups will fit together. The elderly resident becomes defensive, feeling that others on the board are leaving her out. And the social worker certainly lets her bias about preventing gang activity be known. Thus, from the same stimulus, advisory board members re-create the message to fit their own interests and then respond to further strengthen those positions. Try "How Well Do You Listen?" to see if you can identify the listening styles and listening barriers evident in your groups' interaction.

Improving Listening

Remember that listeners, not speakers, control whether they will listen. And in group situations, you'll have more choices as a listener than as a speaker. What can you do to increase your listening effectiveness in groups? First, try to consciously focus on listening. Second, recognize that listening is a multistep process.

MASTERING GROUP SKILLS

How Well Do You Listen?

Organize yourselves into small groups of no more than five members. For this exercise, it is best if you are grouped with people whom you do not know well. The goal of your group's 20- to 30-minute discussion is for members to get to know one another better. Throughout your conversation, try to identify at least five common elements—for example, what your favorite vacation spots are, how you came to select this school, what you expect your salary to be when you finish college, what television shows you watch, how you picked your major, or what you consider to be unique or unusual about yourself.

When you are finished, talk about the listening process that occurred in this discussion. How did group members demonstrate that they were listening? What made it easier to listen? What made it more difficult? Did any listening pitfalls occur? What could have been done to overcome these pitfalls? Overall, how would you assess your listening effectiveness in this exercise?

Too frequently, listening is associated with hearing, yet excellent hearing does not ensure good listening. Listening is both a physical and a perceptual process. After you actually hear the sound of others talking (the physical process), you must make sense of it (the perceptual process). What was said? What does it mean to you? How will you reply? These stages occur rapidly, making it difficult to distinguish one stage from another, and listening errors can occur in any of these stages. You can improve your listening by paying attention to the process and making a conscious attempt to practice effective listening.

The consequences of poor listening in groups include poor working relationships, ineffective group outcomes, and time lost to faulty group processes. When a group finds that it is rehashing the same material or that individual tasks are not being carried out, faulty listening may be to blame. Replace these ineffective listening habits with **active listening**—paraphrasing what the speaker has said, asking questions to confirm what was said, taking notes, and so on. Listening actively means trying to paraphrase what the previous speaker meant. But don't stop there. Ask for confirmation or correction of what you heard. To illustrate, notice how Matt uses this active listening technique during a meeting with Rea and Clinton:

REA: If we want to pursue this science and public issue grant, I think we need to find out which problem is more serious.

CLINTON: Yeah, but isn't it obvious that the ozone problem is worse than the respiratory disease project?

MATT: Guys, I'm not sure what we're proposing. Clinton, it seems that you favor the ozone project and Rea hasn't made up her mind yet. (This statement clarifies for others what Matt has heard.)

REA: Well, yeah. But the ozone project is okay with me.

CLINTON: Okay, let's talk about the ozone problem first. See, to me, if there's this huge hole in our atmosphere caused by CFCs in some places and a concentration of ozone in other places, that causes this build-up, or the greenhouse effect. Scientists think that this is what is causing the increase in respiratory disease. So, it seems a moot point to worry about respiratory problems when that issue itself is probably determined by ozone. Right, Rea?

REA: Well . . .

MATT: Let me see if I got this right. You believe that environmental issues are connected and that some problems are more primary than others. And, more importantly, you believe that the ozone problem may actually be that primary problem. Is that right? (This response is Matt's paraphrase of what Clinton said.)

CLINTON: Right. I agree totally. (This statement is Clinton's confirmation that Matt understood him correctly.) But now that I think more about it, I am wondering if an ozone project may be too big of an issue for this group to tackle before the grant due date.

This technique may seem cumbersome in a group conversation, but it is well worth it in the long run as the group avoids recurring discussions and miscommunication. You have probably been a member of a group in which each member left the meeting thinking he or she understood the instructions. But when the group reconvened and members compared their results, it became obvious that there were great differences in their understanding of the instructions.

Most group members have to consciously practice the art of active listening. You can improve your own listening by monitoring your use of clichéd responses such as "right," "yeah," and "I know what you mean." Some people are extremely good at using these phrases to indicate that they are listening when, in reality, they are not paying close attention to the content. They simply use these phrases to move the conversation along.

Taking notes is another good way to improve your listening skills. This is not to suggest that you write down everything that is said, never looking up at the group members who are speaking. Rather, you should listen and then jot down a paraphrase of someone's comment. This gives you a good record of the group's interaction, and enables you to reflect on important points and to assess how your opinions and ideas can move the group toward its goal. Another way to increase your listening effectiveness is to ask questions. If you have a question, other group members are likely to have similar ones. If no one asks a question, then the group has skipped an important step in the critical evaluation process, and a poor idea may go unchallenged. You can also increase listening effectiveness by looking at the speaker. If you do not, you will miss nuances and nonverbal cues that get you involved in the conversation. You also sabotage listening effectiveness if you use group time to take notes on another meeting or to plan your next day's schedule.

Is it worth your time to develop good listening skills? One study revealed that group members who were rated "most like a leader" were also rated "good listeners" (Bechler & Johnson, 1995). The development of effective listening skills seems to enhance others' perceptions of individuals' leadership ability. Moreover, those group members who were perceived to be poor listeners were more likely to be eliminated from consideration as leader of the group.

In settings with friends, relatives, and romantic partners, listening has been equated to being heard by others (Halone & Pecchioni, 2001). That is, individuals want others to really hear what is being said and to put their thoughts aside so as to be able to concentrate on what is being said to them. Individuals also expressed a desire for others to not just listen but also respond to what is being said. Overwhelmingly, individuals reported that they wanted to be understood and wanted others to pay attention to what was being said. Thinking of listening in this way underscores the relational consequences of listening, and provides a framework for how people conceptualize others as competent listeners.

Task Communication

Task communication is comprised of the verbal and nonverbal messages that are instrumental to the accomplishing of group tasks and activities. In essence, task communication is the social tool created and used by group members to perform their tasks (Hirokawa & Salazar, 1999). Broadly, task messages are those in which group members offer or request direction or action for how to engage the task, advance or ask about a belief or value that is relevant to the task, and report or request factual observations or experiences (Bales, 1950, 1953). Thus, task messages often focus on what group members know, what group members can do, or what level of effort they can or will expend. However, group members must be persuasive in getting others to respond positively to these offerings (Hirokawa & Salazar, 1999).

Task messages are instrumental in that they direct the activities of the group (Strijbos, Martens, Jochems, & Broers, 2004). For example, task messages coordinate a group's time (e.g., "Let's meet again next week, same time"), coordinate group activity (e.g., "Who will make an inventory of all our resources?"), describe the group's goal (e.g., "Tim asked us to consider alternatives to providing volume discounts"), and identify when differences about the task or goal exist (e.g., "There are several proposals on the table"). As a result, task messages are frequently evaluated relative to the quality of the group's outcome.

Given the wide range of tasks and activities that groups can engage in, the type of task or activity dictates what counts as a task message (Poole, 1983). If the group is a problem-solving group, then task messages that introduce, develop, critique, modify, and integrate and synthesize ideas would be the mechanisms through which the group solves the problem. However, if the group is a football team, then its task messages are likely to be instructions or talk about procedures. Can you image the quality of play if members of a football team introduced, developed, critiqued, modified, and then integrated ideas on the playing field? The context of the group and the type of task or activity dictates what is a logical task message.

Recall that all groups have task and relational dimensions. Thus, even a family group can communicate task messages. These messages may be problem solving when the family is planning a vacation, or instructional and procedural when the mom is directing the family in cleaning up the garage.

Relational Communication

When we think of our best and worst groups, our memories often hinge on the relationships we developed with other group members. Even if a group's primary goal is task-oriented, it's the positive and negative feelings about our relationships that stand out. Simply put, the development and maintenance of relationships enhance or detract from how a group's task or activity is carried out. Thus, **relational communication** refers to the verbal and nonverbal messages that create the social fabric or social reality of a group (Keyton, 1999b).

At their most fundamental level, relational messages (a) demonstrate friendliness or unfriendliness, (b) show tension and anxiety or reduce it, and (c) demonstrate agreement or disagreement with what is said (Bales, 1950, 1953). More specifically, relational messages are those that emphasize attraction, dislike, conformity, deviance, cooperation, connection, autonomy, similarity, flexibility, rigidity, cohesion, withdrawal, consensus, domination, stereotyping stigmatization, and satisfaction—all which affect how relationships among group members develop (Barker et al., 2000). Frequently, relational messages are evaluated for the way in which they influence group member satisfaction or cohesion.

First experienced in our family groups, relational messages remain important because they provide us with feedback we use in creating and adjusting our identities and how we fit into groups. For example, a group of six alumni from the University of Kansas meet before each home basketball game to have dinner. Then they carpool to the game where they sit together. In fact, that's how the three couples were introduced. The couples did not know one another before they happened to be assigned seats in the same row. For more than 10 years, the couples in this group have enjoyed the company and companionship of one another. The wives would often get together socially for lunch and shopping and the husbands often went together to a local bar to watch the game when the team played out of town. But this year, the university changed how it assigned seats. Now seats are assigned based on how much money ticketholders gave to the university's athletic fund. As a result, the couples are now scattered throughout the arena. One couple has choice seats at midcourt; one couple sits close to the floor but at one of the corners; the third couple has seats fairly well up into the first tier. The couples still get together for dinner and carpool to the game. But their inability to interact with one another at the game influenced the strength and quality of their relationships and how they identify with one another as a group. Their inability to share the game experience together and to communicate about it while the game was being played diminished the groupness, or group feeling, the couples enjoyed. Watching the game together is this group's primary activity, the reason these couples bonded, and the primary stimulus of the group's communication. Eating dinner together and carpooling were activities that supported their game experience. Without sharing the game together and missing the opportunity to relate to one another while the game was being played, the group identity faltered.

While all groups use relational communication, they vary widely in quantity and quality. Family and friendship groups use relational messages more frequently whereas a basketball team and a group of firefighters use relational messages less frequently. However, some task groups provide unique contexts for relational communication to occur. For example, a group of women taking a self-defense class reported that learning these skills as a group provided the opportunity to reveal their vulnerabilities and their past traumas, which led them to taking the class. Self-disclosing in this way created an intense cohesiveness among group members. Still, group members recognized that "it's a task-oriented group really, it's not a friendship group. We got together to do a task" (Fraser & Russell, 2000, p. 406). Some groups, like social support groups, have distinct types of relational messages, such as communicating to heal and to vent emotion (Cawyer & Smith-Dupre', 1995). Regardless of the context, these affective or expressive messages, positive or negative, create connections and social influence among members, which result in a group's climate.

Integration of Task and Relational Messages

Task and relational messages are distinct, they are also interdependent. Failure to respond to task messages impedes a group's performance of its task or activity. Failure to respond to relational messages impedes a group's sense of identity. A group is a social setting, and, as such, requires group members' attention to relational messages even when the group is primarily focused on a task. The influence of relational messages is so strong that it is often the predictor of group members' commitment to the task or activity of the group (Bayazit & Mannix, 2003).

While it would simplify things to think of task and relational messages as direct or overt, many of the messages we send in group settings are not as direct as the task message "Jason, are you going to do the group's report?" and the relational message "You know, I like you, Jason." Frequently, our interpretation of what constitutes the task or relational component of a message is based on how a message is said. Think of the many ways in which the two messages to Jason could be delivered. The first message delivered loudly with sarcasm would clearly give Jason an idea of how his membership was valued in the group. The second message delivered with direct enthusiasm may compel Jason to take on a task for which group members had not made an assignment. Thus, the nonverbal aspects of a message are very important and are frequently the cause of miscommunication. In the instance of the first example, the leader of the group believes she sent a task message to Jason, but Jason interprets her sarcastic tone of voice and cues primarily in on the relational message that she doesn't like him.

Despite this complexity, relational messages among group members help the group create a shared history and can create a supportive or positive context in

Group Identity, Interdependence, and Group Goal

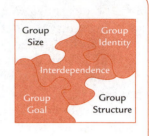

Identify one of your current groups or teams, selecting one that you believe is successful or effective. How would you describe the task messages you send to other group members? How do these task messages help the group achieve its goal? How would describe the relational messages you send to other group members? How do these relational messages strengthen the group's identity?

Now thinking about both sets of messages, what is the balance of task and relational messages in the group? How does that combination strengthen the interdependence among group members?

which its task or activity is performed. The importance of relational communication has been underscored by research that discovered that interpersonal problems were reported as a primary reason for work group ineffectiveness (Di Salvo, Nikkel, & Monroe, 1989). Likewise, members of decision-making groups reported that affiliating with other members is a predominant activity in their meetings (Scheerhorn, Geist, & Teboul, 1994).

Group Communication Outcomes

As a result of task and relational messages, group members can create synergy. **Synergy** exists when the performance of a group goes beyond the capabilities of individual group members (Schweiger & Sandberg, 1989). When synergy occurs, individual group members feed off one another's energy and interest. How does synergy occur? Plainly, effective and appropriate communication among group members promotes positive synergy (Salazar, 1995). In essence, group members can accomplish a great deal because their communication about the task does not threaten their relationships. Thus, reciprocally, strong relationships among group members allow the group to work effectively on the task.

You are probably familiar with synergy but know it by another name—team spirit or teamwork. Whatever you call it, you probably are aware of the effects of synergy. For example, suppose marketing employees in an organization are charged with the responsibility of recruiting new business. Individually, each makes cold calls and follows up on leads on potential clients. As individuals, they are fairly effective, gaining at least ten new customers each week. But when the marketing employees start to work interdependently as a team, they increase their goal to fifteen new customers a week. To meet this goal, they exchange information and expertise with one another. Thus, if Melody experiences problems with a potential customer, she has Jose and Dave join her on a conference call to be more persuasive and contribute their specialized knowledge. The marketing team meets regularly before work, before lunch, and in the middle of the afternoon to see where they are in terms of meeting their goal, to pass on information, and to encourage one another. And after a few weeks, they increase their goal to twenty new customers—something that would not have been possible without the synergistic effects of working together as a team. Clearly, the marketing employees could have worked individually and maintained their performance of ten new customers a week. But their willingness to communicate as a group integrated their efforts, which allowed them to capitalize on one another's strengths and create group synergy.

Interaction among group members strengthens **collective efficacy** or the belief that the group can be effective (Guzzo, Yost, Campbell, & Shea, 1993). In other words, group member efficacy is the sense an individual member has about the group and its capabilities. Efficacy can only develop if members are sharing their ideas about the group's task or activities. Individual members' positive beliefs about their group's capabilities can result in **group potency**, or the group's collective belief that the group can be effective (Guzzo et al., 1993).

Does group potency make a difference? Yes, when comparable groups are evaluated against the same standards, the group with the strongest and most positive beliefs about its task capabilities and group member relationships performs better, while groups whose members have dissimilar beliefs perform worse. Thus, it's not enough for one member to believe that the group can be successful (Jordan, Field, & Armenakis, 2002). It is the collective belief that is important, and this belief is created through group interaction. More importantly, potency develops over time through group members' relational communication (Lester, Meglino, & Korsgaard, 2002). As members recognize the potency of their group, individual members' collective efficacy about the group begins to exceed their self-efficacy, or their beliefs about their own abilities. Because group members are interdependent and working on a group goal, it becomes clear that group success depends less and less on any one member, and more on the contributions of all group members (Baker, 2001). Thus, member sentiment turns from "I can do this" to "We can do this."

As you might suspect, when potency is high, group members are more motivated to work to accomplish the group task. Moreover, groups with high potency develop strong expectations for their continued success. As a result, these groups have higher goal aspirations because members believe that the group can perform. This belief, in turn, actually strengthens its ability to perform, which leads to group performance that is self-fueling (Hackman, 1990).

However a group or team comes together, members' initial interactions have an enduring effect on the group (Hackman, 1990). Thus it is essential that a group get off to a good start. If the initial meetings are positive and productive, the group will establish a solid base on which to draw if it has a crisis. But if the initial meetings are unproductive, group members may not be able to draw on the resources of the group to survive a crisis later on. Thus a group must establish its structure and develop an identity by acknowledging an interdependent goal. And to be successful, the group needs an adequate number of members who satisfy the group's task and relational needs.

Summary

The study of groups spans many disciplines, but the communication discipline has its own unique perspective. Group process relies on verbal and nonverbal interaction; without it, a group ceases to exist. Therefore verbal messages are central to group communication.

To be most effective, group members need to use concrete rather than abstract words and to recognize that groups are capable of creating unique meanings for words and phrases. Verbal communication also helps structure the group, with feedback creating patterns of symmetrical or competitive messages that contribute to each group's uniqueness. Remember that, although it is important to actively participate in a group, consuming too much of a group's time will adversely affect others' perceptions of you. Likewise, how you communicate is as important as what you communicate.

Nonverbal communication is also important in group settings. Your use of vocalics, kinesics, proxemics, haptics, chronemics, and artifacts creates messages and meanings for other group members. Nonverbal communication fulfills functions within groups that are sometimes difficult to communicate verbally. But interpreting nonverbal messages requires a great deal of skill because multiple meanings abound in these messages.

Remember that verbal and nonverbal communication are intertwined. How you interpret messages from others depends on both the verbal and nonverbal components. But when verbal and nonverbal messages are inconsistent, receivers tend to rely on the nonverbal message.

Listening is another type of critical communication in group settings, because groups always have more receivers or listeners than senders. Listening pitfalls are prevalent in groups, and all group members are occasionally guilty of poor listening. Competent listeners are group members who really hear what others say, work to understand the sender, and can respond appropriately.

Task communication is comprised of the verbal and nonverbal messages that are instrumental to the accomplishing of group tasks and activities. Although a group's task or activity dictates what counts as a task message, generally speaking, group members use task messages to offer or request direction or action for how to engage the task, advance or ask about a belief or value that is relevant to the task, and report or request factual observations or experiences. Thus task messages often focus on what group members know, what group members can do, or what level of effort they can or will expend. Task messages are frequently evaluated relative to the quality of the group's outcome.

Relational communication refers to the verbal and nonverbal messages that create the social fabric or social reality of a group. Group members use relational messages to demonstrate friendliness or unfriendliness, show tension and anxiety or reduce it, and demonstrate agreement or disagreement with what is said. Relational messages affect how relationships among group members develop. Thus, relational messages are evaluated for the way in which they influence group member satisfaction or cohesion.

All groups, regardless of their task or activity, use both task and relational communication. Failure to respond to relational messages impedes a group's performance of its task or activity. Failure to respond to task messages impedes a group's sense of identity. A group is a social setting, and, as such, requires group members' attention to relational messages even when the group is primarily focused on a task.

Synergy exists when the group performs beyond the capabilities of individual group members. Interaction among group members strengthens individual members' collective efficacy—the belief that the group can be effective—but it can only develop if members are sharing ideas about the group's task or activities. When group members' beliefs are similar and positive, group potency, or the group's collective belief that the group can be effective, emerges. Because group members are interdependent and working on a group goal, member sentiment turns from "I can do this" to "We can do this," creating a positive and self-fueling effect on task and activity performance.

Discussion Questions and Exercises

1. Attend a public discussion group. This might be a group on your campus (a student government or student organization meeting) or in your community (an advisory hearing or a support group). Pay particular attention to the words group members use. How specific and clear are members in describing concepts? How can you tell if group members share meanings for the words that are used? How do members display attentiveness or lack of attentiveness through nonverbal communication? Does any member display particularly annoying nonverbal behavior? How well do other group members listen when someone is speaking? Can you identify any listening pitfalls? Write a short evaluation of your experience. Identify three things you learned from watching this group.

2. In groups, develop a list of arguments that support the statement "Group members need to be good listeners." Rank-order your list of arguments, and provide a rationale for your rankings.

3. Think of the next group or team you will attend. What types of task and relational messages would be appropriate for this setting? What types of task and relational messages do you want other members to communicate to you? How do these task and relational messages influence the group's effectiveness?

3 Communication That Structures

GROUP SKILLS PREVIEW

In this chapter, you will learn to do the following:

- Distinguish between a decentralized and centralized network
- Describe the different networks that can emerge in a group
- Determine if a group's conversation has functional and topical coherence
- Identify the formal and informal interaction roles enacted in a group
- Analyze whether formal and informal roles are meeting the task and relational needs of a group
- Explain the power of norms on a group's interaction
- Describe how norms develop in a group
- Describe the five stages of group development
- Analyze which stage a group is currently enacting

Group structure develops from the relationships among group members. As members talk to one another, patterns start to emerge. Once formed, group structure also predicts how group members will interact in the future. In fact, a group's structure can be so prominent that it is difficult to change. Group structure creates a foundation for the group. When structure is present, members can more easily identify with the group. In turn, this enhances members' interdependence and commitment to group goals. Group members create the structure of their groups through their communication. As a result of their task and relational messages, group structure can be analyzed by the communication networks that exist among members, the coherence of the group's conversation, the formal and informal interaction roles that members enact, the norms the group creates, and the stage of development the group is in.

Communication Networks

As group members communicate task and relational messages through verbal and nonverbal channels, a network appears among group members. This **communication network**, or a structure of who talks to whom, is the interaction pattern or flow of messages between and among group members. A network creates structure for the group because the network facilitates or constrains who can (or will) talk to whom.

A network is a social structure that consists of group members and the relationships or ties among them. While we generally think of who talks to whom, or communication ties, there are other types of ties among members (Katz, Lazer, Arrow, & Contractor, 2005). Formal ties describe who reports to whom or any other power-laden relationship. Affective ties describe who likes or trusts whom. Material ties describe who gives resources to whom. Proximity ties describe who is spatially close or electronically linked to whom. Finally, cognitive ties describe who knows whom. In a group, it is likely that describing the network among group members would look different based on which set of ties or relationships you were examining. Thus, the terms *communication*, *formal*, *affective*, *material*, *proximity*, and *cognitive* describe the nature of ties or relationships you have with other group members.

Ties or relationships among members in a network can further be described by their communication attributes. Ties can vary in direction. That is, communication may flow one way between two group members, or equally between both. Ties can also be described based on the content of the communication, the frequency of the interaction, and the medium or channel used for communication among group members.

Network ties can also be described as strong or weak, based on the intensity and reciprocity in the relationship. You probably have stronger ties with your family and friends than you do with members of your work group because ties in groups where your relational needs are met require a greater amount of trust than ties in work groups that may be temporary or situational. Similarly, ties can be described as being positive or negative. Identifying a tie as strong or weak and positive or negative is really your evaluation of the importance of the tie to you.

Networks in groups and team are multiplex, meaning that relationships among group members can be described or evaluated across a number of these dimensions. Moreover, describing group relationships according to one type (e.g., formal ties) will reveal a different network than describing relationships according to a second type (e.g., proximity ties). Creating a sociogram, a type of visual representation of the group members' relationships, for any particular type of tie reveals the number and pattern of network ties among group members. Because a sociogram reveals the network among group members, it is easy to determine if subgroups or cliques exist. Figure 3.1 displays two sociograms for a baseball team based on formal and affective ties. Notice both the similarities and differences in the interdependence of member relationships in the two different networks.

Two propositions of network theory can help us understand the importance of thinking of groups as networks (Wellman, 1988). One proposition of network theory proposes that group members' behavior can be predicted by the nature of their ties to one another. That is, group members tend to use their existing networks to get information, seek resources, and request support. Thus, a network presents a set of opportunities if a group member is well connected, but can also act as a constraint if the member is connected only weakly to just a few other

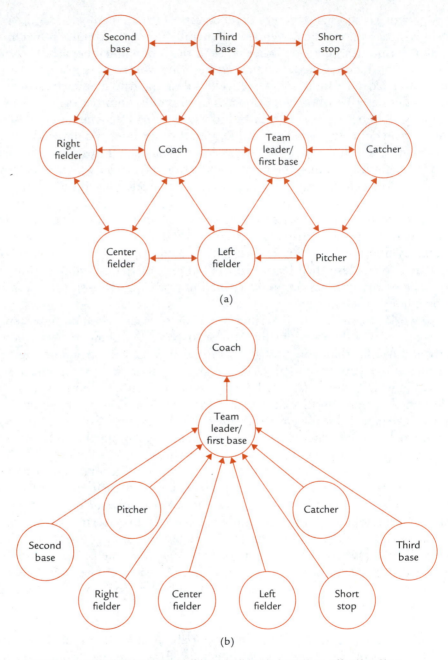

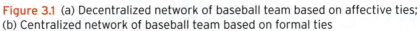

Figure 3.1 (a) Decentralized network of baseball team based on affective ties; (b) Centralized network of baseball team based on formal ties

members. While networks are comprised of sets of relationships between two members, another proposition suggests that every two-member relationship must be considered relative to how that particular relationship is situated within the larger network of the group. In other words, it is the pattern of all of the relationships that is important, not a specific relationship between two group members. How members are connected influences the flow of information and resources. That is, a member who is connected to only one other group member could still receive most of the information distributed in the group if the person he or she is connected to has relationships with all of the other group members.

Notice that networks emerge among group members because they are working interdependly on a task or activity, but that the ties among members are based on both relational (e.g., affective) and task (e.g., formal) dimensions. Simply put, what group members talk about and how group members talk to one another creates structure for the group, and, obviously, different structures will emerge based on the nature of the ties among members. In the case of the baseball team, the group's activity influences who talks to whom in a group. If you are the catcher for your softball team, you will talk to the pitcher and infielders more frequently than you will talk to the outfielders. By virtue of your position on the team, you must talk to the pitcher to plan your approach to opposing batters and to the infielders to coordinate your team's defense. A primary way to evaluate networks is to examine their centralized or decentralized structure.

Decentralized Networks

Most groups use a decentralized network that allows each group member to talk to every other group member. This pattern is **decentralized** because group members communicate without restrictions, and it is typical of most group interactions. Although this is the best communication network to use for group tasks such as discussions, problem solving, and decision making, it may slow down other types of group activities. A decentralized network is also good for building group and team cohesiveness. The affective network of the baseball team in Figure 3.1 is decentralized. The team has been together for a several years. Although there are formal positions of coach and team leader, nearly everyone is the same age, as the team is comprised of individuals who played baseball in college and now play as a team in an amateur adult league. Team members take frequent road trips together, and for many players the team has become their primary social outlet. Thus team members get along well with one another and communicate frequently about topics other than baseball.

An open, or decentralized, network provides the most input, but it can also produce **communication overload**—too much or too complex communication from too many sources. When overload occurs, messages may compete or conflict, causing stress and confusion. Even in discussions, groups using an open network need a facilitator or coordinator to monitor turn taking so that everyone has a chance to be heard. Still, when a group works on a complex task or activity, a decentralized pattern is more effective (Brown & Miller, 2000).

Centralized Networks

Any type of network that imposes restrictions on who can talk to whom is **centralized**. The constraints might be real or perceived. For example, a real constraint is that members of the baseball team are asked to bring issues about uniform repair to the team leader. If they can't be resolved there, then the team leader takes the issue to the coach. A perceived constraint is that a relatively new member of the team feels uneasy about asking the team leader for new equipment. There is no rule or policy to suggest that he can't make this request, but he doesn't because he believes other players are not making similar requests.

When networks are centralized, some members may experience **communication underload**—too infrequent or too simple messages. Group members in an underload situation often feel disconnected from the group. A centralized network can develop if one group member acts as the controller of messages, passing out information to other group members. From this central and controlling position, the member in the role of leader talks to other group members individually. Group members do not talk with one another; they communicate only with the leader. This type of pattern often develops when there is a strong, domineering leader. If this is the only communication pattern within the group, group members are likely to be dissatisfied with the group experience. This pattern also restricts the development of a group identity and weakens the interdependence of group members.

But in the case of the baseball team, the formal centralized structure is based on the team's task. The team needs someone to represent them at league meetings and to negotiate team travel arrangements. The team also flourishes under the instruction given by the coach. Members respect his coaching ability. The team leader is also in a centralized position within the group. He functions like a team captain, taking equipment and uniform requests from members. For this team, the formal centralized structure exists simultaneously with the decentralized affective network. The strong personal and trusting ties among members provide a relational balance to the formal centralized structure necessary to be successful at their task.

Assessing Your Group's Network

Most groups think they use a decentralized or open network in which group members are free to talk to whomever they want. But roles and norms that develop in groups affect who talks to whom and who talks most frequently. Status and power differences among members also affect a group's communication network. As a result some group members will end up talking more, some will be talked to less, and some will talk only to specific other members.

A second way to evaluate group network is look for **faultlines**, or characteristics or attributes of diversity that are salient for a particular group and its task (Lau & Murnighan, 1998). Faultlines can divide members into subgroups because group members commonly communicate more frequently with members who they perceive to be similar. For example, a work group is discussing their organization's new early retirement and family leave policies and their impact on the workplace. Older members or female members may create subgroups in the larger discussion as age and gender are salient to the discussion, and because older group members will easily identify with the potential of retirement and female employees will more likely identify with the potential of taking family leave. When faultlines occur in a group discussion, subgroups can emerge. One way to avoid or decrease these types of demographic faultlines is to create other relational ties among members on other dimensions. In this case, providing employees with a common goal for their unit that requires the skills and talents of all group members will encourage them to create a network that minimizes these differences.

So, which network should your group use? This depends on several factors. Although the task or activity of the group is often the primary determinant (Hirokawa, Erbert, & Hurst, 1996), do not forget about the effects of a communication network on a group's social or relational development. On the one hand, centralized networks place a heavy burden on the person at the center of the network. At the same time, a centralized pattern limits the opportunity for group members to get to know one another, to develop relationships within the group setting, and to create a group identity.

On the other hand, decentralized, open communication networks may slow the group's work on the task. Yet members communicating in this fashion are generally more satisfied with the group and its activity and are more committed to the group. You can ask yourself these questions to determine which communication network will work best for your group situation. More than likely multiple networks will be required to satisfy both the relational and task dimensions of your group.

MASTERING GROUP SKILLS

Analyzing Group Networks

Videotape a drama or situation comedy on television that focuses on a group's interaction. Individually or with others in your class, watch the show to identify the different communication networks that exist among group members. In addition to identifying the basic communication network of who talks to whom, also identify the affective and formal ties between group members. How would you analyze these three networks? Are the ties weak or strong, positive or negative? In general, do messages flow from a few members to the rest of the members of the group to create a centralized network? Or do messages create a more decentralized network? If you could give advice to this group, what three recommendations would you make to enhance the task and relational dimensions of their group?

1. What is more important to the group right now—working on this task or developing relationships and commitment to the group?
2. How difficult is the task? Is it simple or complex?
3. To what extent do all group members need to develop leadership and followership skills? Or are roles and functions specifically set in this group?
4. Have demographic faultlines created subgroups? What other networks could be facilitated if subgroups are hindering group success?

Coherence of Group Conversations

In group conversations, members communicate both task and relational messages through both verbal and nonverbal channels. Coherence is another way to examine the structure that results from these interactions. **Coherence** occurs when group members' utterances are connected to one another in some orderly and meaningful way (Craig & Tracy, 1983). By examining what one speaker says relative to the preceding speaker two types of coherence can be evaluated for both task and relational groups (Pavitt & Johnson, 1999).

Functional Coherence

The first, **functional coherence**, occurs when the group is accomplishing its purpose in an orderly and meaningful manner. For example, group members take turns discussing an alternative in a decision-making group. One member asks a question about the alternative, and another member offers an opinion or provides an answer. This question-response sequence demonstrates coherence, or a logic or order, to the conversation. Functional coherence also occurs, for example, in a friendship group when Janine recognizes the nonverbal tension of Dalton, who is having a hard time entering the conversation. In Janine's next conversational turn, she focuses her attention on Dalton to give him an opportunity to participate. In these examples, respectively, the functions of decision making and relationship building are being accomplished through group members' interactions in a logical, orderly, and expected manner.

Four types of functions (Bales, 1950, 1953) can be observed in most types of groups. Two socio-emotional functions represent positive and negative reactions. Two task functions represent task-oriented questions and answers. Each of the four is further described by three functional behaviors. For example, the positive socio-emotional function is satisfied when group members show solidarity or seem friendly, reduce anxiety in the group by releasing tension or being dramatic, and agreeing or showing acceptance of what other members have said. The functional descriptions for each of the four functions is shown in Table 3.1.

With this coding scheme, known as Interaction Process Analysis, you can identify each message or utterance in a group's interaction as task or relational. As long as meaning can be assigned to a behavior, nonverbal behavior—including facial expressions, gestures, bodily attitudes, and emotional signs—can also be

Table 3.1 Functional Categories of Group Interaction

Function	Functional Description
Socio-motional: Positive reactions	1. Shows Solidarity/Seems Friendly: Shows positive feelings toward another person 2. Shows Tension Release/Dramatizes: Reduces the anxiety that a person or group may be experiencing 3. Agrees: Shows acceptance of what another person has said
Task: Attempted answers	4. Gives Suggestions: Offers direction/action for how to engage the task 5. Gives Opinions: Advances a belief or value that is relevant to the task 6. Gives Orientation/Information: Reports factual observations or experiences
Task: Questions	7. Asks for Orientation/Information: Requests factual observations or experiences 8. Asks for Opinions: Requires a belief or value that is relevant to the task 9. Asks for Suggestions: Requests direction/action for how to engage the task
Socio-motional: Negative reactions	10. Disagrees: Shows rejection of what another person has said 11. Shows Tension: Indicates that a person is experiencing anxiety 12. Shows Antagonism/Seems Unfriendly: Shows negative feelings toward another person

assigned a function. Thus this functional categorical scheme focuses on the purposes messages serve within the group's conversation. By focusing on the function, rather than the content of what was said, messages can be described as contributing to either the task or relational dimensions of the group's interaction.

This functional categorical scheme reflects the ongoing tensions individuals experience in groups. Task-oriented interaction creates deterioration in the group's social structure. Conversely, as group members spend time repairing or strengthening their interpersonal bonds, the task suffers. Thus, task and relational functions are in constant conflict. As group members interact, they must find a balance between task and relational needs that is appropriate for their task or activity.

Topical Coherence

The second type of group conversation coherence is **topical coherence**, which occurs when members' interactions stay focused on a topic (Tracy, 1982). For example, a city council member introduces the topic of tax abatement to attract new businesses to the city. The next council member to speak asks about the tax abatement experiences of other cities in the area. But before his question is answered, another member says that she is in favor of tax abatements and that the city needs to act quickly to avoid businesses selecting locations in surrounding cities. In the first response, topical coherence is *global* in that the relevance of the second council member's utterance was to the larger topic of tax abatement. In the second response, topical coherence is *local*, as this comment brings the conversation back to the topic of tax abatement in this city.

In other words, global topic shifts relate to the conversation topic in general whereas local topic shifts relate to the conversation specifically. The most dramatic change is when a group member's contribution changes the topic completely. Of course, some utterances do not change the topic of conversation, but simply continue or extend the current topic. Examine the following conversation among members of a breast cancer support group. Each utterance, or complete thought, is coded for its topical coherence.

Initial topic: breast cancer dance

DONNA: This is a, you know, busy week. You know that the Stepping Out against Breast Cancer Dance is this Friday night, from 8 to 12 P.M.

Local topic shift: cookies for dance

DONNA: They are expecting our cookies, but if you don't feel like baking cookies, don't worry about it at all, but if you do, please take them to the hotel between 12 and 6 P.M. that day.

Local topic shift: date of dance

ALICE: Is it Friday or Saturday?

Local topic shift: help getting ready for dance

DONNA: Friday. That would be great, and they can use anyone who wants to blow up balloons and help decorate tables from 12 to 3 that afternoon.

Local topic shift: date of dance

ALICE: On Friday . . .

↓

DONNA: On Friday. Yeah . . .

Local topic shift: costumes for dance

DONNA: They're asking . . . I mean, they're suggesting come in costume.

New topic: physician who will attend dance

DONNA: Dr. Aroosian?—do you know her? She is going as a tree. And I'm real curious, because her office staff . . .

Local topic shift: physician's office attended dance last year

GEORGIA: Didn't they go as a group last year?

Local topic shift: costumes for last year's dance

DONNA: Yeah, she was a tornado last year because the office staff goes as a unit. They were the Wizard of Oz; they were wonderful.

Local topic shift: office group won costume contest

REBECCA: They've won the last few years.

GEORGIA: If she's a tree, I wonder what the rest of the office will be? (*laughter, multiple conversations*)

Global topic shift: speculation about this year's costumes

↓

RAMONA: A tree and a dog . . . (*members: laughter*)

↓

ANITA: How about a fire hydrant under the tree? (*laughter*)

↓

DONNA: Well, it should be fun. The tickets are $25 and are available at the door.

New topic: Tickets for dance

DONNA: And, of course, part of that goes to the Breast Cancer Action, which is our umbrella organization.

Local topic shift: dance supports breast cancer organization

RAMONA: Speaking of one, I brought mine (she pulls out her pink breast cancer umbrella).

Topic shift: pink umbrella

RAMONA: And everybody says, it's bad luck to open it inside, so you'll just have to see it again outside.

Local topic shift: superstition about umbrellas

ANITA: They're very nice.

Local topic shift: evaluation of umbrella

RAMONA: They were $7.99.

Local topic shift: Price of umbrella

RAMONA: And they said every dime of it goes to the Cancer Society.

New topic: fund-raiser for breast cancer

ALICE: There was a display at the store today. Special K now has breakfast bars and they have a pink ribbon thing on them. The bars are $2.00 a box, but for every pink ribbon box top you send in, they send in a dollar.

Global topic shift: another product that raises funds for breast cancer

JANET: That's a big percentage.

Local topic shift: evaluation of fund-raising

ALICE: Half of the price of the breakfast bars.

Local topic shift: evaluation of fund-raising

ALICE: There are other products, too.

Global topic shift: other products that raise funds for breast cancer

JANET: Don't forget that the post office has the breast cancer stamps.

Global topic shift: another product that raises funds for breast cancer

DONNA: It's nice to know that there are that many people who are getting behind it.

New topic: Gratitude for fund-raising

GEORGIA: There are. Lots of things.

↓

First, notice how the conversation unfolds from Donna's initial comment that starts the meeting. The seven members of this support group have been meeting weekly for several years; thus, members know the group, its format, and its members well. While the conversation last only a few minutes, the group engages in five topic shifts after Donna introduces the breast cancer dance. Subsequently, the group discusses a physician and her office staff who go to the dance, tickets for the dance, and two types of fund-raising; then two group members express gratitude for the fund-raising. Despite this number of new topics, the conversation has overall coherence in that none of the new topics of conversation is a radical, or even a distinct, departure from the initial topic. In other words, new topics introduced are logical—topics that might be expected given the initial topic, the regular occurrence of the dance as a fund-raiser, and the group's history. Within this series of related topics, members use both local and global topic shifts to add new information, provide explanations, or ask questions about the current topic. Members also do not linger on a topic of conversation, as there are few continuations of any topic. Thus this segment of the conversation is coherent in its overall structure and relevance to the group. It is also coherent in its internal structure, as the conversation within topics appears to satisfy members' need to discuss these topics.

Group Member Roles

Group members' communication create structures for the group, as evidenced by their networks and the coherence of their conversations. Structures are also created by group members as they interact in their formal, or expected, roles and their informal, or negotiated roles (Kramer, 2002). Formal roles are those we can easily label: leader or chair, vice-chair, secretary or recorder, program planner, and so on. Each of those roles has rights and duties, and the roles are consciously performed (Hare, 1994). Accepting or taking on the responsibility of such a role, however, does not ensure that the task and interaction responsibilities of the role will be enacted effectively. For example, Arliss may agree to be the group's leader after much prodding from other group members. But if Arliss places more importance on other activities and misses group meetings, she is not engaging in the leadership role. At times like these, informal roles emerge to substitute for missing or ineffective formal group roles.

While formal roles are developing (or are not being fulfilled), informal roles emerge through group member interaction. For example, any group member can perform leadership duties for his or her group without being the formal leader. Thus, when Arliss misses a meeting and does not notify other group members, Cathy emerges as the group's informal leader. Other group members respond favorably when she gets them organized and focused on the group's task. Informal roles do not always emulate the formal roles of a group. For instance, someone who is good at keeping the group on track by asking questions has developed an informal role for which there is no formal equivalent. After all, we do not elect "back-on-trackers." As formal and informal interaction roles develop, a group further develops and defines its system of interaction, or its structure.

Formal Roles

There are several ways a group can acquire its formal role structure. **Formal roles** are those roles or offices that a group must have to get its work done. Sometimes roles are appointed, as when the mayor appoints a task force to explore opportunities for developing summer jobs for low-income high school students. And when she appoints members to the task force, she may appoint a chairperson or leader of the group. Groups can also elect members to formal roles. Most of the clubs and organizations on your campus use this procedure for filling formal group roles.

Alternately, groups allow roles to emerge from the group's interaction. Thus the member who is most dominant and who attempts to direct the group's activity becomes the leader; the member who takes notes without being asked becomes the group's secretary. Groups are often happy that members want these responsibilities. When someone adopts a role and then accepts implicit confirmation for that role from group members, it saves the group from having to hold an election. However, it may not be obvious to all group members exactly who the leader is. As you might guess, role emergence is not the most effective way for groups to identify their formal role structure. If your group chooses to allow formal roles to emerge, encourage members to discuss role responsibilities to avoid confusion.

Groups of all types can benefit from carefully considering at least three formal roles. Although the role profiles and titles may be unique for each group, the roles of leader, secretary or recorder, and critical advisor are three central roles that can help groups stay focused. Formal roles help group work more efficiently on their task or activity because they help coordinate group activity (Strijbos et al., 2004).

First, many groups need a **leader**—someone to plan for and facilitate meetings, encourage and motivate group members, and be the group's link to its external environment. Even though leaders are required for most groups, students placed in small groups with their peers often simply wait for a leader to emerge. This enables motivated, enthusiastic members to make a claim for leadership by demonstrating their worth to the group. Group members who allow this to happen may want to avoid the humiliation of an election defeat or the high profile or responsibilities of leadership. But sometimes a leader does not emerge until it is too late. When this happens, the group gets behind in its task and can even find itself in a crisis because no one has laid the foundation for the group's work.

In groups in which a natural hierarchy exists (for example, in length of service in the group or in the quality of skills), the highest-ranking person often takes on the leadership role. Although it may seem natural, this norm does not guarantee that this group member will be the most effective leader. Moreover, such a norm does not encourage other members to develop leadership skills.

Sometimes group members assume that several people can share the leadership role. However, when leadership is shared, responsibility for achieving the group's task may be so diffused that the group finds it difficult to move ahead. If one member of the group does not perform the minimal leadership duties of setting time deadlines, encouraging a sense of responsibility and accountability among members, and establishing group agendas, there is a greater likelihood that the group will fall apart. When group leadership is shared, it is recommended that coleaders take on distinct role responsibilities and that other group members determine who is responsible for what. (While leadership is most often associated with decision-making and other types of task groups, groups with relational goals can also benefit from someone leading or facilitating the group. The meetings of peer support groups are often led or facilitated by a member who is coping with the same disease or disability as other group members. In other cases, a medical professional serves in the facilitator role. Despite the difference in the type of group task, a leader of a relational group still plans for and facilitates group meetings, encourages and motives group members, and acts as the group's link to other groups or organizations, as well as the public.)

A second formal role that should be considered for each group is **secretary or recorder**. Groups that meet over time need someone who is formally charged with keeping a record of what happens in the group. The secretary or recorder can also make a list of who is responsible for what assignments and create an agenda for the next group meeting. It is also a good idea for the secretary or recorder to review his or her notes with the group at the end of the meeting. That way, differences in perception can be checked, and all group members can reach agreement. Having a history of its action can help the group avoid repeating mistakes or wasting time.

While a secretary or recorder is particularly crucial for task and decision-making groups, relational groups often appoint or elect someone to other record-keeping roles. For example, at an Alcoholics Anonymous meeting, a treasurer collects money from those in attendance to pay for the meeting space. In other support groups, one member often keeps track of members who miss meetings so contact can be made and support offered. Although these activities are different than what is required of a secretary in a task-oriented group, these roles still provide structure for the groups and help the groups achieve their respective goals.

A third formal role is that of **critical advisor**—also known as the devil's advocate. However, *critical advisor* is preferable to *devil's advocate* because of the negative connotations of the latter. A role primarily reserved for task and decision-making groups, the task of the critical advisor constructively criticizes ideas brought before the group. Evaluating ideas in a tactful manner creates an environment in which other group members feel free to join in the constructive evaluation. Group members who are talkative and enthusiastic about the group's task often want to take on this role. But allowing one individual to dominate this role may cause that group member to be perceived as troublesome or negative. Also, concentrating the functions of this role in one person relieves other group members from any responsibility for critically examining the process or actions of the group.

A better way to establish the function of the critical advisor role is to formally assign the role by rotating it among members on a regular basis. Then, when someone constructively criticizes an idea before the group, other group members are more likely to attribute the criticism to the formal role the person is enacting, and not to any negativity in that individual. The critical advisor can also help the group by reminding members to stay on course with the problem-solving or decision-making procedure they chose to use. Groups that use the critical advisor role make better decisions because they are less likely to use poor information processing, make faulty assumptions, or allow one group member to dominate the group's discussion (Schultz, Ketrow, & Urban, 1995).

Together, these three formal roles—leader, secretary or recorder, and critical advisor—provide a basic functional structure for your group. Your group might require other formal roles as well, such as parliamentarian or program planner. In any case, if the group waits to see who emerges to fulfill these roles, it wastes time and might leave some roles unfilled. Thus group members should either assume responsibility for these roles or assign them. Imagine trying to play softball without knowing your assignment. The batter hits the ball, and everyone dashes to center field to get the ball, leaving the runner free to circle the bases.

Informal Interaction Roles

In addition to formal roles, group members create **informal roles** as conversation becomes patterned and they repeatedly perform interaction functions for the group (Benne & Sheats, 1948; Mudrack & Farrell, 1995). Members are not elected to or assigned informal roles. Rather, informal roles are sanctioned by other group members through interaction.

Informal roles can develop in response to formal role assignments when the formal role structure does not provide for all the activities necessary for the group to be effective. They can also develop in opposition to the formal roles of the group (Homans, 1950). For example, if the formal leader is too dominant or too strict, a group member may develop an informal role that encourages social behavior to balance the leader's strict adherence to the rules. In other situations, roles develop and are accepted as group members gain a better understanding of the roles to be played. For example, Sheila tries to coordinate the activities of the members and provides information when it is requested. Because this behavior helps the group accomplish its task, she may become the group's informal leader.

Task roles are those that function to move the group forward with its task or goal. **Group maintenance roles** help define the members' relationships and develop the group's climate. This type of group role framework is different from the formal roles just discussed in that any group member can step into these roles. They also differ from formal roles in that informal roles tend to develop over time as the group interacts. Informal roles become established through repetition when other group members accept or encourage a group member's behavior (Bormann & Bormann, 1988).

Because these are informal interaction roles, they are contextually bound in terms of appropriateness and definition (Biddle, 1979). This means that a role that is appropriate in one group setting can be inappropriate in another. For example, the type of informal task role you exhibit in your work group probably will not be appreciated when your family is celebrating a holiday. You also should remember that roles are not always enacted similarly in different groups. For example, a group maintenance role in your circle of friends is likely to be more personal because you know these individuals so intimately. In your community group, maintenance roles will focus more on the professional relationships among group members. Finally, you should recognize that not all roles will be evident or needed in all groups. The type of group task or activity and the relationship histories among group members will have a great deal to do with which roles develop. The specific informal task and maintenance roles (Benne & Sheats, 1948) in each category are described as follows:

Informal Task Roles

Coordinator	Pulls together related ideas or suggestions; clarifies the relationships between various ideas or suggestions; tries to coordinate the activities of various members or subgroups
Elaborator	Expands on suggestions; offers a rationale for suggestions previously made; tries to figure out how an idea or suggestion will work if adopted by the group
Energizer	Tries to prod the group into action or to a decision; attempts to stimulate or arouse the group to greater or higher-quality activity
Evaluator/critic	Gives a critical analysis of a suggestion or idea; evaluates or questions the practicality, logic, or facts of a suggestion; holds the group to a standard of accomplishment
Information giver	Offers facts or opinions; relates his or her own experience directly to the group task or problem
Information seeker	Asks for facts, opinions, or interpretations; seeks clarification of suggestions made
Initiator/contributor	Proposes tasks, goals, or actions; suggests solutions, procedures, or ways of handling difficulties; helps to organize the group
Opinion giver	States beliefs or opinions pertinent to a suggestion made or to alternative suggestions; emphasizes what should become the group's view of pertinent values, not primarily relevant factors or information
Opinion seeker	Asks for a clarification of the values pertinent to what the group is undertaking, rather than

primarily the facts of the case; considers values involved in a suggestion or in alternative suggestions

Orienter/clarifier	Defines the position of a group with respect to its goals by summarizing what has occurred; points to departures from agreed-on directions or goals; raises questions about the direction that the group discussion is taking
Procedural technician	Does things for the group; performs routine tasks such as distributing materials, taking notes, typing, and photocopying
Recorder	Writes down suggestions, records group decisions, or notes the product of discussion; provides group memory

Informal Maintenance Roles

Compromiser	Tries to offer a compromise among conflicting ideas or positions (for example, by yielding status, admitting error, maintaining harmony, or meeting the group halfway)
Encourager	Praises, agrees with, and accepts the contributions of others; acts friendly, warm, and responsive to others; offers praise and acceptance of other points of view, ideas, and suggestions
Follower	Passively goes along with the ideas of others; serves as an audience in group discussions and decision making
Gatekeeper/expediter	Attempts to keep communication channels open; encourages the participation of others; tries to make sure that all group members have the chance to participate
Harmonizer	Attempts to reconcile disagreements among group members; reduces tension; gets people to explore differences
Observer/commentator	Comments on and interprets the group's internal process
Standard setter/ego ideal	Expresses standards for the group to achieve or applies standards in evaluating the quality of group processes

As you read through the list, you likely recognized that you have enacted several of these roles. Group effectiveness depends on how complementary members' roles are to one another. Too many members in task roles or in maintenance roles will create an imbalance in the group. Although research has demonstrated that task role behavior is seen as most valuable by other group members (Mudrack & Farrell, 1995), a lack of members in group maintenance roles is likely to diminish member relationships. Not only do formal roles need to be balanced with informal roles, but there must be a within-group balance of both formal and informal role structures.

Whereas task and group maintenance roles help the group become more productive and cohesive, **individual roles** are typically counterproductive for the group, diverting attention from the group and its activities. Sometimes group members perform these behaviors consciously; other times they are oblivious to the impact of their behavior on the group. Roles such as those described below are dysfunctional, as they are enacted with negative and disrespectful communication (Keyton, 1999a) and shift the focus of the group to the member communicating in this manner.

Informal Individual Roles

Aggressor	Expresses disapproval of the acts, values, or feelings of others; attacks the group or the group's problem; shows envy toward another's contribution or tries to take credit for it; jokes aggressively
Blocker	Tends to be negative; resists the direction in which the group is headed; tends to disagree and oppose beyond reason; attempts to bring back an issue the group has bypassed or rejected
Dominator	Tries to assert authority or superiority and to manipulate the group or certain group members (for example, through flattering members, giving directions authoritatively, or interrupting the contributions of others)
Evader/self-confessor	Uses the audience that the group setting provides to express personal interests, feelings, or opinions unrelated to the group's purposes; stays off the subject to avoid commitment
Help seeker	Attempts to call forth sympathetic responses from other group members by expressing insecurity, personal confusion, or self-deprecation
Player	Displays a lack of involvement in the group's processes (for example, through cynicism, nonchalance, or horseplay)
Recognition seeker	Works to call attention to self (for example, through boasting, referring to personal achievements, or acting in unusual or inappropriate ways)

Special interest pleader   Speaks for those with low status in the group, usually cloaking any prejudices or biases in the stereotype that best fits individual needs

Why do some group members engage in these informal but negative roles? One set of explanations focuses on the individual. This group member believes he or she has the correct interpretation of the situation and that other group members are wrong, believes that he or she knows what is right or best for the group, or is simply exhibiting more emotional energy than required by his or her other role in the group. A second set of explanations focuses on the group. A group member can enact dysfunctional individual roles because formal roles are not well defined, group norms are ambiguous or weak, or other group members have tolerated this member's idiosyncrasies in the past. This second set of explanations is more troubling because blame for this member's dysfunctional behavior rests partially with other group members. From this point of view, the dysfunctional group member is able to engage in negative individual role behaviors because other members supported or encouraged that behavior, even if they didn't mean to do so (Keyton, 1999a; Stohl & Schell, 1991).

Improving Your Role Effectiveness

There are several important issues to remember about group roles. First, group members perform roles in both the group's formal and informal role structures. When you assess your role effectiveness in a group, do not forget to examine which roles you play in both structures. You might also want to assess how congruent your formal role is with your informal role. For example, if you have been assigned the formal role of recorder and have also assumed the informal role of blocker, other group members may not trust your abilities to help keep the group

---

PUTTING THE PIECES TOGETHER

Group Structure, Interdependence, and Group Size

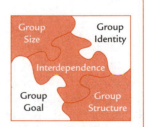

Identify a recent group activity in which there was a specific task or goal. Think about how the roles played by group members provided structure for the group. How did you know that all necessary roles were fulfilled? Did the formal and informal roles fit together comfortably and effectively? How did role behavior affect the interdependence among group members? How did the size of the group affect role development? Were enough formal roles needed by the group so that each member could contribute to the group's formal role structure? If not, what informal roles did these members develop? If there were not enough members to fill all the formal roles, what happened?

focused and on track. Make sure that your informal role is not sabotaging your formal group role.

Second, there will likely be competition for roles. For instance, members frequently compete for the formal role of leader. When this happens, a member may perform task and procedural functions as an informal leader for the group until the formal leadership role is settled. Or the role may go unfilled, resulting in an unproductive group. When there is too much competition for group roles, the group can be sidetracked and lose sight of its goal. Try "Group Structure, Interdependence, and Group Size" for some practice in analyzing group roles. Once established, formal and informal roles often become fixed or accepted by other group members. When group members come to expect that certain people will continue to effectively (or ineffectively) play certain roles, norms have been created.

Group Norms

We all bring a set of norms to our group experiences. A **norm** is a shared expectation that can either constrain or drive group member actions (Graham, 2003). Because a norm influences how group members interact, it can be considered a prescription, or code of conduct, for what is appropriate behavior in a group. Due to this prescriptive quality, group members are sanctioned when they violate group-held norms. While group members do not talk explicitly about norms, they are constructed, understood, and shared among group members through group conversation (Rimal & Real, 2003). But group members do talk about customs, traditions, standards, rules, or values—each of these a synonym for norms. Whatever norms your group establishes, they are the least visible yet most powerful form of social control that can be exerted in a group (Bettenhausen & Murnighan, 1985). The closer group members feel to one another and the greater the number of communication linkages among group members, the more powerful norms are in influencing group members' behavior (Festinger, Schachter, & Back, 1968).

Norm Development

Norms can develop in a variety of ways. A norm can be brought into a group from other experiences of group members. Think of this as a script—or a sequence of activities to follow—that a group member used in a previous group experience. For example, in her musical group, Jasmine suggests that someone should be responsible for calling each performer before the next group rehearsal to remind them of when they will be meeting and what music they will be practicing. This was done regularly in Jasmine's musical group at her previous school, and she thought it was really helpful. If Jasmine offers to be the group member to call and remind others, the norm has a chance to develop and take hold in this group. And if the norm helps the group rehearse more effectively, then other group members may offer to take on this responsibility. However, if group members find the

reminder call annoying or if Jasmine calls them too late for the call to be beneficial, the group may fail to adopt this norm.

Norms can also develop in reaction to some unique event in a group. In this
case, group members implicitly compare their reactions to the event. If their
reactions or interpretations are dissimilar, group members must develop a group-
based understanding of the novel situation (Bettenhausen & Murnighan, 1985).
This group-based understanding becomes the group norm. For example, Zeb,
Caitlin, and Dorothy belong to an honors fraternity on campus. To help the
organization reach its goal of collecting 1,000 children's books, Zeb, Caitlin, and
Dorothy meet to discuss strategies for getting merchants to donate or purchase
books. During their meeting in the lobby of a campus building, Professor Darwin
approaches the group and says, "If you'll let me know where to drop them off,
I'll give you ten books." The threesome's immediate reaction is "Great!" As they
continue to talk, however, they realize that no one has class with Professor Darwin
or knows why he offered to donate the books. Caitlin says that he must have over-
heard them talking. Zeb suggests that some other honors student must have told
Professor Darwin about the book drive. Dorothy's not sure what to think, but she
says, "If Professor Darwin is willing to donate ten books, wouldn't other professors do the same thing?"

The group immediately shifts its focus to ways of approaching professors
for book donations. The building's directory lists 21 professors, so they divide
up the list and start knocking on professors' office doors. When they meet back
in the lobby, they find that together they have secured pledges from thirteen
professors for ten books each. The group is excited about its success, and Zeb
suggests that the group meet the next afternoon in the another building to try
the same approach. The group is developing a norm about how to complete its
task. Something happened (Professor Darwin's offer to donate books) that was
unexpected. When group members discussed this unique turn of events, their
interpretations for why he offered to donate books were dissimilar. But now that
the group has achieved some success toward its goal, the members explicitly agree
to try the approach again. Thus a pattern emerges in their behavior, and they
accept it as a norm because they believe it is effective.

Norms also develop when one member's behavior deviates from what is typical within the group. Even when group members have not explicitly talked about
what they expect from one another, one person's behavior can be at odds with
how other members believe they should behave. When this happens, members
feel as if a norm has been violated. Let's return to Zeb, Caitlin, and Dorothy.
Approaching professors for book donations has turned out to be so successful
that the group has dropped its idea of approaching local merchants. For the last
four days, the threesome has met after classes to solicit books from professors.
But today, when Dorothy meets Zeb and Caitlin, she is dressed in her exercise
clothes, her skin is damp with perspiration, her face is flushed, and her hair is a
mess. Sensing Zeb and Caitlin's disappointment, Dorothy explains that her afternoon class was cancelled and so she took the opportunity to get in a workout
at the gym. The group has never talked about being dressed a certain way when

approaching professors, and Dorothy simply assumes that it will not make a difference. But Zeb and Caitlin clearly are distressed. Without having to address the issue directly, Dorothy concedes, "Okay guys, I won't do it again." Without knowing it, the group has developed and accepted a dress norm when approaching professors to donate books.

In this case, Dorothy challenged the norm. But the group could have had one of three reactions. First, the other members could have ignored Dorothy's appearance. This could have undermined the norm, encouraging members to dress however they wanted, or it could have deepened the conflict between Dorothy and the other group members. Second, Dorothy's appearance could have prompted the group to talk about how to dress. After some discussion, members could have agreed that it did not really matter, that professors were accustomed to seeing students in a variety of attire. Third, the group could have perceived Dorothy's appearance as a real threat to the norm, reinforcing its belief in the norm. This third reaction is what happened with the group.

Why Talk About Norms?

Regardless of how a norm is created, norms tend to evolve from generalized forms to more clearly defined and concrete forms. This is demonstrated in a study (Graham, 2003) that followed students from their face-to-face introductions at a 4-day orientation through the remainder of the course, which was conducted online. As part of that orientation, students were divided into groups to develop norms that should guide their online interactions. At this point they agreed upon norms, such as "communicate frequently," "pull your weight," "be efficient," and "offer and accept constructive criticism." Although the students agreed upon these as norms, it is easy to see that each one is fairly ambiguous. What does "communicate frequently" mean to you? To someone else? Still, the students believed that they *shared* common assumptions or norms about how to communicate and participate in the online course.

As the students participated in the online course, their norms became more defined, more concrete. By the time students had finished their first group project, the "communicate frequently" norm had developed into "team members should check email twice daily, A.M. and P.M." Students agreed that clarifying the norm made it more useful to them. One team even further clarified this norm with "team members must make phone numbers available so that they can be contacted in an emergency," and "the team should use A.M. and P.M. with the appropriate time zone rather than military time." One of the strongest influences on norm development was unintentional violation of the norm, with members sanctioning themselves and apologizing to other group members when they violated a norm. The experiences of these students are a pertinent reminder that, to be useful, norms must be clearly defined and clearly communicated.

Although most people are hesitant to do so, group members should spend some of their first meeting time talking about how the group will operate. Explicitly stating rules of conduct for group interactions can help groups avoid

---

SKILL BUILDER

Identifying Norms in Your Group

Thinking of one of your current groups, identify one norm. What specific evidence can you give that this is a norm for the group? How does this norm help or hinder the group with its task or activity? How has the norm changed during its development? In what way has it become more specific over time? How would a group member be sanctioned for violating the norm? Based upon the effectiveness of the norm for your group, what task and relational messages would you communicate to other group members to either enhance or minimize the influence of this norm?

---

two problems: (a) the difficulty of confronting a member whose behavior is detrimental to the group, and (b) the development of destructive group cycles.

Moving from implied or informal norms to explicit norms is more difficult than people realize. To do so requires conscious attention to the rules and procedures that group members are willing to adopt. The more such rules and procedures are discussed, the more likely all group members are to feel that they have had a part in their development, and thus the more likely they are to adhere to them.

How Groups Develop

This chapter focuses on different structures a group creates when its members communicate task and relational messages through verbal and nonverbal channels. The last type of group structure explores the group's trajectory over time, or its development. There are a several theories of group development. Here we'll focus on five phases that are common to many of the theories.

We'll describe each of the phases of group development as you might expect they would occur, but it is not necessary to think of a group developing in such a linear way. Some groups move steadily through each phase but do not spend equal time in each phase. Other groups may appear to be developing and then regress and repeat certain phases. After describing each of the phases, we'll explore why group development is not always linear.

Phases of Group Development

Generally, researchers identify five stages or phases of group development: inclusion and dependency; conflict; negotiating goals and roles; and task and activity orientation (Arrow, Poole, Henry, & Moreland, 2004; Tuckman & Jensen, 1977; Wheelan, 1994). The communication within the group during each phase has distinct characteristics.

Inclusion and Dependency Phase When the group first comes together, members explore issues of inclusion and dependency. They ask themselves, "Will I be accepted by others in the group?" and "What will I have to do in this group?" Often group members express anxiety because they are unsure about their roles in this particular group or have concerns about how well the group will function. Because group members are focusing on "I" questions instead of "we" questions, the group has not really become a group yet, as this is the forming phase of the group.

In this phase, almost all comments are directed toward the formal leader or toward the person group members perceive will become the leader. Members include comments that provide cues to their identity and status outside of the group because their connection to the group is not strong. There is little basis for trust at this stage because most members take a wait-and-see attitude. Usually, the discussion is superficial because the issues are tentatively addressed until members discover where others stand. And little effective listening occurs as group members try to establish who they are and what they will agree to do in this group. As you can see, in this stage, the group is new and its process is unfamiliar as members try to identify what is acceptable behavior in this group.

Let's see how one student project group working on recommendations for a revised professor evaluation system interacted in this phase:

CYD: Okay, I'm ready to get started. What do you want me to do?

PEARL: I want to work on the questions on the form. Is that okay?

TAL: (says nothing, looks down to avoid eye contact with others)

DARCY: If no one wants to be leader, I could . . .

CYD: Have you been leader of a group like this before? I haven't.

DARCY: Yes, I know what we need to do. I'm the president of the Student Honors Association and I'm vice-president of the Panhellenic Council. Anybody else want to be leader?

PEARL: Can I work with somebody on something since I'm new to campus?

CYD: I could introduce you around to my friends in my sorority.

PEARL: Thanks, let's talk after class; I belonged to Delta Delta Delta at my other university, but there's not a chapter here on this campus.

DARCY: Tal, do you have anything to say?

TAL: I've got another class after this one—a test; I need to study.

DARCY: (ignores his comment and continues) I suggest we brainstorm a list of issues that need discussion and then divide up the work before today's session is over. Agreed?

PEARL: What about the time frame for delivering results back to the students? Don't you think students should get feedback on how well the professors are doing?

DARCY: Okay, that's two issues: questions and time frame for feedback. Anything else?

TAL: (sits reading his chemistry textbook)

This group is in the initial stages of forming. Little trust is being demonstrated toward others in the group, and most comments are self-oriented, not group-oriented. Very quickly, the group allows Darcy to take on the leadership role. From that point on, she dominates the conversation without including the less talkative Tal. But also notice how Cyd and Pearl are making statements that describe their desire to be included in the group ("What do you want me to do?" and "I want to work on the questions on the form") and how Pearl and Cyd are creating a dependency relationship as Cyd offers to introduce Pearl, who is new to campus, to her friends.

There are several things group members can do to help move the group through this initial stage (Wellins, Byham, & Wilson, 1991). First, group members should increase their one-to-one communication with one another. They should get to know other group members and be able to identify them by name. Second, the group should clarify its purpose. In clarifying its purpose, group members will get to know one another while building commitment toward a larger unifying goal. Tension will increase if individuals sense conflict with other group members—especially conflict in reaction to the ambiguity of the group's task. The key here is to relax, use a calm voice, and attempt to view activities from others' points of view. It's also important to participate in group meetings so that members can get to know one another. Sitting back and taking it all in will only increase the tension in this developmental stage.

Conflict Phase The second phase is typically a period of conflict, or storming, during which group members assert their individual preferences. Thus conflict occurs as part of the group's natural development. As group members bring their talents, skills, and knowledge to the group, they may find themselves competing with one another for roles, for attention from other group members, and for status and power. Members may also feel internal conflict because they are being asked to handle tasks or activities that are new to them. And they may feel time pressures as they try to fit these new activities into their schedule.

Generally, participation by all members is high in this phase. As a result, conflicts arise, which further encourages members to use assertive and dominant styles. As group members express their positions on issues, subgroups and coalitions begin to form. Allegiances and feelings of commitment are stronger in the subgroups than in the group as a whole, which can dampen the cohesiveness of the group. Because of the natural outbreak of conflict in this stage, group members must pay attention to their conflict management skills. If a group cannot learn to manage its problems in this stage, it is unlikely to manage them well later on.

Let's take a look at the professor evaluation group now:

DARCY: Okay, you presented your viewpoint, Pearl. Let's move on!

TAL: I don't think I can agree with Pearl.

DARCY: No one can, Tal. Let's move on!

CYD: What about the questions? Has anyone looked at the questions I've developed?

DARCY: We can't deal with the questions just now, Cyd. We've got to figure out the time frame for reporting results back to professors.

TAL: Professors should get their own results first.

PEARL: Why can't they go to the library and look them up like students have to do?

TAL: That's humiliating. Would you want to do that if you were a professor?

PEARL: I wouldn't mind.

TAL: I'm telling you they'll mind and turn down our proposal altogether!

DARCY: Ladies! Gentleman! I'm going to make an executive decision here. Let's table all evaluative comments until we can agree on a time line.

CYD: You know, Darcy, you're not always right.

DARCY: But right enough to move us along. Okay, let's draw the time line on the board. . . .

This group is definitely experiencing conflict. There is conflict over what task deserves the most attention, and there is conflict over Darcy's assumption of the leadership role. Members are not listening to one another because they are too focused on competing with one another. And it is not even clear that all members would agree that they are working on the same task.

How can a group move through the storming phase? There are both group and individual strategies that can help stabilize a group during this phase (Wellins et al. 1991). To maintain group unity following the conflicts that arise during this stage, group members should review their charter or goal statements. Knowing that there is an ultimate outcome or goal can help members more productively manage conflict. At each meeting, the group should review its performance in light of its implementation plan developed in the first stage. Storming can also be a stage of learning because when conflicts arise group members learn more about individual opinions and positions. Group members should try to manage their conflict through problem-solving or collaborative strategies (see Chapter 9). Getting members to agree to meeting management procedures (see Chapter 11) and helping group members see the value of feedback and observation (see Chapter 12) can help a group overcome problems encountered in this stage. In the conflict phase, individual group members should become accomplished at leading and participating in meetings, as well as at supporting other members in their group roles. Doing so provides a sense of integration with other members and can decrease conflicts. Because many ideas will surface in this stage of group development, members should be open to diversity, valuing differences rather than rejecting them. Faith and patience are the keys to moving through conflict to the third phase, negotiating goals and roles.

Negotiating Goals and Roles Once the conflicts are resolved, the group enters the third phase in which members develop trust and come to accept one another. This phase is sometimes called the norming phase because members are familiar with what their roles are and how the group will proceed with its activity, group members can openly negotiate differences while maintaining positive social relationships. The conflicts and diversity the group struggled with in the conflict phase are now integrated effectively into the group, as the group is defining a structure that encompasses its task and members' relationships. Group members feel as if "we're all in this together" (Wellins et al., 1991). The group's communication structure becomes more flexible. Members are likely to report high levels of satisfaction with, cooperation in, and commitment to the group, and group members are able to laugh together (Moosbruker, 1988). "We" is used more frequently than "I."

Let's see how our group has made the transition from storming to norming:

TAL: We've got a plan now. Good!

DARCY: Okay, let's review. We've decided on the time frame for returning feedback to professors and students. Cyd, tell us about how the revisions to the questions are coming along.

CYD: Well, of the thirty questions, we've made changes to about half. It really helped putting the questions on everyone's email and having you send your comments back. That way I could synthesize everyone's ideas. I'll have a final version to show you next meeting. I'm meeting with the president of the faculty senate to get her input before I finish it all up. She said she would be glad to meet with us.

DARCY: Pearl, with the time line done, what's the next task you want to take on?

PEARL: As I review our original plan, there's only the computer coding to consider. I'd be happy to go see the analyst in Information Systems to discuss what we'd need.

DARCY: Thanks, Pearl. That would be great.

TAL: Can I help you, Pearl?

PEARL: How about meeting with me after I go to Information Systems? At that point, I'll need some help figuring out how to meet their guidelines.

TAL: Sure!

This certainly is a different group now. Personal and task conflicts are minimized and the group seems to be working effectively toward one goal that all members agree on. Members appear to be integrating their tasks and are open to sharing information with one another. If it maintains this type of communication, the group will likely finish its project on schedule and be able to take pride in its accomplishment.

But caution should be exercised at this stage. Just because the group is more cohesive at this stage does not mean that it can ignore its processes. Groups can become myopic—that is, their vision can narrow—during this stage. Because the group is working well, it can become vulnerable to making wrong choices.

Procedures that initially seemed overwhelming may now help the group be more productive (for example, using decision-making procedures; see Chapter 7). This is also a good stage to introduce or continue feedback and observation. Now that the group is working well together, group members can use feedback information to make it work even better.

Task and Activity Orientation   The fourth phase is when the task activity of the group is accomplished. Now that both procedures and relationships have been developed and are stable, there is clarity and agreement on the group's goals. It is during this phase, sometimes called the performing phase, that the group works on its task or activity. Problem solving or decision making is more easily accomplished because group members promote and support open discussion and have expectations that they will be successful as a group. Trust among group members is also at its highest level. During this performance stage, group members are so tightly integrated with the team that they find it difficult to distinguish themselves from the group.

So how does our group communicate now?

DARCY: Pearl, will you help Cyd proofread our report one more time? Thanks.

TAL: I've got to paste in these graphics and then we're ready to print.

PEARL: When you get done, Tal, let me know, and I'll look that over as well.

TAL: Sure.

CYD: Oh, problem here. Look at page 14. Is this a mistake in the sentence or a mistake in our logic?

DARCY: Pearl, you worked on this part with Tal. You two take a look at it.

PEARL: (after conferring with Tal) No, just a problem in our grammar. The computer logic is fine. I think we wrote this section fairly fast. Must be our mistake. But we can fix it.

TAL: Okay, let me know when you're ready to print that page again. We're about ready to put this project to bed.

Our group has settled into effective role sharing in the performing stage. Trust is high, and the likelihood that anyone will be blamed for the grammatical mistake is quite low. This group is now successful (and satisfied with) using open discussion and problem solving.

How can a group maintain this stage? Groups that want to stay together and take on new activities must actively work to maintain the positive characteristics and attributes found in this stage (Wellins et al., 1991). By now, the group should be regularly involved in feedback and observation, rotating this responsibility among members.

Termination Finally, the group reaches its ending point or point of adjournment, or its **termination**. Some groups have a specific ending point, or a point at which members are removed or remove themselves from the group. Other groups dissipate more slowly over time, reversing their trajectory through the phases (McGrew, Bilotta, & Deeney, 1999). Whether a group's ending is specific and identifiable or involves a process of decay, group members may feel anxiety as they become unsure about their future participation on this task or with these members.

Different types of groups have different types of endings. Some groups are formed for a specific purpose and terminate when the project or task is completed. For example, your friends join together as a softball team in a summer league, and when the softball season is over, the team is finished. In contrast, your group of friends from high school who did everything together probably dissolved over time as one member after the next left for college, the military, or to full-time work. The ending to this group was gradual, and not planned in advance.

When groups end, members typically have emotional reactions. Some members may have enjoyed the group experience so much that they do not want the group to end. Thus they feel happiness and pleasure at having had a good group experience, but they also feel sadness and loss that the group is over (Rose, 1989). When group members have had less positive experiences, they may be glad the group is over and express this emotion by distancing themselves as completely and as quickly as possible from the group activity and other group members.

Groups that are part of a larger organizational structure (your volleyball team in a church league, your project team at work) need to pay attention to how the group dissolves or terminates (Keyton, 1993). The interaction climate during the period of dissolution will affect the willingness and motivation of individuals are asked to join another team. Both substantive issues and symbolic ones should be addressed. The group should review what it accomplished and assess those accomplishments against its original objectives or goals. Some groups might need to prepare a formal report and decide who will be responsible for further inquiries about the group's outcome after the group is dissolved.

Groups that plan to work together again should summarize what the group accomplished, evaluate the effectiveness of procedures used for the task activity and group discussion, and assess the quality of relationships developed within the group. Additionally, differences and conflicts that were not fully resolved during the group's interaction should be addressed. In taking these steps, groups learn lessons about past group performance. In addition, the identities of individuals within the group are strengthened. This helps members maintain a connection to the group even when the group is inactive. Encouraging members to recognize the ending of the group and giving them opportunities to say goodbye to one another reinforces the existence of the team (Adato, 1975).

Celebrating success is an excellent way to solidify individuals' connections to the group when the group is done with its activities. Many groups conclude their work in a frantic or harried fashion, devoting little time to relationships or to individual or group reflection. Setting aside a time to celebrate helps group members bring closure to the group activity while strengthening group relationships.

For instance, sports teams often celebrate the end of the season with a banquet or picnic. This is a good time to review highlights of the season and to thank people who helped support the group's activities. Even work groups should be encouraged to formally recognize their conclusion. It gives members an opportunity to make sense of their experiences, compare mental histories, and relive stories.

Progressing Through the Phases

Recall that the five phases are typical of group development but not all groups move directly through one phase to the next. Groups develop their structure in response to many factors. For example, a group composed of members who do not know one another is likely to spend considerable time in the first three phases as the group works out its structure. This is frequently the case with your classroom groups. You must spend time getting to know one another before you can work effectively on the assigned task. In contrast, individuals who frequently find themselves together in groups will move quickly through the first three phases.

Other groups move through all phases for each activity, in effect recycling their development for each subsequent task. This is particularly true of groups with stable membership that are given different types of tasks over long periods. Group membership does not change, but each task the group works on creates new challenges to which the group must adapt its roles, structure, and relationships. If a new task is sufficiently different and challenging, a group will find itself repeating the group development cycle.

As mentioned previously, groups can slip backward instead of progressing forward through the phases (Wellins et al., 1991). Why does this occur? Sometimes groups acquire new members, and this causes the group to revisit the earlier phases until the new member is integrated into the group. A team's progression can also be upset by a crisis or other critical event. If the event is significant enough to cause emotional upheaval among group members, the group may find itself back in the conflict phase. This is likely to happen if the crisis renders useless what the group has accomplished. Now, once again, the group has to move through conflict to refocus on its goal. In addition, groups can regress through the phases if group members fail to pay attention to issues of group development. Length of time together does not ensure steady progression through the phases of group development.

Thus, there is not one pattern of group development that describes all groups. What is clear, however, is that group members' communication can be differentiated across the five phases. By looking at how group members are communicating and what their messages are about, you can determine how the group is adjusting to its task or activity (Wheelan, Davidson, & Tilin, 2003; Wheelan & Williams, 2003).

Summary

Group members' task and relational messages sent through verbal and nonverbal channels create structures for the group. Networks among group members are based on the relational ties among members. A communication network is a structure of who talks to whom. Other types of group member networks are based on formal, affective, resource, proximity, and cognitive ties. Each of these creates a social structure based upon the relationships or ties among them. Relational ties in group networks can vary in direction and frequency, and by content and channel. Relational ties can be evaluated as strong or weak, and positive or negative. In all groups, relationships among group members can be described or evaluated across a number of these dimensions. Networks are decentralized, allowing each group member to talk to every other group member, or centralized, which imposes restrictions on who can talk to whom.

The coherence of group members' interactions is another type of group structure. Coherence can be functional or topical, and occurs when group members' utterances are connected to one another in some orderly and meaningful way. If a group's conversation is functionally coherent, then group members are using task and relational messages to accomplish their purpose. If a group's conversation is topically coherent, then group members are staying on topic.

A combination of formal and informal roles creates a structure for the group and its members. Formal roles are those that are required by the group—president, vice-president, secretary, and so on. Typically, group members are elected or appointed to these roles. Even when a group does not have formal roles, group members should consider selecting a leader, recorder, and critical advisor to help the group manage its communication and activities.

Informal roles are those that emerge through group members' interaction. All group members take on some informal roles, whether those are task roles or maintenance roles. But too many members in the same informal role creates an imbalance and often leads to competition. Sometimes a group member will take on an individual role, which is counterproductive for the group.

Norms are group members' shared expectations that can either constrain or drive group member actions. Because a norm influences how group members interact, it can be considered a prescription, or code of conduct, for what is appropriate behavior in a group. While group members do not talk explicitly about norms, they are constructed, understood, and shared among group members through group conversation. Norms tend to evolve from generalized forms to more clearly defined and concrete forms. An expectation only becomes a group norm when behavior violation is noticed by group members. To be useful, norms must be clearly defined and clearly communicated.

There are five recognizable phases of group development. In the inclusion and dependency phase, group members maintain a strong self-orientation because trust is not high in the group. As members state their individual preferences and opinions, the second phase, conflict, occurs as a natural part of the group's development. Members may compete for attention from one another, as well as for roles. Once the conflicting issues are resolved, a group negotiates goals and roles. Here group members are comfortable with their roles and responsibilities and work well with others. The group finds that it is a "we" rather than a collection of "I's." The fourth phase is a task and activity orientation, in which the group completes its task activities. The group has reached clarity and consensus on its goals, and group members are tightly integrated. Finally, a group reaches termination, the ending point of the group. Depending on the quality of interaction among group members, this may be an anxiety-producing phase, a phase full of regret, or a phase characterized by a sense of loss over the group's conclusion. Celebrating the success of a group with a party is an excellent way to solidify group members' connections to the group and to recognize collective and individual achievements.

Although there is the assumption that groups progress steadily through the five phases, not all groups spend equal time in each phase. And groups may double back and revisit previous phases when new members enter the group or when the group encounters new tasks or crises.

Discussion Questions and Exercises

1. Observe a group in action (for example, the city council, an advisory group, or the student council), and analyze its communication network. Identify the type of communication network that emerges in the group's interaction. After evaluating the strengths and weaknesses of the network, what suggestions would you make to the group and to individual members for changing the network structure?

2. Obtain a transcript of a group meeting. Examine the transcript for the group's functional and topical coherence. Are group members able to create a functional coherence appropriate for the type of group and type of task or activity? Is the topical coherence related to the group's task or activity? In what ways are the group's functional and topical coherence related?

3. Many of the roles discussed in this chapter were developed for problem-solving or decision-making groups. What do you believe are the essential formal roles in a support or therapy group? in a group of friends who regularly play on the same sports team?

4. Think back to one of your positive group experiences. Identify the formal and informal roles of each group member. How did the formal and informal roles of the group members interact? For example, did one member's formal role carry over into the group's informal role structure? Did the integration of roles differ in a negative group experience? How so?

5. Groups frequently develop norms for the following group interaction elements: (a) specificity about meeting start times, (b) patterns of who talks to whom, (c) proportion of talk about the group goal or purpose versus talk about relationships or group maintenance issues, (d) the ways decisions are made, and (e) the means by which necessary information is passed along to group members outside the group environment. With two specific but different groups in mind, write an analysis comparing and contrasting the groups on these five elements. Try to identify what led to

the differences in norm development. What influences encouraged norm similarity?

6. Interview a member of a fraternity or sorority. Develop questions that allow this group member to talk about what changes in the group's structure—roles, norms, and communication network—occur each year as members graduate and new members enter.

7. Talk with someone who is a member of a work group or task team where they are employed. Ask them questions that allow them to reflect on how their group started and developed. Do you find evidence of the five stages in their responses?

4 Group Tasks and Activities

GROUP SKILLS PREVIEW

In this chapter, you will learn to do the following:

- Identify a variety of group tasks and activities
- Explain why both task and relational groups engage in many different tasks and activities
- Analyze a group's tasks and activities
- Recognize the influences of participation, time, diversity, and technology on group tasks and activities
- Evaluate group outcomes based on task quality, satisfaction with the group process, and group continuity

When people are asked to define the word *team*, the variety of synonyms and metaphors they provide demonstrate how many types of teams or groups and how many types of tasks and activities people associate with the word (Gibson & Zellmer-Bruhn, 2001; Gribas & Downs, 2002). Sports metaphors, such as football team or basketball team, imply that team members coordinate their activities in a competitive performance to win while another team loses. This type of team task relies heavily on member skill and ability. Similarly, some individuals use military metaphors such as alliance or brigade, which focuses on coordinating with others to win but also to survive. Metaphors such as friends and family suggest that groups are socially or relationally oriented and imply a desire to focus on personal bonding, cooperation, and respect as members fulfill others' affection, emotional, and attachment needs. Still other individuals use metaphors such as community and neighborhood, emphasizing that teams can work together to help others.

Interestingly, three attributes are consistent across the synonyms and metaphors. Overwhelmingly, individuals recognized that teams and groups were structured in some way. That is, teams had some type of *organizing structure* based on the *interdependence* of members. Some organizing structures emphasized common interests; others emphasized abilities or commitment to a particular goal. Regardless of what organized individuals into a group, they recognized that group members had to interact and work together. Not surprisingly, then, the second attribute is that teams and groups require *cooperation* among members. Some labeled this as support or encouragement; others labeled this as trust or getting along. The third attribute is *group purpose*. Individuals recognized that teams and groups have goals and objectives and that group members' communication is the process that helps the group accomplish them.

Thus, in general, individuals conceptualize teams and groups as having an organizing structure based on the interdependence of members who cooperate to achieve a purpose or goal to attain some state of fulfillment. Moreover, this framework crosses a wide spectrum of contexts and situations—from a church choir to a debate team, a family to a police SWAT unit, a fraternity to a children's play group.

Types of Group Tasks and Activities

Despite these similarities, the type of group makes a difference in how members interact and participate. But in most groups, the task will have more influence on how members communicate because tasks have a direct impact on group performance (Goodman, 1986). A key issue is interdependence. How much interdependence is required of group members to effectively complete their task? And as you have probably realized, any one group task is really many smaller tasks and activities. Few group tasks can be described in terms of one single task. For example, in helping your friend move, you probably made decisions about where to start, how to load, when to stop, and how best to get the 8-foot sofa through the 7-foot door frame.

Most group activities can be broken down into subtasks. When this happens, it is likely that the subtasks will differ even though they all contribute to the same overall group goal. Morover, the tasks frequently are interrelated, making it difficult to clearly identify where one task ends and another begins, as decisions in one task affect what will happen with other tasks.

A number of activities are common across both task and relational groups. These are planning, generating ideas, making choices, negotiating, competing, performing, deliberating, building relationships, and providing social support (Cline, 1999; Jarboe, 1999; Keyton, 1999b; McGrath, 1984). Depending on the type of group, these activities might be the group's primary task, or group members might use several of these activities in accomplishing their goal.

Planning

With **planning tasks**, groups are responsible for generating plans to carry out previously made decisions or decisions made by others. For example, a family engages in planning tasks when family members plan a vacation or a backyard clean-up. Particularly in organizations, it is common for an executive group to make decisions and for a task force to carry them out. For instance, my university has changed its registration process. Although university administrators made the policy decision, each department is responsible for planning how best to communicate these changes to students, advise them, and get them registered. Here, a group at a higher level makes the initial decision, and a group at a lower level decides how to implement or carry out the initial decision.

Generating Ideas

With creativity tasks, the group is responsible for generating ideas or alternatives. When a group is charged with the responsibility of being innovative, it needs to use an idea generation technique to enhance its group process. Two objectives must be considered: (a) The technique should not create social influences that could inhibit individual creativity, and (b) the technique should provide social support and reinforcement, or rewards, for participating and contributing. For creativity to occur, group members must be encouraged to think outside of the box. To facilitate this, the procedure the group chooses should minimize the possibility that group members' ideas will be prematurely evaluated. Embarrassing group members by ridiculing or criticizing their ideas will inhibit their participation. One technique that satisfies both objectives is brainstorming (see Chapter 7).

Making Choices

Decision-making tasks are the most common group activity. With such tasks, the group's objective is to reach conclusions through information sharing and group members' collective reasoning. This type of interaction focuses on choices; this activity is different from disseminating information, coordinating and organizing, motivating and encouraging, and developing affiliations (Scheerhorn et al., 1994).

Most decision-making tasks do not have one correct answer, but many groups behave as if one exists. Sometimes groups make the mistake of focusing on one solution as *right* rather than on which solution is *better*. False adherence to a correct outcome (or the hope that one exists) consumes group interaction and keeps the group from moving forward in the discussion of viable alternatives. Groups that develop policy are more at risk for this type of false consensus. Rather than basing their decision on information that is unique to their task, they base it on the norms, values, and beliefs of the group's larger culture.

Negotiating

Group members negotiate when there are differing viewpoints that are difficult to resolve. Although there may be agreement on goals and purpose, there is disagreement among group members on the positions taken and on how those viewpoints are reached. In other words, group members have difficulty understanding how other group members developed the positions they express. In these cases, disagreement actually exists at two levels, making it difficult to untangle the conflict. The more personally involved group members are in the group task or activity, the more likely this type of disagreement will develop. For example, city council members disagreeing over where in the city's budget to increase and decrease spending are engaged in cognitive conflict. Even when council members finally agree, they still do not understand how or why other councilpersons support their preferred proposals.

Negotiation is more complex and time consuming when not all group members share a common interest, goal, or motive. In this situation, group members believe that the group's decision affects them directly as individuals and that the pay-off will benefit one group member at the expense of others. In this type of task, the interests of individual group members conflict because members do not agree on what constitutes an optimal outcome. Will groups working on this type of task experience conflict? You bet. A good example of a negotiating task appeared in a local newspaper. A group of Hispanic businesspeople approached a local chamber of commerce hoping to establish a voice in their otherwise Caucasian and African American city. A group of chamber representatives agreed to meet with the Hispanic group, hoping to encourage them to join the chamber. But the two groups could not establish one goal that satisfied both parties; the motivations of the two groups were not compatible. One group wanted to be heard, to be recognized as a minority in the city. The other group wanted to increase membership by folding these businesspeople into their already existing minority business council. Nothing was accomplished because they could not establish a mutually satisfying goal.

Competing

Groups compete when they engage in a contest, battle, or other form of competitive task. During your childhood, you may have played dodgeball and, later, softball, volleyball, and other competitive team sports. In these types of tasks, one group wins and the other group loses. It is an all-or-nothing proposition. Your goal as a group and motivation as a group member is to beat the other team. Although the two teams may have to cooperate to play together, one team still wins in the end.

Other types of groups also operate in a competitive environment. You may be part of a sales team that is competing against sales teams in other regions. Or you may be in the military and regularly participate in exercises against other units. With these types of tasks, the most important group elements are how well the group performs and whether the group wins.

Performing

Group members perform when they engage in a physical activity, and the performance of that activity is measured against standards of performance or excellence. Unlike a competition in which the group's focus is the opponent, here the group's focus is on meeting a standard that is in place before the performance begins. For instance, a community theatre group is engaged in this type of task. Generally, this group receives good reviews from a local critic, and maintaining this standard is what motivates the members of the group to rehearse and perform. Other examples of group performance are the group presentation you deliver in the classroom or the team presentation you deliver to a prospective client.

Deliberating

While decision making is fairly straightforward in that the group is making choices, deliberation is more complex and often requires more group time and energy. Deliberation is conversation with the goal of seeing things holistically while retaining the connections among parts, learning about others and their viewpoints by inquiring about their assumptions, and creating shared meaning where it didn't previously exist (Barge, 2002). Groups deliberate when they hold face-to-face conversations to carefully weigh information and views, and use democratic processes so anyone who chooses has an opportunity to speak. Often used when different frames of reference and divergent thinking are known to exist, the goal of deliberation is to acknowledge diverse points of view and bridge differences (Burkhalter, Gastil, & Kelshaw, 2002). Often found in political and community settings, groups that deliberate policy and other issues of concern to the community include school boards, city councils, and citizen interest groups. Although the group may later solve problems or develop recommendations, the deliberation task is separate from and precedes these eventual outcomes.

Building Relationships

Building relationships is an activity that occurs in all types of groups when group members create and maintain social ties (Keyton, 1999b). Relationship building often starts with introductions into groups and continues as members use respectful and positive interaction to help individuals identify with the group. Relationships can vary widely in strength and intensity. For example, relationships among one group of coworkers may be restricted to the work environment, while another group of coworkers' relationships carry over into time away from work. In another example, two groups each label themselves as friends. One group maintains loose contact throughout the year except during the winter holiday season, when they meet every weekend to go caroling. The other group of friends communicates more frequently because they volunteer to supervise activities for the parent-teacher organization at the school their children attend.

Providing Social Support

Social support occurs when group members experiencing a shared dilemma search for common solutions through informal interaction. Social support helps group members manage uncertainty they have about a situation, themselves, or others with the goal of enhancing control over their experiences (Cline, 1999). Men in an anger management group provide social support to one another as they make public in the group their personal troubles, uncertainties, and misgivings about their abusive behavior. Such conversations encourage group members to recognize that they are not alone, as others have also struggled with these same issues (Whatule, 2000).

Although providing social support is most often associated with support groups, support can be given to individuals by other members in all types of groups. For example, employees at a telecommunications company know that the CEO is making an announcement at noon about the company's future. Expecting the worst, employees in the training department gather in the break room to talk. Conjecturing about what might happen, members of this work group make suggestions to one another about potential employment at other telecom companies. As the conversation continues, however, the group switches to talk about how their skills might be used in other jobs and industries. Although at work, group members are voluntarily sharing their uncertainties about a common problem and looking to one another for help in resolving their anticipated joblessness.

Analyzing Group Tasks and Activities

Too frequently, groups don't take the time to analyze their task or activity. Failing to do so may waste time as groups try interaction strategies that are not conducive to their task. For example, if your group is going to engage in a competitive task, someone needs to act as the group's cheerleader and motivator. If your group needs to make a plan to carry out actions, some type of time or project scheduling process will be helpful. Even members of a support group must decide how best to serve the needs of its members. Different group activities require different group processes.

Although decision making may be your group's primary concern, remember that most groups and teams have different objectives at different points in their life cycle and need to perform other functions in addition to decision making. A group whose main task is to make policy decisions also needs to coordinate schedules, inform others of the group's outcomes, and encourage others to follow newly developed policy. Often support groups focus on motivating and encouraging members, but occasions may arise when even support groups need to make

SKILL BUILDER

Breaking the Group Charge into Tasks

Before breaking into small groups, as a class identify several important issues that need resolving on your campus. Potential issues to consider include how to increase participation in volunteer activities, how to solve the parking problem, how to expedite class registration, and how to determine the frequency and usage of student activity passes. Assign one issue to each group. Identify all of the types of tasks and activities that you believe the group will need to complete to provide a full recommendation for the identified problem. Remember that complex tasks are made up of many subtasks and subactivities. Some of your tasks will be decision tasks; others will be activities that must be performed. Report back to the class on the types of tasks your group would need to complete and the type of task and relational messages required.

a decision. For example, a weight control group may need to make decisions regarding meeting times, speakers, membership fees, and so on. Moving from one type of task to another can create confusion or conflict in a group that is unaware of the different demands new tasks create for members. "Breaking the Group Charge into Tasks" will help you practice breaking down big goals into small tasks.

Task and Activity Characteristics

Given the variety of group tasks and activities, it is impossible for one set of characteristics to represent all of their attributes. But there are several task and activity characteristics that group members should use in analyzing their tasks and activities, as these characteristics influence group members' interactions and their abilities to accomplish goals, or feel that the group is successful or effective. Task difficulty, solution multiplicity, intrinsic interest, population familiarity, acceptance level, area of freedom, and social complexity are described in this section.

Groups are usually given difficult tasks—tasks that require a sizable amount of effort, knowledge, or skill. The more effort, knowledge, or skill needed, the greater the **task difficulty**. Having many individuals work together on difficult tasks spreads the workload and increases the chance that the group will be successful. Most tasks are complex, with no one *right* answer. This means that group members must pursue several avenues of solutions in solving difficult tasks. Think of the many paths investigators take in solving a murder. Two senior officers lead the investigation and coordinate the team. A forensics specialist collects evidence and works with the coroner in analyzing it. An officer is appointed as a liaison between the investigation team and family members to keep the family informed and ask additional questions. Solving the crime requires the expertise of each these members and their abilities to collectively make sense of the situation. The task is difficult because it is not routine, a great number of skills and a variety of expertise is required, and information is not easily obtained (Herold, 1978).

A closely related feature is **solution multiplicity**, which refers to the number of alternatives available for solving the problem (Shaw, 1973) or to the number of ways in which the activity can be accomplished. For instance, there is one way to balance a checkbook: subtract debits, add credits, and make sure there is enough money in the account to cover the debits. But there are many ways to create a community child care center. Consider all the child care centers you know and the different services they provide. Do they offer educational programs? What ages of children can enroll? What meal services are offered (breakfast, lunch, dinner, snacks)? What types of meals are available (vegetarian meals, nondairy diets)? Regardless of the differences you have identified, these organizations all call themselves child care centers. Group members responsible for designing each child care center came to distinct and separate solutions for providing this service.

Some tasks and activities are more interesting than others. When they are, you are motivated to perform well and are attracted to the group, the task, and its members. This is known as the motivating potential or **intrinsic interest** of the task (Shaw, 1973). But what is intrinsically interesting to you may be boring to someone else. Individuals are attracted to different types of group tasks based on their preferences, experiences, and desires to be challenged. For example, Darci likes being on sports teams. In fact, she loves it that when anyone is planning an intramural game, they think of her as a potential team member. She enjoys demonstrating her athleticism and competing against others. In contrast, Gene avoids physical activity. If all group members are interested in the group task, they are more likely to participate in the group and to strive to be effective members.

Group members who are familiar with the task or activity and one another, those who have **population familiarity**, are likely to work together effectively and efficiently. For example, Kate is a member of a steering committee that plans student research forums on campus. At her first meeting, she did not know the other members and was not clear about what the group was trying to accomplish. As relationships developed and as the task became clearer, Kate's committee was able to plan a successful forum. When it came time to plan the second forum, the group worked together more effectively and efficiently because members were able to use what they had learned about the task and one another from their first experience. By the time the committee was planning the third and fourth forums, distinct group member roles had developed, with each member responsible for particular aspects of the forum planning.

However, when the committee is preparing for the transition to next year's committee, it becomes apparent that the group has become too specialized. Committee members who are returning for next year's committee do not know how to manage public relations for the forums because a member who is graduating has been doing it. Familiarity breeds interest and helps a group be effective. However, overfamiliarity can lead to the feeling of being in a rut or to exclusion from certain aspects of the group's task. Worse yet, overfamiliarity can produce the attitude that one member must do a task for the group without help from other group members. If a group member feels solely responsible for some group task, resentment may result.

Groups can come up with great ideas, but a good idea is useless if it is not accepted or appreciated by others. A decision must be not only technically correct but usable by others; it must have a certain **acceptance level** to be useful. The practicality of a group's proposal should be considered from the frame of reference of both group members and others who are involved with the group or who may use the group's decision. Some people may consider the group decision to be ineffective if the decision is not acceptable to them.

Suppose that, responding to budget cuts, the campus security team decides that security officers will no longer lock campus buildings at night. Rather, they announce that administrators in each building will be responsible for locking up at night and unlocking in the morning. But this team neglects to assess the feasibility of the new policy from the viewpoint of administrators who frequently travel in their jobs. Who will open the buildings while they are at conferences? Who will lock up after night classes, given that administrators go home at 5 P.M.? Although this decision is perceived to be practical by the security team, it certainly is not acceptable to campus administrators.

If a group has considerable authority or responsibility for managing its own affairs and interactions, then the group has autonomy, or an **area of freedom**. For example, Don facilitates a self-help group sponsored by his church. While the church provides the meeting space and lists the meetings on its calendar, Don and other members of the group are responsible for all of the activities of the group. Together they decide what topics the group talks about, if guest speakers or health professionals should be invited, and how conversations should be facilitated among group members. Along with this considerable freedom, members of the self-help group must accept responsibility for their effectiveness. When a team has autonomy, it is important that group members plan and organize things well. Doing so requires a great of communication so group members can come to agreement about their tasks and how they are going to achieve them (Molleman, Nauta, & Jehn, 2004).

Relational or social demands placed on groups can affect other task characteristics (Herold, 1978). Elements of **social complexity** include the level of ego involvement of the group members and group members' agreement on how to proceed and on what should be accomplished. When relationships within a group are positive and strong, demands like these are easier to resolve. But when relationships within a group are negative or weak, other issues surface. Groups with weak relationships require more interaction time to be effective. Members often become more focused on healing poor relationships than on completing tasks. If group relationships cannot be mended, members will evaluate task outcomes negatively even when they are otherwise acceptable. A group that ignores the social demands that occur when individuals work together threatens the group's ability

---

PUTTING THE PIECES TOGETHER

Interdependence and Group Goal

Focus on one of your current social groups. What kinds of tasks or activities does this group do? To what extent do the task characteristics—task difficulty, solution multiplicity, intrinsic interest, population familiarity, acceptance level, area of freedom, and social complexity—describe your group activities? Think carefully and creatively. Do not assume that your social group does not 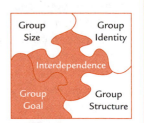 work on tasks or that social activities cannot be assessed with these characteristics. How could you use the characteristics to assess the surprise birthday party your group had for one of its members? How well do these characteristics describe the group goal—for example, throwing a surprise birthday party? To what extent does interdependence among group members create social complexity, acceptance level, and population familiarity in your social group?

to effectively complete its task or activity. "Interdependence and Group Goal" demonstrates how your group is influenced by its various task characteristics.

Influences on Group Tasks and Activities

Traditionally, communication scholars have studied task or decision-making groups like those found in organizations. More recently, however, their focus has widened to include sports teams, public groups who deliberate and discuss rather than make decisions, family and friendship groups, children's groups, and life-enrichment groups that focus on community, religious, and social activities. Adding additional variety is the movement of some types of groups—support groups and work groups, in particular—to the online environment. While it is convenient to designate groups as being primarily focused on tasks or relationships, it should be clear that both types of groups engage in both task and relational communication to satisfy and balance the task and relational dimensions of their activities. Underlying group tasks and activities are several dimensions that influence how group members communicate. Degree of participation and the influence of time, diversity, and technology are described next.

Degree of Participation

Only through their participation do group members have the opportunity to share information with other group members. Three principles are important to keep in mind. First, for better or worse, the more a group member speaks, the more impact he or she has on the group and its task. Second, participation among group members is not equal, thereby giving those who talk the most greater influence on the group and its task. Third, participation is also a function of group size. When a group is a small, members feel greater pressure to participate and contribute. When a group is large, it is less noticeable if one or two members do not participate (Bonito, 2001).

The type of task can influence how members participate and structure their conversation. Some tasks or activities—for example, the process of getting acquainted at the beginning of a meeting or a group of friends celebrating the end of the school year—imposes few restrictions on who talks to whom and the topics of conversation. This type of social activity also directs communication to individuals in the group rather than the group as a whole. Alternately, decision-making tasks will favor the participation of members who have the knowledge the group needs to resolve the problem, but their messages are more likely to be directed to the group rather than individuals (Bonito & Hollingshead, 1997).

Most individuals will participate, or contribute to the group, when they believe they have task-relevant information to add. But group members participate and contribute more when they share common information (Bonito, 2001). For example, a group of friends are talking about restaurants and making recommendations to Jayson for a special dinner with his girlfriend.

JEN: I think you should take her to Pacchi's. It's expensive, but the food is so good!

DAPHNE: You're right, it is good, but not too expensive if you don't order appetizers and dessert. Tell her to have a snack before you go to dinner.

SAM: I haven't been there, but I've heard it will really set you back! Is she worth it?

DAPHNE: I'm curious, are you giving her a ring or something?

Notice that while each member is participating, each contribution reinforces Jen's point that the restaurant is expensive until Daphne changes the subject. When Jen suggests a particular restaurant, Jen's comment activates Daphne and Sam to contribute information that others will recognize and respond to (Bonito, 2002)—that is, the restaurant is expensive. While this type of participation keeps the group on topic (helping Jayson select a restaurant), group members are not contributing unique information only they could provide about other restaurants. This phenomenon is not unusual. In many types of groups, members are more likely to contribute information that that is shared among or known to other group members rather than contributing unique task-related information (Franz & Larson, 2002).

Thus, before drawing a group conversation to a close, members should consider whether they have contributed the task- and activity-relevant information they possess. But just participating and providing information is not enough. Group members must then evaluate and use the information provided to accomplish their task or activity. Not all information is of equal value or importance. Communication among group members may change the value and importance of a piece of information, and determine if and how the group uses that information in its task or activity (Propp, 1999). Returning to the restaurant discussion, if Jayson reveals that he is giving his girlfriend an engagement ring, then the group may decide that taking her to an expensive restaurant is a suitable choice for the occasion.

Influence of Time

Time both enables and constrains group members, their communication, and their work on tasks and activities (Ballard & Seibold, 2000, 2004). Group tasks can vary widely on two temporal dimensions: pace and time flexibility. Both dimensions influence when groups talk, how much time they have to talk, and how much information they share.

Some tasks require a faster **pace**, or tempo or rate of activity, than others. For example, your community arts center is producing *The Nutcracker* ballet as its holiday fund-raiser. Given the complexity of the production, children and adults work in small task groups to learn choreography, create the sets, design and sew the costumes, design and hang the lighting, and promote the event and sell tickets. The pace of the activities, and the resulting intensity of interaction, for each group varies by its task and where that specific task fits into the production schedule. The dancers, set builders, and costumers get started first, early in October, and their activities are scheduled week by week to be ready in time for the dress rehearsal. Because of the large number of people involved and the coordination required among groups, the art center board has requested that no extra rehearsals or design sessions be called. The lighting team can only begin its work after the sets are built and installed and the movement for the dancers is set. Furthermore, because of safety issues, they choose not to hang lights while children are in the theater. Although their work starts mid-November, they still must be done by the rehearsal date. Therefore the lighting team schedules intense late-night work sessions over just a few evenings. The promotion team begins their work much later than anyone else. After creating and posting a few advertisements early in November as teasers for the production, they take a break until they become very busy late in November and stay busy selling tickets through the day of the last performance.

Thus for this event each work group takes on different pace and intensity. The choreographer knows that children can only absorb so much at each practice. Therefore the pace of the children's dance groups is slow and steady, with two regular sessions each week. Although the children are aware of the December performance dates, the choreographer keeps them focused on the shorter time horizon to what happens in this session and what happens in the subsequent session, which influence the topics of their conversations. Meeting twice a week also allows the choreographer to give them regular feedback as well as information about costume fittings and ticket availability. However, adults learn more quickly so the choreographer works with them only one session per week. This group task has greater intensity, meaning that the adult dance group must process more communication about the choreography and other topics related to the performance at each session. Alternately, the primary activities for the promotion team require an accelerated pace and greater intensity within a short period of time just before and during the production. When group tasks, like these, require a high degree of interdependence, communication will be high-paced, as failure to communicate in a timely fashion can put a group behind schedule and threaten the interdependence among groups.

Group members may have flexibility in structuring their activity or task and in dealing with time deadlines or pressures. Groups with **time flexibility** have greater autonomy about what they do and when they do it. For example, friendship groups do not have time pressures imposed on them by outsiders, unlike work groups that complete their tasks under both short and longer term deadlines set by supervisors. Alternately, when time pressures are high, groups are more likely to move quickly toward consensus. Sometimes this creates a **false consensus**, such that group members believe they all agree when they do not. Because group members know there is no additional time to gather information or debate issues, they fail to introduce or adequately discuss opposing viewpoints. When time pressures are not as severe, group members have time to deliberate. However, when group members do not perceive time to be critical or relevant, groups may spend their energy on more interesting activities that are not as important as their primary task.

Many of your classroom groups have been constrained by time pressures. For instance, suppose that, knowing you have 6 weeks to work on a group project, you encourage other members to put off meeting until the week before the project is due. When the group finally meets, it feels the pressure of having to perform well enough to get a decent grade. Now there does not seem to be adequate time to meet, find resources in the library, prepare overhead transparencies and handouts, and rehearse the presentation. You may now wonder why you chose to wait so long to meet.

Influence of Diversity

Gender diversity and cultural (or racial, ethnic, and national) diversity are the primary ways in which group members distinguish themselves from one another. Group members who differ on these or other salient characteristics will contribute to different patterns of interaction. Why?

Individuals of any culture share common symbols, values, and norms, which result in a particular communication style with its own rules and meanings. Enacting this style in a group, individuals are perceived by others to be different. When interaction styles are shared among group members, they perceive themselves similarly and as belonging to the same cultural group. However, when interaction styles are not shared among group members, group members perceive themselves as different from those with a different interaction style. Not only does this influence a group's member self-identity, it can also cause the group's identity to weaken or for subgroups to emerge (Larkey, 1996b).

Diverse groups may require extra time and effort in order for group members to develop relationships and for cohesion to build. With respect to group task, it is not clear if heterogeneous groups have performance advantages over homogeneous groups. Culturally diverse groups can benefit from the different perspectives group members bring, or they can allow their differences to fuel conflicts and prevent cohesion from forming (Watson, Johnson, & Merritt, 1998; Watson, Kumar, & Michaelsen, 1993). Thus how a heterogeneous group handles its diversity is a key factor in task success.

Although it is clear that cultural differences can influence group interaction, it is not apparent why this occurs (Oetzel, 2002). One explanation is that diverse groups can result in status differences related to ethnicity, nationality, sex, tenure, knowledge, and organizational position. Status anchored on these characteristics can affect member participation and result in negative group interactions because observable differences are used to assign group members to hierarchical positions within the group. As a result, group members are more likely to use biases, prejudices, or stereotypes in communicating with one another (Milliken & Martins, 1996). In this case, status is assigned to individuals simply because they possess or represent certain attributes.

Another explanation is that diverse groups must manage cultural differences, or the patterns of values, attitudes, and communication behaviors associated with specific groups of individuals. This explanation focuses on how differences are created through a group's interactions. Types of differences can influence relational communication as well as member participation and turn taking, which ultimately can influence how well group members work together on their task.

One of the difficulties in giving practical advice about communicating in diverse groups is that the group's context influences the way in which individuals identify with their culture and express that identity through communication patterns (Larkey, 1996b). For example, a group of engineers from a variety of cultures will likely have fewer communication difficulties when they are working on an engineering task. Their professional identity and task familiarity may provide a similar communication style that is strong enough to overcome interaction difficulties associated with their different cultural communication styles.

Nevertheless, you are more likely to interact in culturally diverse groups at work, and should be aware of how cultural differences can manifest. Cultural diversity often results in unequal group member participation because some members will only start conversations with similar individuals and overtly exclude those who are different. Cultural distinctions can be even more apparent and negative if group members make implicit or overt cultural, racial, or sexual slurs. Finally, misinterpretation of another group member's intent or simple miscommunication between culturally diverse members can occur (Larkey, 1996b).

Remember, though, that diversity issues go far beyond gender, race, and ethnicity to include social and professional attributes and other demographic categories. Not all of these types of diversity are equal, yet it is difficult to completely isolate one element of diversity from another. Thus cultural diversity is really a combination of differences rather than a difference on any one dimension. **Cultural distance** takes into account the integration of these differences. It is the degree to which you differ from another group member on dimensions of language, social status, religion, politics, economic status, and basic assumptions about reality (Triandis, 1995b). When cultural distance is pronounced between two group members, they will have greater difficulty working together.

The type of group or group activity in which you are engaged creates a unique context in which diversity issues become salient. For example, your work group may be more sensitive to diversity in educational level and political differences than to diversity in race and gender, especially if all group members are from the same department and have similar lengths of service with the organization. In this case, the differences that you might assume exist due to race and gender are not as influential in the group because the group members know one another well and work on tasks regularly and effectively. In contrast, the cultural distance that can be created by race and gender differences may be maximized when members also represent different departments and are new to the group and its task. Group members in this situation have not had the chance to explore their differences and similarities or to develop as a group.

SKILL BUILDER

Are You Ignoring Diversity?

Put yourself in the following situation: You have been asked to serve on a neighborhood action group. You are surprised to be asked to join the group because you recently moved into the neighborhood and do not even know everyone on your block. Your neighbors believe that your neighborhood lacks some important city services and wants the action group to draw this to the attention of the city council. What types of diversity will be represented in your neighborhood action group (gender, race, nationality, age, religious affiliation, occupation, and so on)? To what degree will diversity facilitate the group process or inhibit group members from working well together? What group communication skills might you contribute to help the group overcome any diversity problems it faces?

However, as group members gain more experience interacting with diverse others, group member participation is more equal, cooperation among group members is higher, and group members are more satisfied, which leads to fewer intercultural conflicts and prejudice (Larkey, 1996b; Oetzel, Burtis, Sanchez, & Perez, 2001). As a result, task performance is enhanced when group members move from obvious surface-level or easily detectable differences to discussing different ideas or concerns relative to the task (Harrison, Price, & Bell, 1998). Moreover, there is evidence that groups with high levels of diversity have stronger beliefs about their abilities to complete the task. That is, when there are group members from many different racial and ethnic backgrounds the group does not fall into majority-minority subgroups. As a result, communication is more effective, which facilitates group members' work on the task (Sargent & Sue-Chan, 2001).

Influence of Technology

The increasing availability and variety of technology has caused many organizational groups and support groups to use technology as their primary method of communicating to accomplish tasks and activities. Today, some groups members who regularly complete complex projects on time or support one another through chronic illness or difficult life circumstances have never met face to face. Interestingly, geographical distance among group members is not the prevailing reason for using technology. Group members may be across an ocean or around the corner.

Rather, technologies such as the internet, email, instant messaging, video and audio conferencing, group support systems, and collaborative software (e.g., Blackboard, Lotus Notes), have increased the use of virtual, or distributed, group interactions, giving individuals additional opportunities to become a group. Technologies support a wide variety of group activities, including discussing ideas, planning, generating ideas, and making choices, as well as collaborative document creation and editing. At first, technology was used primarily for work and task groups, but the widespread availability of computers in home and public buildings led to an explosion of online support groups. Given the proliferation and pervasiveness of technology, it is impossible to estimate how many groups use technologies to accomplish their tasks or activities.

The obvious advantage is that groups using technology have flexibility in when they meet. Groups may work asynchronously, as group members are not required to read or send messages at the same time. There is no specific meeting day or time. Group members log on and communicate according to their own preferences and needs. Many work groups and most online support groups work on their tasks and activities in an asynchronous mode. Asynchronous group communication has several advantages. Members do not have to compete for talking time. They also have the opportunity to reflect on what is posted before responding. In general, group members have greater opportunity to participate as they are not closed out by powerful or talkative members. The asynchronous mode also allows any group member to introduce ideas into the discussion, as there are fewer opportunities for controlling the group's task or activity (Gallupe et al., 1992). Other groups use technology for synchronous communication, interacting at the same time even though they cannot be face to face.

Virtual groups can also work on their tasks without members knowing their identity. Interacting anonymously is common in online support groups, and also used in work groups when status differences among members might influence idea generation or decision making (Scott, 1999). Regardless, groups that use technology are distanced by space, even if they are in the same building. Moreover, group members' communication is mediated by the technology (Bell & Kozlowski, 2002). This is not a moot point. Members must use and rely on technology-mediated communication to link them together as a group. In addition, groups must take the time to adjust to or learn about their mediated environment. Not doing so will negatively influence task completion and harm member relationships. Thus, groups who expect to work together on a task over a long period of time are better suited to using technology than groups for which the time horizon is very short (Walther, 2002).

Generally, a more complex task requires greater coordination among group members and more immediate feedback to ensure interdependence among team members. While there is little difference in task effectiveness on less complex tasks between groups that meet face to face and groups that meet virtually, groups perform better on complex tasks when they meet face to face. Thus, two recommendations can be made when groups must work virtually (for example, a team is spread across continents). First, groups will have greater task success if the technology is rich enough to include synchronous and coordinated interaction and easy methods for sharing of documents, drawings, and other graphical information (Bell & Kozlowski, 2002; Scott, 1999). Second, because technology limits the development of relational ties among members, virtual groups should consider meeting initially face to face to help group members create a group identity with one another and develop agreement about the group's goal or task (Meier, 2003),

Another influence of the use of technology is that virtual teams often cross functional, organizational, and cultural boundaries. Because technology makes it easier for groups of people to meet, virtual groups often include members with different backgrounds, knowledge sets, motivations, and communication styles. Technology often makes communication in these groups more difficult because members have more trouble conveying meaning and in knowing when they are not understood. It is also difficult for groups using technology to form relationships and organize themselves (Kiesler & Cummings, 2002). To overcome these potential difficulties, groups can develop procedures or rules for interacting and creating linkages among members by assigning tasks to subgroups of members with different backgrounds (Bell & Kozlowski, 2002). Group members also need to address relationship development because groups using technology whose members have developed collective positive attitudes and beliefs about their group's ability to perform are more effective at their tasks (Pescosolido, 2003).

Evaluating Group Outcomes

All groups have two general functions or purposes (Arrow, McGrath, & Berdahl, 2000). The first purpose is to engage in or complete some task or activity. The second purpose is to fulfill members' needs. Effectively accomplishing a task enhances members' identities with the group. When members are more identified with the group, they are more willing to participate in and help the group be successful at its task. The pursuit of one purpose or outcome affects the other, requiring that the task and relational dimensions of group member interaction work as a system.

Groups, however, differ in the extent to which they favor task or relational outcomes. Moreover, a group may alternate between favoring one over the other. Thus, the balance between the two types of outcomes will vary based on the immediate needs of the group and its members, or as the group adapts to new challenges or opportunities in its environment (Arrow et al., 2000). However, both task and relational outcomes must be fulfilled to some minimum degree for members to identify with the group and consider themselves group members.

Given the wide variety of groups and their tasks and activities, it would be impossible to describe each of the task and relational outcomes groups can produce. But three outcomes—task quality, satisfaction with the group process, and group continuity—are important to all groups.

One of the most obvious ways to gauge group effectiveness is to monitor the quality of group decisions or activities. Standards of quality, quantity, and timeliness are commonly used to judge group output. Questions of quality include the following: Did the group make the best decision? Did the team play well enough? Were members' needs met? Questions of quantity include these: Did the decisions made allow the group to accomplish all of its objectives? Did the team practice long enough to be competitive? Questions of timeliness include these: Did the group use its time wisely? Was the project handed in on time? Individuals outside the group can also monitor or evaluate your group's decisions and activities: Were

MASTERING GROUP SKILLS

Consider Influences on Group Tasks

Select one of your groups that meets face to face and its task or activity. In what ways does the degree of participation among members influence the task? How does time influence the group and its task? What about group member diversity? If you perceive these dimensions as negative influences on the task, what task and relational messages do you believe you should communicate to the group to overcome that negativity? If you perceive these dimensions as positive influences on the task, what task and relational messages do you believe you should communicate to the group to further enhance the influence of these dimensions? Now consider moving your group and its task or activity online. What would change in your group? Why? What would you suggest to the group to manage its online environment?

the group's recommendations acceptable to the vice-president? Did your team meet the early entry deadline? Did your ticket-selling team sell enough tickets? In fact, the degree to which the group's output meets the standards of the people who receive, review, or use that output can be more important than how the group views its outcomes. Obviously, if a group generates an outcome that is unacceptable to others, it is one indication of the group's ineffectiveness. Particularly in organizational settings and in other contexts in which a group is tightly connected to its environment, the future of the group and its members may be more dependent on a subjective assessment from others than on any objective measure of the group's output.

In an ideal world, each group and group member will strive for decisions and actions of the highest quality. Unfortunately, this is not always the case. Sometimes quality is not the most important issue. Time pressures may be so extreme that finding a solution—any solution—becomes the primary focus of the group. Quality is also diluted when member involvement in the group process is low or when group decisions do not directly affect group members. It is hard to be committed to a group decision when you are not responsible for it. If someone outside the group imposes a quantity standard, group members may work to fulfill the standard without maximizing their abilities.

Member satisfaction with group process is a second outcome that groups should seek. When members do not trust or believe in the process the group is using, apathy develops, which distances group members from both other members and the task. Members are more likely to be satisfied when their participation is encouraged. When the process of carrying out the group's work enhances the ability of members to work together, satisfaction with the task and the group increases. Although decision quality is more focused on task orientation, group process is relationally oriented.

Group continuity is the third outcome. Simply put, group members become more committed to the group, its members, the decisions or other tasks the group

MASTERING GROUP SKILLS

Designing Group Tasks

As a group member, it is easy to become accustomed to having group tasks assigned. However, most professionals are charged with the responsibility of supervising groups and designing their tasks. For a group to which you belong, follow these steps to design a task for the group:

1. Generally conceptualize what you want the group to do.

2. Write the group's charge in one sentence. Revise the group charge until it is clear to all group members.

3. Develop a list of each of the tasks or activities that the group will have to complete for the charge to be achieved.

4. Determine which of these tasks and activities will require that members work as a group.

5. For one of these, analyze its task difficulty, solution multiplicity, intrinsic interest, population familiarity, acceptance level, area of freedom, and social complexity.

6. Identify the internal and external constraints that will affect group members working on this task.

7. Review the group charge. Does it need to be revised? How will you explain this charge to the group? Develop a plan for how you can motivate group members to continue with the group task given the constraints they are likely to encounter?

must perform, and the processes the group uses when group members know they will be together over time. This future orientation helps group members recognize that their current actions will affect their future as a group. Advocating a future orientation also helps a group focus on its goals.

Chances for group continuity are increased when group experiences contribute to the growth and personal well-being of the group's members. This criterion focuses on the individual group member rather than on the task or group member relationships identified in the other two outcomes. Group experiences should contribute to the skill development of each group member. Learning new meeting procedures, enhancing communication abilities, or addressing some other individual need (for example, increased visibility in the organization) are a few examples of how group experiences contribute to the well-being of individuals. When group members feel that their individual needs are met through their group experiences, they are likely to be more satisfied with the group experience and more motivated to continue interacting with these group members.

Not every group achieves these three outcomes. Conflicts and disagreements create hostilities, which dampen group members' enthusiasm for working together. Ineffective information flow may cause subgroups to form, hampering the information sharing necessary for effective relationship building. Groups with more positive interaction strategies create effective interpersonal relationships, which strengthens the ability of group members to work together. Group members who work well together make complex or undesirable tasks easier to accomplish. Because effective interpersonal relationships are already in place, group members can proceed more quickly with the task or activity. This type of relationship resiliency is essential when groups are challenged by difficult tasks.

Summary

There are many types of groups and many types of group tasks and activities. In general, however, individuals conceptualize teams and groups as having an organizing structure based on the interdependence of members who cooperate to achieve a purpose or goal to attain some state of fulfillment. Thus members of both task and relational groups can engage in planning, generating ideas, making choices, negotiating, competing, performing, deliberating, building relationships, or providing social support.

Several task and activity characteristics influence group members' interactions and their abilities to accomplish goals, or feel that the group is successful or effective. Tasks can be evaluated for their task difficulty, solution multiplicity, intrinsic interest, population familiarity, acceptance level, area of freedom, and social complexity. By analyzing your group's task before you start, you will have a better understanding of how the task will challenge the group.

Underlying group tasks and activities are several dimensions—participation, time, diversity, and technology—that influence how group members communicate. Only through their participation do group members have the opportunity to share information with other group members. Group participation is generally not equal, giving the person who talks "most" greater influence on the group and its task. Typically, group members participate more when they share common information. Group tasks can vary widely on the temporal dimensions of pace and time flexibility. Both dimensions influence when groups talk, how much time they have to talk, and how much information they share. Although diversity among group members can be influential, participation becomes more equal, cooperation and satisfaction increases, and belief about the group's abilities increases when members have more experience in interacting in diverse groups. When groups interact through technology, they may work synchronously or asynchronously, and even, perhaps, anonymously. Regardless, group members use and rely on technology-mediated communications to link them together as a group.

All groups have two general functions or purposes: to engage in or complete a task or activity, and to fulfill members' needs. The pursuit of one purpose affects the other, requiring that group members find the balance between task and relational dimensions that fits their needs. Both task and relational outcomes must be fulfilled to some minimum degree for members to identify with the group. Three outcomes—task quality, satisfaction with the group process, and group continuity—are important to all groups.

Discussion Questions and Exercises

1. Develop a list of at least ten groups that you belong to. Next identify the tasks and activities of these groups. What similarities and differences are there in the types of tasks and activities these groups pursue? Do any of your groups work on a task or activity that is not described in the chapter?

2. It's fairly easy to describe some tasks to others. For example, many people understand the task orientation of planning, generating ideas, making choices, negotiating, competing, performing, and deliberating. But how would you explain building relationships and providing social support as tasks to others?

3. Watch a situation comedy, drama, or film. Identify the types of groups and the types of group tasks portrayed. Are the portrayals positive or negative? Do the portrayals seem real to you? Why or why not? How well do the portrayals reflect your experiences with similar types of groups?

4. After your instructor gives you the parameters of a group task, put yourself in the following situation: You are responsible for helping the group with its task, but you will be out of town when the group meets. To help the group know what to do, write out instructions for completing the task. In class, exchange your written instructions with another student. Assess each set of instructions for completeness and clarity.

5. Interview a family member about his or her group experiences. Create a set of questions to understand the influence of participation, time, diversity, and technology on his or her group experiences. Based on the answers, what principles or advice would you give to others about these influences?

5

Building Group Communication Competence

In this chapter, you will learn to do the following:

- Describe what people often identify as the ideal group member
- Adapt your communication behavior to meet the interpersonal needs of other group members
- Communicate competently, with a balance of appropriateness and effectiveness
- Distinguish between the communication apprehension of other group members and their potential need to remain silent
- Explain how to help a group member overcome negative attitudes toward groups
- Select the communicator style that is most effective and appropriate for a specific group situation
- Explain the ways in which group diversity can pose challenges for a group
- Sustain ethical practices as a group member

The focus of the previous chapters has been to introduce you to a definition of *group* and *group communication*, and then to explore how people communicate in groups using verbal and nonverbal communication, listening, and task and relational messages. Next we looked at how those individual messages created structure for the group in terms of networks, coherence, roles, and norms, and how those structures evolved over time. Finally, we examined the variety of tasks and activities that groups accomplish through those interactions and interaction structures, and how participation, time, diversity and technology influences group member participation, and, as a result, the task or activity outcomes of groups.

Now our attention turns to you—what knowledge, skills, and abilities you bring to the group or team, including your communication competencies. We have seen that, although individuals make up a group, effective group interaction and group productivity involve more than merely people coming together. When unique individuals come together to form a group, communication difficulties can arise. Examining your communication competence will allow you to better

SKILL BUILDER

How Important Are Communication Skills?

Reflect for a moment on your present group experiences. In the task skills box, give yourself a score of 1 to 10 on the following scale:

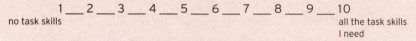

1 __ 2 __ 3 __ 4 __ 5 __ 6 __ 7 __ 8 __ 9 __ 10
no task skills   all the task skills
                                                               I need

Task skills include all the technical knowledge and skills you need to be successful or effective in working on the group's task or activity. Now give yourself a score of 1 to 10 in the communication skills box on the following scale:

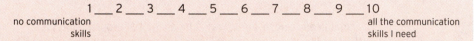

1 __ 2 __ 3 __ 4 __ 5 __ 6 __ 7 __ 8 __ 9 __ 10
no communication   all the communication
skills   skills I need

Communication skills are a person's abilities associated with the effective sending and receiving of messages in the group.

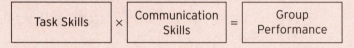

| Task Skills | × | Communication Skills | = | Group Performance |

Now, multiply your score for task skills by your score for communication skills. How well did you score? Regardless of how skilled you are at the task, your level of communication skills moderates your task performance. Even if you gave yourself a 9 in task skills, that score multiplied by a 6 in communication skills will reflect your overall effectiveness. Are you satisfied with your overall group performance score? What steps could you take to enhance your score and your effectiveness in your group?

Source: Adapted from Wellins, Byham, and Wilson (1991).

identify how you can help your group or team overcome these difficulties, as well as identify ways in which you can make other meaningful contributions to the group. Try "How Important Are Communication Skills?" to assess how your communication skills influence group performance.

The Ideal Group Member

What is a good group member? In two studies (Bonito, 2004; Schullery & Schullery, 2002), college students identified these themes when asked to describe an ideal group member:

1. is open-minded
2. knows what he or she is talking about
3. demonstrates good communication skills
4. gets along well with others

5. contributes to the group

6. listens to others' points of view

7. doesn't criticize what others say

8. actively participates in the task or activity

9. shares ideas

10. is willing to work hard

11. provides leadership

12. helps the group stay on task

13. enjoys people and being in a group

14. is flexible

From a student point of view, a good group member is a competent communicator who possesses desirable relational skills and participates in the group interactions to contribute to the group task or activity. Thinking of these characteristics in another way, they are a framework, or set of expectations, of how group members hope others will communicate task and relational messages and participate in a group.

Conversely, when students were asked about their group experiences and what areas of communication they could improve on, they identified deficiencies in the following areas (Schullery & Gibson, 2001; Schullery & Schullery, 2002):

1. being intolerant of others' opinions

2. reluctant to speak up or argue a point in hopes of avoiding conflict

3. not liking groups and not trusting others to work to my standards

4. being too shy

5. being impatient with slow progress in groups

6. having difficulty in organizing and presenting ideas

7. lacking leadership skills

8. having communication anxiety

9. having trouble maintaining focus or motivation

10. dislikes being in groups

11. lacks leadership skills

In this case, students identified a variety of communication competencies that needed improvement, including a number of skills related to their ability to create relationships with other members, and work cooperatively and productively on group tasks and activities.

Many of the ideal and deficient characteristics identified by students have been documented in research on groups and teams (Cannon-Bowers, Tannenbaum, Salas, & Volpe, 1995; Stevens & Campion, 1994). Over time, scholars have identified the following set of teamwork skills:

1. Being flexible and adaptable
2. Expressing an orientation to or having an awareness of the team or group
3. Giving, seeking, and receiving feedback
4. Leading and motivating other group members
5. Maintaining group member relationships through cooperation, collaboration, and conflict resolution
6. Coordinating and planning team and group activities
7. Communicating and listening effectively
8. Participating in decision making or problem solving
9. Helping the group or team establish specific goals

Despite the variety of sources, the three lists are remarkably similar, suggesting that these competencies are important to working effectively in groups and teams.

Given these three lists, it is not surprising that researchers have identified three sets of characteristics—(a) knowledge, skills, and abilities, (b) values, beliefs, and attitudes, and (c) personality traits, and cognitive and behavioral styles—as group member competencies. Having positive attributes in each of these three sets helps group members contribute effectively to the completion of tasks and activities as well as to group interaction, and create and maintain positive relationships with others in the group (Arrow et al., 2000). Task-relevant knowledge, technical skill to complete the activity, and the ability to communicate effectively are examples of the types of knowledge, skills, and abilities competencies we expect of other group members. The degree to which a group member values teamwork, a member's beliefs about the importance of consensus decision making, and a member's like or dislike of groups are examples of values, beliefs, and attitudes commonly expressed in groups. Finally, extraversion, cognitive complexity, and aggressiveness are, respectively, personality, cognitive, and behavioral style attributes that may be expressed in group situations. Regardless of what characteristics you believe you possess, it is the set of characteristics that are observable by others in the group on which you are evaluated.

Obviously, given the variety of group tasks and activities described in Chapter 4 and the different types of groups in which you participate, no one single set of attributes or characteristics will be effective in every group. Some attributes are group or team generic. These attributes directly influence group outcomes regardless of which team or group you are in; as such, they are transportable to other teams. Communication skills, skills associated with developing and maintaining relationships, and attitudes toward working in groups are examples. Other attributes are group or team specific. These attributes are observable only when you work with a particular group of people, or on a particular type of task. For example, having knowledge from shared experiences with some group members would be group specific, as would your attitudes about outcomes for a particular group project. If you can transport or use a characteristic in any group setting, then it is group generic; if not, then it is group specific (Cannon-Bowers et al., 1995).

Several communication attributes that are group generic are the focus of this chapter. However, remember that to be an effective and competent group member you must possess the necessary technical skills for group membership. These include the basic knowledge, skills, and abilities required for the group's activity. For example, to help your team win at a game of Frisbee golf, you need a reasonable amount of skill in throwing the Frisbee and some skills in motivating and cheering on other team members. Second, you must possess personal characteristics that enable you to work with others. In a problem-solving group at work, for example, you need to demonstrate intelligence and creativity to help your group accomplish tasks that meet the standards set by your boss. The technical and personal skills required depend on the type of group and the type of group task. Regardless of the type of group, members must display both the desire to contribute and the capability of collaborating and cooperating with others.

Your Group Interaction Style

Your interaction skills in group settings contribute to how others perceive you. How you present yourself and your ideas is a major factor in how others evaluate your worth as a group member. In fact, other members of your group are more likely to use your negative communication traits or lack of communication skills in forming impressions of you (Zimmermann, 1994). Thus how you communicate with other group members affects how your identity develops within the group and how well you work with others.

Members of organizational work groups and individuals who participate in meetings overwhelmingly report that interpersonal problems and poor communication skills contribute most to unsuccessful group meetings (Di Salvo, Nikkel, & Monroe, 1989). Skills most frequently reported as contributing to group dysfunction are poor listening (for example, not paying attention when others are speaking), ineffective vocal quality (not speaking up so as to be heard by all group members), poor nonverbal presentation (fidgeting with notebooks while speaking), the inability to clearly state the topic (taking an unnecessarily long time to describe a simple concept), the overuse of jargon or technical language, and the use of slang.

Other communication behaviors that negatively affect group interaction include dominating conversations or otherwise acting in ways designed to indicate one-upmanship or power, joking around too much, getting sidetracked during a group's conversation, and interrupting the speaker or talking over others. Participants in the research study also complained that some group members did not participate and that their lack of participation detracted from the group's success. There were three primary reasons given to explain why some members did not participate: (a) lack of interest in the group, (b) shyness, and (c) a desire to avoid responsibility. Finally, group members reported that individuals who bring poor, defensive, or negative attitudes to their groups or meetings detract from the group's success. Thus a variety of negative group communication skills can hinder group progress. Are you guilty of any of these? Most of us are. Lack of motivation or commitment may cause you to communicate ineffectively. Time pressures or role conflicts may make you communicate differently than you would normally. For most of us, even if we believe we are effective group communicators, there are still a few skill areas that could be improved.

Each member brings a unique set of communication skills to the group setting. The more skilled you are and the more comfortable you are in displaying those skills, the more likely you are to be perceived as an effective group member. It is important to increase your group skill level because skill deficiencies can obstruct the democratic process or create inequities in levels of participation. Often those perceived as having the most skill are given more opportunities to talk and to direct discussion toward their concerns. When this happens, the skilled group member has a bigger impact on the group's overall interaction (Gastil, 1993).

Your group communication skills depend on five factors. The first factor is your need to associate with other individuals. Your level and type of interpersonal need fundamentally controls how you communicate in groups. The second factor, communication competence, refers to the characteristics by which other group members evaluate your group effectiveness. Despite your level of competence, you are likely to have some apprehension about working in groups in general, in some types of groups, or with some group members. Communication apprehension, or your level of anxiety or apprehension about working in a group or meeting with others, is the third factor. If you are not apprehensive, you are more likely to join in the group's discussion and to be a member of many groups. The fourth factor, your feelings and attitudes about working in groups, can also influence your degree of participation and your motivation to help the group succeed. The final factor is your personality, which is largely responsible for the type of communication skills you display. Personality-driven communication behaviors have been identified as communicator style. These factors—interpersonal needs, communication competence, communication apprehension, your attitude toward groups, and communicator style—are discussed in the following sections.

Interpersonal Needs

Individuals have social needs—situations or conditions that can only be met by other people. This is what draws us to one another in groups to live, play, and work. There are three basic interpersonal needs—inclusion, affection, and control—that dictate your communication behavior in group settings (Schutz, 1966).

Inclusion is the need to establish and maintain satisfactory relations with others. You do this through interaction and association. Joining and communicating in groups allows you to work alongside those who have mutual interests, and identifying with other group members can help you fill this need. Each of these actions satisfies your need to be included and to include others. **Control**, which refers to the need to establish and share power and control with others, is often evident in group decision making. The degree to which you believe in your own competence and accept responsibilities is evaluated against the respect you hold for other members' competence and responsibilities. If you believe you are more competent, you take control; if you believe others are more competent, you let them take control. **Affection** involves the need to establish psychologically close relationships with others. You do this through developing and maintaining close personal ties to others you meet in group settings. Affection is based on liking, and you usually develop affection for those you like.

Expressing and Wanting Needs

Each of these dimensions—inclusion, control, and affection—is evident in group interaction in two ways. First, each dimension can be expressed by a group member. Expression of a dimension emphasizes the sender role. Each dimension can also be desired by a group member. The desire for a dimension from other group members emphasizes the receiver role. Thus a group member's communication behavior is affected by the degree of need on six variables: expressed inclusion, wanted inclusion, expressed control, wanted control, expressed affection, and wanted affection. Each group member has his or her own unique three-dimensional profile that is a mixture of expressed and wanted needs. For example, a group member with expressed control needs may also desire inclusion and affection from other group members, causing him or her to communicate more frequently in the group (Anderson & Martin, 2002).

If group members do not feel included, member identity with the group is likely to suffer. Thus members may drift away (physically or psychologically), hindering group member interdependence. If no one takes control, a group can easily lose its way and not accomplish its goal. More submissive members may even desire that one group member control the activities of the group. Although it is not necessary to develop intimate friendships with other members of a group, it is necessary for a moderate amount of affection to develop among members. Trust among group members often follows liking. Members of a group without any expressed affection may become suspicious or hostile, negating the opportunities to work together effectively.

Group members are sometimes very subtle in indicating when they have needs to be expressed or want needs to be satisfied by others. Let's join Kat, Patrick, Hanna, and JJ as they work on a new brochure for their university's department of communication. The department chair has asked members of the communication students' honor association to help design a new brochure. Let's see how they are doing and how interpersonal needs influence group members' conversation.

KAT: Are you done?

PATRICK: Okay, I just want to work out the details on the last paragraph before I give it to Hanna.

KAT: Okay. I'm sorry.

HANNA: "Our proposal is to consolidate information into a small pack, a pamphlet, that could easily incorporate deadlines, phone numbers, points of contact, and the like. This plan is to be the model for the remainder of the university while being the prototype for the communication department." I stop there.

PATRICK: I like it. Doesn't everyone like it?

HANNA: And I've also started a cover letter, but it's . . . it's just the normal basic stuff.

KAT: I have one small problem. The advising center repeatedly tells us that the goal of the university is not to educate us to graduate. If we keep emphasizing this in our copy . . .

PATRICK: I think Kat's right.

KAT: . . . if we keep emphasizing only graduation, I think we'll turn them off. Then they won't use the pamphlet.

PATRICK: Right.

KAT: That's my only problem.

HANNA: I don't believe it. It's impossible for you to have only one problem. Let's hear the rest.

KAT: It's not just the goal of the university I'm talking about; it's the goal of the pamphlet. Maybe we reword that . . .

PATRICK: Yeah.

KAT: No, I liked it. I just . . .

HANNA: I always like to do a rough draft and just throw it out. Okay, here, Kat. Fix it.

KAT: The advising center makes such a big deal about that, and I think that if we're selling it to the university, we really ought to broaden the goal statement.

JJ: Hmm, I made some possible goals . . . just wrote them out, and there are a whole bunch of them here. I'm just playing with words, but maybe you'd like it better if we could use the phrase "for students seeking a degree through the communication department," so our specific goal is to get students through the program with something, not just to graduate because they have the necessary hours.

PATRICK: Okay.

JJ: I don't know. It's your decision.

HANNA: Well?

KAT: Hold on. I just had a brief flash of inspiration that may not be worth mentioning. We were trying to come up with a phrase that could combine, you know, education and communication and graduating. Okay, I've lost them already. But something along the lines of, ummm, "information for students seeking to educate themselves in communication with the objective of graduating with a B.A. degree from the University of Wabash."

Can you identify Hanna's need to express control? Her need is expressed as she tries to direct the group's conversation and their work on the task. Can you identify Kat's desire to be included? She communicates it throughout the interaction, an indication that her desire to be included is not being fully met. How might you evaluate Patrick's expressed and wanted needs? It appears he has a need to be liked, or an affection need. Even though he is contributing to the task, he agrees with what other members are saying and doing, and at one point, he directly asks if others like what he has contributed.

Achieving Need Compatibility

Compatibility in groups—and ease in communication—is achieved when there is a balance of group members who want to express a need and those who want to receive it. Generally, members whose interpersonal needs are compatible with other group members are more satisfied and effective as a group (Keyton, 1992). Compatibility should not be confused with liking; rather, it refers to how well group members are able to work together. Compatibility is more a reflection of how complementary group members are to one another.

How much compatibility of needs must there be in a group for it to be effective? This depends on the type of group and the type of task or activity. An effective social support group has high compatibility on the inclusion and affection dimensions. A decision-making group needs compatibility on the control dimension. Must the numbers of group members who want a need be equal to the number of members who express that need? No. Groups can very efficiently satisfy the expression and want of needs. One dominant group member can satisfy several other members who need or want to be controlled, and one friendly member can satisfy the needs of several other members who need a great deal of affection.

When a need incompatibility exists, however, the group must spend time working out these differences. Incompatibility can also create confusion. Five of the six election officials of a voting precinct need to control others, but only Warren is willing to accept being controlled. As a result, Warren is unclear about how to proceed in setting up the voting booths because he gets several sets of conflicting instructions. Lydia is one of four officials with a high need to give affection to others. She is confused when Warren responds with a cold shoulder to her attempts to be friendly. She does not realize that with so many people trying to give Warren affection he is afraid this group may become more personal and intimate than he desires or can handle. Thus, when an incompatibility of needs exists within a group, anxiety is likely to develop. Once again, group members will need to address these issues to effectively work on their task.

Communication Competence

Competent group communicators know how and when to communicate. Thus, **communication competence** is the ability and willingness to participate responsibly in a communication transaction. To be considered competent in group interaction you need to communicate with both appropriateness and effectiveness (Spitzberg & Cupach, 1984, 1989). **Effectiveness** is achieved when the goal of the interaction is reached. If a group needs to make a decision, group members are effective only to the extent that they arrive at an acceptable decision. **Appropriateness** is achieved when group members communicate without violating behavioral expectations for that group context. Appropriate communication does not weaken relationships among group members, nor does it threaten any member's self-esteem. Appropriateness is synonymous with tact and politeness. Within a decision-making context, group members are appropriate when they do not shout at one another, make derogatory comments, or call one another names. Recognize, however, that behavior considered inappropriate for decision-making groups may be appropriate for sports teams—for example, if the name calling is in jest and is a norm among players.

Three skills are needed to achieve competence as a group communicator (Littlejohn & Jabusch, 1982). First, competent communicators comprehend the group situation and dynamics. Group members who can describe and then analyze the group process are reflective. They think back to the group situation and reflect on what happened, why it happened, and what could have been done to create a better group environment. To be reflective, you have to analyze both your own behavior in the group and the behavior of other group members. Once you train yourself to reflect on your group experiences and analyze what happened, you will be able to select more appropriate and more effective behaviors in similar situations in the future. Ask yourself these questions to gauge your ability to reflect upon a past group experience: Can you identify the norms for communicating that the group is establishing? Do you know what informal and formal roles other members are performing? Do the roles you fill fit effectively with the roles of other group members and help the group accomplish its goals? The better you understand the dynamics of the group's conversation, the better you can choose how to participate.

Second, competent communicators are sensitive to the feelings of others. They watch for clues in the group's interaction to help them adapt messages to other group members. For instance, suppose you notice that Natty is not saying much and looks troubled. During a break in the meeting, you ask her if she is okay but do not pry when she says that she does not want to talk about it. Back in the meeting, you sit next to her, give her encouraging smiles, and nod when she does participate. In a classroom discussion on affirmative action, you demonstrative sensitivity by initiating the conversation by tactfully asking how members refer to their ethnic and racial identities. Your attempt to be sensitive to others' feelings may keep some group members from using labels or identifiers that anger or offend others. When you are sensitive to other group members and use situationally appropriate behaviors, your behavior will be interpreted as attentive and empathic. This contributes to a supportive environment for the group.

Third, competent communicators have verbal and nonverbal skills that contribute effectively to the group's conversation. A skilled communicator can give feedback, ask and answer questions, discuss ideas without getting sidetracked, and

MASTERING GROUP SKILLS

How Competent Are You?

Think about your most recent group situation. For each of the following items, rate yourself as weak (having little or no skill in this area), competent (having the necessary skills in this area), or strong (having exceptional skills in this area).

1.	Is skilled at initiating and managing topics of conversation	weak	competent	strong
2.	Is able to ask open-ended questions	weak	competent	strong
3.	Uses complete sentences	weak	competent	strong
4.	Avoids uses of nonverbal fillers ("uhhh," "ummm")	weak	competent	strong
5.	Looks at others while speaking	weak	competent	strong
6.	Nods to encourage others while they speak	weak	competent	strong
7.	Avoids fidgeting while speaking	weak	competent	strong
8.	Speaks clearly (tone and speed)	weak	competent	strong
9.	Focuses body posture toward other group members	weak	competent	strong
10.	Avoids irrelevant responses	weak	competent	strong
11.	Describes ideas in detail	weak	competent	strong
12.	Is able to express opinions without being overly emotional	weak	competent	strong
13.	Provides clarifications	weak	competent	strong
14.	Monitors talking time to create equality	weak	competent	strong
15.	Laughs and smiles appropriately	weak	competent	strong
16.	Uses gestures to emphasize conversation	weak	competent	strong
17.	Shows appropriate facial expressions	weak	competent	strong
18.	Expresses empathy to others	weak	competent	strong

How do you rate your communication competence as a group member? Do you notice any patterns in your responses? Are your verbal competencies stronger or weaker than your nonverbal competencies? Which aspect of your competency needs the most improvement in terms of effectiveness or appropriateness for you to be successful? Are there other skills or competencies not listed here that you believe you should monitor in this group?

listen to others and to new ideas. The only way to increase your group communication skills is to participate, assess your interaction abilities, make adjustments, and try new communication strategies.

A group member can communicate appropriately but be ineffective, and an effective communicator can offend other members while achieving the group's goal. Thus it requires both effectiveness and appropriateness to be competent.

With this level of communication competence, you will demonstrate flexibility. Thus, to be competent, you must select the behaviors that fit the given group situation. "How Competent Are You?" will give you a good idea of your communication competence.

Communication Apprehension

Communication apprehension has been defined as fear or anxiety in relation to either real or anticipated communication with other people (McCroskey, 1977). This communicative predisposition can influence how well you function as a group member (McCroskey & Richmond, 1987). When you are apprehensive about communicating in groups, other group members may perceive you as shy or reticent. In fact, communication apprehension may have greater negative implications in the small-group setting than in any other communication context (McCroskey & Richmond, 1992). It is almost impossible to avoid being in groups, and in each group, all other members will evaluate your communication performance.

What causes communication apprehension? Perhaps you had poor group experiences early in life, or you may have general communication anxiety—anxiety about speaking to others in many situations. Everyone experiences some group anxiety at some time. You may have been anxious about joining a particular group because did not know the other group members. You may have felt anxious in a group meeting when your views were different from those being expressed. You may dislike groups because your experiences have taught you that being in a group means that you have to do the work of six, not the work of one.

Communication apprehension is most often thought of in public speaking situations, but many people express apprehension or anxiety about interacting in groups. In fact, individuals who are reticent—or anxious about interaction in general—interact less frequently in small groups than nonreticent individuals (Burgoon, 1977; Heston, 1974; McCroskey, 1977). More importantly, the contributions of group members who display anxiety to others are typically judged to be less relevant than the contributions of nonreticent group members. Apprehensive group members are also perceived by other group members as less credible and less effective, are less likely to be solicited for an opinion within a group, and are less likely to emerge as the group's leader than nonreticent individuals (McCroskey & Richmond, 1976; McKinney, 1982). Why does this happen? The more apprehensive you are, the more likely it is that your voice is not powerful or forceful enough to be heard by other group members. Or your voice may express nervousness. Your apprehension may be so strong that you remain silent even when you have something useful to say.

Being apprehensive in group situations can also affect your self-perception. Highly apprehensive group members have lower opinions of themselves, and they rate themselves as possessing and demonstrating fewer leadership skills (Hawkins & Stewart, 1991). And other group members agree with those assessments and rate them as being less socially and task attractive than people who are less apprehensive.

Talking less may seem to be a good way to manage your apprehension, but in fact it may be interpreted by others as an unwillingness to communicate and thus help the group. When you do feel anxious in a group, find another group member and develop a one-on-one relationship with him or her. Sit near this person in group meetings so you feel supported. Volunteer for group tasks you know you can accomplish (before you are assigned a task you are not comfortable with). This will build your confidence in speaking out in the group setting and contributing to the group's outcome. It is important that you assess your level of group apprehensiveness and work to control or overcome those feelings. Being anxious about communicating in group settings affects how you interact with others and can result in them perceiving you as not caring about the group or its task.

Your Attitude Toward Groups

Everyone has a predisposition or attitude about interacting in groups. Indeed, many people have **grouphate**, or negative feelings that cause them to dislike working with others in group settings (Keyton & Frey, 2002). Grouphate captures the tension between an individual's orientation to working alone and orientation to working with others. Grouphate is not the same as communication apprehension or anxiety about working in groups. In fact, the two are not related. A group member who is not apprehensive can simply lack the communication skills that allow for smooth interpersonal interaction to occur from which relationships are developed and group tasks accomplished. Without those skills, a persistent negative attitude about working in groups develops. Alternatively, grouphate may develop when an individual's inclusion, control, and affection needs are not met by group members.

Interestingly, grouphate is not related to characteristics people often associate with difficult group situations. This suggests that individuals come to group situations with an understanding that group interaction will manifest interaction difficulties (e.g., It's hard to get all group members to agree), and that these difficulties are more like challenges and are normal in group and team interaction. The good news is that grouphate can be minimized. In general, grouphate is reduced when individuals have positive experiences in group settings, such as when individuals use the group or team as an opportunity to improve their communication skills and meet new people, and when group interactions result in more input or information for working on the group task.

A group member who has a negative attitude about working in groups will have lower performance expectations than other group members (Baker, 2001). If you suspect this about one of your group members, you could demonstrate your group communication competence by creating a relationship with that member so that you can more easily include that person in the group's conversation. By doing so, you'll be more likely to satisfy his or her interpersonal needs and provide information about the group and its task, which might change negative attitudes to positive. Once your relationship has developed, you can further help this member to learn more about other group members and by identifying how his or her talents could help the group—both steps that will help create a more positive group experience and overcome grouphate.

Communicator Style

Another way to examine your interaction in groups is in terms of your **communicator style.** When you communicate with others, you leave an impression about your way of communicating both verbally and nonverbally (Norton, 1983). Your communicator style sends signals to others about how to process the content of your messages. Style adds color, tone, and rhythm to your messages; it creates a distinct signature to your communication. Thus style gives direction, form, or guidance to others about how the content of your messages should be understood.

Communicator style is characterized by nine dimensions: **dominant**, **dramatic**, **animated**, **relaxed**, **attentive**, **open**, **friendly**, **contentious**, and **precise** (Bednar, 1981; Montgomery & Norton, 1981). The way you communicate content is inextricably part of any message. Thus, not only should you be aware of the style, but you should also develop style flexibility to meet the changing demands of group interaction. One style profile (friendly, open, and relaxed) may work well in creating relationships, but you may need another style profile (dominant and precise) in defending your point of view when others question it. The "Determining Your Communicator Style" questionnaire, on pages 114–115, can help you describe your current communicator style. In addition to your self-assessment, you might want to ask a group member whom you trust to complete the communicator style assessment for you. Another person's perspective on your style will give you a broader picture of how you communicate. If the assessment reveals some weakness (for example, you have low relaxed and attentive scores), you can monitor your behavior in future group situations and work consciously to be more relaxed and attentive—perhaps taking a few minutes before the meeting to concentrate on the group's task, removing distractions, and increasing eye contact with other members.

Identify your three highest scores (of those 10 and higher); this is your predominant style, the one you're most likely to use. We'll use Virginia and Anika as examples of how dimensions combine to create a group member's communicator style. Virginia is contentious, dominant, and animated. This forceful communicator style works well for her as she leads her community group in political activities. But her style might be overwhelming for other group members when the group is working to establish trusting relationships. Anika is friendly, open, and relaxed. It is easy for her to engage others in conversation. However, she seldom starts a conversation; she almost always waits for other members to initiate the conversation. Others might interpret her style in terms of submission or unwillingness to take on responsibility.

Each of the style characteristics can be effective or ineffective depending on the group situation. As you assess and interpret your style, be careful that you do not make assumptions about a particular characteristic. For instance, if you have a dominant style, don't assume that your contributions are always constructive

Examine these photos showing group members with different communicator style. The styles are dominant and contentious (top left), animated and dramatic (top right), and friendly and open (bottom). Imagine being in a group with each of these individuals. How would their communicator styles contribute to or inhibit the group's interaction?

or effective. Quantity does not equal quality. You may talk a lot in the group but contribute little of substance to the conversation (Hansford & Diehl, 1988). Situationally, some groups will require that you contribute more; others will require that you contribute less.

How effectively does your style work for you? Is your style more effective in some group situations than others? The more scores you have of 10 or higher, the better you can move flexibly among communication strategies. How do you assess your flexibility? Consider yourself to have well-developed flexibility if you scored 10 or higher on at least five characteristics. Flexible communicators can respond to different groups and different types of group situations. With practice, you can increase your flexibility and your ability to select the most effective style based on the communication situation.

Whatever your group interaction style, your communication competence in group and team settings will also be evaluated by others based upon two abilities:

Determining Your Communicator Style

Thinking about how you generally communicate in groups, rate yourself on each item using the following scale:

0 = never   1 = infrequently   2 = sometimes   3 = frequently   4 = often

1. I readily express admiration for others. — 0 1 2 3 4
2. To be friendly, I verbally acknowledge others' contributions. — 0 1 2 3 4
3. My speech is free of nervous mannerisms. — 0 1 2 3 4
4. I am a very relaxed communicator. — 0 1 2 3 4
5. When I disagree with somebody, I am very quick to challenge them. — 0 1 2 3 4
6. I can always repeat back to a person exactly what was said. — 0 1 2 3 4
7. I am a very precise communicator. — 0 1 2 3 4
8. The rhythm or flow of my speech is smooth and easy. — 0 1 2 3 4
9. Under pressure I come across as a relaxed speaker. — 0 1 2 3 4
10. My eyes reflect exactly what I am feeling when I communicate. — 0 1 2 3 4
11. dramatize a lot. — 0 1 2 3 4
12. I deliberately react in such a way that people know that I am listening to them. — 0 1 2 3 4
13. I don't mind telling strangers information about myself. — 0 1 2 3 4
14. I tell jokes, anecdotes, and stories when I communicate. — 0 1 2 3 4
15. I tend to constantly gesture when I communicate. — 0 1 2 3 4
16. I am an extremely open communicator. — 0 1 2 3 4
17. In arguments or differences of opinion, I insist upon very precise definitions. — 0 1 2 3 4
18. In most situations, I speak very frequently. — 0 1 2 3 4
19. I like to be strictly accurate when I communicate. — 0 1 2 3 4
20. I physically and vocally act out when I want to communicate. — 0 1 2 3 4
21. I readily reveal personal things about myself. — 0 1 2 3 4
22. I am dominant in conversations. — 0 1 2 3 4
23. I am very argumentative. — 0 1 2 3 4
24. Once I get wound up in a heated discussion I have a hard time stopping myself. — 0 1 2 3 4
25. I am an extremely friendly communicator. — 0 1 2 3 4
26. I really like to listen very carefully to people. — 0 1 2 3 4
27. I insist that other people document or present some kind of proof for what they are arguing. — 0 1 2 3 4
28. I try to take charge of things when I am with people. — 0 1 2 3 4
29. It bothers me to drop an argument that is not resolved. — 0 1 2 3 4
30. In most situations I tend to come on strong. — 0 1 2 3 4
31. I am very expressive nonverbally. — 0 1 2 3 4
32. Whenever I communicate, I tend to be very encouraging to people. — 0 1 2 3 4

33. I use a lot of facial expressions when I communicate.   0 1 2 3 4
34. I verbally exaggerate to emphasize a point.   0 1 2 3 4
35. I am an extremely attentive communicator.   0 1 2 3 4
36. As a rule, I openly express my feelings and emotions.   0 1 2 3 4

Transfer your scores to the following chart. Then add across the rows for a total score for each row. Your scores for each row should be between 0 and 16.

1 _____	2 _____	25 _____	32 _____	Total _____	Friendly
3 _____	4 _____	8 _____	9 _____	Total _____	Relaxed
5 _____	23 _____	24 _____	29 _____	Total _____	Contentious
6 _____	12 _____	26 _____	35 _____	Total _____	Attentive
7 _____	17 _____	19 _____	27 _____	Total _____	Precise
10 _____	15 _____	31 _____	33 _____	Total _____	Animated
11 _____	14 _____	20 _____	34 _____	Total _____	Dramatic
13 _____	16 _____	21 _____	36 _____	Total _____	Open
18 _____	22 _____	28 _____	30 _____	Total _____	Dominant

1. Circle your three highest scores of 10 and above. These represent your predominant communicator style, the one you use most often and the one you believe is normal for you. How successful is your style in a group setting? What are the disadvantages of your style in group interaction?

2. Read the descriptions of the styles that follow. Which styles do you believe you need to develop to be more successful and effective in group settings?

Animated   This communicator uses expressive nonverbal behaviors such as facial expressions, eye contact, gestures, and body movements that reveal feelings; is lively and expressive; has emotional states that are easy for others to read.

Attentive   This communicator attends to others in ways that let others know they are being listened to; is closely related to friendly; is considered a good listener and empathetic; pays attention to the speaker; listens carefully and reacts deliberately.

Contentious   This communicator has a tendency to be argumentative and wants to debate points; is also quick to challenge others; demands that others back up their assertions with evidence.

Dominant   This communicator desires to take charge and control interaction; is confident, forceful, active, and self-assured; talks more than others and more loudly; is less compliant.

Dramatic   This communicator has a tendency to dramatize points through exaggeration, emphasis, jokes, story telling, and other dramatic devices; uses metaphor, rhythm, and voice to emphasize content.

Friendly   This communicator gives positive recognition to others through behavior that encourages and validates; is closely related to attentive; is affectionate, sociable, and tactful; encourages others, consistently acknowledging others' contributions.

Open   This communicator is frank, approachable, and willing to disclose information about self; is outspoken, gregarious, extroverted, and easy to read; readily reveals personal information about self.

Precise   This communicator reflects a concern for accurate and precise communication of ideas.

Relaxed   This communicator displays little anxiety and appears relaxed to others; is calm, collected, and confident; is relaxed even when under pressure, not tense.

Source: Adapted from Norton (1978).

(a) your ability to communicate effectively with group members who are culturally different, and (b) your ability to communicate ethically. Both of these competencies are addressed in the next two sections.

Communicating in Diverse Groups

Undoubtedly, you have experienced diversity in groups. And as our society and organizations become more diverse, you will have more opportunities to socialize and work with group members who are different from you. These differences will be expressed in the variety of experiences, values, abilities, and skills members bring to a group. And these differences can be highly beneficial. Groups with members who represent distinct and different demographic characteristics and social affiliations (for example, nationality, ethnicity, race, gender, age, and profession) are **heterogeneous.** Some of these distinctions may be obvious to you when you first join a group. Other distinctions will become more obvious as you interact over time and become better acquainted with and learn more about your group members. Alternately, **homogeneous groups** are those in which members are similar with respect to their demographic characteristics and social affiliations. Members with similar social affiliations are often perceived as sharing basic assumptions that guide their attitudes, beliefs, and values.

Cultural differences can create interesting variety in groups and provide multiple perspectives from which to consider issues or problems. In a more homogeneous group, it is easier to attribute uniqueness to the special qualities of an individual member. In a heterogeneous group, the same uniqueness may be falsely attributed to a group member's cultural background. As workers of all races and ethnic identifications are drawn into all levels of the workforce, each of us will have more opportunities to work in a group with others who are unlike us in basic values, attitudes, beliefs, and assumptions. Certainly, this can create stress, but these difficulties are not insurmountable.

Culture Orientations

The extent to which a culture promotes individualism or collectivism is one of the most important dimensions of cultural difference. Individualistic and collectivistic cultures approach activities and communication differently (Hofstede, 1984, 1991; Oetzel, 1995). **Individualistic** cultures are those that value individual recognition more than group or team recognition. As a result, group members from individualistic cultures are more likely to be task-oriented and to expect confrontation from other members. They also expect members to speak up and say what is on their minds. Generally, people from the United States, Great Britain, and Australia champion this set of beliefs. Groups composed of individualistic members believe that high productivity or quality decision making is a reflection of their group effectiveness.

Alternately, other cultures promote **collectivistic** values in which work by groups or teams is valued over individual accomplishment. In this type of culture, "we" is more important than "I." People from collectivistic cultures are more relationally oriented and expect harmony in their groups. This heightens the tendency for group members to feel obligated to the group. Direct confrontation is perceived to be rude and impolite. When groups are composed of individuals from collectivistic cultures, group effectiveness is evaluated according to group members' abilities to develop cohesiveness and commitment. Japan, China, and Taiwan value this orientation, as do some Central and South American countries.

An awareness of the distinction between individualistic and collectivistic can be helpful as you work in culturally diverse groups. But you need to be cautious in trying to identify a group member's cultural orientation as being at one or the other end of the individualistic-collectivistic continuum. In one way, American culture is individualistic, but you can probably think of many instances in which a team, or collectivistic, culture is promoted. This means that you must be careful about categorizing group members according to their culture, as individuals from the same culture do not always agree on basic values (Cox, Lobel, & McLeod, 1991). As a result, you must also be cautious about overgeneralizing in relation to individuals' societal orientations. You cannot rely on simple guidelines to cultural orientation (for example, that group members who are German will engage in frequent argument). Why? Because cultural differences do not subsume individual differences. Remember that when you read about particular cultures you are reading a generalized view of the culture. Within that culture, individual differences and individualized communicator styles still exist.

For most groups, there are multiple dimensions on which members will differ. Gender and cultural diversity are the obvious ways in which people identify themselves and respond to other people. But diversity is seldom limited to one type of difference. Although all dimensions of diversity can create more communication difficulty for group members, not all types of diversity affect a group's interaction in the same way (Pelled, Eisenhardt, & Xin, 1999).

Thus you should be sensitive to wrongly identifying a group problem as a diversity problem. It's far more likely that different ideas are just that—different ideas. Differences are generally not connected to demographic differences (Rodriguez, 1998). This tendency to identify group problems as diversity problems is especially acute when proportional representation exists. For example, in a group composed of five White students and one Asian American, it is easy to assume that any differences in communicator style exhibited by the Asian American member is due to her culture and ethnicity. But maybe these differences are merely individual differences. She may be different from other group members, but not different *because* she's Asian American. It's easy to let personal differences become cultural differences when they are not (Li, Karakowsky, & Siegel, 1999).

Overcoming Diversity Problems

If you do perceive diversity problems in your group, you are likely to react in one of several ways (Kirchmeyer, 1993; Larkey, 1996a; Thomas, 1995). By identifying

A group with cultural differences can create similarities by focusing on the group's goal or task.

KOFI ANNAN   TARJA HALONEN

your own reactions and assessing the interactions of other group members, you can proactively work to influence your group's positive response to cultural diversity.

One of the most obvious problems in diverse groups is unequal participation. This can occur for many reasons. Often group members from the majority culture dominate the group's interaction, at the expense of members from minority cultures. Emphasizing cultural differences in this way can cause team members to overestimate their similarity to members of the same culture and to overestimate their differences from members of other cultures (Northcraft, Polzer, Neale, & Kramer, 1995). Simply, we talk more to people we perceive to be similar to us and less to people we perceive to be dissimilar.

This type of exclusion can occur in two ways: (a) verbally, as when majority group members start conversations only with other members who are similar to them, and (b) nonverbally, as when a majority group member physically turns away from minority group members as if to direct interaction only to certain group members. By not participating in group conversations, the excluded members lose information, contacts, and opportunities to help the group. Moreover, when this happens, the group generates greater conformity or uniformity in its ideas, which severely limits the group's potential. Diverse groups can produce greater diversity of ideas and be more creative. Usually, the greater the diversity of ideas to choose from, the better the idea ultimately selected.

Some group members may have an unconscious response to diversity. This often is demonstrated when group members deny that diversity exists in the group. When members deny that diversity matters, they may offend other group members who want their diversity to be recognized. A group member who denies that diversity exists may try to suppress minority group members with put-downs —for example, asking "How long have you been a member of this group?" to remind minority group members of their minority status.

Practicing segregation within the group is also a denial tactic. When majority group members cluster together on one side of the meeting table, their behavior is a reminder to minority group members that they are not welcome or that they are not seen as equals in the group. How can you overcome this reaction to group diversity? One way is to monitor other group members' reactions to you, especially the reactions of group members who are culturally different. You may be unaware that you are practicing segregation, verbally or nonverbally. Once you become aware of others' reactions and feedback, you will find it easier to monitor your communication behavior and become more inclusive.

One way to overcome diversity issues in groups is for members to monitor their own communication style for its effectiveness and appropriateness, and to practice convergence by adapting their communication to the style of others. Another way is to emphasize equal status by using group discussion procedures to equalize the amount of talking in the group. It is easy for members who do not feel comfortable to refrain from talking and for those who do feel comfortable to not recognize that they are monopolizing the conversation. Building cohesiveness can help group members feel more comfortable with one another. When group members feel comfortable, it is more likely that all will participate in group discussions (Bantz, 1993). Emphasizing the team's own unique culture helps it develop group unity and promote equality.

Focusing on goal interdependence, especially long-term goals, is another way to overcome diversity problems (Bantz, 1993; Triandis, 1995a; Wong, Tjosvold, & Lee, 1992). With goal interdependence, members create a common vision that helps to ensure that each member's success contributes to the goal attainment of other group members. Although conflict is inevitable in diverse groups, group members who can communicate to other members that their primary interests are in long-term cooperation will move through periods of conflict more easily.

Another way to address problems associated with heterogeneous groups is to increase similarity while decreasing dissimilarity among group members (Triandis, 1995a). Even though group members are different, they may still share certain beliefs and values. Taking time to explore the similarities that exist among group members can help a group overcome perceived differences due to cultural diversity.

Perhaps the best advice for overcoming diversity problems is to emphasize personal identity, not social identity (Oetzel, 1995). Rather than seeing yourself and others as belonging to categories (for example, White, American, male, manager), view yourself and other group members as individuals—each with a unique identity and personality, and able to contribute uniquely to the group. When group members are viewed as individuals, more equal participation results.

Effective and ineffective groups differ more in how they manage their diversity than in the extent to which diversity is absent or present. When a group is composed of diverse individuals, group members need to take proactive steps to create a supportive climate in which integration and congruence can occur. By creating a team culture from the diversity of its members, the group can take advantage of diversity by making it a resource for the group (Adler, 1986; Cox, 1995).

Ethical Group Membership

What is ethical communication? How important is it to group situations? How do group situations affect an individual member's ethical behavior? These questions and others like them are gaining in importance as we increasingly rely on groups to fulfill a variety of personal and professional needs. Ethical group communication is based on two dimensions of interaction: caring and responsibility (Littlejohn & Jabusch, 1982).

The first dimension—caring—means that an ethical group member is concerned about the well-being of all participants. This is evident when a member is more interested in promoting group goals than individual goals. The good of the group comes before the good of the individual. The second dimension—responsibility—means that group members share in the responsibility for the outcome of the group's interactions.

Because groups can act collectively, allowing for actions that could not occur individually, new moral or ethical responsibilities surface (May, 1987). As a member, you represent the group. Your actions alone can affect how people think about and react to other members of your group. Thus, as a member of a group, your moral or ethical responsibility has increased. You are no longer merely responsible for yourself; now you are responsible for and to every other member of your group.

Other moral and ethical issues surface in group settings as well. In particular, issues of deception (such as lying or not revealing all that you know) can hamper the development of group member relationships and the group's ability to proceed effectively with its task or activity. In developing a list of ethical guidelines, however, it is easy to see that ethical behavior is situational. In groups, one ethical guideline may conflict with another because there can be competing claims on the group. Should group members always tell the truth? Should group members withhold some information if it can potentially harm relationships among group members? Let's take a look at a list of ethical guidelines for group interaction (Johannesen, 1983).

First, be candid and frank when you state your personal beliefs and feelings. "I don't think so" should mean just that, and not, "I'd like to tell you but don't feel that I can right now." Not only should statements of disagreement be direct and supported with a rationale, but so should statements of agreement. This kind of direct and straightforward communication keeps other group members from making assumptions about how you think and feel about a problem or issue before the group. Second, and sometimes in opposition to the first guideline, when social relationships among group members are valued, it is better to maintain those relationships than to completely divulge what is on your mind. For example, in your family, you may have information about your brother-in-law but believe that telling your sister that information will hurt her. In this case, you have to decide whether you should tell your sister what you know, causing her some short-term pain but preparing her to deal with her husband later, or should remain silent and let her discover the information on her own. Thus ethical behavior is situational: You have to make choices between being candid and harming others.

Third, when you share information in group settings, that information should be communicated without distortion or exaggeration. For example, suppose you take on the responsibility of checking on the availability of the clubhouse for your group's party. After checking several dates, you are frustrated: The only date available is one on which you have another obligation. Reporting back to the group, you claim, "The clubhouse isn't going to be available. They're booked all the way through June!" You probably did not intend to exaggerate your claim to make it appear that the clubhouse was not available, but that is the message you delivered to your friends. If you do this intentionally, this is unethical. The ethical way to handle this is to report back what you actually found out, with the additional information that you want to attend the party but cannot on the only date the clubhouse is available.

Fourth, in group settings, it is easy to cut someone off from speaking or to change the subject. This is unethical if you do it intentionally. Each group member should have the opportunity to speak and to fully explain him- or herself. The fifth ethical guideline concerns trust. Although trust is rarely offered explicitly or fully without a relationship history, you should be willing to extend your trust to others in the group and to act in a trustworthy manner. This means that you are open-minded and willing to listen to what other members have to say; you are not closed-minded, refusing to accept others' points of view. This also means that you can be trusted with information given to you and with responsibilities assigned to you. Sixth, particularly in decision-making situations, each group member should be allowed to make up his or her own mind without coercion or manipulation. Consensus or agreement is best developed through discussion rather than force. Seventh, because group members represent the collective, each should be responsible for defending the decisions of the group to others. If you cannot do this, say so during the group's decision-making deliberations.

Groups often must make ethical choices during their decision making, and complex decisions deliberated in group settings often center around ethical dilemmas (Dukerich, Nichols, Elm, & Vollrath, 1990). Frequently, the ethical choice has some negative consequences or is not the popular choice. For example, a production team realizes that it has produced a pallet of cardboard boxes that do not meet the manufacturing specifications. The production error doesn't weaken box integrity, but the error will be noticed by the customer who has a long-standing contract with the manufacturing facility. Normally, team members would confer and agree to rerun the job. However, the team is also behind and it's the Friday before a 3-day holiday. Does the production team decide to rerun this job according to the specifications and push back other customers' work? Or does the team agree to sign off on the job ticket and put it on their supervisor's desk just as they're walking out for the long weekend?

Both choices have ethical consequences—for the product, for the team, and for the organization. Why might a group risk making an unethical decision? The environment in which decisions are made can create additional demands or pressures on groups (Street, Robertson, & Geiger, 1997). For example, if group members feel incapable of making a decision, they may opt for an unethical alternative because they feel defeated. Or group members may feel that they have invested so much time and energy in the project that the selection of any alternative, regardless of its ethical implications, will do. A group may start out wanting to do what is best and what is right, but as time passes and risks and costs to the group increase, moral intent and moral behavior can be affected. In this type of pressure-filled environment, an unethical alternative can be regarded as viable.

Different groups may face different ethical dilemmas, but all group members should be ethical members of their groups. It is difficult to develop guidelines, but following some basic ground rules can help you avoid ethical dilemmas (Hargrove, 1998). Here are some basic guidelines that are especially helpful in groups:

1. Treat everyone as a colleague, with respect and politeness.
2. Speak with good intent. Everything you say has meaning for others.
3. Ask questions to satisfy your curiosity, not to reveal your cynicism.
4. Openly express your disagreements.
5. Avoid making attributions about other members' motives or thinking.
6. Help facilitate the group by suggesting a different process or procedure.
7. Avoid coming to decisions too quickly.
8. Acknowledge that a group problem is an opportunity to make the group more effective.
9. Respect confidentiality. Some things said in your group must stay in your group.
10. Clarify your opinions and statements with examples.
11. Acknowledge others' viewpoints and accept them as real.

Summary

To the extent that you want to appear to others to be competent, group communication skills are important. In fact, your communication skills moderate everything you do in groups. Whether individuals are asked to identify ideal or deficient group member characteristics, numerous elements of interaction style related to creating relationships with other members, and working cooperatively and productively in a group are always mentioned. Three sets of characteristics—(a) knowledge, skills, and abilities, (b) values, beliefs, and attitudes, and (c) personality traits, and cognitive and behavioral styles—comprise both group-generic and group-specific group member competencies.

At the most basic level, communication in groups is based on members' interpersonal needs. Needs are expressed on dimensions of inclusion, control, and affection. Reciprocally, individuals want to receive inclusion, control, and affection from other group members. Compatibility in groups—and ease in communication—is achieved when there is a balance of group members who want to express a need and members who want to receive it. When need incompatibility exists, a group will spend more of its time working out these relational differences than it will effectively working on the task.

Evaluations of your group communication competence are based on how effectively and appropriately you communicate. Effective communicators achieve their goals, and appropriate communicators do so without damaging the self-esteem of others. Flexibility in communicator styles allows you to be responsive to individuals in all types of groups.

Some individuals are communication apprehensive, particularly in group situations. Anxiety may result from earlier negative group experiences, or it may arise when you do not know other group members or are unfamiliar with the group's task. The only way to overcome communication apprehension is to put yourself in comfortable group situations so that you can practice talking with others.

Many people have grouphate or negative feelings that cause them to dislike working with others in group settings. Grouphate is not the same as communication apprehension or anxiety about working in groups, nor is it related to characteristics people often associate with difficult group situations. Grouphate can be minimized when individuals have positive experiences in group settings.

Your communicator style is the impression you make on other group members based on how you communicate verbally and nonverbally. There are nine communicator style characteristics: dominant, dramatic, animated, relaxed, attentive, open, friendly, contentious, and precise. Your predominant communication style, or the style you most commonly use, is comprised of your highest scoring dimensions. However, you should assess your style to determine if it is appropriate and effective in different group situations. The greater your flexibility using different style profiles, the more likely you are to be successful in groups.

Finally, all group members need to communicate ethically. An ethical group member communicates in a way that balances caring for the well-being of all participants with responsibility for the group and its task. Ethical issues to be considered involve deception, lies, information sharing, exaggeration or bias, trust, and coercion and manipulation. To avoid making unethical decisions, groups should use problem-solving and decision-making procedures.

PUTTING THE PIECES TOGETHER

Group Identity and Group Goal

Think of a recent group experience. In this group, what are the ways in which you demonstrated that you were a competent group communicator? Be specific. In what ways did you communicate to meet others' interpersonal needs, communicate appropriately and effectively to help an apprehensive group member or a group member with a negative attitude overcome those difficulties, demonstrate flexibility in your communication style, and communicate competently despite cultural obstacles or ethical dilemmas? In total, to what degree did your communication competence enhance group member identity and the group's ability to be successful or effective in meeting its goals?

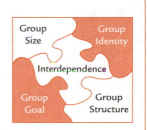

Discussion Questions and Exercises

1. Watch a sitcom, drama, or film that features group interaction. Pay particular attention to the main characters. Do the characters display any evidence of communication apprehension or grouphate? How do other characters relate to these displays? What advice would you give to the character who seems apprehensive? What advice would you give to the character who displays negative attitudes in the group?

2. In small groups of five to seven members, develop a communication profile of the ideal group member. Describe this member's interpersonal needs, level of communication apprehension, communicator style, and communication competence. How different are you from this ideal group communicator? Do you wish you had any of these attributes? What could you do to be more like this ideal communicator?

3. Think of three group members with whom you had difficulty communicating in the past. Using expressed and wanted needs, identify the interpersonal need profile for each individual. How did your communicator style meet or address the needs of these individuals? How could you have changed your communicator style to better meet their needs?

4. Recall a group situation in which there was cultural diversity. What evidence do you have that the distinctions you noted about group members were based on cultural differences? Individual differences? Evaluate the steps you took to help the group overcome any cultural obstacles.

5. Recall a group situation in which you questioned your own ethical behavior or the ethical direction or decision of the group. Now that you have some distance from that situation, what would you do differently? Why?

6 Building Relationships in Groups

GROUP SKILLS PREVIEW

In this chapter, you will learn to do the following:

- Diminish your dependence on and enhance your interdependence with your group members

- Contribute to developing a supportive group climate

- Assist your group in developing cohesiveness

- Maximize your satisfaction in a group and help create satisfaction for other group members

- Maintain the trust of group members

- Socialize new members into a group

A group is a social context in which people come together to perform some task or activity. This cannot be done without creating relationships among group members. This chapter will explore the communication relationships among group members that help to form a group's communication climate and the degree to which communication contributes to cohesiveness and satisfaction among group members. The strength and resiliency of group member relationships is a critical factor in the equity and trust group members perceive in the group. Thus how you build and maintain relationships with other group members will influence whether and how well the group completes its task.

Relating to Other Group Members

Being in a group creates interdependencies among members, which are related to the group's goal. As a result, relationships among members will develop as the group interacts to accomplish its task or activity. These relationships can be positive or negative, productive or destructive. How group member relationships develop depends on a number of factors. But two primary factors are your expectations about the relationships you develop and your willingness to accept the relationships offered you by other group members. Being dependent on other members of your group is very different from being interdependent with the other group members. Let's take a look at those differences.

Being Dependent on Other Group Members

Some group tasks and activities force your dependence on other members within the group. At the interpersonal level, **dependence** means that there is a connection between you and the group and its members, but this connection has you in a subordinate position. Perhaps you are a new member and have not yet found your role within the group. Or perhaps by nature you are more submissive than dominant. This is likely to put you in a more dependent relationship with other group members. In a dependent relationship, the reciprocity is imbalanced—one person gives more than another. This is not unusual in groups. However, you certainly do not want to be dependent on all other group members. In such a situation, you will not be perceived as contributing to or being a useful member of the group.

For example, Jamal's class group is having a great deal of trouble dealing with an overly dependent member. Initially, Paula seemed to be an integral member of the group, contributing to and bringing outside resources into the group. But gradually Paula's participation has declined, and now she is habitually coming late to group meetings, failing to complete her assigned group tasks, and contributing very little to the group's interaction and output. Jamal believes that Paula considers other events in her life to be more important than this group. And other group members agree with Jamal's interpretation.

Interestingly, though, other group members helped Paula become dependent. As her contributions lessened, others took up the slack. They graciously brought her up to date when she was late. Jamal double-teamed with her on many assignments so he was always ready to present her part if Paula did not come through. In fact, Jamal and the other group members helped to create the overdependence as much as Paula did. When Paula perceived that the other group members were willing to help her out (she did not ask, and she did not provide a reason for her lack of participation), she contributed even less. In this case, Paula's dependence on others was not because she was a new member. Initially, Paula's interaction style was not submissive. The group simply reacted to her declining participation and through their own behavior reinforced Paula's behavior as acceptable. In this case, dependence is unhealthy for both Paula and the group.

Being Interdependent with Other Group Members

In contrast to dependence, recall from Chapter 1 that interdependence means that both group and individual outcomes are influenced by what other individuals do in the group. Simply, interdependence occurs when group members rely on and cooperate with one another to complete the group activity. When interdependence among group members is high, there are equally balanced relationships within the group. All group members are influencing other group members in a positive way, which in turn contributes to the group's ability to perform its task or achieve its goals.

Remember that interdependence is one of the key elements in defining a group. Without interdependence, a group fails to exist. Truly effective interdependence can develop only when group members have managed or resolved their problems. When interdependence exists, expectations develop about how group members will interact. Norms, or standards for behavior, become established. Having such a level of interdependence allows the group to focus more quickly on its task or to work through relational issues when they arise.

A wonderful illustration of interdependence in groups is found in a description of the Detroit String Quartet, a subgroup of the Detroit Symphony Orchestra (Hackman, 1990). The interaction in the group is described as smooth; group members know their roles both as musicians and as task managers of nonmusical activities, with each taking on different responsibilities, such as scheduling performances, arranging music, and scheduling rehearsals. Apparently, this group knows how to work through its task and relational issues, using what is called "invisible management." You might also think of it as seamless management—everything fits together so well that it is hard to tell who does what. Interdependence in the group is so well developed, established, and accepted by group members that management of the group seems invisible.

This group has clear and elevating goals; each member, as well as the group as a whole, is fully committed to performing well. As a result, the group has a shared sense of direction, and members experience a strong collective responsibility for their work. And their work is challenging, as it is highly unlikely that any quartet will give a perfect performance (Hackman, 1990). Contributing to the group's success is that it is self-managing; the members alone decide who will be invited to fill vacancies and what norms will guide their behavior. All of this is astonishing for members of a part-time quartet who are not even paid for performing. And this depth of interdependence could not have been imposed on the group by others. Rather, it emerged from the quartet members' communication with one another. Thus interdependence represents the culmination of each group member's contributions to the group.

Not all groups, of course, achieve this level of interdependence. Some groups fail to develop interdependent interaction because communication among members is not frequent enough or of high enough quality to help members achieve the group's goal. Thus the degree of interdependence can vary and is group specific based on the group task and members' communication preferences. As interdependence influences task activity, it also influences relational activity. Interdependence can affect group members' abilities to develop and maintain relationships, which, in turn, influences the group's communication climate and group members' level of cohesiveness toward and satisfaction with the group. We will look at each of these in the following sections.

Group Communication Climate

A group's **communication climate**, or the atmosphere group members create, results from group members' use of verbal and nonverbal communication and their listening skills. Assessing your group's communication climate will help you present your ideas and opinions in ways that make them more likely to be accepted. By paying attention to your presentation strategies, you are also likely to strengthen your relationships with others in the group and to avoid unnecessary confrontation. Thus a group's communication climate is the tone, mood, or character of the group that develops from the way in which group members interact with and listen to one another.

Early research on groups (Gibb, 1961) demonstrated that climates in groups range on a continuum from defensive to supportive. Of course, you do not want to be a member of a group that has a **defensive climate**—a climate based on negative or threatening group interaction. Initially, you may believe that all groups should have a **supportive climate**, or a positive environment. But, to be most effective, you must be able to assess and then create the level of supportiveness you desire in your groups. For instance, a counseling group needs a more supportive climate than a task force making decisions about personnel policies. And the task force needs a more supportive climate than a group of prison supervisors deciding on discipline for inmates. All groups require some level of a supportive climate, but groups vary in their position on the supportive-defensive continuum.

A group's communication climate is built on group members' use of six categories of communication behavior: (a) evaluation versus description, (b) control versus problem orientation, (c) strategy versus spontaneity, (d) neutrality versus empathy, (e) superiority versus equality, and (f) certainty versus provisionalism. Bringing together a group of people to establish and fulfill a group goal always creates a unique interaction context and presents some challenging interaction moments—moments you will recognize as you read the descriptions of the six categories.

Evaluation Versus Description

To arrive at a good idea, group members toss many ideas into the interaction for consideration. Not every idea is great, and when a group member suggests an idea that is considered less than ideal by other members, there is a tendency to evaluate the person rather than the idea. This is the basic notion behind evaluation and description. **Evaluation** occurs when a group member uses evaluative language or content that criticizes the other person. A good example is when a group member uses "you" language to assess the person who introduced the idea. For example, John appears critical of Betsy when he says, "You know, your idea isn't very good; in fact, they never are!" This type of language, particularly when it is accented with a dismissive tone of voice, is likely to cause Betsy to withdraw to some extent—maybe even to the point of not participating. And other group members may withdraw in fear that they will also be evaluated harshly when they introduce ideas.

As an alternative to evaluation, **description** occurs when a group member describes the idea in terms of its weakness and strengths. A better way for John to give Betsy feedback about her idea is to say, politely and tactfully, "I appreciate your idea, Betsy; how can that fit within our budget?" Asking for more information and analyzing an idea and not the person provide a more constructive framework for the entire group. Describing what is wrong with an idea gives the group member who introduced it the opportunity to clarify its presentation or to amend the idea for consideration by the group. Describing the idea may also stimulate other group members to join in and help transform the poor idea into a better one. Description is almost always preferable to evaluation because group members benefit when they know why an idea is rejected. Evaluation simply humiliates the person and is likely to result in a defensive relationship and a defensive group climate.

Control Versus Problem Orientation

Controlling behavior causes a defensive reaction because implicit in controlling is the assumption that controllers know what is best for those whom they are attempting to control. Controlling language or nonverbal behavior makes others feel ignorant, uninformed, or immature. "You meant to say that the budget is $250,000? Isn't that what you meant?" said in a belligerent voice, with a wide-eyed glare, belittles the group member in front of others and asserts the dominance of one member over the other. To make the most of group situations, members need to exhibit the spirit of group participation and democracy, and control does not fit well with those concepts. When controllers assert their superiority, it decreases the likelihood that everyone will participate.

An alternate to controlling behavior is **problem orientation.** A group member practicing problem orientation strives for answers and solutions that will benefit all group members and satisfy the group's objective. A member with a problem orientation does not assume that there is a predetermined solution to be found. Asking honest questions like "Is the budget we're working with $250,000?" is a method for seeking collaboration on solving the problem. When group members adopt this attitude and it is reflected in their interactions, it is easier for them to receive cooperation from one another and to achieve group cohesiveness and productive outcomes.

Strategy Versus Spontaneity

At the outset, **strategy** sounds like a good thing. In this case, however, strategy denotes manipulation of others. Strategy is apparent when a group member places him- or herself above the group or its task. In other words, the member is perceived as having a hidden agenda and wants group members to unknowingly help him or her achieve it. For example, to achieve your own goals, you might withhold necessary information or ask others to perform tasks for you that might otherwise put you at risk. When a group member fakes sincerity or tries to hide motivations, the member is likely to be accused of being strategic.

At the opposite end of this dimension is **spontaneity**. A group member who acts spontaneously is open and honest with other group members. This group member is known for his or her immediacy in the group and willingness to deal

Six different types of behavior contribute to a defensive communication climate; each is based on some type of threat or other negative interaction. Another six behaviors contribute to a supportive communication climate; each is based on positive or friendly interactions. Although most groups generally prefer a supportive climate, groups differ in the amount of support they need.

with issues as they come up. If a member is straightforward with others, the other group members are likely to reciprocate that honesty and openness, which creates a more supportive communication climate for completing the group's task or activity.

Neutrality Versus Empathy

We have all had bad days and not performed at our best in group situations. In a supportive group climate, other group members express empathy for our situation because we have expressed empathy for them. **Empathy** does not mean that another group member is excused from doing his or her assigned tasks; rather, it means that group members express genuine concern and are helpful if their help is requested. Empathic communication conveys members' respect for and reassurance of the receiver. Nonverbal behaviors are especially good at conveying empathy. For example, a smile, a kind gesture, and respect for someone's privacy are ways group members can express empathy for one another.

In contrast, **neutrality** is expressed when group members react in a detached or unemotional way. When group members react with a lack of warmth, other members often feel as if they are not important. For example, Detria comes to the group hesitant to ask for more time to complete her assignment. A series of unfortunate events—her mother's illness, a poor performance on a biology test, and a roommate who just announced she was leaving at the end of the month—prevented Detria from completing her responsibilities to the group. A group member responding with empathy would say something like "Sure, Detria, we understand you need until Monday. Is there anything we can do to help you out?" Said quietly and respectfully, this response demonstrates concern for Detria's situation but doesn't let her disregard her responsibility to the group. Detria would have been met with neutrality if a group member had responded with an offhand "okay, whatever" to her request for more time.

Superiority Versus Equality

Each of us has our strengths and weaknesses, but it usually leads to a more defensive communication climate when a group member continually reinforces his or her **superiority** over others. Name dropping is a good example of demonstrating superiority. Another example of superiority is when a group member continually assumes leadership functions in the group without regard for others in that same role. Often other group members will interpret these attempts at superiority as reflecting a lack of substance and style, and begin to polarize themselves from that group member. Attempts at superiority also discourage others from entering into collaborative problem solving.

Groups are more likely to create supportive communication climates when **equality** is stressed. This does not mean that everyone does the same thing. Think of this more in terms of equity. Equitable assignments for group members are one aspect of equality, just as are trust and respect. Remember that trust and respect are earned and given incrementally. It is every group member's responsibility to work for trust and respect, and to give trust and respect when these are due. And because each group member must establish his or her own trust relationship with each other group member, creating a sense of trust within the group is a long-term, complex process. Equality is also expressed in the tone of voice and type of language used. Using a respectful, polite tone and using the same kind of language to talk to different members are important in establishing equality.

Certainty Versus Provisionalism

No one likes a know-it-all, especially in a group. Group members who believe they have all the answers or who *know* what another group member is going to say or do create a defensive environment. Often, when one group member acts with **certainty**, it triggers a chain reaction, causing other group members to respond with certainty in hopes of proving the other group member wrong. For instance, certainty is revealed by a group member when she cuts off the attempts of other members to answer a question or to finish a complete thought.

A more effective alternative is to act with **provisionalism**. This state is one of flexibility and commitment to solving the group's problems. Rather than taking sides, provisional group members want to hear all of the ideas so they can make better, more informed choices. Provisionalism encourages experimentation with and exploration of ideas in the group. To encourage provisionalism in your group, use descriptive and nonevaluative language to summarize the different positions before the group, and then ask group members if you have correctly summarized the major issues. This creates an opportunity for group members to ask more questions, and it can diffuse the dominance of one or two group members.

Altering the Group Climate

Anyone can engage in defensive communication. And, if too many group members use defensive behaviors, the group as a whole can develop a defensive communication climate. As you might guess, the more group members exhibit the behaviors that lead to a defensive communication climate, the more likely the group is to become focused on relational problems. In turn, this deters the group from working on its task, completing its goal, or providing support for members. Each of us is probably guilty of some defensive behaviors. We may even fall into a rut of behaving defensively because of our personality attributes, our negative feelings about past group experiences, our negative feelings about a group member from other interactions, or our negative feelings about groups in general. When negativity and defensiveness become routine and create issues of dominance, power, and conflict, it is typical for a group to become habitually defensive and have difficulty returning to a supportive communication climate (Broome & Fulbright, 1995; Eadie, 1982).

If any of the defensive conditions describe you in group situations, you can help the group develop a more supportive climate in two ways. First, you can monitor your own behavior and adopt more positive behaviors. The behaviors that create a supportive communication climate require you to assess the group situation, think about what you want to say, and evaluate your statements for their potential impact on other group members. And you must follow through. Good intentions alone do not lead to a supportive communication climate. Use description rather than evaluation to assess the input of others. Create opportunities for all group members to participate. Be open and honest, but tactful. Express empathy for others in the group. Create a sense of equality through equitable assignments and responsibilities. Finally, be flexible and open. It is impossible for one group member to have all of the answers to all of the group's questions and needs. If you adopt some of these supportive interaction strategies, you will strengthen your relationships in groups and help your groups achieve more effective outcomes.

Second, you can monitor your reaction to the interaction of other group members and respond to them in a more productive fashion. For example, you may find it easier to react to superiority with superiority, but a more effective way to neutralize superiority is to respond with equality. It is every group member's responsibility to break destructive cycles in group interaction, and the development and maintenance of defensive group climate is one such destructive cycle.

The communication climate is changeable, but first you must recognize what communication habits have been established, what needs to be changed, and what

---

PUTTING THE PIECES TOGETHER

Group Identity and Group Structure

A group's communicate climate is a critical factor in how members identify with and structure their group. Of the six supportive communication climate dimensions— description, problem orientation, spontaneity, empathy, equality, and provisionalism—which of these are more important to developing group identity? Which of these are more important to how norms, roles, and communication networks develop in the group? How have the dimensions you identified been instrumental to the development of your relationships with other members in your groups?

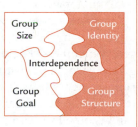

---

your role has been in sustaining a defensive climate or inhibiting a supportive climate. Then you can use supportive communication to create a more positive climate. Even if you have not directly used defensive strategies, you subtly reinforce their use by others simply by tolerating such behaviors.

Group Cohesiveness

Cohesiveness is the degree to which members desire to remain in the group (Cartwright, 1968). When the desire to be a group member is strong, members are more likely to be committed to the group's task. But cohesiveness is an elusive concept. You can sense when it exists within a group, but you cannot see it or touch it. And if you ask group members whether they are cohesive, one might respond yes, and another no.

One group member cannot build cohesiveness alone, but one member's actions can destroy the cohesiveness of the group. Although we say that the group is cohesive, cohesiveness actually results from the psychological closeness individual group members feel toward the group. Cohesiveness can be built around interpersonal attraction to other members, attraction to the task, coordination of effort, and member motivation to work on behalf of the group (Golembiewski, 1962). That is, when group members believe that their task and relational needs are being fulfilled, they perceive the group as cohesive (Carron et al., 2004).

Sometimes people refer to cohesiveness as the glue that keeps the group together; others describe cohesiveness as the morale of the group. In either case, cohesiveness serves to keep group members together because of their attraction to the group. There are three specific advantages to building and maintaining a cohesive group. First, members feel that they are a part of the group. Second, cohesiveness acts as a bonding agent for group members. Members of cohesive groups are more likely to stick with the group throughout the duration of its task (Spink & Carron, 1994). This, in turn, creates more opportunities for norms to be developed and followed (Shaw, 1981). Third, cohesive groups develop a "we" climate, not an "I" climate.

A variety of factors can influence how groups develop cohesiveness. The way a group is initially structured is one factor that can impact the cohesiveness of group members (Fuehrer & Keys, 1988). If too much structure is imposed on the group early in its history, members may become more concerned with meeting requirements imposed by the structure than with building relationships with other group members. For example, if your group has too many rules, members can become lost learning and trying to follow the rules rather than spending time getting to know one another. At the same time, groups without adequate structure can be frustrating for group members because they have too few guidelines to help them select appropriate behavior in the group. When this level of ambiguity exists, members are uncertain about what path to use in developing effective group relationships.

Developing Group Cohesiveness

One method you can use to help develop cohesiveness in your task group is to give members frequent opportunities to talk about the task and about working with others. You might want to devote time at the end of each group meeting to building cohesiveness. This provides closure for this meeting and a bridge to the next one. By giving group members the opportunity to discuss their feelings about the group's task and performance, you enhance the group's cooperation, cohesiveness, and future task performance (Elias, Johnson, & Fortman, 1989).

Researchers have demonstrated that some membership factors can affect the amount of cohesiveness a group is likely to develop. For example, a group whose members complement one another's needs for interpersonal dominance is more likely to be cohesive than one in which all members display high or low interpersonal dominance (Dyce & O'Connor, 1992). Groups whose members are all high in dominance will have more conflict, which ultimately will decrease cohesiveness. Members who display little dominance will not talk very much, which hampers their ability to develop and maintain relationships in the group. Cohesiveness cannot develop on its own. In some groups, it never develops; in others, it requires persistent efforts by group members.

Cohesiveness and Group Performance

The degree of cohesiveness in the group can affect how well the group performs. The more cohesive the group, the more likely the group is to perform effectively (Cohen & Bailey, 1997). This relationship between cohesiveness and performance is often reciprocal (Greene, 1989). When an ongoing group performs well, it is also likely that its members will generate additional cohesive feelings for one another or at least maintain the current level of cohesiveness in the group. Cohesiveness in a group can also affect individual group member performance. Members of groups with high task cohesiveness put more energy into working

Groups with cohesiveness demonstrate this both verbally and nonverbally. Although cohesiveness is generally linked to friendly groups and positive group interaction, a cohesive group can sustain productive periods of conflict interaction.

with and for the group (Prapavessis & Carron, 1997). In other words, individual members have greater adherence to the team task when the group's task is attractive to them. Thus group members are successful because they have helped the group become successful.

However, the relationship between cohesiveness and performance is not a straightforward one. The degree of interdependence needed to perform a group's task affects the cohesiveness-performance relationship (Gully, Devine, & Whitney, 1995). When a group task requires coordination, high levels of interaction, and joint performances from group members, the cohesiveness-performance relationship is stronger. But when task interdependence is low, the cohesiveness-performance relationship is much weaker. A surgical team of nurses and doctors is an example of a group that requires a high degree of interdependence to successfully complete its task. The coordination and communication efforts during an operation are very high. Thus the more cohesive the group, the more effective the team will be in its surgical tasks, because high cohesiveness also motivates individual group members to perform well.

Alternately, tasks with low interdependence provide less opportunity for members to communicate and to coordinate their actions. Even if cohesiveness develops, there is less opportunity for it to be demonstrated and for it to affect group performance. A sales team is a good example of how low interdependence and low cohesiveness-performance interact. The salesperson approaches a client while the service manager makes the follow-up call. Back at the office, two administrative assistants talk the new client through the initial steps of filing forms and preparing documents. Once the goods have been delivered, the salesperson stops back to say hello. This task has low interdependence because the steps of the task are not done simultaneously and because team members are responsible for unique tasks. Thus cohesiveness is likely to be low among sales team members.

What benefits can cohesive groups expect? Members of cohesive groups are less likely to leave to join other groups. For groups with long-term goals, this can be an especially important benefit because the group does not have to spend time finding, attracting, and developing new members. More cohesive groups also exert greater influence over their members. Thus norms are less likely to be violated because cohesiveness exists. In addition, this level of influence encourages group members to more readily accept group goals and tasks. Generally, there is greater equality in participation in cohesive groups because members want to express their identity and solidarity with the group (Cartwright, 1968).

Can a group ever be too cohesive? Yes. The cohesion-performance link is not straightforward. Some groups can develop such a high level of cohesiveness that members become complacent. But the optimum level of cohesiveness will vary, depending on the group's task or activity and the type of attraction group members hold for the group. When cohesiveness is based on interpersonal attraction, groups are more susceptible to groupthink and to producing ineffective decisions. When cohesiveness is based on task attraction, groups are less susceptible to these deficiencies (Mullen, Anthony, Salas, & Driskell, 1994). When your group has strong interpersonal relationships and cohesiveness is high, the group leader or facilitator may want to take extra precautions to prevent groupthink from developing.

Group Member Satisfaction

Closely related to cohesiveness is satisfaction with the group. **Satisfaction** is the degree to which you feel fulfilled or gratified as a group member; it is an attitude you express based on what you have experienced in the group. When your satisfaction is high, you are likely to feel content with the group situation. As an individual group member, you perceive some things about the group as satisfying (such as being assigned to the role you requested), but you may also perceive some group elements as dissatisfying (for instance, having to meet too frequently).

The types of things that satisfy individuals in group settings are quite different from those that cause dissatisfaction (Keyton, 1991). As long as the group is moving along its expected path, group members are likely to be satisfied. This occurs, for example, when group members feel free to participate in the group, when they feel that their time is well spent, and when their group interaction is comfortable and effective. Alternately, dissatisfaction develops when group members spend too much time playing, when the group lacks organization, and when members display little patience. Thus dissatisfaction is more likely to result from negative assessments you make about the group as a whole (such as the perception that the group is in chaos) than from an evaluation of your individual interaction opportunities.

As with cohesiveness, your satisfaction with the group may be based on interpersonal elements, task elements, or a combination of both (Witteman, 1991). Generally, when you are satisfied with the activity of the group, you try harder to communicate more effectively. As a result, you are satisfied with communication within the group. How a group handles its conflict also affects member satisfaction. Members of groups that identify viable solutions to conflict have greater satisfaction than members of groups that avoid conflict. Thus, even groups that experience conflict can have a satisfying group experience, especially when group members use these behaviors: (a) make direct statements about the conflict rather than try to avoid it, (b) work to find a solution by integrating the ideas of all group members, and (c) are flexible, which demonstrates goodwill toward other group members. Note that it is how group members handle conflict that influences group member satisfaction, not its absence.

Improving Cohesiveness and Satisfaction

Building cohesiveness and satisfaction in your group cannot be accomplished alone. But there are some tactics you can undertake as an individual to help the process along. For example, you can adapt and monitor your communication so that your interaction encourages positive climate building in the group. Your interaction should be more supportive than defensive. You can encourage your group to celebrate its successes; this creates a history and tradition for the group. But do not wait until the project is over; each time the group accomplishes a subgoal, recognize the achievement. If you facilitate or lead the group, adopt a reward system that encourages all members, and not just a few, to participate. Basing rewards on group output rather than individual output builds cohesiveness. To make this work, however, group goals must truly be group goals. Additionally, group members should have input in developing goals. Each time the group gets together, group members should be aware of how their communication and activities contribute to the pursuit of these goals.

There are three cautions in developing closeness in groups. First, groups that are not cohesive and in which members are not satisfied are unlikely to produce positive outcomes. But high levels of cohesiveness and satisfaction among group members do not always lead to acceptable output (McGrath, 1984). Cohesiveness in a group can be so high that members overlook tasks in favor of having fun. Cohesiveness can also insulate a group, making it less able to fully explore its task or options. Instead of making a group more vigilant, overly high cohesiveness among group members can make the group susceptible to faulty thinking. With respect to satisfaction, group members may be satisfied because they like one another and as a result become focused on the relational aspects of the group while minimizing their attention to tasks.

MASTERING GROUP SKILLS

How Satisfied and Cohesive Are Your Group Members?

Camaraderie among group members should exist when a group is cohesive and its members are satisfied. This scale can help identify your group's success in achieving camaraderie. Think of a recent group interaction, and respond to each item by circling one number on the continuum.

1 = strongly disagree   2 = disagree   3 = slightly disagree   4 = undecided
5 = slightly agree   6 = agree   7 = strongly agree

1. The group was characterized by group members having mutual respect for one another.   1 2 3 4 5 6 7

2. The group was characterized by loyalty among people who were trying to reach the same goal.   1 2 3 4 5 6 7

3. The group was characterized by social harmony.   1 2 3 4 5 6 7

4. Group members showed concern for one another as people independent of the task.   1 2 3 4 5 6 7

5. The group was characterized by positive interaction whether the goal was achieved or not.   1 2 3 4 5 6 7

6. The group was characterized by emotional closeness that bound the group together.   1 2 3 4 5 6 7

7. Group members were mutually supportive.   1 2 3 4 5 6 7

8. The group created an atmosphere that was open to members' thoughts and ideas.   1 2 3 4 5 6 7

9. Group members demonstrated a helpful attitude toward others.   1 2 3 4 5 6 7

10. The group consisted of people who treated one another equally.   1 2 3 4 5 6 7

11. The group was characterized by positive relationships that could handle stress as well as success.   1 2 3 4 5 6 7

12. Group interactions were based on trust.   1 2 3 4 5 6 7

13. The group was characterized by a partnership that felt like everyone contributed to a great extent.   1 2 3 4 5 6 7

14. The group was characterized by a pervasive trust that could withstand pressure.   1 2 3 4 5 6 7

15. Group interactions were smooth and comfortable.   1 2 3 4 5 6 7

16. Group members worked well together.   1 2 3 4 5 6 7

17. The group consisted of people who worked in sync.   1 2 3 4 5 6 7

18. Group members had similar convictions.   1 2 3 4 5 6 7

19. The group was characterized by the integration of members' talents.   1 2 3 4 5 6 7

20. Group members worked together to find a solution within the group.   1 2 3 4 5 6 7

21. Group members showed respect for one another's ideas.   1 2 3 4 5 6 7

22. Interactions were positive whether the goal was achieved or not.   1 2 3 4 5 6 7

23. Interactions were characterized by freedom and flexibility.   1 2 3 4 5 6 7

24. The group was characterized by feelings of members being accepted within the group.   1 2 3 4 5 6 7

25. Group members had a willingness to work together.   1 2 3 4 5 6 7

26. The group consisted of people who treated one another honestly.   1 2 3 4 5 6 7

27. The group was characterized by the integration of members' abilities.   1 2 3 4 5 6 7

28. The group coordinated varying personalities into action.   1 2 3 4 5 6 7

29. The group consisted of a positive collection of easygoing, laid-back people.   1 2 3 4 5 6 7

30. The group was characterized by feelings of members being comfortable within the group.   1 2 3 4 5 6 7

31. Group members came together to provide support for the team.   1 2 3 4 5 6 7

32. The group was characterized by a sense of teamwork.   1 2 3 4 5 6 7

33. The group consisted of members who were loyal to one another.   1 2 3 4 5 6 7

34. Group members were highly loyal to the task at hand.   1 2 3 4 5 6 7

Add your responses together to find your total score: _____.

Discussion Questions

1. How close is your score to 166? If your group scores at this level or above, your group should be experiencing enough camaraderie to be successful. With a score below this cutoff point, group members may not feel cohesive or satisfied enough with one another to work together effectively.

2. Do you believe your score reflects the level of camaraderie in your group? In what ways do you believe camaraderie is similar to or different from cohesiveness and satisfaction?

3. Go back and circle each item on which you scored 5 or higher. Are any patterns evident among these high scores?

4. If your scores reflect camaraderie in the group, what communication skills will you use to maintain that level? If your scores do not reflect camaraderie in your group, what communication skills can you use to achieve it?

Many people want to believe that cohesiveness and satisfaction are so tightly related that, as one increases, so must the other. This is the second caution. If group members become overly cohesive, they may start to reject or ignore their task. For instance, if you are attracted to a genealogy group because you want to learn more about how to research your family's history, you will probably not be very satisfied if the group regularly focuses its conversations on other topics. Although the cohesiveness of the group might enhance the discussion of any topic, your satisfaction with the group may actually decrease because you are not accomplishing your goal.

The third caution involves group size. When a group grows too large, creating greater complexity than can be handled by the communication structure of the group, there are fewer interaction opportunities among group members. This diminishes cohesiveness and satisfaction. Both cohesiveness and satisfaction develop from the opportunity for members to interact on a regular basis. You have probably drifted apart from your best friend in high school because you see each other less frequently; the same phenomenon occurs in groups. Frequency and quality of interaction are important to establishing cohesiveness and satisfaction. Try "How Satisfied and Cohesive Are Your Group Members?" on pages 138–139 to learn more about those dimensions in one of your groups.

Trust

You have probably heard that trust is earned, that trust is not automatic or given freely to others. **Trust** is a group member's positive expectation of another group member, or a group member's willingness to rely on another's actions in a risky situation (Lewicki, McAllister, & Bies, 1998). In other words, when we trust someone, we expect that they will be helpful, or at least not harmful. Thus, trust resides in one group member's relationship with another group member, is based on previous experience with one another, and develops over time as relationships unfold and confidence builds. When you trust another group member, it helps you predict how this group member will behave or react. The establishment of trust, then, usually occurs after a moderate level of rapport has developed in the group among all group members.

But here is the problem: You do not establish rapport with the group; rather, you establish rapport with each group member. That is why establishing trust in group settings takes such a long time. Trust is also extended slowly and incrementally. For example, Russ trusts you a little, and you trust him a little in return. Russ begins to feel comfortable with how your relationship is developing (and you are not doing anything to erode the trust you have established), so Russ extends a deeper level of trust to you. Extending trust is risky, which is why we are unwilling to give full trust to new people in new settings.

Trust is also multifaceted, based on honesty, openness, consistency, and respect (Larson & LaFasto, 1989). As you might suspect, it is difficult to trust a group member who is not honest. It is also difficult to trust a group member who is not open. Sharing part of yourself with the group by revealing personal or professional information helps others to get to know you. Not only must you share with others, you must also be receptive to receiving personal and professional information about other group members. Openness cannot be one-sided. Being consistent in your group's interactions helps others understand you as well. When you interact in an inconsistent manner, others become hesitant around you because they are never quite sure how you will react.

Finally, trust is based upon respect. It is hard to trust someone who does not respect others or who does not command respect. Your behavior and interactions are always being evaluated by other group members. If you tell offensive jokes about someone when that person is not present, other group members might assume that you tell jokes about them when they are not around too.

How can you build trust in groups? First, be aware of your communicator style in the group and work to minimize your apprehensiveness. This will increase your ability to develop positive interactions with others. Second, use the supportive climate interaction characteristics discussed earlier. If you interact in a defensive manner, it is unlikely that others will extend trust to you. Third, use appropriate self-disclosure. We have all met people who tell us more than we want to know about them in our initial meeting with them. Extend only the personal and professional information about yourself that you believe will be perceived by others as positive contributions to the group. As group members warm up to one another, self-disclosure often becomes more personal. Remember, however, that in decision-making and other task groups, revealing too much personal information may be considered unprofessional. Moreover, personal information can be used against you—once you reveal it, you lose power over the information. Fourth, focus on developing a positive and collaborative climate with *all* group members. For instance, Jack may resist extending his trust to you because you treat Margaret more favorably than other group members. Finally, monitor your interaction behavior to ensure that you are not overusing defensive behaviors or behaving in such a way that other members label you as dysfunctional. Trust is seldom extended to

SKILL BUILDER

How Fragile Is Trust?

Reflect on one of your current group experiences. What is the level of trust in that group? Specifically recall behaviors you have used to help develop or maintain trust within the group. Have you done enough to reinforce trust among group members? What else could you do to strengthen the level of trust among group members? Consider the following: (a) Do you always follow through on commitments you make to the group? (b) Have you ever broken a confidence inside or outside the group? (c) Do you ever withhold information from other members? (d) Have you ever indicated that you would do one thing for the group and then did something else? Identify what you would do and communicate to sustain or enhance trust among group members. What communication skills are most central to sustaining and maintaining trust?

group members who are perceived negatively. "How Fragile Is Trust?" explores the effect of lack of trust on group interaction.

Socializing New Members into Groups

Building relationships with group members is particularly important when a new member joins an established group. Sometimes membership changes are temporary, as when a nurse takes a 2-week vacation and is replaced by a nurse who floats among assignments at the hospital. At other times, membership changes are permanent. Members may leave the group when they quit or retire from the organization or transfer to other units. Also, members may simply grow tired of the group and drop out. Each of these membership changes are member initiated.

Membership change in groups can be critical because a change in the composition of the group also changes the cluster of knowledge, skills, and abilities within the group (McGrath, Berdahl, & Arrow, 1995) and the relationships among group members. Let's explore some of the issues surrounding membership change to assess its impact on groups (Arrow & McGrath, 1993). First, when membership change increases or decreases the number of members in the group, other aspects of the group—group roles, norms, and communication networks—must change as well.

For example, Kara's honors study group meets with its honors advisor to work on a research project. For over a year, the group—the professor and four students—has met in the professor's office. After much discussion about whether to add other students, the group decides that adding one more student will help lighten the workload of running the experiments. Unfortunately, the group does not think about how an additional group member will affect the group's meetings. The professor's office is crowded with stacks of books and computer printouts. There is a couch that can seat only three people, as well as a visitor's chair, and the professor's chair. When the group with its new member gathers to meet for the first time, someone has to sit on the floor. This seating arrangement creates awkward dynamics among group members and impedes the group's ability to work together on coding data. Certainly, the group could move to a new meeting location, but that would cause another disruption in the group. Although adding a member seems to be a gain for the group because it will lighten the workload, it also creates an unexpected negative consequence.

Second, it is important to know why there is a change in group membership. Group members react differently to situations in which membership change is member initiated, and not controlled by someone outside the group. You are more likely to accept a new member who persuades you to let her join than a member who joins because your boss says she must. Sometimes groups actually recruit new members because they need skills other group members lack. Does a group ever purposely change members? Yes. Sometimes a group member creates a logjam, making it difficult for the group to accomplish anything (Cohen, 1990). Groups can get stuck when strong, self-oriented individuals are in the leadership role, and groups can fail to meet their potential if there is a weak link. Changes to replace ineffective members are made deliberately to help the group out of its entrenched patterns. We expect professional sports teams to use this strategy, and we should want our groups to do the same.

The timing of a change in group membership is also important. Most of you expect that your membership in classroom groups will remain stable throughout the term or the course. What will happen to your group and how will you respond if 3 weeks after your group forms, your instructor adds a student to your group? Making changes after your group has formed and while members are developing a group identity and structure likely will disrupt your group.

The frequency with which groups change membership also reflects on the stability of the group, on the group's ability to chart a course for itself, or on the group's leadership. For example, an executive team that cannot hold any person in the position of administrative assistant for longer than 6 months makes you wonder more about the executive team and less about the individuals rotating through the administrative role. Groups that have regular turnover like this are often questioned about members' ability to work together. The assumption is that their inability to do so effectively drives off the administrative assistants.

Fourth, it is important to know which members are leaving, because group members are not interchangeable. A group that loses an effective leader upon whom other group members relied will experience disruption and frustration. Sometimes another group member can assume that role and take on new responsibilities; other times, however, the group has a hole that must be filled. For example, your relay swim team relies on the swimmer who can assess how the other teams are doing in relationship to your team and then really kick in for a quick finish. Thus, if you lose the member who normally swims in this position, your group has a hole to fill.

What is affected by changes in membership (Arrow & McGrath, 1993)? Obviously, membership dynamics and relationships will change. Any change in group membership will alter to some degree the interactions among group members. Not only does the structure and the process of the group change, but members' performance is also likely to be affected. The more interdependence among members of the team, the more the team will feel the effects of membership changes. And the more central the member is to the team, the more the team will feel the effects of the change.

Group members build a history together, and each group develops a memory of how and why it does certain things in certain ways. At the very minimum, a new group member will be unfamiliar with a group's habits and routines (Gersick & Hackman, 1990). These need to be explained, or the new group member will feel left out. And the new group member cannot share in the memory of the group—there is simply no way for the new group member to know what it feels like to be a part of this group (McGrath et al., 1995). Assumptions or old knowledge that other group members use in making decisions simply are not available or do not make sense to the new group member.

Also, there is no guarantee that current members will be able to make the behavioral adjustments needed when a new group member enters. However, a group can overcome these effects by realizing that membership change actually creates a new group. The group must allow members time to resocialize and to reidentify the role structure. The challenges of membership change are (a) to initiate the new members into the team, (b) to learn from the new member's fresh perspective, and (c) not to sacrifice the pace and focus of the team (Katzenbach & Smith, 1993).

When group membership changes, socialization, or the reciprocal process of social influence and change by both newcomers and established members occurs (Anderson, Riddle, & Martin, 1999). Group socialization is an ongoing process, but it becomes especially salient to group members anytime an established group finds itself creating or re-creating itself or its activities.

Obviously, group members do not join a group as a blank slate. Individuals bring knowledge, beliefs, and attitudes about group work with them, just as they bring their own motivations for joining the group and their own sets of communication skills. The socialization process really commences as an individual begins to anticipate what it will be like to be a member of a particular group. For example, you are thrilled that you were selected to be a member of your university's ambassador team but also a little concerned about how you will blend in with students who have already served on this team for several years. And even as you are anticipating joining the team, the existing team members also have anticipatory expectations about you. They might be wondering if you'll be able to devote the time these group activities demand. They might also be hoping that you'll live up to the performance level you claimed you could achieve in the interview.

The first day you meet with the ambassador team, you and the other members begin to adjust to one another, and to negotiate the formal and informal roles, norms, and communication networks of the group. There are many ways to introduce yourself to other group members. If you get there early, you can greet the other members as they arrive. Always be sure to introduce yourself to anyone you do not know well. When you do this, you help establish a friendly and supportive climate and create a sense of openness to which others will respond.

At your first meeting and in subsequent encounters with other group members, you need to continue to assimilate yourself into the group. One way to get to know others is to sit next to someone you do not know at all or do not know well. You can start a conversation by bringing up an easy topic (weekend activities, hobbies, your role in this group). The objective here is to create an opportunity for interaction that will help you get to know the other person. But the topic of conversation should not be threatening or invasive.

Now, as a member of the team, you are influencing the group, just as the group and its other members are influencing you. You are fully integrated, or assimilated, into the group culture when you and the other team members establish a shared group identity by working effectively and interdependently within the group's structures toward a common group goal.

Of course, current members should also help to welcome and socialize new members into a group. During a meeting, you can assimilate new group members by asking them to comment on what the group is talking about ("Mary, what do you think of this plan?"). This is especially important because as new members they may believe that their opinions are not welcomed, given that they have little or no history with the group. Creating opportunities for new members to contribute to the group's task or activity also provides a mechanism for them to create interdependence with other group members, from which relationships flow.

Summary

Working in groups means building relationships with others. You are likely to develop dependent relationships with some group members, but be careful. Dependent relationships create superior-subordinate interaction. Alternately, interdependent relationships are those that are more equally balanced. When group members perceive interdependence with one another, they can use communication to resolve differences. Interdependence also creates a seamless communication flow among group members.

Group communication climate is the atmosphere group members create from the content, tone, mood, and character of their verbal and nonverbal messages. A group will develop a defensive or negative climate if group members send messages that are based on evaluation, control, strategy, neutrality, superiority, and certainty. Alternatively, a group will develop a supportive or positive climate if group members send messages that are based on description, problem orientation, spontaneity, empathy, equality, and provisionalism. While groups will vary in their need for a supportive climate, all groups require some level of supportiveness to maintain interdependence among members to accomplish the group task or activity.

When members believe that their task and relational needs are being fulfilled by the group, they perceive the group as cohesive. Group cohesiveness contributes to the development of interdependence. When a group is cohesive, members want to remain in the group, whether they are attracted to the group's task or to group members. Cohesive groups often perform more effectively, but cohesiveness does not ensure good group performance. In fact, too much cohesiveness can actually interfere with the group's ability to critically examine alternatives.

Like cohesiveness, satisfaction develops from interdependent relationships. Members are satisfied when they are fulfilled or gratified by the group, particularly when the group is moving along its expected path. The source of dissatisfaction is more specific, created by group members who waste time or fail to use effective procedures. When group members are satisfied, however, they are willing to work harder and be more committed to the group.

Trust is a group member's positive expectation of another group member, or a group member's willingness to rely on another's actions in a risky situation. Thus, trust resides in group member relationships, and is developed as relationships unfold over time and individuals build confidence in each other. Trust is based on honesty, openness, consistency, and respect. Group members must earn trust in one another through their interactions. Trust is fragile; once broken, it is hard to reinstate.

Building relationships with group members is particularly important when a new member joins an established group, thereby changing the group's cluster of knowledge, skills, and abilities, as well as the relationships among group members. Socialization, or the reciprocal process of social influence and change by both newcomers and established members, occurs any time membership changes in a group. Both new and established members are responsible for making the transition a smooth one.

Discussion Questions and Exercises

1. Think of a recent group experience, and write a short essay analyzing the communication climate within the group. Give specific examples to support your conclusions. Provide three recommendations for maintaining or increasing a supportive climate.

2. Suppose you've been asked to be a consultant to a team at work that is experiencing relational disharmony. What advice will you give this group for developing and maintaining positive and productive group member relationships?

3. Describe three things that you see as evidence of group member cohesiveness and satisfaction in one of your groups. Do these descriptions apply to all groups? or only to groups like yours? or only to your group?

4. Think back to one group in which trust was high and to another group in which trust was low. Write a short paper responding to these questions: What accounted for the difference in level of trust? How did the level of trust affect the group's communication? How did one group build trust? What happened in the other group to erode trust?

5. Based upon your experiences in joining groups and teams, what advice would you give to a friend who is joining an established sports team? Changing teams at work? Welcoming a new member into the family? Would your advice be similar or different across these three contexts? Why or why not?

7

Solving Problems and Making Decisions

GROUP SKILLS PREVIEW

In this chapter, you will learn to do the following:

- Describe the task, relational, and procedural skills group members need for effective decision making

- Describe the critical functions needed for effective decision making

- Explain why and when groups are better than individuals at making decisions

- Explain why groups should consider using a decision-making procedure

- Select the best procedure for a group decision-making situation

- Lead your group through the use of several decision-making procedures

Decision making in groups is fundamental to many different types of groups. Family groups make decisions about where to spend their vacation or how to organize a garage sale. Groups of friends make decisions about where they are going on Friday night or how to surprise one member with a birthday party. At work, groups and teams make decisions in developing new products and enhancing customer service. Some of these decisions are more straightforward than others. Still, for any of these decisions, a group needs to engage in two processes: problem solving and decision making. Problem solving represents the group's attempts to analyze a problem in detail so that good decisions can be made. This includes generating alternatives for the group to consider. Once these are developed, the group can turn to a decision-making procedure to make a choice between alternatives. Before we look at procedures groups can use in decision making, let's turn our attention to the skills group members need to effectively make decisions in groups.

Decision-Making Skills

Across the range of decisions that groups make, group members need task, relational, and procedural skills (Gouran, 2003). In fact, the quality of group members' contributions and a group's ability to make effective decisions depends on these skills. Different decision-making tasks place different demands on members and the group. Some decisions require a great deal of discussion and deliberation, and, as a result, require a higher degree of skill and a greater variety of skills. Simple decisions require little discussion and fewer skills, as group members make a choice from known alternatives, each of which is agreeable to them. Although we identified the skills college students used to describe an ideal group member in Chapter 5, these three sets of skills are specific to group decision making.

Task Skills for Decision Making

Group members need task-related skills to manage the content or substance of the decisions made in the group. First, group members must have skills with **problem recognition and framing**. A group cannot make a decision if its members cannot identify the decision that needs to be made or if they frame a decision inaccurately or inappropriately. In other words, group members have to agree upon what the decision is really about. For example, the mayor and council members of one town debated vigorously through one entire meeting when to schedule subsequent city council meetings. The issue, of course, wasn't really about scheduling meetings, but about who had the power to control what the council did (Barge & Keyton, 1994). Clearly this group misframed the problem as one of scheduling. The council failed to recognize the problem as one of authority. The group needed to make a decision about who had authority to set council meetings. This example demonstrates how difficult it can be for group members to recognize or articulate the issue before the group.

Inference drawing is another task-related decision-making skill. As group members solve problems or make decisions, they will be required to use analysis and reasoning and then communicate that analysis and reasoning as judgments or claims that go beyond the available information. Inferences can be drawn by using analogy or cause-to-effect reasoning. For example, a human resources task force draws a conclusion about the effectiveness of a sexual harassment policy they are ready to submit to the employees' union because the discrimination policy they submitted earlier was well received. Inferences drawn using analogy are based on the similarities of different objects or situations that are believed to have the same qualities. Members of the task force also draw inferences with cause-to-effect reasoning as they argue that having a discrimination policy in place (the cause) will influence employees to behave more respectfully (the immediate effect) and thereby decrease the number of complaints (a longer-term effect).

The third task-related decision-making skill is **idea generation**. To make effective decisions, groups must have adequate alternatives from which to select. When groups limit themselves to a few obvious choices, they unnecessarily restrict their opportunity to make an effective decision. For example, a policy team was created for the purpose of generating ideas for stimulating regional economic growth. As soon as introductions were completed, Charles, a member with high status in the community and a vice-president of a large organization, went to the podium and began a slide presentation that described his idea. The group, whose members had not worked together before, were impressed with his preparation. When he was finished, group members asked Charles questions for about an hour; then they took a vote to pursue his idea. The problem: All of the group members were high-status members of the community and had the potential to generate a number of useful ideas for economic development. While Charles's idea was sound, the policy team did not consider other alternatives that may have proven to be better than the only idea discussed. Brainstorming, a group technique for generating ideas, could have helped this group create additional proposals to consider; it will be described in detail later in this chapter.

The fourth task-related decision-making skill is **argument**. Group members need to be capable of generating and presenting reasons for a position they support or reject. Novel arguments, or arguments not considered by group members prior to discussion, can be especially influential in decision making (Meyers & Brashers, 1999). In the policy team example earlier, Charles was skilled at presenting arguments with sufficient evidence, which influenced the group. Moreover, his arguments were novel, as the other group members could not have possibly considered them before the meeting since they had no idea what Charles would propose. Although in the minority, Charles skillfully used argument to convince the majority of the group into accepting his proposal. The obvious tension between the policy group's failure to generate other ideas and Charles's skill in presenting arguments demonstrates why multiple skills are required when groups make decisions.

Relational Skills for Decision Making

While problem recognition and framing, inference drawing, idea generation, and argument are required for group decision making to occur, relational skills—or skills that focus on members rather than the task—can enhance decision-making effectiveness. **Leadership** is a skill that can counteract the cognitive, affiliative, and egocentric constraints that can arise in group interaction (Gouran & Hirokawa, 1996; Janis, 1989).

Cognitive constraints, or difficulties and inadequacies in processing information, occur when there is little information available or limited time for making a decision, or when the decision is more difficult than group members can comfortably or normally handle. When decision making occurs under these conditions, group members believe they have limited capacity or motivation to make an effective decision.

The second type of constraint is **affiliative constraints**—those that are based on the relationships among members of the group. When relationships, or the fear that relationships will deteriorate, are the dominant concern, some group members exert undue influence on other group members.

The third type of decision-making constraint is **egocentric constraints**, which occur when one group member has a high need for control over the group or its activities or has a personal or hidden agenda.

A leader with effective communication skills can help group members reduce the impact of these constraints by refocusing the group's relational energy and shifting the group's focus back to decision making. Facilitating discussion among all group members, assisting the group in information gathering, helping members to verbalize unstated positions, and focusing conversation on the group's goal are three techniques anyone in the group can use to provide leadership for the group and minimize the negative influence of cognitive, affiliative, and egocentric constraints. Leadership is described in detail in Chapter 10.

The second relational skill needed for decision making is **climate building**. As described in Chapter 6, a positive or supportive climate develops when group members communicate with equality, spontaneity, and empathy, and avoid evaluation, control, and certainty. To help build a supportive climate for decision making, group members should be friendly with and respectful of others. Doing so helps group members to feel valued and that their input is welcomed. Climate building is as easy to accomplish as it is to overlook. Members of a project team who do not know each other well will meet each Friday until their marketing plan is developed. To help members become comfortable in the team, each meeting begins with members providing a brief update of what they accomplished during the week in their respective departments. By sharing this type of information, team members get to know one another better because they learn about the skills each member possesses, as well as getting a feel for how the team's output will influence activities across the organization. Most importantly, this opening procedure ensures that everyone has talked, which deemphasizes role and status differences among group members.

Conflict management is the third relational skill needed for decision making. It's not conflict per se that creates a problem for group decision making. Conflict about ideas can actually help groups make better decisions. But when conflict about issues is not managed or when conflict is focused on personal differences, then the struggle between group members takes precedence over the decision-making task. To help manage conflict, group members can steer the conversation from personal issues back to task issues and to helping those who are experiencing conflict find common ground. Other skills for managing group conflict can be found in Chapter 9.

Procedural Skills for Decision Making

Finally, there are two procedural skills, or skills that help the group move from discussion to decision making. The first procedural skill is **planning**. Members with this skill help the group by communicating what needs to be first, second, and so on, and by suggesting a decision-making procedure to use. Planning, of course, can only be based on a goal, so group members engaged in planning need to remind others about the goal and help them reach agreement on it. The second procedural decision-making skill is **process enactment**, or helping the group through the decision-making process. Even with the best planning, a decision-making group will have to address unforeseen circumstances. Thus members with process-enactment skills can help the group manage these difficulties and stay on track. A group member might set up procedures for the group (for example, concluding each meeting with a review of assignments or creating mechanisms to help the group track its work, like posting information on the group's website). These skills are not difficult; any group member can contribute to the group's decision making by using planning and process enactment skills.

While we consider decision making one type of group task or activity, effective decision making is only accomplished when skilled group members engage in a number of different tasks or activities throughout the decision-making process. The types of decisions that most groups make are either ones that are fairly complex (for example, managing a program for evicting drug dealers from rental property; see Keyton & Stallworth, 2003) or ones in which group members are personally involved (for example, an activist group developing plans for a protest; see Meyers & Brashers, 2003). Reviewing these task, relational, and procedural skills reminds us why some groups have difficulty with their decision making, but also how group members can use their skills to help their group through the decision process.

Decision-Making Principles

Regardless of the procedure or process your group uses, four principles seem to fit most group problem-solving and decision-making situations (Hirokawa & Johnston, 1989). First, group decision making is an evolutionary process. The final decision of the group emerges over time as a result of the clarification, modification, and integration of ideas that group members express in their interaction. A student government group may know that it needs to make a decision about how to provide child care for university students, but the final decision results from the group bringing new information to meetings and other group members asking for clarification and development of proposed ideas. Thus, a group will have a general idea about a decision that needs to be made, but not necessarily its specifics.

Relatedly, the second principle is that group decision making is a circular rather than a linear process. Even when they try, it is difficult for group members to follow a step-by-step approach to group decision making. Group decision making is circular because group members seldom bring all the needed information into the group's discussion at the same time. Let's say that your group decides to hold the fund-raiser on June 3, close to the end of the spring semester. Your group needs to make this decision first to secure a date on your university's student activities calendar. Now that the date is settled, your group can concentrate on what type of fund-raiser might be best. But you have to take into consideration that it is late in the semester. Not only will students have limited time because of term papers and final exams, but their funds likely will be depleted. That information will affect the type of fund-raiser you will plan. But wait! At that point in the semester, students really enjoy having coffee and doughnuts available in the early morning, after all-night study sessions. And your group can sell lots of coffee and doughnuts to many students for very little money. In this way, group members move information about the date and type of event back and forth to integrate into a final fund-raising decision.

The third principle is that many different types of influences affect a group's decision making. Group members' moods, motivations, competencies, and communication skills are individual-level variables that affect the group's final decision. These are individual-level variables because each member brings a unique set of influences to the group. The dynamics of the interpersonal relationships that result in group member cohesiveness and satisfaction also affect a group's decision making. Finally, the communication structure or network, developed in the group impacts information flows among group members. The quality of information exchanged by group members affects a group's decision outcomes. And forces outside a group also generate influences. An example of this type of external influence is the generally accepted societal rule about making decisions quickly and cost-efficiently.

The fourth principle of group decision making is that decisions are made within a system of external and internal constraints. Few groups have as much freedom of choice as they would like. Groups are constrained by external forces such as deadlines or budgets imposed by outsiders and the preferences of the people who will evaluate or use the group's decision. Internal constraints are the values, morals, and ethics that individual members bring to the group setting. These values guide what the group does and how it does it.

These four principles reveal that decision making may be part of a larger problem-solving process. Problem solving is the communication group members engage in when there is a need to address an unsatisfactory situation or overcome some obstacle. Decision making and problem solving are often used interchangeably, but they are different. Decision making involves a choice between alternatives; problem solving represents the group's attempts to analyze a problem in detail so that effective decisions can be made (Sunwolf & Seibold, 1999). Hence, this problem: Groups often make decisions without engaging in the analysis associated with problem solving. For anything but the simplest matters, groups are more likely to make faulty decisions when they do not take advantage of the problem-solving process to address the contextual details or do the thoughtful analysis good decisions require.

Why Groups Are Better at Making Decisions

Why are groups better at decision making than individuals? For complex decisions or problems, it is unlikely that any individual will possess or have access to all the knowledge and resources necessary to make a good decision. Second, groups generally bring a greater diversity of perspectives to the situation, so it is more difficult to become locked onto an idea that lacks merit. Third, and probably most importantly, when more people are involved in decision making, the group has the opportunity to check out ideas before one is selected and implemented. This opportunity to try out ideas allows groups to be more confident than individuals in making decisions (Sniezek, 1992).

Groups produce better decisions through communication. The quality of communication among and the full participation of group members are central to their ability to work together to select high-quality solutions (Mayer, 1998; Salazar, Hirokawa, Propp, Julian, & Leatham, 1994). Even when group members have high potential (are highly skilled or highly knowledgeable), communication is the process that allows the group to do its best. Groups that spend their time on goal-directed communication to evaluate task-relevant issues and generate ideas create superior group outcomes.

Decision making is a social process. The presence of others creates a context of social evaluation that motivates people to find the best possible solution (Kameda, 1996). For decisions that affect many individuals, involving them in the process increases their commitment to upholding the decision as it is implemented. To carry out some decisions, the cooperation of many people is needed. Including those people in the decision-making process helps to ensure their cooperation, as well as overall satisfaction with the decision. Moreover, involving them in the decision making increases their understanding of the solution so that they can perform better in the implementation stage.

To take advantage of their strengths, however, groups need some structure in the decision-making discussion (Van de Ven & Delbecq, 1971). Using a procedure to structure group discussion and decision making helps groups in three ways. First, the content of the discussion is more controlled and on task than when discussions are left unstructured. Second, group member participation in the discussion is more equal when some type of procedure is used. Alternative viewpoints from group members cannot help the group unless those viewpoints are revealed during discussion. Third, the emotional tone of a group's discussion is less likely to become negative or out of control. Think of a procedure as a map to follow or a guidebook to show you the way. You could get there from here—but it is easier with some help.

Advice from Functional Theory

Before turning to specific procedures, let's examine the characteristics group decision-making procedures need to satisfy. Obviously, the goal of any group is to find the solution best suited to solving the problem or making the decision. To do that effectively, group members need to accomplish five functions: (a) thoroughly discuss the problem, (b) examine the criteria of an acceptable solution before discussing specific solutions, (c) propose a set of realistic alternative solutions, (d) assess the positive aspects of each proposed solution, and (e) assess the negative aspects of each proposed solution. According to functional theory, these are the five critical functions in decision-making and problem-solving activities (Gouran & Hirokawa, 1983; Hirokawa, 1982, 1983a, 1983b, 1988; Hirokawa & Pace, 1983; Hirokawa & Salazar, 1999; Hirokawa & Scheerhorn, 1986). A function is not just a step or a procedure, but an activity required for the group to make a decision. When the five functions are not addressed, a group diminishes its chances for identifying an effective solution or making a good decision. Your group can accomplish these functions by using one of the formal discussion procedures described later in the chapter.

First, group members need to achieve an understanding of the problem they are trying to solve. The group should deliberate until it believes all members understand the nature and seriousness of the problem, its possible causes, and the consequences that could develop if the problem is not dealt with effectively. For example, parking is generally a problem on most campuses. But a group of students, faculty, staff, and administrators addressing the parking problem without having an adequate understanding of the issue is likely to suggest solutions that will not really solve the problem. The parking problem on your campus may be that there are not enough parking spaces. Or it may be that there are not enough parking spaces where people want to park. Or perhaps the parking problem exists at only certain times of the day. Another type of parking problem exists when students do not want to pay for parking privileges and park their cars illegally on campus and in the surrounding community. Each parking problem is different and so requires different solutions. When group members address this function —understanding the nature of the problem before trying to solve it—their decision-making efforts result in higher-quality decisions (Hirokawa, 1983a).

Second, the group needs to develop an understanding of what constitutes an acceptable resolution of the problem. In this critical function, group members need to understand the objectives that must be achieved to remedy the problem or the specific standards that must be satisfied for the solution to be acceptable. This means that the group needs to develop criteria by which to evaluate each proposed alternative. Let's go back to the parking problem. In this step, group members need to consider how much students and employees will be willing to pay for parking. Group members also need to identify and discuss the type of solutions campus administrators and campus police will find acceptable. The group probably also should consider if the local police need to agree with its recommendation. In other words, the group has to decide on the objectives and standards that must be used in selecting an appropriate solution. Any evaluation of alternatives must be based on known and agreed-upon criteria (Graham, Papa, & McPherson, 1997).

Third, the group needs to seek and develop a set of realistic and acceptable alternatives. With respect to the parking problem, groups frequently stop generating alternatives when they generate a solution they like. Look at the following dialogue:

MARTY: Okay, I think we should think about building a parking garage.

LINDSEY: Where would it go?

MARTY: I don't know. But there's all kinds of empty lots around campus.

HELEN: What about parking in the church parking lots?

LINDSEY: That's an idea, but I like the idea of our own parking garage better.

TODD: I like that, too. It would be good to know that whatever time I go to campus a parking spot would be waiting for me.

MARTY: Any other ideas, besides the parking garage?

LINDSEY: No, I can't think of any. I think we need to work on the parking garage idea.

TODD: Me, too.

HELEN: Shouldn't we consider something else in case the parking garage idea falls through?

MARTY: Why? We all like the idea, don't we?

If a group gets stuck in generating alternatives, as our parking group does, a brainstorming session or nominal group technique (discussed later in the chapter) may help. A group cannot choose the best alternative if all the alternatives are not known.

Fourth, group members need to assess the positive qualities of each of the alternatives they find attractive. This step helps the group recognize the relative merits of each alternative. Once again, let's turn to the parking problem. Students and employees probably will cheer for a solution to the parking problem that does not cost them money. Certainly, no-cost or low-cost parking will be attractive to everyone. But if this is the only positive quality of an alternative, it is probably not the best choice. For example, to provide no-cost or low-cost parking, your recommendation is that during the daytime students park in the parking lots of churches and that at night they park in the parking lots of office buildings. Although the group has satisfied concerns about cost, it is doubtful that those who manage church and office building properties will find this alternative attractive. This leads us to the fifth function: Group members need to assess the negative qualities of alternative choices.

When group members communicate to fulfill these five functions, they increase the chance that their decision making will be effective. This is because group members have worked together to pool their information resources, avoid errors in individual judgment, and create opportunities to persuade other group members (Gouran, Hirokawa, Julian, & Leatham, 1993). For example, the members of the parking group bring different information to the discussion because they come to school at different times of the day. Those who come early or late in the day have a harder time finding a place to park than those who come early in the afternoon. By pooling what each participant knows about the parking situation, the group avoids becoming biased or choosing a solution that will resolve only one type of parking problem.

In addition, as the group discusses the problem, members can identify and remedy errors in individual judgment. It is easy to think that parking is not a problem when you come in for one class in the early afternoon and leave immediately after. In your experience, the parking lot has some empty spaces because you come at a time when others have left for lunch. And when you leave 2 hours later, the lot is even emptier, making you wonder what the fuss is about in the first place!

Discussion also provides an opportunity to persuade others or to be persuaded. Discussion allows alternatives to be presented that might not occur to others and allows for reevaluation of alternatives that initially seem unattractive. Let's go back to the group discussing the parking problem:

MARTY: Okay, where are we?

HELEN: Well, I think we've pretty much discussed parking alternatives. I'm not sure.

LINDSEY: What about using the bus?

TODD: You've got to be kidding.

LINDSEY: Why not? The bus line goes right by campus and the fare is only 50 cents.

MARTY: Well, it's an idea.

HELEN: Well, what if the bus doesn't have a route where I live?

LINDSEY: Well, that may be the case for you, Helen, but I bet many students and employees live on or near a bus line.

MARTY: I wonder how many?

LINDSEY: Why don't we call the bus company and get a copy of the entire routing system.

MARTY: Good idea, Lindsey. We were looking for parking alternatives and hadn't thought about other modes of transportation.

Groups that successfully achieve each of the five critical functions of decision making make higher-quality decisions than groups that do not (Hirokawa, 1988). However, the functional perspective is not a procedure for making decisions, because there is no prescribed order to the five functions. Rather, it is the failure of the group to perform one of the five functions that has a profound effect on the quality of the group's decision making. But do the five functions contribute equally to group decision-making effectiveness? An analysis across hundreds of groups indicates that the most important function is group members' assessment of the negative consequences of proposed alternatives. Next in importance were thorough discussion and analysis of the problem, and the establishment of criteria for evaluating proposals (Orlitzky & Hirokawa, 2001). The procedures described in the next section will help your group satisfy the five critical functions. But first, try "Identifying Decision-Making Functions" to get some practice in analyzing group decision making.

Using Decision-Making Procedures

You may think that it's natural for all groups to use some type of procedure or set of guidelines in making decisions. But many groups are unaware of procedures that can help them. Even when a group uses some procedure or structure as an aid to decision making, group members may not be aware of the rules their group uses (Johnson, 1991). Why should groups use procedures to help them generate ideas, make decisions, and solve problems? Procedures help guide a group

MASTERING GROUP SKILLS

Identifying Decision-Making Functions

Select one of your favorite television shows to record (hourlong dramas are a good choice for this exercise). First, watch the show and jot down what characters say as part of the decision-making process, paying particular attention to statements or questions you believe are important. Next, check your list for the following:

1. Statements or questions that helped the group understand the problem or decision. If there were none, how did characters know and agree upon what the problem or decision was?

2. Statements or questions that helped the group understand what might constitute an acceptable choice. Did the characters identify any criteria against which to evaluate the decision?

3. Statements or questions that identified alternatives to consider.

4. Statements or questions indicating that the group was assessing the positive qualities of the alternatives.

5. Statements or questions indicating that the group was assessing the negative qualities of the alternatives.

Now watch the show again to see if you can fill in any of the categories. Then answer the following questions:

1. Specifically, what was the decision or problem on which the group was working?

2. Did the characters make a final decision or resolve the problem?

3. What was the decision, or how was the problem resolved?

4. How many alternatives did the group consider?

5. To what extent did the characters apply the five functions of group decision making?

6. To what extent do you believe the group's decision making was effective?

7. In what areas does the group need to improve?

8. If the situation were replicated in real life, what recommendations would you give to the group about its decision making?

through the process of decision making and help it overcome problems or limitations that routinely arise when groups make decisions. Without procedures, a group's conversation is more likely to result in problems like the following:

- The group has trouble staying focused on what it needs to accomplish.
- The group has difficulty sticking to the meeting agenda.

- The group performs superficial rather than detailed analyses of alternatives.

- The groups' members have little motivation for working on this decision, or the group has fallen into a rut.

- The group relies on the perceived expert or the person who seems to care the most about the problem.

- Group members consider one alternative and then drop it for discussion of the next alternative without comparing alternatives.

- Group members go straight to decision making without problem solving.

- The group accepts the first solution mentioned.

- The group fails to think of a complex decision as a series of smaller decisions.

- The group does not use its time wisely.

- Group members will make a choice without evaluating its merits.

When groups do not use procedures to help them manage the decision-making process, social or relational pressures can result in pressures to conform or unnecessary conflict. Why does this happen? Without procedures, some group members will not speak up or will not have the opportunity to contribute to the discussion, as the most talkative or high-status group members control the discussion. Simply, without process procedures, members have difficulty balancing the task and relational dimensions of their group (Sunwolf & Seibold, 1999).

The procedures described in the following sections—standard agenda, brainstorming, nominal group technique, consensus, voting, and ranking—vary widely in the amount of control and the type of help they provide to groups. Procedures can vary according to how group members participate in decision making (style) and according to how much group members participate (quantity). Procedures also differ according to whether participation is voluntary or forced. Some procedures are formal; others are more informal (Schweiger & Leana, 1986). Some procedures help structure a group's communication during decision making and problem solving. Other procedures provide an analytical function to help members to evaluate, question, and investigate their ideas. Some procedures help a group with its creativity. Finally, some procedures assist a group in managing conflict and developing agreement (Sunwolf & Seibold, 1998). Groups that use these procedures generally outperform groups that do not. Although the use of such procedures does not guarantee group effectiveness, using procedures maximizes opportunities for groups to achieve the results they desire. Actually, groups should be able to use a variety of decision-making procedures. Few complex decisions have a single *right* answer; thus groups may need to use several procedures to identify solutions and make the best decision.

Each of the procedures described in the following sections provides guidelines or ground rules for members to follow. One procedure that is not discussed here is parliamentary procedure, which is a highly formalized method to help larger groups (for example, parent-teacher organizations and community groups; Weitzel & Geist, 1998) structure their discussion, decision-making, and business activities. If you are an officer in an organization that uses parliamentary procedure, you will want to become familiar with its many protocols. However, small task groups or informal groups rarely follow these procedures. We will start with the standard agenda.

Standard Agenda

The **standard agenda**, also known as reflective thinking, is a strict linear process that groups follow in considering decision alternatives. A group using this procedure passes through a series of six steps—each focusing on different aspects of the problem-solving process. The six steps are (a) identifying the problem, (b) analyzing the problem, (c) identifying the minimal criteria for the solution, (d) generating solutions, (e) evaluating solutions and selecting one as best, and (f) implementing the solution. This step-by-step process creates a structure for group members to use in thoroughly analyzing the problem it is dealing with. Each step must be completed before going on to the next.

The first step in the standard agenda is problem identification. Here the group must clarify what it wants to do or what it is being asked to do. A good way to start is to ask this question: What exactly is the problem before the group? Too frequently, groups overlook this step. When this happens, each group member can have a different idea of what constitutes the problem and assume that other group members have the same problem in mind. For example, suppose a student group is seeking a solution to the lack of food services on the north campus. All of the food outlets are at least a mile away from this part of campus. So what precisely is the problem? Is it that students, faculty, and staff do not have access to food for lunch and dinner? To be sure, the group members canvass students to examine the problem from their point of view. This helps them be certain that they are on track before going ahead with the rest of the project. Before going on to the next step, each group member should be able to state the problem clearly and succinctly.

The second step is problem analysis. Here group members gather information, data, and even opinions to help them understand the history and causes of the problem. Group members need to decide how serious or widespread the problem is. Considering solutions that will resolve a problem for a few isolated people is quite different from considering solutions that will resolve a problem that affects many. Continuing with the previous example, the group surveys students for the type of food service they might prefer. Their next step is to contact the food services department on campus to discuss the types of services they could make available on north campus. With both sets of information, the group can compare the foods that are easily accessible from food services with the foods students want. And, although the general focus is on problems, group members also need to think about any hidden issues. One hidden issue—and the real reason food is not available on this part of campus—is that custodial staff is limited on this part of campus, meaning that there are not enough custodians to keep the food areas up to health department standards of sanitation.

The third step involves identifying the minimal criteria for the solution. In the food problem, the primary criterion is money. How much are students willing to spend for the convenience of eating near their classes? How much money can food services allot in their budget to establish food service on the north campus? How much money will be required for extra custodial help? In discussing these issues, the group finds other criteria that need to be considered. For example, where will these new food services be located? Who will give permission to install food outlets in classroom buildings? Because space is so tight, the only place that can reasonably hold a food outlet is the theatre department's ticket office. But the group does not pursue the issue of what will happen to the ticket office if it is moved to accommodate food outlets. The more criteria group members can think of for evaluating solutions, the more complete and the more useful their decisions will be.

In the fourth step, group members generate solutions. As you might guess, it is difficult to keep from doing this throughout the discussion generated in the first three steps. But groups that generate solutions too quickly can come to premature conclusions without fully investigating all potential solutions. For example, the group studying the problem of food on the north campus fails to generate other solutions such as independent food cart vendors, which do not require permanent space. It is a good idea to allow at least two meetings for idea generation. That way, group members have the opportunity to think about the problem individually before coming back to the group.

The fifth step is evaluating solutions and selecting one as best. If the group has followed the standard agenda, this step will be relatively easy because the group has access to all needed information. Using the criteria generated in the third step, the group should evaluate the advantages and disadvantages of each solution generated in the fourth step. What about our campus food group? Unfortunately, they get stuck early on in the process. That is, they become so focused on moving the ticket office and installing a fast food outlet that they have no other options to evaluate at this stage. As a result, they force themselves into recommending a solution that will not be approved.

The sixth step of the standard agenda is solution implementation. But follow-through can be a weak area for groups. Sometimes the charge of the group does not include implementation, so group members get little practice in this area. Other times the group has used all of its energy in making a decision and has little left over for implementing the decision. Thus they simply stop after selecting a solution. Because implementation is a common weakness for groups, we will explore this step in detail in the next chapter.

Using these six steps maximizes group effectiveness in decision making because it provides equal opportunity to all proposals, no matter who makes them. Highly cohesive groups benefit from using the standard agenda procedure because members of such groups can feel inhibited about criticizing an idea or proposal before the group (Pavitt, 1993). Following the steps of the standard agenda allows group members to question ideas and ask for clarification.

Although the standard agenda is often seen as the ideal procedure for most decision-making activities, it is not always practical (Jarboe, 1996). Some groups may find it difficult to follow the steps of the standard agenda. The sequence of steps structures the type of discussion the group has at each point in the process, and the procedure certainly takes time. However, this procedure satisfies the five critical functions that a group must perform to make effective decisions.

The other five decision-making procedures can be used in the various steps of the standard agenda. Each procedure can contribute to the group's decision making in different ways. In practice, groups may use several different procedures throughout their decision-making activity.

Brainstorming

Brainstorming is an idea generation technique designed to improve productivity and creativity (Osborn, 1963). Thus the brainstorming procedure helps a group to function creatively. In a brainstorming session, group members first state as many alternatives as possible to a given problem. Creative ideas are encouraged; ideas do not have to be traditional or unoriginal. Actually, the wilder and crazier

Using brainstorming procedures, group members alternately generate ideas, post ideas, and discuss ideas. Each group member has the opportunity to contribute ideas, to ask questions about ideas, and to vote for his or her top choices.

the ideas, the better. But it's important that all ideas be accepted without criticism —verbal or nonverbal—from other group members. Next, ideas that have been presented can be improved upon or combined with other ideas. Finally, the group evaluates ideas after the idea generation phase is complete. The group should also record all ideas for future consideration, even those that are initially discarded. A group member can act as the facilitator of the brainstorming session, but research has shown that someone external to the group may be more effective in this role. The facilitator helps the group maintain momentum and helps members remain neutral by not stopping to criticize ideas (Kramer, Fleming, & Mannis, 2001).

This brainstorming procedure helps groups generate as many ideas as possible from which to select a solution. Generally, as the number of ideas increases, so does idea quality. Members may experience periods of silence during idea generation, but research has shown that good ideas can come after moments of silence while members reflect and think individually (Ruback, Dabbs, & Hopper, 1984). So it may be premature to end idea generation the first time all members become quiet.

When should a group use brainstorming? Brainstorming is best used when the problem is specific rather than general. For example, brainstorming can be effective in identifying ways to attract minority employees to an organization. But the problem—what does a group hope to accomplish in the next 5 years—is too broad. Use a brainstorming session to break it down into subproblems, and then devote a further session to each one. Brainstorming works best with smaller rather than larger groups. Finally, members are more likely to generate a greater number of unique ideas if they write their ideas down before presenting them to the group (Mullen, Johnson, & Salas, 1991).

Brainstorming can help increase group cohesiveness because it encourages all members to participate. It also helps group members realize that they can work together productively (Pavitt, 1993). In addition, group members report that they like having an opportunity to be creative and to build upon one another's ideas (Kramer, Kuo, & Dailey, 1997), and they usually find brainstorming fun. However, groups do better if they have a chance to warm up or to practice the process (Firestien, 1990). The practice session should be unrelated to the subject of the actual brainstorming session. Practice sessions are beneficial because they reinforce the procedure and reassure participants that the idea generation and evaluation steps will not be integrated. Posting the five brainstorming steps so they are visible during the session helps remind participants of the procedure's rules.

To summarize, the brainstorming procedure should include the following steps:

1. State as many alternatives as possible.
2. Encourage creative ideas.
3. Examine ideas that have been presented to see if they can be improved upon or combined with other ideas.
4. Accept all ideas without criticism.
5. Evaluate ideas after the idea generation phase is complete.

Notice that brainstorming is a procedure for generating ideas, and not for making decisions. As a result, brainstorming by itself cannot satisfy the five critical functions of group decision making. However, it is especially effective in helping a group seek and develop a set of realistic and acceptable alternatives and in coming to an understanding of what constitutes an acceptable resolution, and moderately effective in helping group members achieve an understanding of the problem.

Nominal Group Technique

The same basic principles of brainstorming are also applied in the nominal group technique (NGT) except that group members work both independently as individuals and interdependently in the group. Thus the **nominal group technique** is an idea generation process in which individual group members generate ideas on their own before interacting as a group to discuss the ideas. The unique aspect of this procedure is that the group temporarily suspends interaction to take advantage of independent thinking and reflection (Delbecq, Van de Ven, & Gustafson, 1975). NGT is based on two principles: (a) Individuals think most creatively and generate more alternatives working alone, and (b) group discussion is best used for refining and clarifying alternatives.

NGT is a six-step linear process, with each step focusing on different aspects of the problem-solving process. In step 1, group members silently generate as many ideas as possible, writing down each idea. It's sensible to give members a few minutes after everyone appears to be finished, as some of our best ideas occur to us after we think we are finished.

In step 2, the ideas are recorded on a flip chart by a facilitator. Generally, it is best to invite someone outside the group to help facilitate the process so all group members can participate. Members take turns, giving one idea at a time to be written on the flip chart. Duplicate ideas do not need to be recorded, but ideas that are slightly different from those already posted should be listed. Ideas are not discussed during this step. The person recording the group's ideas on the flip chart should summarize and shorten lengthy ideas into a phrase. But first, this person should check with the member who originated the idea to make sure that editorializing did not occur. When a member runs out of ideas, he or she simply says "pass," and the facilitator moves on to the next person. When all members have passed, the recording step is over.

In step 3, group interaction resumes. Taking one idea at a time, group members discuss each idea for clarification. If an idea needs no clarification, then the group moves on to the next one. Rather than asking only the group member who contributed the idea to clarify it, the facilitator should ask if any group member has questions about the idea. By including everyone in the clarification process, group ownership of the idea increases.

In step 4, group members vote on the ideas they believe are most important. For instance, if your group generates 40 ideas, consider asking group members to vote for their top 5. By not narrowing the number of choices too severely or too quickly, group members have a chance to discuss the ideas they most prefer. If time permits, let group members come to the flip charts and select their most important ideas themselves. This helps ensure that members select the ideas that are important to them without the influence of peer pressure.

In step 5, the group discusses the vote just taken. Suppose that, from the 40 ideas presented, 11 receive two or more votes. Now is the time for group members to further elaborate on each of these ideas. Direct the discussion according to the order of ideas as they appear on the flip chart, rather than starting with the idea that received the most votes. Beginning the discussion in a neutral or randomly selected place encourages discussion on each item, not just on the one that appears most popular at this point in the procedure.

With that discussion complete, step 6 requires that group members repeat steps 4 and 5. That is, once again, members vote on the importance of the remaining ideas. With 11 ideas left, you might ask members to select their top 3 choices. After members vote, the group discusses the three ideas that received the most votes. Now it is time for the final vote. This time, group members select the idea they most favor.

The greatest advantage of NGT is that the independent idea generation steps encourage equal participation of group members regardless of power or status. The views of more silent members are treated the same as the views of dominant members (Van de Ven & Delbecq, 1974). In fact, NGT groups develop more proposals and higher-quality proposals than groups using other procedures (Green, 1975; Kramer et al., 1997). Another advantage of NGT is that its specified structure helps bring a sense of closure and accomplishment to group problem solving (Van de Ven & Delbecq, 1974). When the meeting is finished, members have a firm grasp of what the group decided and a feeling of satisfaction because they helped the group reach that decision.

To summarize, NGT includes the following steps:

1. Individuals silently generate ideas, writing down each idea.

2. Have a facilitator record the ideas, one at a time, on a flip chart.

3. As a group, discuss each idea for clarification.

4. To narrow the number of ideas, vote on the ideas believed to be most important.

5. Discuss the ideas that receive the most votes.

6. Repeat steps 4 and 5 until only one idea remains.

When is it best to use NGT? Several group situations can be enhanced by the NGT process (Pavitt, 1993). NGT is most helpful when proposal generation is crucial. For example, suppose your softball team needs to find new and creative ways to raise funds. Your team has already tried most of the traditional approaches to raising money, and members' enthusiasm for selling door to door is low. NGT can help the team identify alternatives without group members surrendering to the ideas of the coach or the best players. NGT also can be very helpful for groups that are not very cohesive. When a group's culture is unhealthy and cohesiveness is low but the group's work must be done, NGT can help the group overcome its relationship problems and allow it to continue with its tasks. The minimized interaction in the idea generation phase of NGT gives everyone a chance to participate, increasing the likelihood that members will be satisfied with the group's final choice. Finally, NGT is particularly helpful when the problem facing the group is particularly volatile—for example, when organizational groups have to make difficult decisions about which items or projects to cut from the budget. The conflict that is likely to occur through more interactive procedures or unstructured processes can be destructive. The structured process of NGT helps group members focus on the task because turn taking is controlled.

With respect to the five critical functions of group decision making, NGT satisfies four. Because interaction is limited, especially in the idea generation phase, group members are not likely to achieve understanding of the problem. The discussion phase of NGT, however, should be effective in helping group members come to understand what constitutes an acceptable resolution to the problem, develop realistic and acceptable alternatives, and assess the positive and negative qualities of alternatives considered.

Consensus

Consensus means that each group member agrees with the decision or that group members' individual positions are close enough that they can support the group's decision (DeStephen & Hirokawa, 1988; Hoffman & Kleinman, 1994). In the latter case, even if members do not totally agree with the decision, they choose to support the group by supporting the decision. Consensus is achieved through discussion. Through members' interactions, alternatives emerge and are tested. In their interaction, group members consult with one another and weigh various alternatives. Eventually, one idea emerges as the decision that group members can support.

To the extent that group members feel they have participated in the decision-making process, they are satisfied with the group's interaction. That satisfaction is then extended to the consensus decision. Thus, when all group members can give verbal support, consensus has been achieved. To develop consensus, a group uses discussion to combine the best insights of all members to find a solution that incorporates all points of view. For example, juries that award damages in lawsuits must make consensus decisions—everyone must agree on the amount of money to be awarded.

Too frequently, consensus building is seen as a freewheeling discussion without any sort of process, plan, or procedure. But there are guidelines a group can use to achieve consensus. This procedure is especially useful for groups that must make highly subjective decisions (for example, a panel of judges deciding which contestant best represents the university, or the local United Way board of directors deciding how much money will be allocated to community service agencies) (Hare, 1982). Thus consensus is a procedure that helps a group reach agreement.

To develop consensus, the leader or another group member takes on the role of coordinator to facilitate the group's discussion. This coordinator does not express his or her opinions or argue for or against proposals suggested by the group. Rather, he or she uses ideas generated by members to formulate proposals acceptable to all members. Another group member can act as a recorder to document each of the proposals. Throughout the discussion, the recorder should read back statements that reflect the initial agreements of the group. This ensures that the agreement is real. When the group feels it has reached consensus, the recorder should read aloud this decision so members can give approval or modify the proposal.

To summarize, the steps for using consensus include the following:

1. Assign one group member to the role of coordinator to facilitate the discussion.
2. The coordinator uses ideas generated by members to formulate proposals acceptable to all members.
3. Assign another group member to record each of the proposals.
4. Throughout the discussion, the recorder reads back statements that reflect the agreements of the group.
5. The recorder reads aloud the final decision so members can give approval or modify the proposal.

In addition to following these steps, all group members need to be aware of a few basic discussion rules. First, the goal of the group's discussion is to find a solution that incorporates all points of view. Second, group members should not only give their opinions on the issue but also seek out the opinions of other members. The coordinator should make an extra effort to include less talkative members in the discussion. Third, group members should address their opinions and remarks to the group as a whole, and not to the coordinator. Finally, group members should avoid calling for a vote, which has the effect of stopping the discussion.

Consensus can only be reached through interaction. Although each group member should be encouraged to give his or her opinion, group members should avoid arguing for their personal ideas. It is better to state your ideas and give supporting reasons. Arguing about whose idea is better or whose idea is more correct will not help the group achieve consensus. If other group members express opinions that differ from yours, avoid confrontation and criticism. Rather, ask questions that can help you understand their points of view.

As the group works toward consensus, it can be tempting to change your mind just so the group can reach consensus and move on to other activities. Be careful! Changing your mind only to reach agreement will make you less satisfied with the process and the decision. If the group has trouble reaching consensus, it is better to postpone the decision until another meeting. Pressing for a solution because time is short will not help group members understand and commit to the decision. If a decision is postponed, assigning group members to gather more information can help the next discussion session.

PUTTING THE PIECES TOGETHER

Group Goal and Interdependence

Think about a group decision in which you participated for which consensus was the decision-making procedure used by the group. To what extent did consensus decision making help the group achieve its goal? How well did consensus decision making reflect interdependence among group members? Was consensus the most appropriate decision-making procedure for this group and this decision? In what way did the group's practice of consensus match the description of consensus given in this chapter? Considering what you know now about decision-making procedures, what three pieces of advice would you give to this group about its use of consensus?

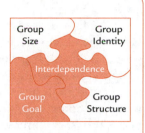

How well does consensus achieve the five critical functions of decision making? As a decision procedure, it is very effective in helping group members achieve an understanding of the problem they are trying to resolve, identify what constitutes an acceptable resolution, and develop a set of realistic and acceptable alternatives. Discussion leading to consensus allows more viewpoints to be discussed, so members are made aware of issues and facts they did not previously know. As a result, group members become more knowledgeable about the problem. Consensus discussions involve everyone, which results in a high degree of integration as at least part of everyone's point of view is represented in the final decision. Thus consensus can help achieve the first three critical functions. However, it is less effective in helping groups assess the positive and negative qualities of the alternatives presented.

There are a few disadvantages to using consensus. First, this procedure takes time. When not enough time is allotted, some members may opt out of the discussion process, allowing the group to come to a **false consensus**—agreeing to a decision simply to be done with the task. Thus the extent to which consensus is effective depends on the voluntary and effective participation of group members. Second, consensus is usually not effective when controversial or complex decisions must be made. A group charged with making a decision that heightens emotional issues for members is likely to make a better decision with a more standardized approach that structures group inquiry. This is why the consensus procedure is not always effective in assessing the positive and negative qualities of the alternatives presented.

Voting

Voting, another decision-making procedure, is simply the process of casting written or verbal ballots in support of or against a specific proposal. Many organizational groups rely on the outcomes of majority voting to elect officers or pass resolutions. A group that votes needs to decide on three procedural issues before a vote is taken.

The first procedural issue centers on the discussion the group should have before members vote. Members do not simply walk into a meeting and vote. Voting should be on clear proposals, and only after substantial group discussion. Here is a suggested procedure to follow in voting (Hare, 1982). Members bring items to the attention of the group by making proposals in the form of motions. Let's say that your communication students' association is making decisions about its budget. Karen says, "I move that we set aside part of our budget for community activities." But subsequent discussion among group members reveals two ambiguities. What does Karen mean by "part of our budget": 20 percent? 40 percent? And what are "community activities"? Do they include teaching junior high students how to give speeches? With other members' help, Karen's proposal is made more specific: "I move that we set aside 20 percent of our budget for community intervention activities that help children appreciate the value of communicating effectively." Now, with a specific motion, Karen can argue for her proposal by stating its merits. Even with a specific proposal, she is going to receive some opposition or face more questions. That is okay because it helps all group members understand her motion more clearly. During this discussion, the group leader makes sure that all those who want to be heard get a chance to talk. However, the leader does not argue for or against any particular motion. To do so would put undue influence on the group. The group's secretary or recorder keeps track of the motions and identifies which ones receive approval from the group.

The second procedural issue is to decide how the vote will be taken. When sensitive issues are being voted on, it is better to use a written ballot. Similar ballots or pieces of paper are given to each group member. This way group members can vote their conscience and retain their anonymity. Two group members should count the votes and verify the decision before announcing it to the group.

A verbal vote, or a show of hands, is more efficient when it is necessary only to document the approval or disapproval apparent in the group's discussion. For example, suppose your communication students' association has several items of business to take care of at the next meeting. Specifically, the association needs to elect officers, approve the budget, and select a faculty member for the outstanding professor award. The budget was read to members at the last meeting and then discussed. Although members will ask some questions before the vote, the group basically needs to approve or disapprove the budget. Because there is nothing out of the ordinary about the budget and little controversy is expected, it is okay to use a show of hands in this case.

However, electing officers and voting for one professor to receive an award can bring up conflicting emotions among group members. Both of these matters are better handled with written ballots. This way group members can freely support the candidates and the professor they desire without fear of intimidation or retaliation.

The final procedural issue that needs to be agreed on before taking a vote is how many votes are needed to win or decide an issue. Most of the time, a simple majority vote (one more than half of the members) is satisfactory. However, if a group is changing its constitution or taking some type of legal action, a two-thirds or three-fourths majority may be preferable. Both the method of voting and the majority required for a decision need to be agreed upon before any voting takes place.

Voting can be efficient, but it can also arbitrarily limit a group's choices. Many times motions considered for a vote take on an either/or quality that limits the choice to two alternatives. And a decision made by voting is seen as final—groups seldom revote. This is why having an adequate discussion period before voting is necessary. As you can see, voting is not the best choice when complex decisions must be made.

To summarize, the procedures for voting include the following:

1. Hold discussions to generate a clear proposal.
2. Decide how the vote will be taken—written ballot, verbal vote, or show of hands.
3. Decide how many votes are needed to win or decide an issue.
4. Restate the proposal before voting.

How well a group develops the discussion before voting determines how well the group satisfies the five critical functions of group decision making. Although voting is often perceived as a way of providing a quick decision, inadequate time for group discussion can severely limit the appropriateness or effectiveness of the proposals to be voted on.

Ranking

Ranking is the process of assigning a numerical value to each decision alternative so that group members' preferences are revealed. Groups often use a ranking process when there are many viable alternatives from which to choose, but the group must select the preferred alternative or a set of preferred alternatives. There are two steps to the ranking process.

First, each member individually assigns a numerical value to each decision alternative. In effect, rankings position each alternative from highest to lowest, as well as relative to one another. Usually, 1 is assigned to the most valued choice, 2 to the next most valued choice, and so on. These rankings may be based on a set of criteria developed by the group (for instance, How well does this alternative fix the problem? Is the alternative possible within the time frame allotted the project?).

Second, after group members complete their individual rankings, the values for each alternative are summed and totaled. Now the group has a score for each alternative. The alternative with the lowest total is the group's first-ranked alternative. The alternative with the second-lowest score is the group's second-ranked alternative, and so on. This procedure, which helps group members come to agreement, can be done publicly so group members can see or hear the ranking of one another's alternatives, or the process can be done on paper so individual rankings are anonymous.

Just as with voting, the ranking procedure is most effective when the group has adequate time to develop and discuss the alternatives to be ranked. Compared to groups instructed to "choose the best alternative," groups that rank-order their alternatives do a better job, as all alternatives must be discussed for members to perform the ranking task (Hollingshead, 1996). Thus the extent to which this procedure satisfies the five critical functions of group decision making depends on the quality of the group's discussion.

To summarize, to use ranking effectively as a decision procedure, a group should take the following steps:

1. Hold adequate discussion that leads to clear proposals.
2. Have each member assign a numerical value to each decision alternative.
3. Sum individual rankings and total them for the group.
4. The alternative with the lowest total is the group's first-ranked alternative.

Although ranking decreases group members' feelings of personal involvement or participation, groups using this procedure report little negativity in decision making. Fewer arguments or conflicts are reported when ranking is used because it is more difficult for one or two individual members to alter a group's decision-making process. Each member gets to indicate his or her preference, and all preferences are treated equally. Thus group members report feeling satisfied with the outcome (Green & Taber, 1980). Group members usually prefer ranking to voting for making a decision when more than two alternatives exist.

Comparing Procedures

Procedures help groups by managing their discussions and decision-making processes. In turn, this enhances the quality of decision making in the group by coordinating members' thinking and communication, providing a set of ground rules all members can and must follow, balancing member participation, managing conflicts, and improving group climate (Jarboe, 1996; Poole, 1991; Sunwolf & Seibold, 1999). Most importantly, procedures help groups avoid becoming solution-minded too quickly.

But which procedure is best? Sometimes the group leader or facilitator selects a procedure. Other times the group relies on familiarity—selecting the procedure it used last time regardless of its effectiveness. Rather than select a procedure arbitrarily, groups should select a procedure or a combination of procedures that best suits their needs and satisfies the five critical functions of group decision making. Table 7.1 summarizes the ways in which each procedure satisfies the five functions.

Thinking of each function as a unique type of decision task, we can see that the standard agenda fulfills all five functions and seems to be the most effective decision procedure. But we should be cautious in recommending it as the most

Table 7.1 The Ways in Which Various Procedures Satisfy Problem-Solving and Decision-Making Functions

	Understand the Problem	Understand What Constitutes Acceptable Resolution	Develop Realistic and Acceptable Alternatives	Assess the Positive Qualities of Alternatives	Assess the Negative Qualities of Alternatives
Standard Agenda	Yes	Yes	Yes	Yes	Yes
Brainstorming	Somewhat	Yes	Yes	No	No
NGT	No	Yes	Yes	Yes	Yes
Consensus	Yes	Yes	Yes	No	No
Voting	Depends on quality of group discussion *before* voting	Depends on quality of group discussion *before* voting	Depends on quality of group discussion *before* voting	Depends on quality of group discussion *before* voting	Depends on quality of group discussion *before* voting
Ranking	Depends on quality of group discussion *before* ranking	Depends on quality of group discussion *before* ranking	Depends on quality of group discussion *before* ranking	Depends on quality of group discussion *before* ranking	Depends on quality of group discussion *before* ranking

effective procedure in all group decision-making tasks. Why? Although the standard agenda identifies which steps need to be completed, it does not ensure that all members will participate. Recall that the type and structure of communication among group members differs across these procedures. Groups need to select the procedure that best fits their communication needs.

Before you select a procedure, you should analyze the type of task before your group. If the task is easy—for example, the group has all of the necessary information to make effective choices—the type of procedure you select will have less influence on the group's ability to resolve the problem or reach a decision. However, if the group task or decision is difficult—for example, members' decision-making skills vary, the group needs to consult with people outside the group, or the decision has multiple parts—the decision procedure selected will have a greater impact on the group's decision-making abilities. Generally, in these situations, the procedure that encourages vigilant and systematic face-to-face interaction will result in higher-quality outcomes (Hirokawa et al., 1996).

Regardless of which procedure your group selects, all members must agree to using the procedure if *any* benefits are to be achieved. Also remember that the

SKILL BUILDER

Which Procedures Will Help Your Group?

Think of three recent group experiences in which decision making was the focus of your group's activity. Which procedures do you believe might have been most beneficial for each group? Why? Could the groups have benefited from using more than one procedure? How might you have initiated the use of procedures in your groups? Would group members have welcomed this type of procedural assistance or resisted it? What strategy or strategies could you have used to get your groups to adopt decision-making procedures? What communication skills could you have relied on to help the groups adopt these procedures? Which communication skills will you use in your next group meetings to encourage the groups to adopt the procedures?

procedure itself does not ensure that all members will be motivated and willing to participate. Decision procedures cannot replace group cohesiveness. To help you distinguish among these procedures, see "Which Procedures Will Help Your Group?"

The Paradox of Using Procedures

Research has demonstrated that groups using formal discussion procedures generally develop higher member satisfaction and greater commitment to the decision. Although the standard agenda procedure helps groups pay greater attention to detail, NGT and brainstorming groups generally produce more ideas and higher-quality ideas, and voting and ranking can make decision outcomes clearer. Yet many groups try to avoid using procedures. This is because discussion and decision-making procedures take time, and groups must plan their meetings accordingly. Group members often are reluctant to use procedures because they are unaccustomed to using them or initially find them too restrictive. Group members may be more willing to try a procedure when they find out that one of the most frequent mistakes groups make is to plunge into their tasks without adequate discussion and thorough review of alternatives. Remember the student group trying to find a solution to the problem of food services not being available on the north campus?

It is often difficult for groups to stick with a procedure once it has been initiated. For example, members may find it difficult to refrain from nonverbal evaluation of ideas in brainstorming. Groups using NGT may believe they have found the best idea in the initial voting and discussion steps and so fail to pursue the rest of the process. Groups find that the standard agenda is difficult to stick with because it requires the diligence of all group members. One group member can successfully dislodge others from using the process. But it is exactly these difficulties that procedures guard against. In each case, the group avoids the procedure to move along more quickly, but efficiency is generally not a characteristic of effective groups.

Procedures help group members resist sloppy thinking and ineffective group habits (Poole, 1991). When procedures seem unnatural, it is often because group members have had little practice with them. If members have not used a particular procedure before, it is best to hold a practice session on a nonrelated topic. Practice can help demonstrate that the use of a procedure keeps groups from falling into traps of ineffectiveness or faulty thinking. Procedures also help groups manage their discussions and decision-making conversations and improve their effectiveness by providing a set of objective ground rules. When all group members know the procedure, it keeps the leader from assuming too much power and swaying the decision process. In addition, procedures help coordinate members' thinking and interaction, making it less likely that a group will go off topic. As member participation becomes more balanced, more voices are heard, and more ideas are deliberated.

To help your group gain experience with procedures, use these seven guidelines (Poole, 1991). First, motivate your group to use a procedure. For instance, provide positive feedback to group members when a procedure is used. Or look for discussion and decision-making problems that occur in your group, and then suggest a procedure to help the group overcome that difficulty. Second, champion the procedure process. For example, know and advocate the value of the procedure, remind the group to use it, and provide advice and help when the group does so. Also, train yourself in several procedures so you can help your group use them effectively. Third, help other group members learn the procedure. The more members who know and can use the procedure, the more likely the procedure is to be used.

Fourth, if needed, tailor the procedure to the group's needs. For example, perhaps your group works so fast at brainstorming that two facilitators are needed to write down members' ideas. This modification helps the group use the procedure more effectively. Tailoring a procedure to a group's particular needs gives the group ownership over the process. Fifth, suggest that your group spend time analyzing its discussion interaction with and without procedures. Getting members accustomed to talking about the group's strengths and weaknesses helps them realize that procedures can become a natural part of the group's activities. Sixth, when conflicts are high or cohesiveness is low, ask someone who is not a member of the group to act as the facilitator. Someone who is neutral, and not intrinsically interested in the group's outcomes, can ensure that a procedure is fairly administered. Finally, help the group set reasonable expectations with respect to using procedures. Using a procedure cannot solve all of a group's problems, but it can help a group discuss alternatives and make decisions more effectively. And make sure the procedure fits the group need. This will ensure that the group achieves greater success and will encourage group members to view the procedure as a tool, not as a panacea for all of the group's troubles.

Summary

Decision making is a primary activity of many groups. To a large extent, our society depends on groups to make decisions—decisions that affect governmental and organizational policies, long-term policies, and day-to-day activities. Family and other social groups also make decisions. Across the variety of group decision-making situations, group members need task, relational, and procedural skills. Generally, groups are better decision makers than individuals when the problem is complex, when the problem requires input from diverse perspectives, and when people need to identify with and commit to the decision.

Regardless of the procedures or process your group uses, four principles seem to fit most group problem-solving and decision-making situations. Acknowledging that group decision making is evolutionary and circular and that there are multiple influences on decisions made within a larger context of constraints allows us to embrace rather than fight the process.

Functional theory advocates five functions as necessary for effective decision making: understanding the problem, understanding what constitutes an acceptable choice, generating realistic and acceptable alternatives, assessing the positive qualities of each alternative, and assessing the negative qualities of each alternative. Groups whose communication fulfills all five functions are more effective in their decision making because information has been pooled and evaluated.

Decision-making procedures can help groups stay on track, equalize participation among members, and balance emotional and social aspects with task issues. Groups can choose from a variety of decision-making or discussion procedures. The standard agenda, or reflective thinking, is a strict linear process that helps groups focus on different stages or aspects of the problem-solving process. By moving through each step, group members can first identify and then evaluate each of the potential alternatives in complex problem solving. Brainstorming is an idea generation procedure that can help groups be creative in thinking of alternatives. The nominal group technique also assists the idea generation process, but it strictly controls the amount and type of communication among group members. Consensus is a technique with wide application in group decision making. In this procedure, one group member helps facilitate the discussion and makes sure that all members have the opportunity to express their points of view. Voting is a popular procedure when groups must make their final selection from a set of alternatives. Like ranking, voting allows each member to equally affect the outcome.

Each procedure can help groups be more effective, but some procedures are better suited to different aspects of the decision-making process. Groups can compare procedures for their ability to satisfy the five critical functions according to functional theory.

No one person or procedure will make group decision making effective. It is the appropriate selection and combination of people, talents, procedures, and structures that strengthens group decision making. By monitoring your own performance and the performance of the group as a whole, you will be able to select the most appropriate decision-making or discussion procedures.

Discussion Questions and Exercises

1. For one week, keep a diary or journal of all the group decisions in which you participate. Identify who in the group is making the decisions, what the decisions are about, how long the group spends on decision making, and what strengths or weaknesses exist in the decision-making process. Come to class ready to discuss your experiences and to identify procedures that could have helped your group be more effective.

2. Using the data from your diary or journal from item 1, write a paper that analyzes your role in the problem-solving and decision-making procedures your group uses and the ways in which your communication skills in that role influence your group's decision-making effectiveness.

3. Select someone you know who works full-time, and ask this person to participate in an interview about group or team decision making at work. Before the interview, develop a list of questions to guide the interview. You might include questions like these: How many decision-making groups or teams are you a part of? What is your role and what are your responsibilities in those groups and teams? How would you assess the effectiveness of your decision making? Is there something unusual (good or bad) that helps or hinders your groups' decision-making abilities? If you could change one thing about how your groups make decisions, what would it be?

4. Reflect on situations in which your family or group of friends made decisions? Using the five key components of a group—group size, interdependence of members, group identity, group goal, and group structure—describe how this social group was similar to or different from a work group or sports group to which you belonged. Selecting one decision event from both types of groups, compare the decision process in which the groups engaged. What task, relational, and procedural skills did you use to help the groups with their decision making? Which of these skills do you wish you would have used? Why?

5. Reflect on a decision made by your family group. In what ways was this decision-making process similar to or different from the four characteristics of decision making (evolutionary process, circular process, influences affecting the group, and external and internal constraints)?

Assessing Decision Processes and Implementing Decisions

GROUP SKILLS PREVIEW

In this chapter, you will learn to do the following:

- Help your group avoid faulty decision making

- Monitor your information sharing in groups

- Maintain vigilant communication to help your group avoid groupthink

- Select appropriate decision-making skills to confront decision-making challenges

- Develop a PERT diagram to implement your group's decision

- Identify appropriate and reasonable criteria against which to measure the success of your group's decision

Once its decisions are made, the group should assess its decision-making effectiveness, in terms of both group members' performance and the group's ability to overcome any challenges experienced during decision making. Challenges include factors that contribute to faulty decision making, constraints that limit or restrict decision making, and groupthink. Groups seldom make just one decision. Analyzing decision-making effectiveness by considering how well (or how poorly) group members interacted and why the group performed well (or poorly) provides helpful information for the next decision or problem the group encounters. Of course, decision making is not complete until the decision is implemented and the implementation is monitored. By taking these final steps, a group completes the problem-solving and decision-making process.

Monitoring Decision-Making Performance

One way to help your group make effective decisions is to monitor how well your group is performing its decision-making or problem-solving activities. Here is a three-part assessment you can use while you are in group decision-making settings to gauge how effective your group is (Hirokawa et al., 1996). First, does your group have access to all the information it needs? If not, what can you do to secure this information for the group? Generally, the more informed members are about the problem or issue, the more likely the group is to reach a quality decision.

Second, how do you rate the effort of group members? Is their effort of high quality, or are they simply putting in their time? How would you rate your effort? Are you helping or inhibiting the group in its decision process? Putting forth a high-quality effort means examining and reexamining information on a single topic, not merely sitting together for long periods and talking about various topics off the agenda. Third, what is the quality of group members' thinking? High-quality thinking involves using logic and reason to reach opinions, not simply relying on superficial opinions ("because I like it"). In what ways did your interactions help the group move forward on its decisions in a logical or rational manner?

While group members intend to contribute to the group decision-making process, their contributions are often not as influential as they hope. Too frequently, group members fail to perform the task, relational, and procedural skills required for effective decision making that are described in Chapter 7. Or they do not encourage the group to adopt the decision-making procedure most appropriate for their group situation. Challenges to decision making can derail group members' best intentions. These challenges are explored in detail in the next section.

Challenges to Decision-Making Effectiveness

Generally, research has shown that groups make better decisions than individuals when the problem or issue is complex, but the relational dynamics among group members can produce negative influences and hinder group decision-making effectiveness. However, these challenges can be overcome.

Information Bias

As explained in Chapter 4, one influence on tasks is the degree of participation of group members. When participation is uneven, an information bias can develop. **Information bias** exists any time the information the group is using is prejudiced toward a particular alternative, or prejudiced in such a way as to favor some group members over others. Regardless of how a group goes about its decision making, group members must communicate to have accurate information to recognize and define a problem, identify potential solutions, establish criteria for evaluating solutions, evaluate alternatives in light of those criteria, and then select one alternative (Propp, 1999). Information is the currency of decision making.

If decision making benefits from different viewpoints, then it would make sense that all viewpoints and information supporting those viewpoints would be used in a group's decision process. Bringing unique information to the group makes all group members more informed, which leads to more effective decision making (Henningsen & Henningsen 2003). However, one type of information bias occurs when some group members, particularly those who are new to the group or have lower status, tend to discuss information that is shared or already known by group members rather than bring new information before the group. One explanation is that these group members repeat or further the discussion of shared information in an attempt to create perceptions of credibility and competence (Wittenbaum, 2000). This type of bias is more likely to happen when group members have a high need for approval or inclusion from other members (Henningsen & Henningsen, 2004). Wanting others to like them or approve of their contributions, members repeat information that the group has already discussed—a strategy that is less risky than introducing new information into the group's discussion.

While a certain amount of discussion about shared information is necessary to ensure topic agreement, groups that fall into this type of information bias trap are not taking advantage of the unique viewpoints or perspectives of all group members. The group's leader or members with more experience or higher status can counteract this tendency by asking questions, such as "What experiences have you had that would challenge what the group is discussing?" "We seem to be coming to agreement, let's consider the negative consequences of this alternative?" or "Are stuck on this one solution? Does someone have an alternative?"

Another type of information bias occurs when majority members have undue influence on the decision outcome. **Majority influence** occurs when a group's largest subgroup uses social pressure to influence decision outcomes. It would be easy to conclude that the largest subgroup should succeed in influencing group decision simply because it has more members advocating for a particular choice. But it's not that simple. Research demonstrates that it is in the consistency in majority members' presentations—not the size of the majority subgroup—that creates the social influence (Meyers, Brashers, & Hanner, 2000). Perhaps you're wondering how the consistent presentation of preference of one alternative by a majority of a group's members can negatively influence decision making? That's a fair question. Frequently, this type of social pressure results in group members agreeing on a conventional or more cautious solution without considering unique or novel alternatives. Moreover, members of the majority can advocate for a position that is inaccurate or incomplete or one will not satisfy the criteria for an acceptable solution. Just because it is the preferred solution or choice of the majority of group members does not make it the best solution or choice.

How can a minority subgroup counteract majority influence? To counteract the influence, it has to be recognized, and one way to identify majority influence is by paying attention to how frequently members of the majority subgroup agree with one another. When members of the subgroup repetitively agree, an illusion of consensus about a position or choice is developed and the group is more likely to accept the majority subgroup's position. Minority subgroups can decrease majority influence by being consistent in their presentation of arguments (Meyers et al., 2000). Being consistent keeps other alternatives in the group's discussion. Recall from Chapter 7 that *argument* is one of the task skills needed in decision making (Gouran, 2003). Thus minority members need to consistently present assertions, propositions, elaborations, amplifications, and justifications for the solutions or choices they prefer. Logical and rational arguments presented in a consistent manner from members of the minority subgroup can influence a group to accept the minority position.

Groupthink

Groupthink is faulty decision making that results from a lack of critical thinking. Groupthink occurs regularly and can have a devastating influence on groups. It is most likely to occur when the following conditions are present:

- Disagreement is absent in the group.
- The group develops an extraordinarily high sense of cohesiveness.
- The group uses language to detach itself from ethical or moral considerations associated with finding a solution.
- The group is not vigilant in its thinking and artificially narrows what it considers to be an acceptable solution.
- Group members feel that the group is infallible, that it can do no wrong.
- Group members protect one another from any criticisms or new knowledge that might demonstrate that the group is wrong.

According to the groupthink hypothesis (Janis, 1982), highly cohesive groups are more likely to adopt faulty solutions because members fail to critically examine and analyze options. Let's explore these issues in more detail.

Groupthink occurs because group members overestimate their power and invulnerability. Group members do not question what they are doing or why they are doing it. Maintaining group harmony or enhancing the desire to build a group identity is perceived by members to be more important than considering information that may temporarily reduce group cohesiveness. When cohesiveness is high, group members are more psychologically dependent on one another and less willing to challenge ideas.

As the group becomes closed-minded, group members reject information that is contrary to the preferred or assumed course of action. By insulating itself from external influences, the group, in effect, isolates itself. Often group members create rationalizations that support their isolation (for example, "We don't need their input anyway" or "Their information wasn't helpful"). At worst, the group would close themselves off permanently from sources of information that could be useful in their decision making.

Groupthink is more likely to occur when group members experience high pressure to conform because of strong relationships between the leader and group members. Pressure and stress are heightened when the stakes are high or when the leader recommends a solution and group members see no viable alternative. This pressure to conform acts as self-censorship, causing group members to believe that consensus exists in the group when it does not. In these cases, members view pleasing the leader as more important than considering other options.

These conditions create a working climate for a group that rewards closeness and cohesiveness and that punishes members for being different. Groups in which members have long and shared working histories and groups that are insulated from the views of others tend to generate this type of closeness. When time pressures and high-risk or high-consequence decision making also characterize a group's environment and activity, these difficulties are amplified (Neck & Moorhead, 1995). These types of groups often fail to use decision-making procedures to help them generate and then analyze alternatives. These conditions lead to full-blown groupthink. However, not all of these conditions need to be met for groups to make faulty decisions or to develop groupthink problems.

A group never intends to let groupthink occur, but groupthink can result when a group's face-to-face communication is ineffective. The absence of disagreement is the primary contributor to groupthink (Courtright, 1978), and that occurs when groups are overly cohesive. Overly cohesive group members are less likely to allow discussion that criticizes the group, its activity, or the ideas it generates. As a result, the group develops premature concurrence that shelters it from critical thinking. Believing that they have arrived at a unanimous decision, group members terminate their deliberations prematurely (Cline, 1994).

There are two ways to avoid groupthink. The first is to encourage full participation by all group members by adopting decision-making procedures. These procedures help groups focus on their tasks, and groups that have high task commitment are more likely to search for and assess alternative courses of action (Street, 1997). These procedures also help groups seek out information that is not currently known. This is important because groups that tend to talk about what all members already know, rather than to seek new information, are more susceptible to groupthink. A decision-making procedure can help offset high group cohesiveness, which can cause a member with valuable information to refrain from sharing it because it does not fit with other information possessed by the group.

The second way to avoid groupthink is to foster full group member participation by monitoring leadership behaviors. A leader who encourages member participation, solicits divergent opinions, and stresses the importance of reaching

---

PUTTING THE PIECES TOGETHER

Group Structure, Group Identity, and Group Goal

Identify one of your groups in which groupthink is most likely to occur or has occurred. What might you do to alter the group's structure (i.e., communication network, norms, roles) to overcome the high sense of cohesiveness or lack of disagreement? Considering group identity and the group's goal, what decision-making procedure would you recommend to help the group move out of groupthink? Do you believe other group members would agree with your assessment and choices? Why or why not? As you analyze your recommendation, does it focus more on helping the group manage its tasks and activities, or helping members manage their relationships?

an effective decision will promote greater depth in the group's discussion. Leaders should open up discussions by encouraging other members to voice their opinions rather than stating their own. A leader's opinion is only one of many that group members should deliberate. Giving an opinion too forcefully and too early may make other members hesitant to speak up. Ultimately, the leader is responsible for developing and maintaining a system of effective communication that allows group members to reach their goal (Flippen, 1999).

Factors in Faulty Decision Making

Many decision-making groups are susceptible to information bias and groupthink, and the negative consequences are well documented. In addition to these two primary challenges, group members should be aware of other factors that create challenges for their decision making (Gouran, Hirokawa, & Martz, 1986). The eight factors described below are common across a variety of groups. At first glance, these factors may appear to be more annoying than troubling, with a minimal effect on group decision making. However, left unattended, each of these factors can create destructive and dysfunctional interaction patterns.

First, some faulty decisions result when group members make assumptions about the facts of a case. When members wrongly assume that they know the facts or have all of the information needed to make a decision, the decision-making base is flawed. For example, recall our parking example from the previous chapter. The group's initial belief that there is not enough parking on campus becomes a fact and affects the type of solutions it develops to combat the problem. However, when group members investigate the issue, they find that it is not a question of how many parking spaces are available, but of where or when the parking spaces are available. This additional information creates a different frame for the group's decision making and changes the type of solution group members propose. Questioning one another and asking for clarification even when everyone believes it is a fact can help a group avoid making faulty assumptions.

A second factor contributing to faulty decision making is a breakdown in the group's reasoning process. Even when group members have all of the needed information, they can still make a poor decision if they allow themselves to jump to conclusions or use faulty logic. Drawing unwarranted inferences is one example of faulty reasoning. Unwarranted inferences are based not on facts, data, or information, but on what group members think to be true. What they believe to be true enters the discussion as fact before anyone checks the validity of the inference. As group members continue to interact, the unwarranted inference becomes a fact, and no one thinks it needs to be checked out. Here is an example of how this can happen:

PAULA: I think we're not having an awards ceremony because the president of the university will be traveling out of the country.

ALTHEA: How do you know that?

Faulty or failed decisions are more prevalent than you might think. Making assumptions about facts, using faulty logic, and being pressured by someone external to the group are just a few of the factors that can contribute to faulty decision making.

PAULA: I heard my dad talking on the phone. He went to a chamber of commerce breakfast and our president was the guest speaker. My dad said the president talked about traveling to central Europe.

LOREN: But when?

PAULA: I don't know. But don't you think it's unusual that the university cancelled an event that's been a tradition for 25 years?

LOREN: Well, maybe there's some other reason.

ALTHEA: I think she's right, Loren. Why else would they cancel the awards ceremony?

Using one of the discussion-making and problem-solving procedures described in Chapter 7 can help group members overcome this type of breakdown in the group's reasoning process. For example, if the group was using the standard agenda, the group's discussion in the problem identification or problem analysis stages would have likely corrected this unwarranted inference about the cancellation of the university's awards ceremony.

Third, faulty or ineffective decisions are more likely to occur when the group is under pressure to make a quick decision or when it believes that it has to pick a particular solution to please someone outside the group. In both cases, group members perceive that no other choice is available them. Even if the pressure is imagined, such a belief curtails the group's discussion and prevents it from exploring the potential negative consequences of the choice. Once this type of perception crystallizes in the group, it can become so salient that it seems impossible to move from this position. You have probably been a member of a class group in which this happened. The teacher tells the groups they can pick whatever topic they want for their presentations. But instead of focusing on topics of interest to your group members, you try to figure out what topic your teacher would like to hear about, hoping to please him or her. Perhaps somebody mentions that the teacher was in the Marines. Before you know it, your group is planning a presentation on why military service should be mandatory rather than voluntary.

Incomplete decision criteria is the fourth factor contributing to faulty decision making. Many groups work to resolve problems that are time or budget sensitive. In fact, groups frequently use a time or budget criterion as the primary or sole criterion. By focusing on this one issue in the exploration of alternatives, a group overlooks other potential negative consequences. For example, a group working under the budgetary pressure to purchase the cheapest available product will select the least costly alternative. Believing they have satisfied their budgetary constraint, group members may overlook the long-term costs or the costs to implement the decision. For instance, buying the cheapest copy paper may cause the copier to continually jam. How do you evaluate the time lost to unjamming the copier in comparison to the pennies saved on the paper?

Fifth, faulty decision making occurs when group members are unable to persuade or convince one another that an alternative decision is better. For example, Kedrick strongly believes that adopting the neuter-spay/reduced animal license fee program will increase pet owner responsibility. But in conversations with others, he has difficulty both presenting and defending this point of view. His inability to persuade others that some pet owners will be lured by the financial incentive to neuter or spay their pets allows the group to reject this alternative. Thus your persuasive ability as a group member can help your group accept a high-quality alternative and reject low-quality ones.

The sixth factor contributing to faulty decision making is the use of ambiguous and vague language (for example, "Do you remember what we were talking about?" "Yeah." "Sure." "Okay, then, here's what we're going to do . . ."). When group members are vague and indirect, other group members may misread the intended meaning. In discussing alternatives, clear and concise language is needed to explore the positive and negative consequences.

Seventh, rigid adherence to role boundaries can create conflict for group members. When role conflict exists, group members rarely venture outside their ascribed roles to collect additional information or to pursue additional alternatives. This occurs more often when roles and prescribed channels of communication are closely aligned. For example, a female secretary who is a member of an otherwise all-male executive committee knows that her primary role is to serve as the group's recorder. In a policy-making discussion about maternity benefits, however, she may wish to communicate to the group her beliefs about what women in the organization want. The information she possesses could help the group in its decision making, but she feels hesitant to change roles from passive recorder to active participant. Feeling pressure to remain in her formal role, she remains quiet while the men discuss maternity benefits.

Finally, failure to ask relevant or obvious questions creates assumed understanding. Frequently, the most obvious question goes unasked because a group member is fearful that he or she will be penalized or humiliated by other members for not knowing the answer. But asking questions gives groups another opportunity to explore details that are often taken for granted. For example, a student group is preparing a graphic presentation of its final project. Wanting to impress their instructor and classmates, they spend extra time putting the computer slide presentation together and practicing with it. The members simply assume—and so no one bothers to ask—that the computer in the presentation room can run the slide presentation program. Minutes before their presentation, the leader pops in the group's disk, but nothing happens. Finally, a message appears on the screen: "Powergraphics cannot open the presentation." Failing to ask obvious or relevant questions can waste a group's time and render other decisions ineffective.

Helping Your Group Make Effective Decisions

How can a group member recognize that his or her group is facing one or more of these challenges? How can you help your group make effective decisions? Three techniques—listening and giving feedback, taking on the role of critical advisor, and using decision-making skills—can help.

Recall from Chapter 2 that listening is the most frequently used group communication skill. Because many people will share talking time, you will spend more time listening than talking. Even if your group has a formal leader, every member is responsible for the group, its interaction, and its decision outcomes. If you believe your group is facing one of these challenges, listen carefully to determine if and how the group's interaction is being jeopardized. Taking notes during the group's meeting can help you isolate the problem and pinpoint specific examples to use when you bring these challenges to the group's attention. This is an important contribution you can make, as it is nearly impossible for group members to alter group communication patterns and structures without someone pointing it out. More information about making observations in your group and giving group members feedback can be found in Chapter 12.

The second technique for improving group decision making is the role of critical advisor. Often referred to as the devil's advocate, the critical advisor constructively criticizes ideas brought before the group. The critical advisor assesses the group's process and asks questions that keep the group on course. In this role, the critical advisor suggests disadvantages to alternatives posed, reveals hidden assumptions by offering analyses of the problem that the group has not discussed, and questions the validity or reliability of information presented. The critical advisor helps the group see errors in its logic and thinking. By asking questions about the quality and number of alternatives examined, and by asking for clarification when assumptions are being made, the critical advisor helps the group avoid stereotypical thinking or premature judgment. The critical advisor challenges what the group is doing, forcing group members to provide support for its decisions (Schultz et al., 1995; Schweiger, Sandberg, & Ragan, 1986).

Only one group member is assigned to the critical advisor role. But, over time, different group members should assume the role. Group members may find that the critical advisor interjects unexpected and alternative reasoning when the group thinks it is on a roll. This is an advantage for the group because it keeps the group from falling into traps of faulty agreement. However, negativity can surface when the critical advisor interjects questions into the discussion. Rotating the role among group members minimizes the likelihood that a single group member will be accused of slowing down the group. Role rotation also strengthens members' skills as each member has the opportunity to fulfill the critical advisor role.

When should a group use the critical advisor role? Group members who have had experience working with one another will probably get the most out of the critical advisor role. Because this procedure has little structure, it can be used when other, more formal feedback procedures would consume too much time. This procedure is also useful when a group must present and support its decision to an external audience. Having responded to the questions of the critical advisor, the group should be able to respond more effectively to outside challenges. The constructive conflict allowed in the critical advisor procedure helps groups produce high-quality decisions.

Let's see how the role of critical advisor works in a group:

TIM: Jody, do you think we can move on the proposal?

JODY: I'm not sure, Tim. We've still got a lot to think about.

NICK: (in the role of the critical advisor) Maybe it would be a good idea to stop and consider what we have left to do.

SELA: Okay, we've got to finalize the budget, draw the time line, get someone to draw the graphs, and write the cover letter.

JODY: I said I'd do the graphs. Did everyone turn in their sketches?

TIM: Sorry, Jody. I forgot. How about tomorrow?

SELA: You've got mine.

NICK: Mine, too. Do we need to look at all of the graphs as a group?

JODY: That's a good idea. I don't want to spend time on the computer and then have someone disagree with what I've done. Let's do that at our next meeting.

NICK: Tim, let's come back to your comment about needing to move on the proposal. Is there some other pressure we don't know about?

TIM: Well, I saw Mr. Campbell at lunch yesterday. He asked about our proposal. Gave me the pep talk, you know.

NICK: Did he say anything to indicate that the deadline was moved up?

TIM: Not exactly. I just got that feeling, you know, that he was waiting on us.

NICK: Maybe we should confirm the deadline for the proposal with Campbell. I'll send him an email just as soon as we're through.

TIM: Well, I didn't want to mention it, but I also saw Ms. Rhoades. She also asked when we'd get the proposal done.

NICK: Is she waiting for our proposal? Or for Campbell's decision?

JODY: Good question, Nick. Previously, she's pushed me to finish something I had to do for Campbell because Campbell takes longer than she likes in making a decision.

NICK: Is that a concern of this group, then?

SELA: Well, it could be. Rhoades is watching what we're doing because I think she has something else planned for us when this is finished.

TIM: I got that feeling, too, Sela.

JODY: Well, maybe we need to get moving, then.

NICK: That could be. But let's confirm the deadline with Campbell. And let's not move so quickly that the proposal we turn in will fail.

Nick's role as critical advisor is to monitor the group's process and ask questions that clarify what the group is talking about. When someone plays this role in a group, the intent is to help the group become its most effective, not to hurt other members' feelings or destroy the morale of the group. Try "Assuming the Role of the Critical Advisor," on page 187, to see how this role could help your group.

Although groups want to be effective, decision-making conversations can present challenges as group members generate ideas, weigh alternatives, and make choices. Thus the third technique for improving group decision making is to assess the skills that you are contributing. Recall the decision-making skills described in Chapter 7. Relative to the task, do you help the group with problem recognition and in proper framing of the problem? In analyzing the situation, are the inferences you draw sound ones? Do you help the group by contributing novel ideas and unique information? Finally, do you present arguments for your positions that are rational and logical?

With respect to relational skills, do you enact a formal or informal leadership role effectively and help the group counteract the influence of cognitive, affiliative, and egocentric constraints? Do you help the group by creating a supportive climate that encourages the participation of all members? And, when conflict is present, can you help the group navigate effectively through it? With respect to procedural skills, how do you help the group plan its activities and proceed in a logical order? Do you help the group stay on track when difficulties arise? Do you encourage the group to use one or more procedures for problem solving and decision making? Encouraging others in the use of these skills will be more effective if you model effective decision-making skills.

Implementing Decisions

Despite the time and energy a group spends in making a decision, the group is not finished when the decision is made. Group members still must implement that decision. This is where the pay-off occurs for group members. The decision is put in place, and the process of embedding it in a group, organization, family, or society becomes the central activity (Nord & Tucker, 1987). How does a group

SKILL BUILDER

Assuming the Role of the Critical Advisor

Think back to one of your recent group experiences in which a critical advisor would have helped the group's decision making or problem solving. What steps could you have taken to emerge as the group's critical advisor, or to ask another group member to take on this role? What arguments would you have needed to persuade other group members that a critical advisor was needed? Reflecting on your communication and group member strengths, identify at least three behaviors that would contribute to your effectiveness as a critical advisor. In your next group situation in which a critical advisor could be useful, use these behaviors to help your group improve its decision-making effectiveness.

evaluate its decision implementation? You might simply ask whether it worked, but there are multiple criteria against which to judge the success of a decision implementation (Nord & Tucker, 1987).

Criteria for Successful Implementation

The first criterion to be addressed is whether the group reached its goal. For example, if the executive board intends to generate, evaluate, and rank projects for the Humane Society, then the first criterion is met if, in fact, these activities took place and the Humane Society now has a list of projects to guide it through the next year. A second criterion is whether the group's output (in this case, the list of projects) has utility or value for the Humane Society. If the projects will help publicize the mission of the Humane Society, increase donations, and increase membership and pet adoptions, then the second criterion of success has been achieved. As the year progresses, another success criterion will be used to measure the effectiveness of each project in achieving one of the goals. In this case, the group will assess the long-term consequences of the group's decisions.

For most decisions, certain costs are involved. Thus another criterion of successful implementation involves staying within budget in terms of supplies, personnel, time, and money. Decisions that use a lot of an organization's resources, require more personnel, take longer than expected, or go over budget are not successful implementations. One success criterion that is less obvious is how the process of decision making affects those who make the decisions. If members of the executive board find that they work well together and are enthusiastic about their relationships with one another, another measure of success is achieved. Thus, when the decision-making process contributes to the growth and personal well-being of team members, this type of success is achieved (Hackman, 1990, 2002).

An additional aspect of decision implementation to consider is whether the decision is routine or radical. If the executive board of the Humane Society simply decides to repeat last year's project in the coming year, the decision and implementation are routine. The people who will implement the decisions and those who will be affected by them have a good idea of how the board's decisions will affect their actions. But if the executive board decides to recommend unique projects, board and organizational members will face uncertainty as they implement the decisions. Generally, the more innovative the decisions, the more the board will have to rely on communication to make sure everyone understands what they are to do; the more radical the innovation, the more likely it is that the status quo will be disrupted. Thus innovative decisions result in a broad range of changes, such as changes in information, values, incentives, power, and other elements (Nord & Tucker, 1987). So, if the board decides to try something different for a fund-raiser—say, an adults-only party at the zoo—the implementation is more complex. Board and organizational members will be dealing with new tasks; thus they will not be able to rely on how things were done in the past. This type of implementation requires greater levels of communication than implementation of standard or routine decisions.

Designing the Implementation with PERT

The implementation stage may create a new series of decisions or problems for the group to consider. One technique to use at the implementation stage is **PERT** (program evaluation and review technique), which helps group members order the activities that must be completed to implement a decision (Fourre, 1968). With PERT, group members plan what actions will be needed and how long it will take to complete each action. PERT is especially useful when implementation is believed to be complex because it encourages group members to consider which, if any, activities can overlap or be completed simultaneously.

A PERT network is composed of events (points or areas on a diagram) that are connected by one or more lines. The events are diagrammed against a time line so that deadlines are visually prominent and logically thought out. Using PERT, a group is through with a decision only when all activities are done and implementation is complete. Look at the PERT diagram in Figure 8.1. The diagram flows from left to right; the time line can be calculated in days, weeks, or months. Of course, few decisions are as simplistic as this one. To implement most decisions, actions can be broken down into smaller activities that are also

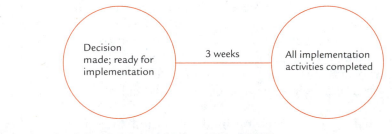

Figure 8.1 Decision Implementation Using PERT

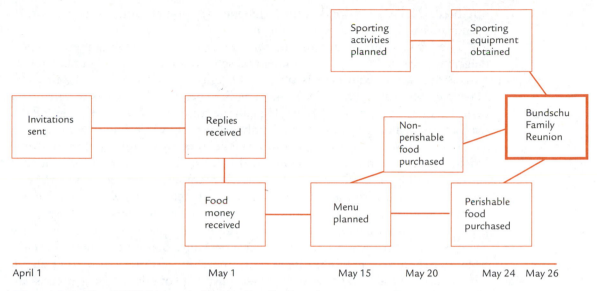

Figure 8.2 The PERT Diagram for the Family Reunion

represented by an event. For example, in planning a family reunion, "food purchased" is the completed action whereas "purchasing food" is the activity leading up to the completion of the action. Generally, individual group members are responsible for some activities but not all of them. At some time in the implementation process, all group members will need to meet to coordinate their activities.

A PERT diagram can help a group identify which activities must be completed first, second, and so on; which activities can overlap or be completed simultaneously; and how long it will take for activity completion. PERT visualizes the full implementation process, which helps group members recognize that many small but significant steps must be taken before other activities can occur.

The following steps will help you develop a more complex PERT diagram (Applbaum & Anatol, 1971; Phillips, 1965). First, identify the final event or activity, the one that will mark the completion of implementation. As an example, we will use the Bundschu family reunion, an annual event that draws together over a hundred family members from 13 states. This event goes in the box at the far right of the diagram (see Figure 8.2). Second, with all group members working together, make a list of all the other events that must happen before the final event. In this step, it is not necessary to list the events in order, but it is essential that the list of events be as complete as possible. Third, review the list of events and start to order the list. This should lead to the discovery that some events can occur simultaneously. For example, in planning the family reunion, food can be purchased by one committee while others are gathering sporting equipment. Ordering the events should also help the group recognize which events are dependent on other events. In planning the family reunion, the food committee cannot purchase food until the menu has been drawn up and the money has been obtained. The buying-food event is dependent upon completion of two other events: menu planned and money obtained.

The group is now ready for the fourth step—to start developing its PERT diagram. Because PERT is a planning and scheduling process, it is unlikely that your group will develop the best flow of events and activities on the first try. Have plenty of paper available. Visualizing the events and activities will help you identify any errors in your planning logic in the third step. Let's look at the PERT diagram for planning the Bundschu family reunion shown in Figure 8.2.

The critical first step in planning the reunion is sending the invitations. Without knowing how many people will be attending, planning for food and activities will be difficult. Notice that family members have been asked to send their money back with their reply. Without knowing how many people are coming and thus how much money there is to spend, the food committee cannot plan the menu. Also notice that the food committee starts planning the menu before the sports committee commences its activity. Menu planning is more difficult, because committee members must take into account differing diet preferences. The food committee will also want to take advantage of sales at the grocery store on nonperishable items. So this committee begins its work first.

In the fifth step, group members assess how much time will be needed for each of the activities. It's important to be realistic here. The group should consider (a) the optimistic time, the time it will take under ideal conditions with no complications, (b) the pessimistic time, the time it will take if every possible delay is encountered, and (c) the most likely time, the time it will take under normal conditions. By looking at time in this way, the group can calculate the expected time—a reasonable estimate of the time involved. How do these conditions apply to planning the family reunion?

From the optimistic point of view, no invitations get lost in the mail, and every family RSVPs (with their money) on time. Further, every time the planning committee gets together, each member shows up and has completed his or her assignments. From the pessimistic perspective, invitations are mailed late and then come back requiring extra postage, and families do not RSVP (or send their

Groups never seem to have enough time! Establishing your group's time frame for decision making and decision implementation is a crucial first step in the decision-making process.

MASTERING GROUP SKILLS

Implementing Plans with PERT

In one of your current groups that is charged with the responsibility of implementing decisions, develop a PERT diagram of the actions and activities you believe are needed. Recall that you must specifically identify the final event, as well as list all other events that support this outcome. Order the events, being careful to determine whether any of them can occur simultaneously. As you design the diagram, list the questions you'd like to ask other group members as you consider the amount of time it will take and the possible sequencing of events. Also list the assumptions you must make to diagram the implementation process. Each assumption should trigger the development of the question for the group. Present your draft of the PERT diagram at your next group meeting to get other members' reactions. Encourage your group to adopt this implementation procedure.

money) on time. The most likely time can be calculated by asking each group member to make independent estimates of the time they believe the group will need for each implementation activity. By talking through committee members' different points of view, they will develop a better idea of the time it will take to plan and carry out the reunion.

These discussions may also focus members' attention on other events and activities that are not on their PERT diagram. For example, these discussions help identify April 1 as the deadline for invitations to go out. The date allows enough time to receive the replies and the money to make the reunion a reality. It also helps the planning committee recognize that it has not thought of alternative sites for the reunion in case of bad weather. As a result of this discovery, another committee is formed to search for and select a backup location. When each group member is satisfied with the flow of events and activities and the time allotted for completing activities, then the PERT analysis and diagram are complete. Try "Implementing Plans with PERT" to get some practice with this technique.

Monitoring and Evaluating Decision Outcomes

Few decisions made by groups can be evaluated as being simply right or wrong. Thus quality of a group's decision is a better criterion (Gouran, 1988). Your group has made a high-quality decision if the decision (a) satisfied the criteria for acceptable solutions, as identified by group members, (b) produced high rewards and low costs, and (c) was acceptable to the group or others who implemented the decision. These standards can be evaluated immediately after the group has made its decision.

Decision evaluation should also be a part of the implementation process. There are three basic questions groups can use to structure these evaluations (Gouran, 1990). The first question is, Did the decision have the effect group members intended? In other words, was the group's goal consistent with what happened? Let's go back to the executive board of the Humane Society. In making decisions about projects to be carried out in the next year, the board intended to publicize the mission of the Humane Society, increase donations, and increase membership and pet adoptions. The set of projects the board approved had good potential, and at the year-end evaluation session, board members are pleased with what they have accomplished. By implementing the projects, the Humane Society has a more visible image in the community, donations are up 15 percent, membership is up 23 percent, and 97 percent of the animals the shelter took in have been adopted.

The second question groups can use to guide their evaluation is, Was the decision reached responsible for the observed effects? For example, how can the board members know that it was their set of projects that helped them to accomplish their objectives? Could it be that people in this community suddenly have become more sensitive to the plight of unwanted pets? Could it be that the national media campaign for the humane treatment of animals over the past 9 months is partly responsible for the success of the projects? Frequently, when groups achieve favorable outcomes, group members attribute those outcomes to the group's effective decision making. In contrast, when the outcomes are not favorable, group members are likely to ignore them or to attribute the failures to factors outside the control of the group. One way for the Humane Society board to be more confident that their projects indeed created the positive outcomes is to conduct a follow-up survey. By asking potential adopters how they found out about the shelter or asking new members what encouraged them to join, the board can more fully understand the impact of their decision making.

The third evaluation question is, Did the decision have any unintended or negative consequences that outweigh or offset the intended or positive consequences? For example, despite the best intentions, the board's projects have an unintended consequence. With the additional publicity and public outreach, the Humane Society drew considerable scrutiny from the local media. Reporters frequently came to the animal shelter to check on the conditions of the kennels. One television news program tried to expose the shelter, claiming that it would not take in stray dogs. In reality, the shelter was full, and accepting more animals would have violated state animal control regulations. Even so, this news report created negative publicity for the shelter during one of its major donation drives. Increasing media scrutiny and potentially negative press and media coverage were not the board's intended goals. Thus, in the final evaluation, the positive outcomes of the many projects had to be balanced by the negative publicity.

Summary

A group's decision-making performance should be monitored for each decision made. Information bias is a challenge to group decision making. Bias exists any time the information the group is using is prejudiced toward a particular alternative, or prejudiced in such a way as to favor some group members over others.

Another type of information bias occurs when some group members, particularly those who are new to the group or have lower status, discuss information that is shared or already known by group members rather than bring new information before the group. Majority influence, another type of information bias, occurs when a group's largest subgroup uses social pressure to influence decision outcomes.

Groupthink is the phenomenon that occurs when groups are pressured by external environments and a sense of cohesiveness, invulnerability, and infallibility. A group that has these characteristics, as well as a charismatic and powerful group leader, retreats from vigilant discussion about decision alternatives and adopts the alternative suggested by the leader with little or no critical evaluation. Other challenges to decision making occur when faulty assumptions are made, when there is a breakdown in the group's reasoning, when there is a time pressure, when the group uses incomplete decision rules or criteria, when group members are unable to persuade one another, when group members adhere too rigidly to roles, and when group members fail to ask relevant or obvious questions. By paying attention to the group's process, groups can overcome each of these problems.

Group members can counteract these challenges by listening and giving feedback, taking on the role of critical advisor, and using, relational, and procedural decision-making skills. A critical advisor is suggested for groups that will be challenged by an external audience. By responding to questions and requests for clarification, a group can maximize the strength of its decision before presenting it to others. To be used effectively, all group members should rotate through this role.

Too frequently, groups spend a great deal of time on making decisions, forgetting that their time and effort are also needed in the decision implementation and monitoring stages. Implementation is the stage at which the pay-off occurs if the group achieves its goal, if the outcome has utility, and if the project stays within the resources budgeted. Implementation is a success if a group can confirm these objectives and indicate that the group developed as a unit throughout the experience.

PERT is a technique that can help groups plan the sequencing of implementation activities. Working on a time line, PERT allows group members to specifically identify which steps of implementation must occur first, second, and so on. PERT is particularly useful when time deadlines are rigid, when time is limited, or when multiple tasks must be accomplished.

Monitoring all decision outcomes is the final step in decision making. Groups should ask three questions: Did the decision satisfy the criteria for acceptable solutions, as identified by group members? Did the decision produce high rewards and low costs? Was the decision acceptable to the group or others who implemented the decision? When the decision is implemented, three additional questions should be asked: Did the decision have the effect group members intended? Was the decision responsible for the observed effects? And did the decision have any unintended consequences?

Discussion Questions and Exercises

1. Obtain an audio- or videorecording of a decision-making group. Analyze the group's discussion for evidence of repetitive agreement about shared information. In what way did this type of repetition keep the group from exploring other alternatives? Was there any evidence that other group members had novel or unique information to share? In a second analysis of the same group meeting, what evidence can you point to that members of a majority subgroup were putting pressure on the minority subgroup? How did the minority subgroup react to this pressure?

2. Think about one of your classroom or work experiences in which groupthink occurred. How were conditions in this group similar to or different from the conditions of groupthink explained in this chapter? Give a full explanation of how groupthink developed and who or what in the group allowed it to continue. Looking back on that experience, what did you learn about the groupthink phenomenon? What will you do in future groups to prevent groupthink from occurring?

3. In one of your long-term groups (at work, in your family), identify the faulty decisions the group has made. Now review the eight factors that contribute to faulty group decision making presented in this chapter. Is a pattern evident? Is it possible that your group continues to make the same mistake? Or are different mistakes made in different decisions? Can you provide an explanation for your group's inability to make effective decisions?

4. Reflect on one of your decision-making groups. What challenges did the group experience? If those challenges occur in the future, which of the task, relational, and procedural decision-making skills would you use to counteract those challenges? How would you encourage others in the group to use those skills as well?

5. Reflect on a recent and important group decision in which you participated but were not responsible for implementing the decision. If you had been responsible for implementation, how would your implementation have differed? Would you rather have someone else or another group implement the decisions you help a group make? Or would you rather be responsible for both decision making and implementation? Articulate your reasons.

9 Managing Conflict in Groups

GROUP SKILLS PREVIEW

In this chapter, you will learn to do the following:

- Explain the advantages and disadvantages of group conflict
- Identify types and sources of conflict
- Explain how gender and cultural diversity influence conflict interactions
- Recognize the relationship between power and conflict
- Identify five conflict management strategies
- Help your group engage in an effective conflict management strategy
- Avoid or respond to nonproductive conflict management strategies

Seldom do individuals—each with unique experiences, perspectives, knowledge, skills, values, and expectations—develop into a group or team without experiencing conflict. In fact, the more complex the group task or activity, the more likely conflict is to occur. Although most people don't like conflict, nearly every group experiences it. Conflict is inherent in group situations because incompatibilities exist among group members. At its worst, conflict interferes with task coordination, creates opportunities for dysfunctional power struggles, and disrupts the social network and communication climate among group members. At its best, conflict can help groups find creative solutions to problems and increase rationality in decision making.

Defining Conflict

In this society, we use the word *conflict* regularly, often not thinking about what it really means. Conflict results from incompatible activities (Deutsch, 1969). To be in a **conflict** means that at least two interdependent parties (individuals or groups) capable of invoking sanctions oppose each other. In other words, one party believes that the other party has some real or perceived power over it or can threaten it in some way, or that the other party will use that power, real or perceived, to keep it from reaching its goal. Generally, conflicting parties have different value systems or perceive the same issue differently, thus creating incompatible activities.

Conflicts occur when each party desires some outcome that, if obtained, causes the other party to not obtain the outcome it seeks. A conflict exists because both parties cannot obtain both outcomes simultaneously. For example, your family may be experiencing a conflict over where to go on vacation. You and your mom want to go to the beach, to enjoy the sun and the ocean; your dad prefers a vacation filled with adventure—hiking, canoeing, and camping. But your family cannot take its only vacation simultaneously in Canada and Mexico.

Conflict is a process that occurs over time or in a sequence of events (Thomas, 1992). A conflict starts when one or all group members realize that an incompatibility exists. Next group members frame the conflict by identifying what the conflict is over, who the conflict is with, and what the odds are for obtaining their goal. The conflict continues with group members interacting, each trying to obtain their goal. Here is where a conflict can become really interesting, because no matter how well you think out a conflict strategy or how well you rehearse what you are going to say, you can never fully predict what the other person will say or do. Thus you have to adjust your intentions and behaviors during the conflict management interaction.

Fortunately, most conflicts have an end. This occurs when each party is satisfied with what it won or lost or when those involved believe that the costs of continuing the conflict outweigh the benefits of continuing the conflict, hoping to win (Watkins, 1974).

Regardless of the outcome, it's important to realize that one conflict episode is connected to the next one. How you evaluate the outcome of the first conflict episode will affect your awareness of the next (potential) conflict. Suppose you are in a conflict with another person and believe that the two of you have reached a mutually agreeable decision. The next time you engage in conflict with that person you will expect to again reach an agreeable outcome. Alternately, if you believe the decision to be totally unfair to you, the next time you become aware of a conflict you will bring these emotions into the interpretation that a conflict exists. In other words, your awareness of conflict in subsequent episodes is heightened by your sense of success or loss in the first one.

The feelings that result from conflict are the **conflict aftermath** (Pondy, 1967). In other words, each conflict leaves a legacy. If the conflict results in a positive outcome, members are likely to feel motivated and enthusiastic about the group as they recognize that conflict does not necessarily destroy group relationships. However, if the conflict is resolved with some group members feeling as if they have lost, they can have negative feelings for other group members and even become hostile toward the group.

How important is conflict aftermath? Conflict aftermath affects group members' perceptions of their ability to work together. When the aftermath is negative, members are less likely to embrace conflict in the future. After all, they believe that they lost this time and do not want to lose again. For instance, Theo is distraught over his group's recent conflict episode because he feels as if he really didn't get a chance to express his viewpoint while all of the arguing was going on. "Man, that wasn't a good situation," he concludes. "Now nobody in the group gets along, and we were just given another project to complete." Theo's feelings —his conflict aftermath—will affect his interaction in the group. His motivation to work with group members, his trust of other members, and his interpersonal relationships with other members are all negatively affected.

But conflict can also create positive outcomes (Wall, Galanes, & Love, 1987). A moderate amount of conflict can actually increase the quality of group outcomes. Conflict can motivate members to participate and pay attention and can strengthen a group's ability to solve problems. When group members manage the conflict by satisfying their own concerns, in addition to the concerns of others, group outcomes are of a higher quality (Wall & Galanes, 1986; Wall & Nolan, 1986). Furthermore, when conflict is managed effectively by the group, high levels of trust and respect are generated (Jehn & Mannix, 2001).

Thus, conflict is an emotionally driven process, and group members experience emotion in positive and negative ways, which results in an evaluation of the group as good or bad. When individuals are vested in the group or its activities, group members identify with the group. Emotions are more salient because group members' identities are affected when conflict occurs and threatens members' positions, ideas, or points of view. This of course can influence their relationships. Thus conflict is emotionally defined, valenced as positive or negative, identity-based, and relationally-oriented (Jones, 2000).

Ways of Thinking About Conflict

One way of thinking about conflict is to consider the past, the present, and the future (Hawes & Smith, 1973). Recall that conflict occurs when people have incompatible goals. The underlying assumption here is that goals direct people's behavior, which means that goals in the present motivate future behavior. If the goals of group members are in conflict (present), then so must be their subsequent behavior (future). For example, suppose your goal is to finish the group project before spring break, Michael wants to finish the project after spring break, and the other group members will be happy as long as the project gets done. As you, Michael, and the other group members interact, these goals will drive your communication. Before long, it will be apparent that there is conflict in the group about finishing the project.

Now let's turn that logic around and look at the past. It is possible to argue that goals only become meaningful after you behave. For example, if you make a jump shot, then your goal to do so is meaningful. If you do not make the jump shot, then you can claim that it is "no big deal." In this sense, you realize that you are in a conflict after the communication episode takes place and someone brings it to your attention. This is not as far-fetched as you might think. During group discussions, there is a great deal going on to which you must pay attention. Suppose that, in a group discussion, you mention that Starr is not your first choice for leader; you prefer Peter and give your reasons. As the discussion continues, you come to realize that everyone else is supporting Starr, and after a vote, she is elected. Following the meeting, Tony says, "Way to go . . . you sure made a big impression. Now the group thinks you're not going to work well with Starr." You realize that a conflict is perceived to exist between you and the other group members. Your goal of supporting Peter has created a conflict because everyone else supported Starr. You were not trying to start a conflict, but the others think you were.

Conflict can escalate quickly when each group member views the conflict in his or her own way. To avoid escalation and the emotional responses it invokes, group members should recognize that they are all in the conflict together. Achieving this recognition will help group members manage their conflicts productively.

Is Conflict Always Disruptive?

Although we often think of conflict as being disruptive, conflict can be productive for groups (Deutsch, 1969). When conflict exists, people are engaged and talking with one another. This means that stagnation is prevented and that interest in and curiosity about the group and its activities are stimulated. Conflict provides an opportunity for members to test and improve their abilities and to create solutions. This is not to say that groups seek conflict. Rather, conflict naturally occurs; it is not something that should be avoided. Conflict about the group's task can keep members from prematurely accepting or agreeing on solutions. In fact, conflict increases the likelihood that the group will engage in effective problem solving (Baxter, 1982).

Although conflict can help groups generate creative and innovative solutions, many groups try to avoid conflict at all costs. Other groups deny that conflict exists and continue with their interactions as if nothing is wrong. Still other groups believe that conflict is disruptive and detrimental. Why do groups hesitate to engage in conflict, given that positive outcomes can be achieved? One reason has to do with the anxiety associated with conflict. When you compare the language and interaction of groups in conflict with that of groups not in conflict, distinct differences emerge. Group members in conflict actually change their verbal patterns. For instance, they become more repetitive and use simpler forms of language, speaking in habitual ways and repeating phrases without adding anything new to the conversation. In addition, their anxiety rises, which affects their ability to take the perspectives of others in the group. Look at the following example:

LUCY: Can we just get on with it?

JIM: Sure, I want us to vote for the incorporation.

ELLA: Right, as if the incorporation will do us any good.

JIM: Well, it will . . . the incorporation, I mean.

LUCY: Can you explain more about the incorporation plan, Jim?

JIM: Well, as you know, the incorporation plan will incorporate all of the surrounding towns into Plainview.

ELLA: If we incorporate, we'll be just like Plainview. No different, but just like Plainview.

LUCY: I've figured out you're against incorporation, Ella. But could someone please tell me what incorporation means?

In this case, the low levels of language diversity or redundancy—such as the repeated use of the word *incorporation* with no explanation of what it means—reinforce the disruptive nature of conflict (Bell, 1983). Anxiety is increased in conflict situations like this, affecting group members' abilities to take the perspective of others in the group. Although group members are using the same word—*incorporation*—there is no evidence that they have similar meanings for it. Because members take positions, they are not likely to have common ground, and, thus, misperceive what others in the group are saying (Krauss & Morsella, 2000).

Is Conflict Inherent?

Conflict occurs because one of three things happens (Smith & Berg, 1987). First, groups often need people with different skills, interests, and values to accomplish their goals. These differences alone can create conflict. How those differences are integrated into group interactions can create or enhance conflict as well. Although group member differences may be necessary, they can also threaten a group's capacity to function effectively. To benefit from diversity, group members must become interdependent in a way that provides unity while preserving differences.

Second, groups have a natural tendency to polarize members as a way of ordering and defining reality. For instance, if one person suggests that a group of friends consider going to dinner and a movie, another person is likely to suggest going to the theatre as an alternative. Although the suggestions may seem similar, they really are polar opposites—the movie option is informal and spontaneous whereas the theatre option means getting dressed up and planning ahead. Although the friends may, in fact, enjoy either option, the polarization or difference between the two options can cause a conflict.

Groups can also polarize members in terms of how they communicate (Bales & Cohen, 1979). Friendly group members will feel that they are in conflict with members who are negative and unfriendly, and submissive group members will feel opposed to members who are dominant, outgoing, and assertive. When differences in levels of group member dominance are great, conflict is likely to occur (Wall & Galanes, 1986). For example, both Shareece and Joe are talkative, bold, and expressive. They usually initiate group conversations and occupy most of the

SKILL BUILDER

Did I Do That?

Think about the last group conflict in which you were involved. At what point did you know that a conflict had developed? What cues led you to this conclusion? What was your role in helping to develop or establish the conflict? Did you say something that someone found offensive, inaccurate, or personal? Or did you neglect to say something when you should have spoken up? Did you behave in a way that demonstrated lack of interest in the group or in what the group was doing? Could you have changed your communication or behavior in any way to help the group avoid or minimize the conflict?

group's talking time. In comparison, Marc and Wendy are more submissive. They really do not like to talk much, preferring to follow Shareece and Joe's lead. But this does not necessarily mean that Marc and Wendy will go along with anything and everything the other two suggest. Wendy, in particular, becomes angry—but does not show it—when Shareece and Joe decide what the group will do. As this example suggests, differences in ideas are often exacerbated when there are differences in levels of group member dominance. More dominant members take responsibility for the group, often without asking other members for their input or for agreement. More submissive members are less likely to take a vocal or overt stand against ideas, making it appear that they agree with more dominant members.

Conflict is also likely to occur when there are differences in group members' orientation (Wall & Galanes, 1986). Some members may have a higher task orientation, whereas other group members have a higher relationship orientation. This difference in orientation affects how individuals perceive their group membership and the primary function and goal of the group. The task-oriented members think the other members are slowing them down, and the relationship-oriented members think the task-oriented members need to relax to allow group members to develop stronger relationships. Frequently, these group members will find themselves locked in a distributive conflict in which one side will win and the other will lose. Try "Did I Do That?" to reveal your role in a group conflict.

Thus group life is filled with many opportunities for oppositional forces to exist and many instances in which members perceive that opposition exists. This means that individuals in groups and groups as a whole will always be managing differences even as they are seeking a certain level of homogeneity (Smith & Berg, 1987).

Third, group members can experience feelings of ambivalence about their group membership, which can cause conflict. You may want to identify with others and be part of a group, but you also want to retain your individuality and be different. Thus you feel both drawn toward the group and pushed away from it: "I'm like them; I'm not like them." The desire to be both separate from and connected to the group can result in individual-to-group conflict. For example, Jones is a member of a fraternity, and he values his affiliation with his fraternity brothers. He wears their logo proudly on a cap and a sweatshirt, and plays on their soccer team and captains their softball team. He even moved from his apartment into the frat house. But Jones's fraternity brothers are notorious for waiting until the last minute to fulfill their service work as campus safety escorts. Because Jones lives in the frat house, he is called on frequently to take shifts when others do not show up. Lately, he has become resentful of others relying on him to take their shifts. "After all," Jones complains, "don't they realize I have a life of my own?"

Conflict can even be inherent in the most common of group tasks. For example, in a brainstorming session to generate ideas to be considered by the group, members produced 64 unique ideas for the group's consideration. When group members voted on their top 5 ideas, 33 different ones received at least one top 5 vote (Warfield, 1993). As you can see from this example, group members' different skills, interests, and values generated a substantial number of solutions for consideration. This is certainly one advantage of working in groups. However, with so many ideas capturing the interests of group members, conflict will surely arise as the different ideas are debated and discussed. According to the **law of inherent conflict**, no matter the issue or group, there will be significant conflict stemming from different perceptions of relevant factors (Warfield, 1993).

Types and Sources of Conflict

As mentioned previously, conflict is not necessarily destructive. It may seem that way when you are involved in a conflict situation, but conflict actually can be productive for the group. Conflict is destructive if it completely consumes the group's energy and time, prevents members from working together, or escalates into violence. Alternately, conflict can be productive if it exposes new ideas, helps clarify an issue, or alerts the group to a concern that needs to be addressed.

When conflict erupts in a group, all group members may view the conflict similarly. But that seldom is the case. Frequently, group members disagree about what the disagreement is. To be effective, groups must express some agreement about the type of conflict or disagreement that is occurring (Pace, 1990). Because conflict can occur over many things and group members can perceive conflicts differently, group members need to agree on the nature of the conflict before they can move toward managing it.

Is the conflict personal? Personalized or **affective conflict** is rooted in interpersonal relationships, emotions, or personalities. Even when group members agree about the group's goals and procedures, this type of relational conflict can keep a group from accomplishing its task. For instance, when Angie refuses to listen to what Scott has to say because Scott makes it clear that she could not possibly understand the importance of his position in the group, the conflict is affective. Scott communicates in such a way that Angie and other members are painfully aware that he is the president of the ski club and that they are *just* members. Affective conflict is based on social or relational issues like status, power, perceived competence, cooperation, and friendliness, and it generally increases emotional responses. Effective groups are those that can experience conflict over ideas without tying the conflict to particular group members. When conflict is linked to a particular group member, it is personalized. This type of conflict is likely to be more dysfunctional because it is like a deep current running through the group, and it is often subtle. Most groups can manage their way through task, or substantive, conflict. But, affective, or relational, conflict may encourage members to leave the group (Bayazit & Mannix, 2003).

Alternately, **substantive conflict** is rooted in issues or ideas, or disagreement about some aspect of the group's task (Guetzkow & Gyr, 1954). For example, members disagreeing about the appropriateness of two alternatives or about the scope of their responsibilities are having substantive conflicts. Managed effectively, substantive conflicts help groups improve their problem-solving abilities and generate member satisfaction with decision making (Witteman, 1991).

Is this a win-lose conflict? Another distinction concerning conflict is whether the conflict exists in a competitive or cooperative environment (Guetzkow & Gyr, 1954). **Competitive conflict** polarizes groups, with one side winning and the other side losing. When this happens, group members are likely to escalate the conflict and become defensive or even hostile toward one another. Alternately, **cooperative conflict** occurs when the disagreement actually helps move the group along with its task or activities. In this case, the climate surrounding the conflict is supportive or positive. As a result, the group is more likely to find a mutually beneficial resolution to the conflict.

How important is the conflict? A third distinction is the centrality of the conflict to the group (Guetzkow & Gyr, 1954). How important is the issue to the members who are in disagreement or to the group as a whole? If the conflict is about a trivial matter (for example, what type of paper to copy the agenda on), then the conflict is not as salient, or important, to the group's objective. If group members are arguing about a critical feature of the group's project, then the conflict is salient, or more important, and has the capacity to create more dysfunction in the group.

Is the conflict over information? A **cognitive conflict** exists when group members disagree about information or data or the analysis of that information (Knutson & Kowitz, 1977). For example, suppose you assert that the university could return professor evaluations to students earlier. Another student government senator says, "No, they've got to go to the professors first, and they don't get them until the middle of the following semester." "But," you argue, "that's not what the dean of students told me." You are having a conflict about how professor evaluations are distributed. One of you has viewed the information incorrectly or made an incorrect assumption about the data collected. In most cases like this, the conflict can be resolved when group members get more or better information. But it must be evidence or data from a credible and valid source. It does not work to say "because I say so." To resolve a conflict over information, data must be available to all group members.

Is the conflict about a procedure or group process? Your group may find itself in disagreement about the type of leadership it needs or find members deliberating about the size of the majority it needs to finalize your group's plans. **Procedural conflicts**, or conflicts about how the work gets done, occur when procedures or processes are not discussed beforehand or when the group encounters a situation for which there is no precedent (Knutson & Kowitz, 1977). Procedural conflict impedes a group's work because the group doesn't have the necessary framework for moving ahead. Suppose a group is having difficulty picking a leader. At least three members are qualified to be the group's leader; two have even said they would like the opportunity to lead the group. But now the group's membership is evenly divided in support of the three members. This conflict could have been avoided if the group had discussed a procedure for selecting a leader.

Is the conflict about expectations? **Normative conflict** occurs when one party has expectations about another party's behavior (Thomas, 1992). In other words, conflict occurs when someone evaluates your behavior against what that person thought you should have done. Sororities and fraternities are notorious for dealing with normative conflict. For instance, Heidi turns in her sorority sister because she violated sorority house rules. Heidi expected her sorority sister to know the rules and abide by them. Normative conflict can evoke an emotional response like blame, anger, or disapproval, and it is usually followed by sanctions intended to produce conformity to the formal rules or implied standards.

When group members disagree about the nature of the conflict (for example, is the conflict affective or substantive, competitive or cooperative, central or trivial, based on valid data, procedural, or based on expectations) these issues need to be addressed before the group can resolve the primary conflict. Disagreements over these issues allow group members to perceive that incompatible goals exist. The more disagreement there is about the nature of the conflict, the more strain there will be on the group's interpersonal relationships. Group members who can come to agreement through interaction on the nature of conflict are more likely to build consensus and cohesiveness (Pace, 1990).

Gender Diversity and Conflict

Gender stereotypes are thought to be prominent in task and organizational group situations, especially when either males or females are numerically distinct. For example, when the CEO is the only female in the executive team or when the only two men on the basketball team are the coach and trainer, the number of women and men are obviously disproportional. Importantly, the group's context may make the numerical distinction more salient or noticeable, and increase the prevalence of gender stereotypes in the group. A recent study suggests that the salience of gender distinctiveness, not the mere presence of gender diversity, in a group explains the occurrence of conflict. That is, majority members of a group are more influenced by a group's gender diversity than are its minority members when the context emphasizes the number of men and women in the group. In these cases, the use of gender stereotypes and affective conflict increase (Randel, 2002).

Cultural Diversity and Conflict

As a member of a culturally diverse group, one of your biggest challenges is recognizing and admitting your cultural biases and coming to terms with them. Generally, people are **ethnocentric**. This means that individuals judge events and people as good or correct when they are similar to events and people in their own culture. This type of perceptual bias is natural as we grow up in cultures that teach us what is appropriate and inappropriate. Yet cultural differences are not necessarily harmful to the group. In fact, these differences may provide the group with additional variety and stimulation.

Sometimes cultural differences are obvious. But remember that cultural differences permeate every conflict (Avruch & Black, 1993). Even a group of culturally homogeneous members represents a wide variety of cultural beliefs. Cultural values, beliefs, and attitudes are not evenly distributed across members of a cultural group. That is, not every female, Republican, Baptist, teenager, or African American has the same values, beliefs, and attitudes; not everyone who shares a common language shares common values, beliefs, and attitudes. Thus, in one way, cultural differences are present in every conflict, not merely in those in which cultural differences are heightened, such as a conflict between Arab and Israeli students.

Having said that, we still need to realize that members of cultures—and even subcultures—vary in how they perceive conflict. In U.S. society, competition and conflict are expected. We assume we will have conflicts with one another because the First Amendment guarantees our freedom of speech, which in reality means that we believe others have the *right* to hear our opinion! Still, Blacks and Whites approach conflict differently (Kochman, 1981). These differences are apparent in how the two groups view confrontation and argument and the appropriateness of emotionality in discussions and negotiations, as well as what constitutes valid arguments, truths, or evidence. Cultural differences are even more pronounced between Americans and Japanese (Oetzel, 1998b). The American view of "what is in it for me?" is quite different from the Japanese perspective of "what is good for the group, is good for me." As a result, those two cultural groups approach conflict differently.

Because of this, it can be helpful to do a cultural analysis in addition to analyzing the conflict. Supplementing conflict analysis with a cultural analysis can help you see how those group members who are culturally different perceive the conflict. What might seem bizarre to you may be normal from another culture's point of view. Be wary of relying on cultural stereotypes (for example, the English are cold). This doesn't mean that you should pay no attention to differences in beliefs and customs. It merely means that you don't perceive all members of one group as being similar. Above all, do not insert cultural differences into any conflict that already exists. It is easy to think that intercultural conflicts are simply that—cultural differences. But rarely do intercultural differences account for all of the conflict among people who are culturally diverse (Avruch & Black, 1993).

Because much communication is habitual, you need to be especially mindful of your communication in intercultural settings (Gudykunst & Hall, 1994). This means that you need to acknowledge the patterns in your communication and analyze them for their usefulness in a given situation. In intercultural conflicts, groups need to use procedures and processes that allow different or alternative ideas to be presented. It also helps to be aware that others bring different perspectives to the conflict.

Power

Anytime you bring people together in groups, power will be an issue and can contribute to conflict. Why? It is unlikely that all group members are equally skilled or knowledgeable, and even more unlikely that all group members perceive that they have equal status. **Power**—the influence resulting from social interactions or created by the possession of or access to resources (Lovaglia, Mannix, Samuelson, Sell, & Wilson, 2005)—is an issue in all types of groups. Think for a moment of your family group. Who has the most power? your mom? your dad? your little brother? Now think of your work group. Who has the most power? the leader?

Power is not inherently good or bad. Having access to power or knowing that others see you as powerful helps you feel confident in group settings. At the same time, we are all familiar with the misuse of power in group settings and the relational damage it can cause. Positive or negative, power resides in the relationships among group members. Some types of power facilitate conflict among group members, and other types prevent conflict from developing. It's how power is communicated and used that determines its influence on and for group members.

Bases of Power

Power exists in relationships among group members. When a group member has power, he or she has interpersonal influence over other group members because they have accepted or allowed the attempt at power to be successful. If you perceive the influence of another group member and alter your behavior because of that influence, power exists. Although power traditionally has been seen as residing primarily in group leaders, any member of the group can develop power and use it in relationships with other group members. Six power bases have been identified: reward, coercive, legitimate, referent, expert, and informational (French & Raven, 1968; Raver, 1993).

You are probably most familiar with **reward power**. Rewards can be relationally oriented, such as attention, friendship, or favors. They can also take on tangible forms such as gifts or money. Group members behave and communicate in a certain way because they are rewarded when they do so. In contrast to the positive influence of rewards, threats represent negative or **coercive power**. In group settings, coercive power results from the expectation that you can or will be punished by another group member. Coercion can take the form of denying a group member the opportunity to participate or threatening to take something of importance away from a group member.

Legitimate power is the inherent influence associated with a position or role in the group. Leaders or facilitators often have legitimate power—they can call meetings and make assignments. Group members allow the member with legitimate power to do these things because the power is formal, or inherent in the role the person has within the group. This type of power exists within the role, not within the person. Without another power base, a leader relying solely on legitimate power will have little real influence in a group.

Referent power is influence given by you to another group member based on your desire to build a relationship with him or her. In other words, you admire or want to be like another group member. Thus you allow yourself to be influenced by this person. For instance, if Wes admires Harvey and wants to be like him, Wes will allow himself to be influenced by Harvey and will follow his suggestions and recommendations. Anyone in the group can possess referent power, which is often based on charisma. And members can have referent power over others without intending to do so. A group member with a pleasant or stimulating communicator style often develops referent power with others, which gives this person additional opportunities to develop power bases with these same group members.

Expert power is influence based on what a group member knows or can do. Group members develop expert power when they offer their unique skills to help the group, and their behavior matches the expectations they have created. Suppose Amber says she can use computer-aided design software to design the team's new office space. Her team members will reward her with this expert power only when she demonstrates this skill and the office layout is approved by the group. Saying you can do something is not enough; your performance must match the expectations you create.

Finally, **informational power** is persuasion or influence based on what information a group member possesses or the logical arguments he or she presents to the group. In a medical team, the medical student, physical therapist, and nurse each can exert informational power on a patient's treatment. For example, the student interprets and reports the findings of the diagnostic tests, the therapist reports on how well the patient is responding to increased activity, and the nurse reports on the patient's general mood and well-being. While these members of the team have less legitimate power than the physician, their informational reports will influence the physician's subsequent treatment of the patient.

Of these types of power, all except coercive power are essential for effective group process. Group members want someone to be in control (legitimate power); like it when others compliment them on their contributions (reward power); find it beneficial when someone is the group's motivator, cheerleader, or contact person (referent power); and expect others to contribute their skills and knowledge (expert, informational, and legitimate power).

A group member can hold little power or can develop power in many areas. But to be influential, the base of power must be essential to the functioning of the group. Position power is not powerful if the position is with another group. For example, the leader of your work team will not necessarily have position power on the company basketball team.

Although we often think that others give us power, that does not happen unless we act powerful. For example, if Andy does not profess his expertise in creating computer graphics for the group's final report, other group members cannot create this power relationship with him. Andy's power arises only if the others are aware of his knowledge and skill. Thus power emerges through interaction. Although the group leader or facilitator typically holds more power than other group members, each member should develop and demonstrate some base of power to augment his or her credibility in and worth to the group. When power is distributed among group members, participation is more balanced, and cohesiveness and satisfaction are enhanced.

How important is it that you develop a power base as a group member? Very. Power used positively creates attraction from other group members. We all like to be associated with powerful people. In fact, power has a greater effect on other group members than status (Bradley, 1978). This is because power is developed within the group's relationships whereas status is generally brought into the group. You may have status or prestige because of where you live, what your parents do for a living, what car you drive, and so on. But these status issues may not be salient or relevant to the group and its activity. Would it really matter to another group member that you drove an expensive car if you did not follow through with your group assignments? Would it matter that last semester you worked for a prestigious law firm if you did not share your knowledge with the group? Try "Group Structure and Group Size" to better understand the power bases of a group experience.

A power source that is often overlooked is control of resources—real or imagined. As groups work on their tasks, information and materials from outside the group frequently are needed. For example, when a group member volunteers

---

PUTTING THE PIECES TOGETHER

Group Structure and Group Size

Think of a recent group experience in which you were not the person in charge, you were not the group's leader, or you took on a relatively minor role in the group. How did the member in charge or the leader use his or her legitimate power? To what extent did the leader use other bases of power to influence group members? How did this use of power affect the structure of the group? What bases of power did other members have or develop? Were there so many group members that it was easier to give most of the power to the leader to coordinate the group's activities? Or was membership small enough that each member could develop some bases of power?

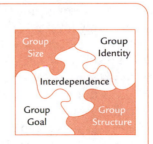

to use her connections to obtain permission to use the dean's conference room for the group's meetings or to have the group's presentation professionally created at her father's graphics shop, she is exerting power over needed resources. Group members are often thankful that someone in the group has access to these resources and impressed that the individual can obtain what they cannot.

However, overusing these connections can create a defensive climate in the group. Here power can be perceived as strategic manipulation. For instance, if Leam volunteers to get the dean's conference room, then it is likely that she will see when its availability fits her schedule. If she volunteers to have the presentation graphics created, and other group members are not there when she proofs them, she can exert editorial control over the copy the group gave her.

Power and Conflict

If power is neither inherently good nor bad, how does power relate to conflict? In two ways (Sillince, 2000). First, those with power use the communication resources of a group differently than those with less power. Powerful members of a group talk more, respond to questions more, issue more challenges, and introduce more new topics into the group than do less powerful members. Using these communication strategies, a powerful member is more likely to set the agenda for the group, and that can cause conflict. Second, less powerful group members often want more power and try to find ways to increase their power base. This can cause conflict because the more powerful members may feel threatened or unappreciated.

Conflict Between Groups

Conflicts can also occur between groups. For example, if you are married, the two sides of your family may be in conflict over which side will host the Thanksgiving celebration you and your spouse attend. Each family is a complete group by itself, but when you go home for Thanksgiving, the two families are brought together by your presence. Forcing this type of interdependence can create competition over family loyalties. Similarly, your basketball team competes with other teams, and your project team at work competes against teams from other organizations for a prospective client's business. How well your groups deal with conflict from external sources can affect their internal interactions.

Within groups, members communicate with one another to develop the image of some other group as the enemy or the competitor and to discuss how the two groups are in conflict with each other and what actions to take to resolve the conflict (Johnson, 1975). In other words, your group frames other groups as the enemy through communication. Until someone in your group identifies a conflict with another group and other members agree with that vision, conflict with the other group does not exist. Think back to high school. How did your football team become archrivals with one of the many high schools in your city or region? The conflict or competition between the teams was generated through

Conflict between groups often results from communication practices within groups. Group members can create competition with another group by labeling that group as the enemy. This type of rhetorical force is responsible for creating intergroup competition.

communication. Even before you entered high school, you probably knew who your archrival was. In high school, there were pep rallies, announcements over the loudspeakers, and banners in the hallways encouraging your team to "Tromp the Wildcats!" or "Make the Cats Meow!" You developed a vision that an enemy or competitor group existed because people communicated that message to you. This rhetorical force is very strong in groups. It takes only a thread of a conversation to construct the reality among group members that another group is competing with them. Generally, as the sense of competition with another group builds, the level of cohesiveness within your group also builds. Because your group has identified an **out-group**—a group different from yours in some way —your **in-group** becomes closer and more meaningful to you. Often, a group can propel itself into conflict with another group through verbal statements. Later this conflict is overtly expressed to others outside of the group, and before you know it, the other group has accepted the fact that it is in conflict with your group.

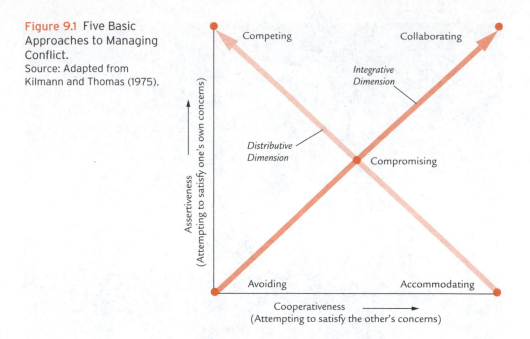

Figure 9.1 Five Basic Approaches to Managing Conflict.
Source: Adapted from Kilmann and Thomas (1975).

Conflict Management Strategies

Conflict resolution or conflict management—which is more appealing to you? You may think that there is little difference between conflict resolution and conflict management, but the two terms represent widely divergent views of conflict. Resolving conflict requires that you view conflict as a destructive phenomenon or as a disruption that you need to eliminate. Thus the only kind of *good* conflict is the absence of conflict. Managing conflict, in contrast, implies that conflict is a normal and inevitable situation that groups must handle. Groups that manage their conflicts take advantage of conflict situations to solicit alternative views not previously addressed. Managing conflict results in creative and innovative solutions.

There are five general conflict management strategies: collaborating, competing, accommodating, avoiding, and compromising (see Figure 9.1). Although you probably prefer one strategy or have a primary orientation for managing conflict, you should know that you can develop new skills for managing conflict. Not all conflict situations are alike and the conflict management strategy you're most comfortable with may not be the best strategy for all conflicts.

Collaborating

Which is the most effective conflict management strategy? Many people would argue that using **collaboration** helps a group achieve a win-win outcome—an outcome with which everyone can agree—because information sharing and collaboration are promoted. Collaboration is an **integrative conflict management strategy** because you attempt to maximize the gains of all conflicting parties.

This promotes rather than inhibits relationships among group members (Canary & Spitzberg, 1989).

In collaborating, the parties replace their incompatible goals with the super-ordinate goal of solving the problem even though their initial ideas for how to solve the problem differ. For example, even though conflict partners might have different ideas for resolving the problem, their common interest is in finding a solution. Thus parties must communicate with one another to redefine the situation so that they can identify a shared or mutually acceptable interest or goal. Besides sharing the goal, the opposing parties must develop or build a common language in order to create a shared frame from which to view the problem.

Ultimately, this means that opposing parties who see each other as enemies must be able to move from that framing device to one in which the other parties are viewed as partners. To effectively work in the problem-solving mode, a new *we* must be created to include all parties involved. This process of reframing adversaries as partners may be easier to accomplish if you think of it this way: You see the other parties as holding positions different from yours; they are your adversaries. But let's turn the tables: They see you as holding a position different from theirs; you are the adversary from their point of view. "But I'm not an adversary," you say. That is what the other parties are saying as well. Acknowledging this type of mirror logic can help you move from self-perception to *we* perception.

Collaboration is an integrative strategy because it relies on parties communicating with one another. How can you initiate this strategy? You can ask other group members how they feel about the problem or let others know that something about the group or its task is bothering you (Jarboe & Witteman, 1996). Or you can self-disclose—a good way to get others to self-disclose and open channels of communication (Sillars & Wilmot, 1994).

As communication between parties begins, look for objective criteria by which to evaluate potential solutions. This cooperative strategy allows both parties to find and develop common ground, and diminishes the emotional and subjective aspects of the conflict. Groups that can achieve integrative conflict management produce higher-quality outcomes and generate higher group member satisfaction (Wall & Galanes, 1986; Wall et al., 1987). Because collaboration requires a good-faith effort from everyone and open communication among everyone, it is easier to initiate and sustain in groups of five or fewer (Farmer & Roth, 1998).

Although collaboration can take time and energy, it is a constructive way of managing differences, and it is the conflict management style people report using most often (Farmer & Roth, 1998). Openly discussing differences, having access to a variety of opinions, and carefully critiquing assumptions help create commitment to the group, as well as trust among and respect for group members (Thomas, 1992). Collaboration also can offset problems caused by initial differences among members or unequal participation caused by diversity within the group (Kirchmeyer & Cohen, 1992). More importantly, collaboration can produce higher-quality decisions and solutions.

What are the alternatives to the integrative strategy of collaboration? There are several, but none can create the same win-win outcome as collaboration. Two strategies—competing and accommodating—are **distributive conflict management strategies,** meaning that they are characterized by a win-lose orientation, or an outcome that satisfies one party at the expense of the other. Group members who use one of the distributive strategies often show anger and use sarcasm. One of these strategies may settle the conflict, but the relational aspects of the group will be damaged because of the strategy's win-lose orientation. When win-lose strategies are used, the quality of the outcome is also lower (Wall et al., 1987).

Competing

Forcing, or **competing**, as a conflict management strategy emphasizes your own triumph at the other person's expense. In a sense, you take from the conflict but give very little. In using a competing strategy and wielding power over others, you are being assertive and uncooperative. So, you are likely to force the issue and dominate the interaction. You believe that you are right and the other person is wrong.

When group members compete, communication channels close down (Deutsch, 1969). In fact, you might go out of your way not to talk to other group members as part of the competition. And even when communication is taking place, you may be suspicious of the information you receive from other parties. Thus error and misinformation abound. Competing also contributes to the view that the solution to the conflict can be of only one type—the type that is imposed by one side on the other.

Accommodating

The other distributive conflict management strategy is **accommodating**, in which you give everything and take very little from the conflict. Here you are cooperative, yet unassertive. You focus on trying to satisfy the other's concerns rather than your own. You try to smooth over issues and relationships by being obliging and yielding. For example, each time Henry brings up a sensitive issue, Nell becomes submissive and quiet. Even when Henry tries to force Nell to talk about the problem, she lowers her head and says something like "Whatever you say, Henry. I'm sure you must be right. You've never led us down the wrong path before." In essence, Nell accommodates Henry and his viewpoint to end the conflict.

Avoiding

Neither integrative nor distributive, the **avoiding conflict management strategy** is nonconfrontive. Group members choosing this strategy try to sidestep the conflict by changing the topic or shifting the focus to other issues. They hope that if they ignore it or do not draw attention to it, the conflict will disappear. How is this strategy used to end a conflict? Generally, people who use the avoiding conflict management strategy verbally withdraw from the conversation. They can also physically withdraw by not showing up. Members of work groups often use the avoiding strategy. One member will acknowledge a problem he has with another group member and then back off (for example, "I get pretty ticked off sometimes, but it's not really a problem"). This type of denial is to be expected, given that members are assigned to these types of task groups, and often do not have a choice in group member selection. This type of forced intimacy can be characterized by nervous tension and denial; thus one party to the conflict withdraws and the conflict ceases to exist. Although not recommended as a strategy for managing most conflicts, avoidance can be the most effective strategy when it allows group members who must work together to focus on their task (De Dreu & Van Vianen, 2001).

Compromising

A fifth strategy, compromising, also deserves attention. **Compromising** is an intermediate strategy between cooperativeness and assertiveness. Although compromising may settle the problem, it also will offer incomplete satisfaction for both parties. You have given up something, but you are still holding out for something better. Although a compromise may be easier to obtain than collaboration, it is at best a temporary fix (Putnam & Wilson, 1983; Thomas, 1977). Groups tend to manage conflict with compromise when they feel time pressures to reach an agreement. Unfortunately, giving in to a compromise may mean that not all ideas or concerns have been heard.

You have probably compromised with a roommate over who will perform household tasks such as taking out the trash. These compromises are okay at first because they solve the immediate problem by ending the fight about who will take the trash out right now. But over the long term, compromises tend not to hold. Eventually, your roommate will forget to take out the trash when it is his or her turn, and you will blow up and start looking for a new living arrangement.

Which Strategy Should You Pick?

In conflict situations, you are managing three views of the situation: (a) your view of the conflict, (b) your belief of what the other person's view is, and (c) your evaluation of the relationship between you and the other person. When conflicts occur, it is typical to start with a strategy that emphasizes your view of the problem. Even if you enter the conflict with little concern about your view, that quickly changes. You would not be in the conflict if your own view of the problem were not important to you. And, as you might expect, your attention to the other person's view often diminishes throughout the interaction. Thus a pattern dominates most conflict situations: People enhance their own view of the situation while minimizing the view of the other person (Nicotera, 1994).

Initially, it seems reasonable to put your view of the conflict first. Attempts to minimize the view of the other person also seem reasonable given that you don't want to lose in conflict situations. And you probably have some interest in continuing a relationship with the other person, as people generally have conflicts with others who matter to them or with members of groups that matter to them. But remember that your conflict partner has the same orientation to the conflict. He or she views the issue as important, is attempting to minimize your view, doesn't want to lose in the conflict, and sees you or the group as mattering to him or her. Essentially, both parties have the same, but incompatible, goals.

How you manage conflicts provides others with a means for evaluating your communication competence. Your conflict messages are assessed according to their appropriateness and effectiveness. In turn, these assessments act as a filter through which evaluations of your competence are made. One conflict episode can influence how your relationship with someone develops. And, certainly, a pattern of conflict over time will influence your ability to maintain relationships with others. Generally, you will be perceived more negatively and as having lower competence if you manage conflicts with competing, accommodating, or avoiding strategies. In contrast, group members who use collaboration to focus on the issue or content of the conflict are perceived more positively (McKinney, Kelly, & Duran, 1997).

Some conflict situations, however, are complex enough to require a mixture of different conflict management styles (Munduate, Ganaza, Peiro, & Euwema, 1999). What combinations of styles are effective? Generally, group members who use some combination of collaborating, competing, and compromising are judged to be effective at conflict management because they are best at creating mutually acceptable outcomes and maintaining relationships. Once a group develops a pattern for managing its conflicts, it tends to use the same strategies in subsequent conflicts. Such a pattern can have far-reaching effects. For example, groups that manage conflict collaboratively increase group efficacy, which in turn encourages members to believe that they can also handle subsequent conflicts (Alper, Tjosvold, & Law, 2000). Moreover, groups that master collaboration as a conflict management strategy incorporate it into their decision making more than groups that rely on confrontation or avoidance (Kuhn & Poole, 2000).

How you manage conflict depends both on what you say and on how you say it. Because conflict creates emotional reactions, the nonverbal messages you

MASTERING GROUP SKILLS

Strategy Effectiveness

Think of a recent conflict in one of your groups. Which strategies did group members use to manage the conflict? How successful were those strategies? Would other strategies have been more appropriate and effective? What was your role in the implementation of the strategies? In the future when a similar conflict situation occurs in this group, specifically what will you say or do to help the group successfully navigate its way through the conflict?

communicate (consciously and unconsciously) and the words you choose influence other group members' responses in conflict interactions. For example, suppose you say, "That's a good point, but I disagree." Said in a polite and respectful tone, other group members might interpret this as indicating a willingness on your part to develop a collaborative solution. But if you say, "That's the dumbest idea I ever heard" as you roll your eyes, you are likely to get a very different response from other group members. Even though the content of the two messages is very similar —that you disagree—the interpretative frames through which the messages are sent and received are quite different.

Which conflict management strategy is best? It depends upon you and your involvement in the conflict situation (Thomas, 1977). Usually, the integrative strategy of collaborating or problem solving will return the best long-term gains, but it takes time and commitment from all conflicting parties. Collaborating should be used when you view the issue as too important to compromise, when you have a long-term relationship with the other party and other conflicts are inevitable, when you could learn from merging your insights with the insights of others, and when you need to build a sense of community and commitment. Although the other strategies may seem effective in certain situations, they also have costs or risks associated with them.

The distributive strategy of competing can be used when decisive action is vital, as in an emergency, or when you need to implement an unpopular action. Competing can be effective when the conflict is with others who would take advantage of you if you used a noncompetitive strategy or when you know you are right (just be sure you are!). Accommodating, the other distributive conflict management strategy, is especially effective if you discover that you are wrong. By accommodating, you demonstrate that you are willing to learn from others. Accommodating can also be effective when you need to satisfy others to retain their cooperation; in other words, the issue is more important to them than it is to you. And, because you value the long-term nature of the relationship, it is important to be reasonable and to demonstrate harmony in and loyalty to the relationship. Thus accommodation can be an effective strategy for managing minor internal group disagreements while the group is resolving more significant problems.

Avoiding is effective when the issue is trivial and you can let go of it or when other matters are more pressing. Sometimes it makes sense simply to walk away from a conflict. Avoiding can be an effective strategy when you perceive no chance of satisfying your concerns. Why fight over something you cannot have? As a teenager, you probably used avoiding with your parents to let everyone cool down and gain perspective before dealing with an important but sensitive issue again.

Compromising may be effective in some conflict situations, especially if you and the other party are willing to accept a temporary settlement. Also, a compromise may be the best you can achieve when both sides are adamantly fixed on opposing or mutually exclusive goals. For example, suppose members of management and union representatives are meeting as a group to discuss a potential strike. What management offers to forestall a strike is likely to be different from what the union representatives want. The only type of settlement likely to be achieved is a compromise. Generally, these two groups are fundamentally opposed to each other's view, so anything more than a compromise is unlikely. Recognize, however, that the resolution achieved through compromise is only temporary. Parties with fundamentally conflicting views are likely to reinitiate the conflict or start another one.

To select the strategy that you believe will be most effective, it can be helpful to analyze the conflict you're experiencing according to four dimensions: (a) the level of emotionality in the conflict, (b) the importance of the conflict, (c) the degree to which there are group norms for handling conflict, and (d) the conflict's resolution potential (Jehn, 1997).

First, identify how many negative emotions are being expressed during the conflict. These emotions might include anger, rage, annoyance, frustration, resentment, or simple discomfort. In your group, yelling, crying, banging fists, or talking in an angry tone are clear signs that negative emotions exist. Second, identify the importance or centrality of the conflict to the group. In other words, is this conflict a big deal or of little importance? The importance of a conflict is often tied to the perceived consequences of being in the conflict. If the outcome of a conflict will greatly influence the identity of a group (for example, splitting a larger team into two separate teams), the consequences can be considerable.

The next step is to identify the norms this group has about conflict, particularly the degree to which group members find conflict acceptable. Do they regularly engage in conflict? Do they perceive it as normal for conflict to occur? For groups in which conflict is not acceptable, members often try to downplay or avoid conflict. For groups in which conflict is a regular occurrence, members may view conflict as a healthy and constructive part of the group process.

Finally, assess the conflict for its resolution potential. The key question is, Do group members *believe* this conflict can be resolved? What's important here is group members' perceptions, not how an outsider might assess the resolution potential of a conflict. Some group conflicts are easy to resolve by gathering additional information or by giving group members additional time to work through difficult issues. However, other conflicts, especially personal or relational conflicts, can be difficult to resolve. Issues that influence members' perceptions of resolution potential include the degree of group member interdependence, the group's history with conflict, uncertainty about the group and its activities, and status and power differences. Regardless of the outcome, one conflict episode is connected to the next one. The feelings that result from the first conflict, or conflict aftermath, influence your awareness of the subsequent conflict and your interaction in it.

Summary

The word *conflict* generally conjures up negative emotions. However, in our society and in working groups, conflict is a normal part of day-to-day activities. When parties are in conflict, they have mutually exclusive goals. Because the parties are interdependent, they cannot all have things their way simultaneously. Conflict can be productive for groups by stimulating interest and providing opportunities to evaluate alternatives.

Conflict is inherent in group interactions because different skills, values, and talents of members are needed to complete complex activities and goals. These differences, although necessary, also allow conflict to occur. Effective communication can help groups manage their differences and find solutions to conflict problems.

Conflicts can be over affective issues or substantive issues, and they can be cooperative or competitive. Conflicts can occur over judgment or cognitive tasks, over the use of (or lack of) procedures, or over incompatible personalities. Conflicts can arise over differing goals or interests, and they can develop when one party evaluates another in terms of what should have been done or accomplished. Because gender and culture are primary ways in which we identify ourselves and others, differences attributed to these characteristics can be salient in conflict interactions. Despite gender stereotypes, there is little evidence that men and women communicate differently in groups. Still when gender distinctiveness is relevant to the group's task conflict can occur. Likewise differing cultural orientations can also cause conflict. In both instances, however, we should remember that gender and intercultural differences cannot explain all instances of conflict. Many conflicts are based on other affective or substantive issues.

When relationships and interdependence develop among group members, power issues are inevitable. Power is created through communication and can be based upon rewards, coercion, role or position, charisma, expertise, or information. Power is best analyzed contextually. The extent to which power develops may be based on formalized power structures and the degree to which a struggle over power occurs. Power is fluid, not static; power in relationships changes frequently. Power can also be created when a group member has control over real or imagined resources.

Conflict between groups is common in our society. We create enemies by talking about our adversaries. We belong to multiple groups and sometimes find ourselves caught in the middle. When our group is in conflict with another, intragroup cohesiveness and commitment build as we distinguish ourselves from the out-group members.

There are five types of conflict management strategies. Collaborating, or problem solving, is an integrative strategy that can produce high-quality solutions and decisions for the group. Through discussion, all parties contribute their ideas to find one solution that satisfies everyone's concerns. The distributive conflict management strategies of competing and accommodating are characterized by a win-lose orientation. In competing, you win and the other party loses. In accommodating, you allow yourself to lose to let the other party win. Avoiding is characterized by verbal or physical withdrawal from the conflict situation. Compromising is an intermediate strategy in that it may settle the problem but also offer incomplete satisfaction for both parties.

Usually, you will select a conflict management strategy that emphasizes your view over those of others. But as the discussion continues, you are likely to change your strategy. In any case, the strategy you use affects how others judge your communication competence. Although each strategy has advantages and disadvantages, most people prefer the integrative strategy of collaborating.

Discussion Questions and Exercises

1. Most television shows revolve around conflict—even situation comedies. As you watch television this week, make a list of the group conflicts you see. Label each conflict according to whether it is affective, substantive, competitive, cooperative, cognitive, procedural, or normative. Also note how the conflicts are managed. What conflict management strategies did characters use? What conflict management strategies would have been more effective?

2. Keep a journal for one week of the groups you are involved with and the conflicts they are experiencing. In addition to classroom groups, include your family or living group and any work groups. Describe and analyze each conflict in terms of the following characteristics: Who was involved in the conflict? When did you become aware that you were involved in the conflict? What were your perceptions of the conflict? How did you communicate with the other person(s)? Did your plan for managing the conflict change as you communicated with the other person(s)? How long did the conflict last? What was its outcome?

3. You probably can remember at least one group conflict that did not turn out as you expected or wished. Think back to that conflict and the ways in which you communicated during that interaction. What part did emotion play in this conflict? Who was most emotional—you or other group members? Now that you have had a chance to think about and reflect on that interaction, how do you wish you had communicated? Write down what you should have said. How can you avoid an overemotional reaction in conflicts like this in the future?

10 Providing Leadership in Groups

GROUP SKILLS PREVIEW

In this chapter, you will learn to do the following:

- Describe the communication behaviors associated with group members who emerge as leaders

- Identify the task, relational, and technical competencies required of effective leaders

- Explain why different group situations require different leadership styles

- Match leadership styles with task concerns, relational concerns, and readiness levels of group members

- Develop the qualities needed to be a transformational leader

Leadership is a process of influence. The person who influences other group members is the leader of the group even though he or she may not be appointed or elected to the formal leadership role. Leaders influence what groups do or talk about. They also influence how groups perform their activities and achieve their goals. Because leadership roles are based on influence, it's not unusual for a group to have members in both formal and informal leadership roles.

Society's conceptualization of what a leader is has changed over time. More recently, leadership theory has focused on the leader as a motivator—someone who can provide the group with energy. But there is one thing you should keep in mind as you read about leadership: Research on leadership has focused almost exclusively on groups that make decisions in formal or hierarchical settings. Thus some of the findings presented here may seem out of place for less formal groups or for groups in which initiating, developing, and maintaining relationships are primary goals.

Defining Leadership

We can define leadership in a number of ways. In its broadest sense, **leadership** is the use of positive interpersonal influence to help a group attain a goal. More specifically, leadership is both a process and a property. As a process, leadership is the way a person uses noncoercive influence to direct and coordinate the activities of the members of a group toward the accomplishment of group goals. As a property, leadership is the set of qualities or characteristics attributed to the person by group members (Stogdill, 1974).

With this definition, group members do not have to view leadership as residing in one person. Rather, many group members can provide leadership. By defining leadership as both a process (something one does) and a property (something one possesses), we make communication central to the discussion. Leadership is a social phenomenon, as group members in the roles of leader and follower need one another for leadership to occur. Leadership vividly demonstrates the type of interdependence found in group situations. Recall that one of the defining elements for a group, given in Chapter 1, is that members must have agreement about a goal. The interdependence created by group members sharing a collective goal forces issues of leadership to surface (Hollander, 1985).

Four caveats are worth mentioning here. First, you are not exhibiting leadership if others are not following. If group members do not respond to your leadership attempts, you are not the leader. Second, being appointed as head, chair, or leader does not guarantee that you will influence others. Group members will follow the member or members who exhibit influence in a positive manner to help them achieve their group and individual goals. Thus leadership influence is not inherent in the position. Third, leadership and power are not synonymous. Leadership may be infused with power (Hollander, 1985), but other group members also control power in the group. Finally, the leader cannot do everything (Hollander, 1985). There are limits to everyone's capacities, knowledge, skills, and motivation in performing this role. As a result, many followers perform leadership roles in groups. Thus the distinction between leader and follower may not be as clear as you might initially believe.

Based on expectations created by societal standards and by experiences in other group situations, members have expectations about how leaders should behave (Pavitt & Sackaroff, 1990). First, group members expect the leader to encourage participation by others. Second, they expect that the leader will keep the group organized by talking about the procedures the group will use, summarizing the group's discussion, and facilitating group discussion. Third, they expect that the leader will work to develop and maintain harmony in the group by managing group conflicts. Finally, they expect the leader to play the role of devil's advocate or critical advisor.

How does a leader meet those expectations? By performing three types of leadership behavior: (a) procedural behavior, (b) analytical or task behavior, and (c) social or relational behavior (Chemers, 1993; Ketrow, 1991). Procedural leadership behaviors are those that coordinate group activities and help members function as a group. Procedures often help a group achieve its goal, and group members look to others in the group for procedural aid. The person who does this best is likely to be selected as the group's leader (Ketrow, 1991). Thus leaders provide team coordination; that is, they successfully coordinate the skills, abilities, and resources available in the group.

Analytical or task leadership behaviors are those that help the group assess and evaluate its discussions. Group members recognize the need for someone to display task behaviors and believe that the member who displays this type of behavior is the most influential person in the group. However, if different members exhibit procedural and analytical behaviors, group members are more likely to choose the procedural member as the leader (Ketrow, 1991). Somewhere between procedural and task behaviors is the expectation that the leader will provide image management. This means that the leader must establish credibility by behaving and communicating consistently in terms of group members' expectations. If a group desires task direction, then to appear effective to the group the leader must be task-directed with them.

Social or relational leadership behaviors are those that help group members cooperate with and express support for one another. Effective leaders also need to address relationship development. In this function, leaders develop and maintain relationships with group members to foster interpersonal ties, increase motivation and goal activity, and create perceptions of fairness within the group. Thus a leader must be able to demonstrate a wide repertoire of behaviors.

Becoming a Leader

When we enter a new group situation, often one of the first things we want to know after identifying the group's task is who is going to be the leader. Leaders come to their positions in one of three ways: (a) They are appointed, (b) they are elected, or (c) they emerge from the group's interaction.

Appointed Versus Elected Leaders

An authority outside of the group can appoint leaders, or group members can elect their own leader. How a leader is selected affects the group environment (Hollander, 1978, 1985). Each method of leader selection validates one person as leader, and each creates a different reality for testing a leader's legitimacy.

When leaders are elected by group members—usually by a simple majority vote—members have a stronger investment in and more motivation to follow the leader than when the leader is appointed by outsiders. When things are going poorly for the group, elected leaders are more likely to be rejected by group members. Thus elected leaders may have a greater sense of responsibility and face higher expectations for leader success than appointed leaders.

For example, suppose your group elects Jason as chairperson. You expect him to take responsibility for the group, yet you will blame him if he fails. One way to interpret this is in terms of the group giving a reward to one group member in advance, with the other group members then expecting the elected leader to *pay back* the group by producing favorable outcomes (Jacobs, 1970). Now let's examine what happens if Jason is appointed leader of your group. Your evaluation of Jason as a leader depends on his performance as leader and your confidence in whoever appointed him. If he does not perform well, you may attribute the group's failure to Jason. You can also attribute the group's failure to whoever appointed him, and you will be more likely to do so if Jason is well liked in the group. Although it may be more efficient to elect or appoint a leader, these procedures do not guarantee that the leader will be an effective communicator or

Any one of these group members could be the group's leader. Leadership exists when one group member uses his or her communication skills to gain the trust and respect of other members. Leaders respond to the needs and expectations of other group members.

that group members will perceive this person as leader of the group. Generally, a leader who is elected by the group after a process of allowing leaders to emerge and be tested is in the strongest position to get things done (Hollander, 1978).

Emerging as a Leader

Some groups rely on **emergent leadership**, whereby a leader who is not appointed or elected emerges as a result of the group's interaction. That is, a group member becomes the leader because other members judge him or her to be one (Pavitt, 1999). Emergent leadership is most likely to occur in leaderless groups or in groups with ineffective leadership. At the start, group members assess the trustworthiness and authoritativeness of members to see who might be leader-worthy (Baker, 1990). The group member most likely to gain influence over other group members is the one with these characteristics:

- Is not hesitant to speak and speaks frequently
- Uses nonverbal movement to communicate a sense of dynamism, alertness, involvement, and participation
- Is supportive of and concerned with the welfare of others
- Says and does the things that others in the group want to hear

- Is charismatic
- Does not control resources to demonstrate power
- Contributes procedural and task-relevant messages

Thus those members who take an active role and talk frequently in the group are most likely to end up in the leadership role (Anderson & Wanberg, 1991; Baird, 1976; Hollander, 1985; Pavitt, 1999). The reverse is also true: Group members who do not contribute ideas for the group task or do not help organize the group are eliminated from leadership consideration (Baker, 1990). Those members who remain quiet and who are vague and tentative will effectively be passed over. In this way, your behaviors and actions serve as a test because leadership must be attempted before you and others can judge your ability to influence other group members (Bass, 1981).

Emergent leaders are generally those group members who use their social intelligence to monitor the situation and to modify their behaviors as required by the task and by other members (Ellis & Cronshaw, 1992). Individuals who emerge as leaders are good at monitoring social cues to assess whether their leadership behavior is appropriate and wanted (Cronshaw & Ellis, 1991). When one group member possesses this type of social and task awareness, other group members are likely to look to this person as the natural leader of the group. In fact, the greater the degree of behavioral flexibility displayed by the potential leader, the more likely that person is to take on leadership roles within the group.

Leadership emergence can occur in two different ways. Let's use Ava as an example. Group members may willingly support the emergence of Ava as leader and encourage her to take on the leadership role. Or they may allow Ava to emerge as leader because they are passive and do not want to assume any of the group's leadership functions. In either case, a leader can only emerge through the sanctioning behavior of other group members. Thus Ava emerges as a leader when other group members perceive her as leader and act as if she is leading them and when her attempts to initiate action or structure the group's interaction are successful (Bormann, Pratt, & Putnam, 1978).

How you communicate within a group is important because other group members are evaluating your potential for leadership by assessing your communication skills (Schultz, 1986). In particular, your ability to communicate clear goals, give directions, and summarize will either identify you as a potential leader or eliminate you from consideration. If several members are competing for the leadership role, the degree to which you communicate in a self-assured manner contributes to your selection as leader. The member most likely to emerge as the group's leader is the one who can identify sources of differences or conflicts within the group and then develop and present a compelling rhetorical vision that can transcend those differences (Sharf, 1978).

Let's see how these principles are revealed in the following group:

NANCY: I'm glad I'm in your group. This should be fun.

QUINTON: Me, too. It'll give me a chance to get to know Andrea better.

JOEL: Yeah.

ANDREA: Uh . . . what's your name, again?

NANCY: I'm Nancy, and that's Quinton and Joel.

QUINTON: Can we get started? I've got another meeting in an hour.

NANCY: Sure. Where should we start?

ANDREA: I'm not sure I know enough at this point to really help out.

JOEL: Me either.

QUINTON: Let's try getting started by identifying what each of us knows about the registration problem.

NANCY: Good idea, Quinton. For me, my enrollment time slot is when I'm in class. It just doesn't make sense to me. The university's enrollment system knows I'm registered for classes this semester. Why am I assigned an enrollment time that conflicts with my schedule?

QUINTON: Joel, what do you think the problem is?

JOEL: I, uh . . . don't really know. I just know it doesn't work.

QUINTON: Andrea?

ANDREA: Well, it seems that . . . maybe I shouldn't say since this is my first semester.

QUINTON: Okay. This is my fourth time to register this way. I agree with you, Joel, that it doesn't work. One thing I've noticed is that the registration form my advisor signs doesn't follow the registration prompts on the computer.

NANCY: Right. That sure makes it confusing.

QUINTON: And I've had trouble trying to give another option when my first course selection is closed out. Well, it sounds like we've had different problems, but it also seems that we believe a different system for registering could be developed. Do you agree?

Who do you believe will emerge as leader of this group? Nancy and Quinton are certainly more assertive, and both are contributing ideas for the group to consider. Joel is both vague and tentative. Andrea bases her hesitancy to help the group on her limited experience at the university. But does that mean she could not be a good leader? If the conversation continues in a similar way, we can expect that Nancy or Quinton will emerge as leader.

A Communication Competency Approach to Leadership

Regardless of how leadership develops in the group, the member or members who take on leadership responsibilities must be competent in those roles. The **communication competency approach to leadership** (Barge & Hirokawa, 1989) can help determine the types of competencies leaders need. Three assumptions are the foundation of this approach. First, according to this approach, leadership is action that helps group members overcome the barriers or obstacles they face in achieving their goals or completing their tasks. This means that a leader must take active steps to reduce ambiguity and manage the complexity faced by the group. In other words, the leader helps the group create a system for working together and accomplishing its goals. Second, leadership occurs through communication. Thus the relationships established and maintained between leader and group members through verbal and nonverbal communication are central to defining the nature of leadership. Third, individuals use a set of skills or competencies to exercise leadership in groups (Barge, 1994).

Effective leaders must demonstrate two sets of competencies—task and relational. **Task competencies** are skills individuals use to help manage the group's task; **relational competencies** are skills individuals use to help manage relationships among group members and the group's overall communication climate. Leaders must know which competencies their groups need. Moreover, they must be flexible, possessing the ability to change to or adopt other competencies when the group needs it.

What competencies will your group require? It depends on two factors: (a) the type of goal your group is working toward and (b) the situational complexity of the group's environment. When the group's goal is primarily relation-oriented (for example, maintaining sorority or fraternity solidarity), the leader probably needs more relational competencies. When the group's goal is primarily task-oriented (such as a sales team developing a marketing plan), the leader needs more task competencies. The degree of situational complexity—goal complexity, group climate, and role ambiguity—also affects the degree to which the leader needs to demonstrate these two types of competencies.

Task Competencies

To help the group accomplish its tasks or activities, a leader should be able to help the group establish operating procedures and plan its work. Specific to decision-making tasks, the leader should demonstrate competency in analyzing problems, generating criteria to evaluate potential solutions, identifying those criteria for solutions or actions under consideration, and selecting the best solution or activity. Some group leaders must also demonstrate competency by coordinating the activities of their groups, especially in competition or performance tasks. Of course, the essential task competency of leaders is to facilitate the group's deliberations and discussions, a skill needed across tasks and activities.

Relational Competencies

As individuals work together to accomplish the group task or activity, it is natural that miscommunication and conflicts will surface, challenging interpersonal relationships among group members. Effective leaders provide four types of relational assistance—interaction management, expressiveness, other-orientation, and relaxation—to help group members maintain, manage, and modify relationships within the group. Effective leaders assist the group in managing its conversations by clarifying and summarizing the comments of group members. Interaction management is also visible when the leader balances participation among group members. Managing conflicts and building consensus are further examples of the types of interaction management assistance leaders can provide.

Relational assistance with expressiveness helps groups avoid ambiguity. An effective leader encourages group members to express themselves clearly by identifying undocumented opinions and irrelevant remarks. In providing an other-orientation, the leader displays concern for and interest in other members, which helps the group develop a climate of trust and respect. Anxiety is a natural state in a group and occurs because individuals are often hesitant to express their ideas for evaluation. An effective leader reduces the amount of social anxiety in the group by creating a relaxed atmosphere of involvement and participation.

Technical Competencies

A third type of competency—technical competency—should not be overlooked. Leaders must demonstrate technical competence relative to the technical demands of the group's activity (Bass, 1981). Leaders who cannot express or share their expertise, or who are unwilling to learn new skills on behalf of other group members, will be disregarded by group members. This does not mean that the leader of, say, a softball team must be the best fielder and hitter, or that the chairperson of the budget and finance subcommittee must be a gifted accountant and a tax law expert. It does mean, however, that the leader must possess enough technical competence to help other group members and to know when outside expertise is needed. Generally, we expect leaders to be qualified or technically competent in at least one area relevant to the group's problem or activity.

Gender Diversity and Leadership

Group leadership is one area in which gender stereotypes are particularly abundant. In mixed-sex groups, we frequently expect that males will emerge as leaders of groups, but this is not always the case. For example, females are more likely to emerge as leaders when groups are dealing with relational issues. Alternately, males are more likely to emerge as leaders when groups are primarily task-oriented (Eagly & Karau, 1991). Thus the type of task or activity the group is working on seems to influence who might emerge or be selected as the group's leader. Regardless of gender, the member who communicates task maintenance messages to the group is likely to emerge as the leader (Hawkins, 1995).

Once the leader role is established, behavior for male and female leaders differs only very slightly (Chemers & Murphy, 1995; Eagly & Johnson, 1990). Still, stereotypes about gender and its effect on leadership ability persist despite the fact that both males and females can be effective leaders (Eagly, Karau, & Makhijani, 1995). Of all the differences that could exist between male and female leaders,

We often make stereotypical assumptions about group members based on gender. Doing so diminishes our ability to view group members as individuals and to recognize their unique talents and skills.

only one has been substantiated. That is, females are more likely to adopt a democratic or participative style of leadership whereas male leaders prefer an autocratic or directive style (Eagly & Johnson, 1990).

Our gender assumptions about leadership are firmly embedded in society (Ridgeway, 2001). One reason for this may be the way in which the male leadership assumption is entrenched in our language. It can be difficult to avoid assuming that males are more likely linked to leadership roles when group members use gender-specific language, as in "the person we elect as leader, well, he should be forceful, strong, and willing to work hard as we do" or "the chairman will decide when the report will be due." You can avoid this assumption and encourage both men and women to consider the leadership role in your group by using gender-neutral language (for example, chairperson, not chairman) when talking about group roles.

Leadership Styles

Research has demonstrated that different leadership styles exist and that each style can be effective in certain types of situations. One way to distinguish among leadership styles is to consider two dimensions of leader behavior: (a) the leader's relational or supportive behaviors (the relationship dimension) and (b) the leader's ability to provide guidance (the task dimension). A leader high on the relationship dimension communicates warmth and friendliness toward group members; a leader high on the task dimension communicates strategies for how the group can best achieve its goal. Although it is tempting to believe that leaders who are high on both dimensions—relationship and task—will be the most effective leaders, leadership should match the needs of the group. The situational leadership model explains how each style of leadership can be successful.

Situational Leadership® Model

The **Situational Leadership® model** (Hersey, Blanchard, & Johnson, 2000) describes differences in leadership based on (a) the amount of task direction a leader gives, (b) the amount of relational support a leader provides, and (c) the readiness level of group members in performing their tasks. Each leadership style can be effective depending on how well the leader selects a style relative to the task and relational contingencies created by the group's situation.

The readiness of group members is the key element in this leadership model. Here **readiness** refers to ability and willingness, and has nothing to do with age or tenure. A member with high readiness is someone who is knowledgeable and able to complete a task, and who is motivated toward task completion. Thus readiness is task-dependent. We'll explore how group member readiness directs leaders to select one of four leadership styles: telling, selling, participating, and delegating. Figure 10.1 shows the Situational Leadership® model and the relationships among the four styles. Notice how the horizontal and vertical axes of the primary diagram represent the task and relational contingencies. Thus each leadership style represents one combination of those contingencies. Notice, too, the readiness continuum, from low to high, in the boxes below the primary diagram.

Telling Style   The **telling leadership style** (high task, low relationship) is best for group members who are both unable and unwilling (low readiness) to take responsibility for group tasks. Perhaps the task is too complex and group members are intimidated by it. In some cases, directions for working on the task may be unclear or incomplete. Or group members may simply be procrastinators. By providing clear and specific directions for low-readiness group members, the telling-style leader has a good chance of succeeding.

What communication behaviors are required to effectively use the telling leadership style? When group members are unable or unwilling to complete group tasks, the leader's primary functions are to help the group get started, clarify its purpose, define its goals, and keep it on track. To help the group get started, the leader initiates action, makes suggestions about member roles, and structures how group members will work together. Clarifying the group's purpose is also important because group members are not able to do it for themselves. To clarify the purpose, the leader should address the common goal of the members, identify the goal as the primary reason for the group's existence, and address how each group member will contribute to goal achievement. Once the group's purpose is clarified, he must define the group's goals. Identifying the specific steps needed for each aspect of the goal is an effective strategy for this type of group. Finally,

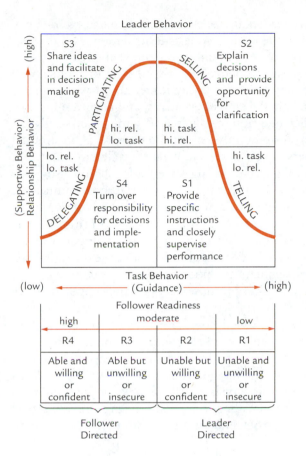

Figure 10.1 Situational Leadership® Model
Source: Hersey, Blanchard, and Johnson (2000).

the leader keeps the group on track by repeating the group's purpose and goal, giving step-by-step instructions, and providing positive feedback.

As you can see, the telling style of leadership is fairly directive. But this doesn't mean that the leader is unpleasant, negative, or overly critical. Nor does it mean that he is aggressively trying to get his way. A leader using the telling style of leadership directs the group's communication structure by providing well-defined methods for accomplishing the group's task. This type of structure helps members establish a model for their future group experiences.

Selling Style   The **selling leadership style** (high task, high relationship) is best for group members who are willing but unable to take responsibility for group tasks. Group members at this readiness level (low to moderate) are enthusiastic and motivated but lack the abilities or skills to complete group tasks. These conditions often surround a new task for which group members have no experience. With this leadership style, the leader offers increased levels of emotional support and acts as a role model. This leader is selling because, by her actions, she is trying to get group members to buy into what needs to be done.

In essence, the selling style of leadership relies on friendly persuasion. When this style of leadership is required, the leader requests information, asks for suggestions from other members, and solicits members' feelings about the group's activities. In doing so, the selling leader is actively seeking the contributions of all group members. The primary functions of the selling leader are to ask questions, guide and encourage responses, help develop alternatives, and advocate for possible solutions. Asking open-ended questions can help clarify the group's activities because these types of questions have no inherent correct answer. Questioning can uncover what group members are thinking and what they already know. But simply asking questions is not enough. The selling-style leader should also guide and encourage member responses by creating a supportive communication climate. This leader helps the group generate options and alternatives to pursue, and advocates for other alternatives if the group becomes stuck. In this case, the leader is teaching group members about the value of a two-way dialogue between leader and members. Even though the leader is making most of the decisions, she carefully explains them and gives members an opportunity to ask questions.

In other words, the selling-style leader promotes an open and supportive team communication environment—an environment in which every group member is encouraged to participate. The selling-style leader has a very active role because she is both helping the group satisfy its task goals and providing high levels of relational support for the group. By practicing friendly and persuasive communication behaviors, this leader hopes to encourage group members to respond in a similar fashion. Although members do not have all of the task competencies needed, they are enthusiastic about and willing to work on the group's task. And a well-developed communication network encourages group members to learn from one another more quickly.

Participating Style   The **participating leadership style** (high relationship, low task) is effective with members who are able but unwilling to take responsibility for group tasks (moderate to high readiness). This level of readiness often occurs when group members demonstrate task knowledge but for some reason are hesitant to take the next step—perhaps because they are overwhelmed or confused. By increasing levels of relational concern, the participating-style leader can overcome any insecurities or anxieties group members may have. This nondirective leadership style includes members in the decision making; the leader's role is to facilitate and communicate.

How does a leader practice the participating style of leadership? The primary function of this leader is to enhance group commitment. He does this by encouraging involvement of all group members, synthesizing and summarizing for the group, and facilitating problem solving. Because group members are task-capable, the leader can focus on motivating them. Thus this leader's style is more relationally oriented than task-oriented. He encourages involvement by creating an open and supportive communication climate and by facilitating discussion procedures in which all group members have an opportunity to provide input. Working with the suggestions and information offered by group members, the participating-style leader integrates what group members offer into one workable solution. Finally, the participating-style leader checks to make sure that all group members are committed to the group's decision. Because group members are task-capable, this leader can focus attention on task accomplishment. Decision making has shifted from leader to members, and the leader actively reinforces the work of the group by complimenting group members.

Although the inclusive style of the participating-style leader requires that he address the relational concerns of group members, his effectiveness is diminished if he responds similarly to all group problems. For example, agreeing with everything group members say is not the hallmark of the participating style. Likewise, avoiding decisions to avoid hurting group members' feelings is not productive for the group.

Delegating Style The **delegating leadership style** (low relationship, low task) is most effective with group members who are both willing and able to take responsibility for group tasks (high task readiness). These group members can operate without a great deal of direction from the leader. They are results-oriented and are comfortable asking for help when they need it. In this case, the leader takes a low profile, delegating as much of the group's tasks as she can to group members.

The primary function of the delegating-style leader is to attend to group members' needs. Listening, showing interest, and taking notes for the group demonstrate to group members that she is attending to them without dominating the group. Because the delegating-style leader is listening for understanding, she may not participate as much as other group members. This is appropriate because group members are able and willing to complete group tasks. Even when the leader isn't giving her verbal input, she can show interest in the group by non-verbally communicating her positive response. Taking notes for the group is a good way for the delegating-style leader to stay involved with the group while letting group members remain responsible for completing their work. Doing these three things provides the delegating-style leader the opportunity to monitor and observe the group, allowing her to participate more fully if needed. Thus the delegating-style leader remains accessible to provide support and resources while group members assume the responsibility for and risks in completing the task.

The delegating-style leader is less active than leaders using the other styles because group members are more involved in the group's primary activity. But this doesn't mean that the leader withdraws psychologically or physically from the group. A leader using the delegating style must be there when group members need her. A quick way to destroy group effectiveness and leader-member relationships is for a delegating leader to avoid the group or to act bored when there. Try "Identifying Your Leadership Style" to learn more about your skills as they relate to these four styles.

Comparing Leadership Styles Let's examine how these different styles might apply to a group of nurses. On the first work shift, Malique is responsible for four nurses who are new to this particular hospital and to nursing in general. So he

---

SKILL BUILDER

Identifying Your Leadership Style

It's likely that you are competent in some of the behaviors required for each of the situational leadership styles—telling, selling, participating, and delegating. To discover your areas of strength and areas that need further development, identify two communication behaviors that you can effectively use and two communication behaviors that need further development. For example, for the telling style, you may be competent in clarifying the group's purpose and helping group members maintain direction as they work on the task. But you need to enhance your skills in motivating members to work on the task and in identifying and addressing the commonalities among group members. In the group meeting in which you contribute leadership, plan to use the skills you have and to practice the skills that need more development. After that meeting, review the communication behaviors associated with the style you were practicing to assess your success.

---

will use a telling style. His team members are technically competent, but they have not been around the hospital long enough to fully know hospital procedures. They are also somewhat unwilling. They are not trying to be uncooperative, but they are hesitant because they only recently graduated from nursing school.

Kia is supervisor of the second work shift, and her team members have between 1 and 3 years of nursing experience; most have been with the same hospital for that length of time as well. Recent changes in nursing procedures have made them more excited about their jobs, but they do have to be checked out for some new procedures. So Kia will use a selling leadership style to overcome that obstacle.

The third nursing shift is led by Deanna. Members of her nursing team have long tenure with the hospital; in fact, many of them helped train some of Malique's new hires. Their reaction to changes in the nursing procedures, however, is not favorable. They believe that the nursing administration is making changes to avoid litigation, not because the nursing procedure needs improvement. Deanna will use the participating leadership style with them.

Finally, Aaron is the leader of the floating nurse team. He and his team members cover all shifts when extra staffing is needed or when other nurses are out sick or on vacation. The nurses on this team are the most flexible because they have to be able to fit in with nurses on the other three teams. Aaron feels lucky to lead such an experienced team, and to a great degree, he can rely on a delegating leadership style. Let's see how each nursing team leader uses his or her leadership style to inform and then convince the teams about the procedural change:

MALIQUE: (using the telling style) Before you start your shift, I need to explain a change in a pharmacy procedure. When people come in to the emergency room with their own medication, we must do three things: first find out why they're taking that particular medication; second, find out how often they're taking it; and third, check the pill against the picture in the *Physician's Desk Reference*. The first one to get a case like this today should let me know. We'll use your patient as a learning case. Okay?

KIA: (using the selling style) Last thing before you go to the floor, there's a change in pharmacy procedures. This is a new one—thanks to Felicia. Her suggestion earned her a $50 bonus. Thanks for making us look good. Felicia, do you want to lead us through the procedure?

DEANNA: (using the participating style) I know you don't need one more thing to relearn, but we've got a change in pharmacy procedure. I've heard the gossip, but I don't think this change has anything to do with lessening hospital liability when you handle patient medication. I think this new procedure has some merit. (Deanna hands out the new procedure.) After the shift tonight, let's discuss how the new procedure went.

AARON: (using the delegating style) Okay, I just want to remind you of one notice on your update sheets. We've got a new pharmacy procedure. Let me know what you think. Nursing administration will want to hear your opinions. Check in with me if you need anything.

Choosing a Leadership Style How does a leader decide which leadership style to use? An effective leader will choose the appropriate style by diagnosing the complexity and newness of the task and by assessing the readiness level of group members. A leader adapts his or her style to the group. The group should not be expected to adapt themselves to the leader's preferred style or way of working. You can determine your strengths in applying these leadership styles by taking the Leadership Adaptability and Style Inventory (Hersey & Blanchard, 1974). Besides identifying your most effective style, it will reveal your leadership style flexibility.

A good place to begin an assessment of the leadership situation is to determine the degree to which the leader needs to help the group structure its discussion (Jurma, 1979). A structuring leader helps the group by making sure the relevant issues of the task are understood, providing information to the group, helping to stimulate and motivate group members, offering constructive criticism to maintain standards of performance, and reminding the group of any time limits (Vecchio & Boatwright, 2002). These behaviors are task-oriented and characteristic of the leader-directed telling or selling leadership styles. Alternately, nonstructuring leaders allow a group's discussion to develop on its own, so the group is self-directed rather than leader-directed. This type of leader is also vague if members ask for structuring assistance. Group members who have a high task orientation may be able to work without a structuring leader, as they are capable of directing and structuring the task on their own. This is more in line with the participating or delegating leadership styles. Thus one contingency or situation that leaders should address is the degree of task orientation among group members. If task orientation is high, the leader can encourage group members to take on some of the structuring responsibilities. If the task orientation of members is low, the leader should assume these responsibilities for the group.

The other dimension to consider is the degree of supportive, or relational, communication group members will require in their task or activity interactions. A supportive leader takes time to listen to group members and keeps the group informed. By being friendly and approachable, a leader demonstrates support by putting others at ease and communicating in such a way as to be easily understood (Vecchio & Boatwright, 2002). These communication behaviors are in line with the participating and selling styles of leadership. Of course, not all groups work on tasks that require this level of leader involvement in the relational dimension of the group. When group members have worked together for a period of time, are familiar with one another, and have good relational ties, they require less relational support from the leader, which is line with the delegating leadership style. The telling leadership style also requires fewer supportive behaviors, as the task dimension of the group's activity is more prominent.

Remember that in the Situational Leadership® model leadership is situational. This means that once a leadership style is selected it will not necessarily remain effective throughout the lifetime of the group. The style that is effective at a given time depends on a group's task readiness. Thus a leader must be flexible, able to perform all four leadership styles. If, after observing group members work on the group's task, the leader believes that their readiness level can be increased, he can use training to enhance their ability or knowledge, or restructure the group's tasks to motivate them to try new behaviors or tasks. It is the leader's responsibility to develop the readiness levels of group members, to the extent that they desire such development.

In the next section, transformational leadership is introduced and explained. You will find that transformational leaders are masters of assessing the situation and then using a wide repertoire of communication skills to inspire group members. Hence, the leadership transforms members, which, in turn, allows the group members' interactions to be more effective and satisfying.

Transformational Leadership

A **transformational leader** is an exceptionally expressive person who communicates in such a way as to persuade, influence, and mobilize others. According to this theory, acting as a role model, the transformational leader sets an example for group members to follow. This type of leader uses rhetorical skills to build a vision with which members can identify. That vision creates a sense of connection with group members and motivates them toward goal completion (Bass, 1985, 1990). Although transformational leaders are perceived by group members to be powerful, they do not rely on their position of power or the use of organizational rewards. Rather, they communicate a sense of urgency and utility—a group vision—that members find appealing.

This type of leader creates power through the use of dramatic and inspirational messages. Thus you can find transformational leaders at all levels of organizations and in group settings in which motivating people and providing services are more important than monetary rewards. For instance, your soccer coach

The passion of a transformational leader is often the characteristic with which group members identify and to which they respond. Communicating both a sense of urgency and utility, transformational leaders use the power of communication to reach and empower group members.

might be a transformational leader, and your church group may be empowered by a transformational leader. Many civic and community groups, particularly grass roots organizations, are led by transformational leaders. As you might guess, transformational leaders are successful at recruiting group members and helping them achieve high-quality performance.

Transformational leadership occurs when leaders broaden and elevate the interests of group members, when they generate awareness and acceptance of the group's purpose and mission, and when they encourage group members to look beyond their own self-interests and work for the good of the group. Thus group members are encouraged to take on more challenges and greater responsibility.

Transformational leaders have charisma. This means that they have confidence in their communication competence and conviction in their beliefs and ideals. Such a spirit generates feelings of faith, trust, and respect from other group members. But, more importantly, transformational leaders inspire others by communicating high expectations. These leaders are animated, which arouses others and heightens their motivation. Transformational leaders are intellectually stimulating, helping group members to be more aware of problems and to pay more attention to problem solving. Most importantly, and the key reason for their success, transformational leaders give special attention to each group member, treating members as individuals. Thus each group member is treated differently according to his or her needs and capabilities.

Transformational leaders are particularly good at getting group members to perform the extra work that is often necessary to achieve performance goals (Avolio, Waldman, & Einstein, 1988; Gardner & Avolio, 1998). How is this accomplished? Transformational leaders inspire their followers. Together leader and followers create a larger collective with which members identify. As identification with the leader increases, so does commitment. Despite time and energy pressures that threaten to keep group members from contributing to group activities, transformational leaders are able to persuade group members to do whatever it takes to achieve group goals. The confidence and inspirational qualities of transformational leaders are the motivating factors for group members.

How can you become a transformational leader? First, you must assess the working climate and task of the group. You might rearrange or restructure work on group tasks to provide more stimulating activities. By knowing the current state of affairs in your group, you can then address what you would like the group climate to be like. Ultimately, these assessments will lead you to strategies that can help group members recognize their individuality, creativity, and responsibility to the group. What you will find as a transformational leader is that you are valuing group members differently. Together your group will have been transformed from "what is" to "what is desirable" and "what ought to be" (Rosenthal & Buchholz, 1995).

Second, if you can answer yes to the following questions, you may have the communication skills necessary to be a transformational leader:

1. Does your communication act as a role model for group members?
2. Can you define and articulate a vision for the group?
3. Do you earn the trust and respect of others in the group?
4. Can you inspire other group members to excel?
5. Can you stimulate group members to think in new ways?
6. Do you avoid criticizing group members in their attempts to try new things?
7. Do you consider and recognize each group member as an individual?
8. Can you coach or mentor group members?

If you consistently answered yes, you possess the four traits necessary to be a transformational leader. First, a transformational leader demonstrates idealized influence by acting as a role model and articulating a vision and goal for the group. Second, a transformational leader creates inspirational motivation by communicating high expectations. Third, a transformational leader creates intellectual stimulation by challenging members to think creatively. Finally, a transformational leader practices individualized consideration by providing a supportive climate that helps each group member develop and reach her or his potential.

Enhancing Your Leadership Ability

Effective team leadership is critical to a group's success (Hirokawa & Keyton, 1995; Larson & LaFasto, 1989). To be an effective leader, you must be in control of three factors: knowledge, performance, and impression. Together these three factors form the basis of how group members evaluate your communication competence and leadership ability.

First, are you knowledgeable about leadership issues? Do you understand a variety of leadership styles, and can you explain why different types of leadership may be needed? Do you know if your group has a greater need for relational support or for task guidance? Can you identify the decision procedure that is most needed by your group? However, being knowledgeable about leadership isn't sufficient to make you a competent group leader. Other group members can't benefit from your knowledge unless you demonstrate your knowledge through your leadership performance.

Second, can you perform a variety of leadership behaviors and functions? Or are you stuck, having to rely on one type of leadership behavior? Is your leadership situationally appropriate? Being flexible and able to adapt to the needs and expectations of other group members is a hallmark of effective leadership (Nye, 2002). Still, there are some leadership behaviors that are effective in nearly all group situations: establishing and communicating the goal or intention of the group, keeping the group focused on its primary activities, taking steps to establish a positive group climate, monitoring or facilitating interactions among team members, and modeling competent group communication skills (Galanes, 2003). These are common leadership expectations across a variety of groups. The leadership performance you communicate to and with other group members is what other group members evaluate.

Third, what kind of impression do you make as a leader? A group leader who is generous with his or her time and energy, is willing to do favors or make sacrifices for others, shows personal interest in others, and praises others' ideas and actions will create a favorable impression with group members (Rozell & Gundersen, 2003).

In many group situations, leadership may be better expressed as facilitating group member interactions leading to goal realization. Too frequently, leadership is conceptualized as an overly directive style, with the leader arguing for his or her position, refuting information that challenges it, and advocating for a decision that supports this position. While this style may satisfy the leader's needs, it is unlikely to satisfy other group members. Moreover, this style of leadership can have detrimental effects on a group. By imposing leader preferences, the flow of information from and among other group members is stifled (Cruz, Henningsen, & Smith, 1999).

Leadership is like walking a tightrope. You must balance task and relational concerns throughout the group process (Barge, 1996). The effectiveness of a leadership style will change as the group matures and moves from a beginning to an ending point. You must be able to anticipate and deal with unexpected problems

PUTTING THE PIECES TOGETHER

Group Goal, Group Structure, and Interdependence

After reading this chapter, you should have developed some idea of your leadership effectiveness. Think about one of your group leadership experiences. How would you describe or characterize your leadership? Specifically, what communication strategies did you use? To what extent did these strategies help the group achieve its goal? In what ways did your leadership enhance or inhibit interdependence among group members? Did other group members find it easier or more difficult to work together? How did your leadership affect or alter the group's structure or its use of decision procedures? Were you the only leader? Were additional leaders required? Did additional leaders emerge? If so, why were other leaders needed? To what extent did each group member exhibit leadership to help the group?

and to regain control if the situation warrants it. Your flexibility as a leader will dictate your balance, sense of control, and confidence—and hence your success as a group leader. Try "Group Goal, Group Structure, and Interdependence" to assess your leadership effectiveness.

Summary

Leadership is a process of influence that occurs when a leader and group members interact. Leadership can also be considered a property, as in the leadership qualities one possesses. Because leadership requires followership, interdependence is created among group members through this social and communicative phenomenon. To be effective, leaders need to demonstrate procedural leadership behaviors, analytical or task behaviors, and social or relational behaviors.

Leaders are appointed or elected, or they emerge from the group's interaction. Elected leaders generally have a greater sense of responsibility and a higher level of accountability than appointed leaders. Emergent leaders are usually group members who are active and dominant in the group's conversation, are trustworthy and authoritative, and can monitor the group situation to meet the task and relational needs of members.

The communication competency approach to leadership is based upon a leader's competence in both task and relational skills. A third competency, technical skills, enhances these other areas. A leader helps organize and manage a group's environment, facilitates members' understanding of obstacles they face, and helps members plan and select the most effective actions. The more complex the group activity, the more complex the leader's communication needs to be.

Different leadership styles can satisfy a group's leadership needs. The Situational Leadership® model describes four different leadership styles based on the amount of task direction and relational support a leader provides. Each leadership style—telling, selling, participating, and delegating—can be effective, depending on how well the leader selects a style relative to the task and relational contingencies created by the group's situation, and on the readiness level of group members.

Transformational leadership theory explains why some leaders are more effective than others. A transformational leader communicates a sense of urgency and utility, which motivates group members. Group members report that transformational leaders are charismatic, inspiring, and intellectually stimulating and that they treat each group member as an individual. Thus this type of leader can empower group members to accomplish more than they originally thought possible.

Effective team leadership is critical to a group's success. You must be knowledgeable on leadership issues and be able to perform a variety of leadership behaviors and functions, and you should leave a favorable impression as a leader. Together these three factors form the basis for how others evaluate your communication competence as a leader.

Discussion Questions and Exercises

1. Select at least two people you know who lead or direct groups, and ask them to participate in informal interviews on their views of leadership. You might select someone who (a) chairs a task force or project team in a for-profit organizational setting, (b) leads a not-for-profit group of volunteers, (c) chairs a committee for an educational or government organization, or (d) leads a religious study or self-help group. Develop at least five questions to guide your interaction with your two leaders. For example, how do they view their role as leader? What functions do they perform for the group? How did they come to be in that particular leadership role? How do they believe other members of the group perceive them and evaluate their leadership? If there is one thing they might do to improve their leadership, what is it?

2. Think of a community, regional, or national leader who is a transformational leader. What evidence do you have to support that claim? Do others agree with your assessment? Is your evidence based on the leader's communication behavior, the communication behavior of the leader's followers, or the outcomes achieved by the group? Which of these do you believe is the best direct evidence that transformational leadership is an effective method for creating and sustaining positive leader-member relationships?

3. Identify the leadership behaviors that you feel comfortable using in groups. Are there leadership behaviors that you could use but that you think need development? What are those behaviors? What leadership behaviors do you currently lack? What could you do to develop those behaviors you identified?

4. Set a timer for 3 minutes. In that time, think of as many labels as you can for "leader." In addition to your own experiences, also think about what leaders may have been called at different points in history, in organizations, in families, in friendship groups, in community and civic groups, and so on. Compare your list with other students' lists. How did your lists differ? What labels did you overlook? How do different labels imply different styles or strategies of leadership?

11 Managing Group Meetings

Group Skills Preview

In this chapter, you will learn to do the following:

- Carry out the premeeting responsibilities as a leader or member of a group
- Design and lead an effective group meeting
- Select and prepare appropriate visuals to help the group record what is happening
- Take effective minutes for your group meeting
- Carry out the postmeeting responsibilities as a leader or member of a group
- Assist your group in overcoming typical meeting obstacles

Your need to hold group meetings certainly won't end when you complete this course. You're likely to be involved in group activities for other courses and to attend meetings as a member of a fraternity, sorority, or other campus organization. If you work, you may have to attend work group or shift meetings. In fact, as you continue your professional career, you'll probably be involved in even more meetings. For instance, if you manage or supervise other employees, you're likely to attend meetings even more frequently. One survey found that the average manager reports spending more than one full day a week in meetings. And as our country shifts more to a service-oriented economy, employees report that they are involved in more project-oriented work that requires more meetings so they can collaborate with their colleagues (McGinn, 2000). Additionally, you're likely to attend meetings at your child's school and to participate in meetings of volunteer and civic organizations. This chapter explores methods of managing group interactions during such meetings and describes the responsibilities of both leaders and group members. Too frequently, meetings become sites of information transmission and fail to make use of group members—and their knowledge and skills—as resources (Myrsiades, 2000). Thus, it is the responsibility of all group members to manage meetings to facilitate group productivity.

Importance of Meeting Management Procedures

Meetings can be valuable in helping group members reach their goal. But they can also waste valuable time. Whether meetings are positive or negative really depends on how prepared you are for the meetings' activities and what meeting facilitation skills you can contribute to the group. Even though some organizations are replacing some meetings with more frequent use of technology that allows employees to meet across divisions in time and geography, the simple truth is that no technology can fully replace face-to-face meetings.

This means that you need to be skilled in basic meeting management procedures. Even simple agendas can provide structure for groups and keep meetings running smoothly. Procedures help group members coordinate their thinking and provide a set of objective rules all members can follow. You have probably been a member of a group that did not accomplish what it intended because another topic was introduced into the discussion. As a result, the group spent most of its time on this new topic, forcing you and other group members to make important decisions in the last 10 minutes without adequate discussion.

Meeting management procedures and facilitation strategies benefit groups by balancing members' participation. When all group members share their input, higher-quality decisions result, and members are more supportive of the group's output. There are many other advantages to using meeting management and facilitation strategies. These techniques help to uncover and then manage conflicts that can steal valuable resources and time from the group. They provide structure that can be revisited if a group takes a temporary detour, and they encourage group members to reflect on their meeting process and progress.

Meeting management procedures and facilitation strategies help teams develop more effectively and overcome obstacles. Being able to help your group manage its meetings and providing it with facilitation expertise are responsibilities that go along with group membership. Fulfilling each of these responsibilities allows you to participate in the group to the best of your abilities. At the same time, you are helping your group's interaction become more effective and efficient. You might think that the leader should bear these responsibilities. But when all group members participate in helping the group's interaction develop effectively, the group's process is smoother and members are more likely to feel satisfied on both task and relational dimensions.

Let us first explore meeting planning. You have probably used some of these procedures in the past, but just because your group has developed an agenda does not necessarily mean that it effectively manages its time together. There is more to formal meeting planning than simply listing items of business.

Meeting Planning

Meetings should not just happen, but many do. Taking a needs assessment (Johansen et al., 1991) beforehand will help you organize the meeting in such a way as to achieve the group's goal—or help you realize that a meeting is not needed at all.

Premeeting Planning and Preparation

When a meeting is called, most of us jot down the time and date and then show up. But that is really not enough. The group's leader or facilitator should do premeeting planning, and every group member should do some premeeting preparation as well. If you need some motivation to do this extra work before your next group meeting, think about this: A typical group meeting generates somewhere between 100 and 600 speaking turns or opportunities for individuals to talk (Scheerhorn et al., 1994). Can you imagine trying to make sense out of so much information without at least an agenda to guide the way?

Leader Premeeting Responsibilities   Before calling any meeting, the leader should first decide if there is enough business to hold a meeting, and, if so, what the meeting's purpose should be. If there is not enough business, or if a clear purpose does not emerge, do not hold a meeting. One way to make these decisions is to list the specific business items you want the group to consider or accomplish during its next meeting. Now look at the items. Can they be organized in some fashion that will make sense and move the group forward? If not, are these issues really ones that the entire group needs to discuss? Could talking individually with some group members take care of these issues?

It may seem obvious to consider the overall purpose of the meeting, but answering these questions can force you to consider why you need a meeting in the first place. Perhaps you are going to call a meeting because your boss requested the vacation schedule for your department. Is a meeting the best way to collect and coordinate this information? If you cannot identify a purpose for the meeting, do not have one!

Now consider the participants. You need to sort out who should be invited to the meeting and who should be informed about it. The two lists are not always the same. If a key person cannot attend, should the meeting be cancelled or rescheduled? Or should the meeting go on regardless of who shows up? Answering these questions can help you determine the importance of those attending the meeting, as well as the importance of the meeting itself.

Once you have decided that there is a valid reason for the group to meet, you need to consider how long the meeting should be. Everyone identifies a start time, but few groups know when they can expect to be finished. Identifying a stop time is important because it can help a group focus on its work. Knowing that time is limited is a motivator that can keep group members from delaying action or making a decision. Group members appreciate knowing when a meeting should be finished. This actually increases attendance because it allows group members to schedule around the meeting and avoid time conflicts. This is important because group members are likely to hold membership in other groups, and time devoted to meetings must be integrated with their other responsibilities.

Time limitations make an agenda that much more important. An **agenda** lists what the group needs to consider in detail and what the order of consideration will be. Group members should receive a copy of the agenda before the group meets. This way, they can plan what they want to say and collect data or information to support their point of view. When group members have an agenda before the group meets, they are better prepared to contribute effectively and efficiently.

The agenda should list the meeting's starting and stopping times, the location of the meeting, the expected attendees, and the overall goal of the meeting, as

Agenda
Project Development Work Group
Thursday, January 29, 1:00 to 2:00 P.M. Conference Room A

Participants: Cynthia, Dan, Lu, Marquita, Tyron
Purpose: Project Update Tracking

Welcome

Introduce any guests

Preview agenda; ask for additional agenda items

Information sharing
   Review developments since January 15th meeting
   Dan, report on final numbers for December's project activity
   Cynthia, tell group about presentation to Federal Express

Discussion items
   Progress on planning of telephone service cut-over
   Evaluation of new project tracking board

Decision item
   Need decision on feasibility of upgrading digital networks
   (bring cost estimates)

Suggestions for next meeting's agenda

Set next meeting date/time

Adjourn

Figure 11.1 A Sample Agenda

well as the specific goal of each agenda item (for example, to share information, to discuss a proposal, or to make a decision). Figure 11.1 shows a sample agenda. Additionally, the agenda should identify or describe any preparations that group members should make, such as "Come to the meeting with ideas on how to help our department pass its accreditation assessment." Notice how the agenda starts with items that are easy for the group to manage and that give group members the opportunity to contribute. Welcoming members, asking for additional agenda items, and sharing information are activities that do not take much time but that can help the group establish a positive or supportive climate. Now that the group has warmed up, it's time to take on more difficult tasks. Unless decisions are interdependent and need to be made in a particular sequence, it's best to make easy

SKILL BUILDER

Developing a Meeting Agenda

For the next meeting you will participate in (for this class, at work, in your community), develop an agenda. If the group typically uses an agenda, try not to rely on a past agenda for form or substance. As you develop the agenda, use the principles described here to identify the meeting's activities, and provide enough information for the agenda to be useful to members before and during the meeting. What would you say to group members to encourage them to use an agenda to help structure group meetings? What specific advantages can your group expect from implementing this meeting procedure?

decisions first and work your way up to the more difficult ones. Wrapping up the meeting by discussing the agenda and date for the next meeting gives members an opportunity to regain their composure if the decision making was contentious. Ending on a positive note with respectful and positive messages completes the meeting cycle (Tropman, 2003). Try "Developing a Meeting Agenda" to test your skills in this area.

Once an agenda is complete and distributed to all group members, you are done, right? Wrong! Now, as the group leader, you still have some work to do. First, given the items on the agenda, what leadership style should you use? What decision procedures will be most appropriate? Will the group meeting require any equipment? Have space and equipment been reserved? Are there enough seats? Can the participants fit comfortably around the table? Does the table and the configuration of the room enable all participants to see and speak to one another easily? Is the room available when you need it? Do you need to make a reservation? Will you need refreshments? What level of documentation is needed? What agendas, minutes, or reports will the meeting require? How many copies will be needed? Who will make them? Will it be necessary to have overheads, flip charts, chalkboards, or technology during the meeting? Do you have to make an equipment reservation?

After your needs assessment, you are ready to plan the meeting and invite those you identified as necessary participants and inform others who simply need to know about the meeting. Make sure to give adequate lead time and send along the agenda and any other documentation they will need prior to the meeting. If you want participants to prepare in some special way for the meeting (for example, to bring lists of budget requests), make sure to tell them that. The more completely you prepare for the meeting, the more quickly the group will be able to work on its business and complete its activities.

Physical Environment and Material Resources   Usually, it is the leader who arranges for or secures the physical environment in which a group will meet. It is important to find a quiet meeting place where the group can have privacy. This type of setting promotes relational development because group members feel more comfortable negotiating differences of opinion in private. To the extent possible, seating arrangements should emphasize equality. Circular tables are more likely to provide this perception because conversational distance between all members is about the same. Circular settings also promote an open network of communication in which each group member can easily talk to every other member or to the entire group at once. When chairs are arranged in a lecture format (all chairs facing forward toward the leader or facilitator), it encourages one-way communication and reliance on the leader. A group member who is part of the audience has to gain formal acknowledgment that it is okay and appropriate to speak. And other group members cannot see him or her easily. These physical conditions inhibit free-flowing interaction and limit the opportunities to develop relationships with other group members.

Besides needing meeting space, groups need time to meet. Time is a resource for most groups and teams, and should be considered by the leader when planning a meeting. When to meet and how long to meet are influenced by the number and length of other meetings group members must attend and by other constraints on their lives.

The greater the level of connectivity and embeddedness among group members, the more difficult it is for a group to find a time to meet. As our organizations become more team-oriented, meeting time and meeting preparation time become even more serious considerations. Groups that meet formally might also require time and space to meet informally in between regularly scheduled meetings. Informal interaction further anchors group member relationships and gives members an opportunity to test ideas with others before presenting them to the entire group. You may think time is only a problem for organizational groups, but this is not so. Given the variety of demands on your schedule, your family, personal, and recreational groups may be even more pressed for adequate time.

The material resources needed by the group to complete its activities are also a responsibility of the leader. Most organizational groups need office supplies (paper, pencils, chalkboards, flip charts, and so on) and access to copy machines so documents can be distributed to all group members. When group members leave the group setting, they need time to accomplish individual tasks, as well as access to information (in the form of data or other people) and technology (phones, fax machines, computers). Clubs and organizations need resources, too, as minutes and notices must be copied and distributed. Informal and social groups also require resources. For example, family groups meeting for recreational events need sports equipment and refreshments. The more loosely connected the members of the group, the more likely the group will not have the resources it needs.

Group Member Premeeting Responsibilities   You have just put your next work group meeting on your calendar. Now what? To be an effective contributor, you should review the agenda (or ask for one if it is not provided) to determine if you need to prepare anything before the meeting. For instance, in looking at the agenda, Dan sees that his group is going to begin considering alternative work schedules at its next meeting. He has not been asked to prepare anything, but he knows that these discussions will be emotional. Even though his group members complain frequently about the schedule they work, changing the work schedule will also cause problems. First, Dan reviews the overtime records to see how much overtime each member has worked. Then he reviews the project record to see if there is any pattern to how projects flow into the department. He notices that only a few projects come in the first week of the month but that the pace picks up steadily each week until many projects must be worked on simultaneously and completed by month's end. This gives him an idea: Why not propose that everyone work flextime the first 2 weeks of the month and take some additional time off? This would balance out the overtime needed during the final 2 weeks of the month. Now, Dan has an alternative based on data to present to the group for consideration.

Preparing for a meeting may require that you talk with other group members. For example, after reviewing her agenda, Marquita believes that she should talk with Dan about the scheduling issues. As a single mother who depends on child care, she has a special interest in changes in schedules. She must get to the child care center by 6 P.M. or face a stiff late penalty and an anxious child. Marquita talks first with other parents in the group to see how they manage their child care arrangements. Cynthia tells her about one child care center that is open until 8 P.M., and Karen tells her that the company is scheduled to open an on-site child care center within a few months. At the meeting, Marquita suggests that the work team lobby the company's executive board about the importance of an on-site child care center. With that benefit, employees like Marquita will be willing to work unusual schedules. Although the child care center issue is not on the agenda, child care considerations affect the group's discussion of work schedules. Without talking beforehand to Cynthia or Karen, Marquita would not know of any alternative child care arrangements or of the company's plans for an on-site child care center. Without this knowledge, Marquita could easily steer the group off its primary topic to more emotional issues.

Conducting the Meeting

The group's leader or facilitator should arrive at the meeting site early to make sure everything is ready. When it is time for the meeting to start, the leader can call the meeting to order, preview the agenda with the group, and ask if other topics need to be added to it. By presenting the agenda as tentative rather than firm, the leader gains group members' support when together they agree that the agenda includes all important items (Schwarz, 1994). Posting the agenda so everyone can see it will help keep the meeting moving along. Before starting the meeting, the group should agree on the ground rules (when the meeting will end, what will happen if there is a tie vote). Finally, the group should review developments since the previous meeting. These should be brief reports to bring group members up to date.

Now the group is ready to move ahead with new business. As leader, taking each agenda item in order, you can announce the item and then ask what process might be most appropriate for this item of business. You can make suggestions but should be open to the ideas of other group members. For example, suppose that, for the agenda item concerning new ways of meeting the production schedule, a group member suggests using PERT (see Chapter 8). If other members agree that this is appropriate, this procedure should be used. With the item of business described and the process decided upon, you proceed with the discussion or action item. Generally, the leader's role is to initiate and structure discussion, not to control the discussion content. It is normal, if not always desirable, for group members to look to the leader for approval. One way to break this pattern and encourage input from everyone is to ask one member to respond to what another member says. This keeps the group discussion from developing into a pattern in which the leader says something each time a group member speaks.

Sometimes members complain, taking up valuable group time unnecessarily. For complaining members, your job as leader is to listen carefully to the complaints for their relevance to the agenda item. If a complaint is really about another topic, ask other group members to respond so you can gauge the extent to which this is a group rather than an individual concern. If it is a group concern, suggest that this issue be made another agenda item for later in the meeting (if there is time) or for a future meeting. If it is an individual issue, let the complaining group member know that you will speak with him or her about it after the meeting. Besides controlling complaining speakers, you may also have to encourage less talkative members to contribute. You can do this by asking open-ended questions (such as "David, you've worked at other companies with rotating schedules. What can you tell us about your experiences?").

When different ideas are presented, summarize these in a compare-and-contrast format. Ask group members if your summaries are complete and accurate. If group members are quiet, do not assume their apparent consensus. Ask questions until you believe that group members really do agree on the substance of the issue. When an argument or conflict begins, do not take sides. Rather, ask group members to clarify their comments and probe for alternative viewpoints. You should reveal your own viewpoint only if it differs from those already expressed. To help clarify what the conflict is really about, ask group members to write down their response to the statement "I believe our conflict is about. . . ." This technique allows each group member to identify his or her perception of the conflict. Then ask group members to read their statements to the group. You may find that there is disagreement over what the conflict actually is about. Once the conflict is identified and agreed upon by all group members, encourage joint problem solving through discussion. When it is time for the group to make a decision, consider the advantages of each of the decision-making procedures described in Chapter 7. Be sure to let group members know if the decision they are making is a binding one or if a vote is simply an opportunity to see how group members are currently thinking about an issue.

Taking Minutes   Groups need a record, or **minutes**, of what they did at each meeting. Minutes should report on who attended the meeting, what was discussed,

Minutes
Project Development Work Group
Thursday, January 29, 1:00 to 1:40 P.M. Conference Room A
Participants: Cynthia, Dan, Lu, Marquita, Tyron
Guest: Jensen
Purpose: Project Update Tracking

Lu called the meeting to order at 1:00; all members of the work group were present. Jensen Clark attended the meeting at Lu's invitation.

Lu reported on three items that occurred since the January 15 meeting: (a) promotion of competing software, (b) manufacturing status of our software, and (c) results from software demonstrations. Competing software has entered the market but has received unfavorable reviews. Our software is still on target for a March 1 release date, and feedback from the demonstrations has been positive. *Decision*: The group decided that additional demonstrations were not warranted. *Action*: Dan will check manufacturing status every Friday and email an update to each member of the group. *Action*: Lu will ask the marketing department to watch consumer reaction of competing software.

Dan reported that December project activity was slightly off due to higher than anticipated vacation days. January numbers appear to be in line with estimates.

Cynthia reported that her presentation to Federal Express

page 1 of 2

Figure 11.2 Sample Meeting Minutes

what was decided, who agreed to take on what responsibilities, and what the group plans to do next. Generally, the group's secretary or recorder takes the minutes, finalizes them, and presents them to the group at the next meeting. Many groups prefer that the minutes be prepared and distributed prior to the next group meeting. This gives members ample opportunity to review the record for accuracy. At the next group meeting, the minutes should be reviewed and corrected, if needed, before being accepted by the group as its formal record of activity. Figure 11.2 shows the minutes that resulted from the meeting conducted with the agenda displayed in Figure 11.1.

Managing Relational Issues Besides conducting the meeting and helping the group accomplish what is on the agenda, the leader or facilitator is also responsible for developing and maintaining a supportive group climate. Greeting group members as they arrive and engaging them in small talk can help establish a friendly meeting environment. If group members do not know one another well, brief self-introductions, name badges, and table tents can help them learn names more quickly.

If the meeting is long, suggest taking a break. This not only gives people time to take care of personal needs or get a snack but also relieves the tensions that can develop in groups. Another way to help group members feel more comfortable is to ask for volunteers for assignments. When someone volunteers, ask other members who know and like this person to work with her or him as a team.

As the leader, you also have primary responsibility for establishing and setting group norms. Group members will follow your lead. As the meeting progresses, analyze norms for their effectiveness. Just because your group has always done it a certain way does not mean that it is effective. When you speak, try to use "we" and "our team" rather than "I" language. These subtle cues help create a team atmosphere other members can accept and adopt.

Because conflict is a natural outgrowth of group discussions, watch for cues from group members that conflicting positions or hidden agendas are developing. Conflict cues include rising voices as the conversation goes back and forth between group members and the use of more dominant nonverbal behaviors—such as a visible tightening of arms and faces, forceful gestures, and averted bodies. Some group members become silent and withdraw from a group's conversation when conflict arises.

A hidden agenda may be developing when one group member dominates the conversation with his or her own input while dismissing input from others. A person with a hidden agenda may ask loaded questions ("So, you don't think I would be a good chairperson?"), causing other group members either to retreat or to respond with the answer the person is looking for merely to keep peace in the group. When you see cues that conflicts or hidden agendas are developing, deal with them. The longer you wait, the more entrenched they become, making them

Part of the leader's responsibility is to make group members feel welcome. This indirectly invites them to participate in and contribute to the group's activity.

more difficult for the group to manage and making the group less effective. (See Chapter 9 for strategies for managing conflicts.)

Using Space Four principles should guide the selection and use of meeting space (Schwarz, 1994). First, all group members should be able to see and hear one another. Many different room configurations can accommodate this goal, but round or rectangular tables generally are best for groups of less than 10. A U-shaped table configuration can work well for groups of 20 or so. But, members should only be seated on the outside of the U so they can easily see one another. Second, if your group will be using visuals (see the next section), the seating arrangement should allow each member to easily view the flip chart or other visual aid. Third, if nonparticipants are invited to the meeting to provide information or simply to observe, they should not sit with the group members who will discuss or vote on issues before the group. Nonparticipants can easily contribute when called upon if they sit in a ring outside or just beyond the participants. This seating arrangement keeps nonparticipants from invading the psychological or relational space of group members. As a final consideration, the space for the group meeting should fit the needs of the group but not be so large as to allow for empty seats among participants. Group members may need space for notebooks or other materials, and they should not feel crowded. But allowing for too much extra space between members may increase the psychological distance among them and impede group progress.

Using Visuals Even the best meetings and the best groups can profit from keeping visual records of what is happening in the group. Although a secretary or recorder may be taking minutes, these generally reflect only group outcomes or the final decisions made by group members. Graphics or visuals can be used to keep track of the group's process and progress (Sibbet, 1981). By keeping and posting a running record of the group's key ideas and central themes, several positive things occur. First, group members know immediately if others are accurately hearing them. As a group posts its ideas on a flip chart, it is easy to determine whether another group member accurately summarized someone's 4-minute statement and to correct misperceptions as needed. Second, writing what people say makes members feel acknowledged and part of the group process. When this type of validation occurs, group members are more likely to continue to contribute to the group discussion, which increases levels of participation, cooperation, and involvement. Third, visualizing or graphing what is going on in a group helps to spark the creativity of group members. Providing a visualization of the interaction helps group members both analyze and synthesize ideas before the group. Finally, visualizing the group's interaction provides a graphic record for the group, helping to reinforce group decisions. In this case, seeing is believing. The visuals can also be used for making minutes more detailed. The graphic record can be referred to in future meetings when the group needs to revisit something it has already addressed.

What does it take to visualize a group meeting? Markers and flip chart pads are the best tools, although chalk and a chalkboard can be used as well. You might be thinking, "I can't do this. I'm not an artist!" It does not require artistic talent, but it does require that you be interested in what is happening in the group and be able to follow the interaction. Most group members can visualize or graph a group's interaction with just a little practice. Here is how the process works.

Any group member can visually track the group's interaction. The role of this person is to capture what people say, not to evaluate ideas. Record everything, as accurately as you can, in group members' words. Your job is to provide some structure or organization to what people say. You might want to use different colors—say, green for positive attributes, red for negative attributes, and purple for questions that still need to be explored. When you have filled one flip chart, hang it up and start another. As you hang charts, place them close together so you can draw arrows from one to another. Periodically stop and ask other group members if you have captured everything accurately and clearly. Use asterisks (*), boxes and circles, and underlining to highlight important items or to indicate what has been decided upon. Use forms (stick people, smiling faces, dollar signs, check marks, question marks—anything you feel comfortable drawing) to help structure or organize the record.

Graphics can take several forms. The one with which you are probably most familiar is the lists groups generate when using the brainstorming procedure (see Chapter 7). As group members contribute ideas, the facilitator writes them one by one on a flip chart. Putting the group's agenda up on a flip chart also helps the group keep moving. It is more difficult to stay stuck on one item when you can see that the group has 12 other things to discuss.

Other visual techniques that can assist your group include mapping, clustering, matrixes, organizational diagrams, and flow charts. In the clustering technique, you place comments together within circles as themes start to emerge in a group's discussion. Starting with just a few spread-out circles helps you cluster items together. And you can draw lines out to other ideas to connect circles (themes). The clustering technique helps groups separate and integrate ideas. The mapping technique is similar to clustering in that it separates and integrates ideas, but it adds elements to reflect the flow of the group's discussion. The group member developing the visual reflects the decisions made during the discussion by noting the questions members ask and the answers the group develops. In mapping, it's a good idea to start on the left side with general ideas and questions and to work toward the right as the group develops the answers. Arrows can be drawn to connect answers to questions and to indicate the sequence of the discussion. Look at the map of a group meeting in Figure 11.3. Can you tell what this group discussed?

The matrix technique helps groups find relationships in a systematic way. Let's say that your group is proposing ways to raise funds. Look at Figure 11.4. By identifying options for making money and then comparing them against criteria the group developed, members can analyze which money-making strategy is best for them. When a group has data to analyze, using a matrix is a good idea.

Another type of visual is an organizational diagram, which is really a treelike sketch. Although most often associated with employees and their work roles or responsibilities, organizational diagrams can be useful with any type of hierarchical

Initial group conversation

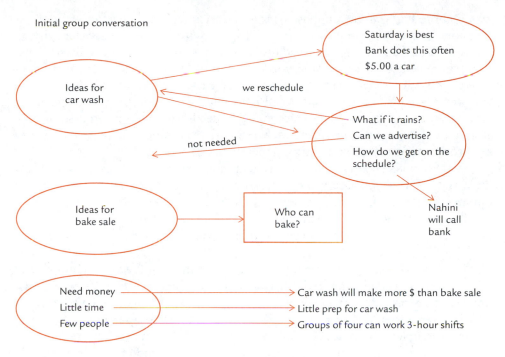

Figure 11.3 A Sample of a Map of a Group Meeting

	need money	little time	few people
Car wash	Can charge up to $5 a car	Only takes about 10 minutes to wash a car	Two people can wash the same car
Bake sale	Items generally sell for $1 or less	Must bake the night before	Would need more people to bake
Magazine subscriptions	Only get 5% of sales	Would have to go door-to-door	Can eight people do this?

Figure 11.4 A Sample of a Matrix of a Group Meeting

information. For example, suppose your fraternity is trying to develop a new structure for the group's many social and service activities. By drawing the existing structure and then editing the structure on paper as group members discuss what is missing, needed, or redundant, you will soon have a new organizational structure to present to the fraternity's board. The PERT diagramming discussed in Chapter 8 is a form of flow chart. In a PERT chart, the diagram acts as a planning tool. It flows from left to right, indicating what needs to be completed first, second, and so on. But your chart can start anywhere and go anywhere as long as it imitates the process and makes sense to group members.

Whatever visualizing or graphing techniques your group uses, do not throw them away. The group's secretary or recorder can use them to write more detailed minutes. Group members might want to refer back to them between meetings to see if an idea was discussed. And because the visualizations are a pictorial record of the group's process, they can even be used to settle disputes.

Making Assignments   Most group meetings reach a point at which additional information is needed. The leader may assign individual members these responsibilities, or group members may volunteer. In either case, you need to develop action statements and get agreement about what is to be completed.

For example, it becomes obvious to Terry that his group needs more information on how to use the company's videoconferencing system before this group will agree to adopt its use. Being comfortable with technology, Terry offers to find information about training for the group. Sounds good, right? But what exactly is Terry going to do? Will he find out when the training is scheduled? Will he explore what is covered in the training? Will he see if there is a handy guide group members can keep near their computers once they have received the training? When should he report back to the group? and how? by email? By specifying what should be accomplished, Terry's expectations will parallel those of others. When assignments are made or accepted in meetings, this action should immediately be noted for inclusion on the next meeting's agenda. It helps create continuity in the group when group members report back on what they have accomplished, and it keeps all group members informed of progress toward group goals.

Ending the Meeting   At the end of the meeting, the group should do two things. First, it should review decisions and plans for action. Taking this step helps everyone understand precisely what decisions were made and who is responsible for following through for the group. Second, if the group does not have a regular meeting time, it should schedule the next meeting and discuss a tentative agenda. This step helps group members view the meetings as having continuity, rather than each meeting being an independent activity.

Postmeeting Follow-Up

Most leaders consider their job done when the group concludes its meeting. However, to make meetings more effective, a few follow-up steps should be

MASTERING GROUP SKILLS

Managing Meetings

Think of a recent group meeting you attended or led. How would you evaluate your group on the following checklist?

1. The meeting was conducted effectively and efficiently.
   a. The meeting started on time.
   b. The meeting space was appropriate for the group's task.
   c. An agenda guided the group's discussion.
   d. Members' contributions were valuable to the group and appropriate to the discussion topic.

2. A record of the group meeting was developed.
   a. Minutes were recorded.
   b. The group's discussion was tracked through graphs and other visuals.

3. The relational dimension of the group was satisfied.
   a. Positive group norms were established or followed.
   b. All members had an opportunity to participate.
   c. Conflict was managed effectively.

4. The meeting concluded effectively.
   a. Members reviewed decisions made by the group.
   b. Members agreed on the next actions to take; assignments were made.
   c. Members generated ideas for the next agenda.
   d. The next meeting date and time were set.
   e. The meeting stopped on time.

Review the list again. This time identify how your behavior and interactions with group members facilitated or inhibited the meeting. For example, did you volunteer to graph the group's discussion? Or, did you keep the meeting from starting on time because you were late?

performed. First, the leader should review the minutes with the person who took them and distribute them to each group member. This should be done as soon after the meeting as possible. This enables other group members to review the minutes for completeness and accuracy so that corrections can be made as soon as possible and the minutes be redistributed. Because the minutes include action statements for which group members agreed to be responsible, this reminds them of their commitment to the group. Second, if a group's actions will have an impact on other groups or individuals, the leader should share the group's decisions with those parties. And, third, as the leader reviews the actions to be taken from this agenda, he or she should begin preparing the initial framework for the group's next agenda.

The leader has another responsibility toward the group. After each meeting, the leader should analyze what went well and what did not work. To a great extent, the leader is responsible for making sure that the group realized its goals during the meeting. Did that occur, and if not, why not? The leader should also think back over the meeting's interaction to assess whether individual group members' goals appear to be in alignment with the group's goals. If not, what could the leader do to encourage or motivate group members?

After important group business is conducted, the leader should also analyze to what extent inequality was an issue in the group. Some inequalities may stem from the leader's influence attempts. Some leaders are too assertive or dominant in their communicator style, which effectively shuts down members' contributions. In a sense, this influence pattern diminishes the need for a meeting, in that the leader is the only group member talking, giving input, and making decisions. Another type of negative influence occurs when a leader always looks to and speaks to the same group members. By consistently relying on only certain group members to answer questions and take on responsibilities for the group, the leader is implicitly saying to the others "You don't count" or "I don't trust you to do this for us." In either case, the leader's influence creates subgroups—the dominant subgroup that performs most of the group's work and a subordinate subgroup whose members are expected to follow along meekly. A leader can avoid these problems by making eye contact periodically with all group members, encouraging more silent group members to give their opinions, deferring the input of more dominant group members, and using decision-making procedures to help equalize any undue influence in the group.

Group members also have postmeeting responsibilities. If you were assigned or took on a responsibility to the group, be sure to fulfill it. If you believe the group forgot to cover something important, tell the leader so he or she can make sure it is part of the next meeting's agenda.

Developing a Group Charter and Code of Conduct

If yours is a group that will meet over an extended period, developing a charter and code of conduct can help your group develop cohesiveness and find unity of purpose. A **group charter** or mission statement describes the goals or mission of the group (Shea & Guzzo, 1987). A **code of conduct** describes behaviors that are appropriate in this particular group. Developed early in the group's history, both documents will help the group move effectively toward its goal.

To develop a group charter, the group must discuss and agree upon what members view as important and what they hope to accomplish in this group experience. Groups goals are generally the primary component of a charter or mission statement. Each goal should be listed individually, and both task and relational goals should be included. What individual members can expect to learn or obtain from the group can also be listed. Figure 11.5 provides an example of a group charter. As you can see, the charter is specific and clear, and provides direction for the group. But it does not dictate how the group will meet its objectives.

Check your charter by answering the following questions (Goodstein, Nolan, & Pfeiffer, 1992): Is the statement understandable to all group members? Is it brief enough that team members can remember it and keep it in mind? Does the charter clearly specify the activities of the team? Does it reflect realistic goals? Is it in line with members' values and beliefs? Is it inspiring or motivating to members? Not

---

Group Charter

Group's Mission Statement: To work interdependently as team members to identify relevant issues, resolve problems, learn new skills, and have fun.

Our group will develop a strategic plan for our organization for the next five years. The plan must: (a) be accepted by the executive committee to which this group reports, (b) be implemented by the rest of the organization, and (c) meet a set of conditions given to us by the executive committee.

In working on the strategic plan, each group member should develop skills in group facilitation, organizational forecasting, and team member effectiveness.

Our goal is to complete the first objective in 6 months from our start date.

Figure 11.5 A Sample Group Charter

only does a charter or mission statement help a group define and solidify its purpose, this document can be used to stimulate group discussion at a later meeting (Heath & Sias, 1999). Posting the charter or mission and asking—"Are we on track?" or "What are we doing to implement our mission?" or "Has our mission changed?" —helps group members either reaffirm or challenge their purpose and goals.

As Figure 11.6 shows, a code of conduct lists those behaviors that members feel are appropriate and will help them be effective in the group. Too frequently, group members do not discuss what they expect from one another in terms of behavior. When this is left undiscussed, members are unsure of what is appropriate or inappropriate behavior. Thus they use behavioral norms from other groups to guide their behavior. Of course, norms from previous groups are not always transferrable to other group situations. Attendance and preparedness are examples of individual behavior to be included in the code of conduct. Group-level behaviors —those related to role sharing within the group, decision-making rules, election procedures, and group structure—can also be described and included (Shonk, 1992). Specifying both individual and group behaviors ensures that all members are aware of what is expected of them in this group.

A code of conduct provides a set of guidelines—much as rules establish the guidelines by which you participate in any sport. Guidelines provided by the code of conduct create equity in the group process because all group members share in their creation. By developing a group charter and a code of conduct, members are more likely to share perceptions about what constitutes effective group membership. Developing these documents also helps a group crystallize its identity and culture.

Code of Conduct
created and agreed to by all group members,
August 14, 2005

As a team, we expect all members of the team to support the team's charter. Our communication, actions, and decisions should emphasize teamwork, not individual accomplishment. Each group member is responsible for being involved in the day-to-day business of the team. Each group member expects to receive information and influence from all other group members.

As a group, we will elect a leader for each month we are together as a team. By rotating the leadership role, we will help to develop each member's leader and follower skills. The leader is to provide overall direction and support for the team. Followers are to carry through their assigned responsibilities and inform the leader if they encounter any obstacles.

We expect to make decisions as a team using the majority vote rule. In cases where a minority vote member is so uncomfortable with the decision outcome that he or she cannot support the group's decision, he or she may ask the group to reconsider the issue.

Group members are expected to attend all meetings. When a member cannot attend, other members will expect his or her assignments to be completed and handed in to the leader before the next meeting. In the event any member finds that he or she cannot fulfill the responsibilities of being a member of this team, he or she may ask the group for a reduction in, or termination of, group responsibilities.

Figure 11.6 A Sample Code of Conduct

Overcoming Obstacles

Despite your best efforts in planning for and conducting meetings, problems can still arise. You have probably encountered one or several of six general obstacles to effective group meetings: (a) long meetings, (b) unequal member involvement and commitment, (c) the formation of cliques, (d) different levels of communication skills, (e) different communicator styles, and (f) personal conflicts (Gastil, 1993). Let's examine each obstacle and consider how you can help your group overcome each one.

Long Meetings

No one likes long meetings, but a lack of preparation by group members actually contributes to this dilemma. It is easy to be prepared for your group's meeting. Review what happened at the last meeting and what the group wants to accomplish at this meeting. At the meeting, speak in a clear but concise manner. Do not ramble, and do not let other group members do so either. If a group member gets off track, ask him or her to clarify the point. If your group has several long-winded talkers, you might want to consider asking group members to establish a time limit for individuals to contribute to the discussion. This can quicken the pace of the meeting. During the meeting, take notes and be attentive; do not take a mental vacation. Keep side conversations to a minimum because one side conversation tends to escalate into several more. Finally, if possible, schedule the meeting for a time of day when everyone is alert. Having definite starting and stopping times for your meetings can help. And if you cannot cover all of the agenda items in your meeting, ask members for their commitment to continuing the meeting or schedule a follow-up.

Unequal Member Involvement and Commitment

It is easy to say that you should interact in such a way as to make others feel more involved and hope that their commitment will increase. However, you cannot be directly responsible for another member's level of involvement. What you can do is to ask questions to encourage their input. Another strategy is to link the interests of each member to the goal or activity of the group. Consider what each individual group member can gain from the group's activity. Pointing out these individual-group relationships to others may help them identify with the group more strongly. Generally, when members identify with the group, they become more committed. Another strategy for increasing involvement and commitment is to allow the group to create and develop its own goals. When members help direct the activities of the group, their involvement and commitment should follow. These strategies can help a group overcome social loafing, or the failure of group members to perform to their potential (Comer, 1995). When group member participation is unequal, less talkative group members may become detached from the group because they feel as if their contributions do not matter.

Formation of Cliques

Cliques, or subgroups, develop when there is a reason or need to communicate outside the group setting. When cliques develop, not all group members will have access to needed information. You probably cannot entirely avoid the formation of cliques based on long-term relationships or common interests, but you can reduce the impact of cliques on the group by having an alternative means of communicating with all group members. You can post the group's minutes, activities, or agenda online or on a bulletin board. If it is going to be a long time until the next group meeting and group members do not have access to a common area, send crucial information to all members. Ask group members to communicate important developments that occur between group meetings to all other members before the start of the next meeting. Finally, be sure to recognize personally each group member early in the group's discussion. Using their names and asking them questions that personally involve them in the group's discussion increases each member's involvement in the full group.

Different Levels of Communication Skill

You may think there is not much you can do to enhance another group member's lack of communication skill, but there is. First, establish a procedure that allows everyone to speak early in the group discussion. You might begin a group session by asking each member to report on what he or she accomplished while away from the group or to reflect on what happened in the previous group meeting. The important thing here is to give each group member an opportunity to speak freely. You can help other members improve their skills by asking them questions that you know they can answer easily but that still contribute to the group. For example, you know that Marianne did a great deal of work checking out three sites for the festival. But you also know that she has some difficulty in giving detailed

Subgroups, or cliques, develop from the communication networks that group members establish. Cliques often form when group members have relationships outside a particular group and when group members do not feel comfortable expressing themselves in the group's meetings.

descriptions. Here is how you can help: Ask Marianne to tell the group about the three sites. When she pauses, ask her which site she prefers. What did she particularly like about that site? What criteria did she use in selecting sites? By asking Marianne questions you know she can answer, you are helping her overcome her anxiety, as well as providing details for other group members so that they can appreciate the work Marianne did.

Usually, each group member can improve his or her communication skills. Even members with typically good skills can find some aspect of their group performance that can be enhanced. Here is one way to encourage all group members to work on their interaction skills. In addition to working on the group's activity or task, have the group identify a particular skill as the practice skill for that meeting. For example, in one group meeting, the group may decide to work on asking good questions; in another, the group could work on not interrupting members when they are talking. By selecting one skill for all group members to work on, you are enhancing everyone's skills without focusing undue attention on any particular group member.

Different Communicator Styles

People differ in their personalities and their communicator styles. But as we discussed in Chapter 5, the more aspects there are to your communicator style, the more flexibly you can interact with others who favor different styles. What can you do to decrease differences among communicator styles in your group? The key is to remain flexible and to accept other styles. If everyone had the same communicator style, the group's interaction could be boring and less productive. Think about maximizing the opportunities that differences offer to the group rather than negating others who communicate differently.

Personal Conflicts

Personal conflicts and personality conflicts are especially likely to happen if the group is feeling other pressures (such as time, resource, or deadline pressures). Rather than panic when these conflicts occur, use them as opportunities to learn more about other group members. Help group members maintain mutual respect by not contributing to gossip. If you work to build a strong and positive personal relationship with each group member, they are less likely to gang up on somebody. Another way to avoid personal conflicts is to create a supportive climate in which members can express their feelings in the group. Sometimes conflicts occur simply because we think someone said something other than what they did. When a conflict does arise, help members work through it by having each side express its views clearly. Finally, if an intense conflict develops, direct the group's attention to the primary conflict issue before continuing with other group activities or business. Failing to deal with the conflict when it arises will likely escalate the conflict later. "Group Identity, Interdependence, and Group Structure," on page 262, will give you further insight into conflict and other meeting obstacles.

Group Identity, Interdependence, and Group Structure

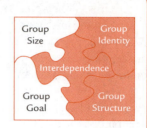

Reflect on a meeting in which your group experienced some of the obstacles described on pages 258-261. First, identify the obstacles that arose. Now, assess each obstacle for its impact on group member identity. For example, did the length of the meeting cause members to resent being in the group? Did the formation of cliques cause negative feelings and emotions and threaten the identity of the group? To what degree did the obstacles that arose affect interdependence among group members? How could you determine that interdependence was adversely affected? Finally, what structural elements of the group—group roles, norms, and communication network—contributed to these problems? Using the principles of meeting management, what suggestions to group structure would you make to prevent these obstacles from occurring in the future?

Successful Meeting Management

How can you evaluate the success of your group meetings? If your group meeting was successful, you and your group members were able to meet each of the following standards:

- An agenda guided the group's discussion.
- The leader and members were prepared for the meetings.
- Members shared a sense of purpose and pursued common goals; moreover, group members were willing to work to meet those goals.
- In addition to accomplishing the goal, members were also aware of and interested in how well the group operated as a system.
- The team was able to identify the resources available among its members and used those resources appropriately. As a result, all group members had power and influence in the group.
- Group members listened to one another and clarified their statements; they valued communication with one another by showing interest in what others said.
- Differences of opinion were encouraged; no one was hesitant to say what he or she thought.
- The team effectively managed conflicts; as a result, the group operated effectively because differences were aired and integrated into a collaborative solution.

- The team used its energy to solve problems, rather than focusing on interpersonal disputes or competitions among members.

- Roles among members were balanced and shared; as a result, the group experienced high levels of group cohesion and morale.

- The team encouraged members to take risks and be creative; mistakes were treated as sources of learning rather than as failures.

- The team responded to changes because members were flexible and open to new ideas and experiences.

- Team members periodically reviewed how well the team was doing, allowing time in the group's agenda to talk about process and procedures, thereby building evaluation of the group's success into the team's interaction.

- A climate of trust was established among group members.

- Minutes of the group's meetings reflected what happened in the meetings and included assignments group members agreed to take on.

Summary

Meeting management procedures and facilitation strategies capitalize on the strengths of groups because they balance member participation. Meeting planning includes premeeting planning and preparation by group members and by the group leader. An agenda, identifying both start and stop times and all matters the group will consider, should be prepared and distributed before any group meeting. Remember: If you cannot identify a specific purpose and goals for a meeting, do not have one.

The group's leader conducts the meeting according to the agenda. However, the leader's role is to initiate and structure discussion, not to control discussion content. Besides helping the group move through its business issues, the leader is also responsible for developing and maintaining a supportive group climate. Introducing members, establishing norms, and managing conflict are some of these responsibilities.

A secretary or recorder should take minutes at each meeting. Minutes should include what was discussed or decided, who agreed to take on what responsibilities, and what the group plans to do next. Minutes should be distributed, and revisions made, as soon as possible.

The space in which a group meets is important. All group members should be able to see and hear one another easily. The size of the space for the meeting should fit the needs and size of the group. Members should feel neither too crowded nor too distant from others in the group. Using visuals and graphics can help a group record what is happening in the group. Listing topics of conversation, drawing a diagram of the group's conversation, clustering ideas together, creating data matrixes, and drawing organizational charts are just a few types of visualization that help a group capture a pictorial memory of its interaction.

In most meetings, group members volunteer for or are given assignments to be completed before the next meeting. These actions should be noted both in the minutes and on the next meeting's agenda. At the end of a meeting, the group should review decisions and plans for actions, schedule the next meeting time, and discuss future agenda items.

Whether you are the group's leader or one of its members, you have responsibilities before the meeting, during the meeting, and after the meeting. Carrying these responsibilities out effectively is part of being a member of the group.

One way to help your group is to develop a group charter or mission statement and a code of conduct. A group charter describes the goals or mission of the group; a code of conduct describes behaviors that are appropriate for this particular group. Both can provide direction and clarity for group members.

Most groups experience some obstacles. Long meetings, unequal member involvement and commitment, the formation of cliques, differing levels of communication skills, different communicator styles, and personal conflicts are common obstacles groups must overcome. Any group member can help a group surmount these barriers.

Discussion Questions and Exercises

1. Think of your most recent group experience—one in which the group will meet again. Write a three- to five-page paper analyzing your group by answering these questions: (a) What did your group accomplish? How does that compare to what it should have accomplished? (b) What is one aspect of the group process or procedure that was effective, and one aspect that was ineffective? (c) Which meeting management strategies would have helped your group? How? Be specific. (d) What did you learn about yourself as a group member that you can carry forward to the next group experience? What did you learn about the group that you can apply in the next group session?

2. Gather the agendas of several different meetings. Compare and analyze them for their effectiveness. If the agendas are from meetings you attended, consider the usefulness of the agenda to the structure and purpose of the meeting. If the agendas are from meetings of other individuals, ask them to what degree the agendas helped them prepare for the meeting (if they got the agenda ahead of time) and to what degree the agenda reflected the meeting's activities.

3. Interview at least three people who have been members of organizational groups or teams, or community or civic groups. Ask each person to describe how the group or team accomplished its work. If these are not mentioned, ask each person about the group's use of agendas, graphics, and minutes.

12 Making Observations and Giving Feedback

Group Skills Preview

In this chapter, you will learn to do the following:

- Explain why a group could benefit from feedback
- Distinguish between types and levels of feedback
- Complete and interpret an interaction diagram
- Persuade your group to try audio- or videotaping meetings to obtain feedback
- Help your group initiate and design a feedback system
- Give effective feedback in one of your groups

Group success depends heavily on the degree to which group members effectively interact with one another. Groups that meet over an extended time—from just a few meetings to meeting every week—are more likely to effectively perform their tasks and create positive relationships among members if the group creates a feedback system (Dominick, Reilly, & McGourty, 1997). A feedback system includes two separate activities. The first is setting up a system for monitoring, observing, or collecting data about group and individual group member performances. The second is setting up a system for using that data as feedback for group members. By considering both positive and negative features of the group and its process, a group can use feedback to strengthen its performance.

What Is Feedback?

Feedback can be information about the quantity or quality of a group's work, an assessment of the effectiveness of the group's task or activity, or evaluations of members' individual performances. To be most effective, feedback should be an objective evaluation of individual group members' performance or the actions of a group, not one member's opinion or subjective evaluation. The feedback described in this chapter is not part of a formal performance evaluation system; an outsider does not evaluate the group. Rather, feedback is generated for the group by the group itself.

Feedback, as we are interested in it, is a group process that serves as an error detection device to help a group identify and begin to solve its interaction problems.

Thus group members generate their own feedback. Group members are both participants and observers, with observations aboveboard and apparent to other group members. Group members who trust one another can assume these additional group roles. The most effective group is one in which all members contribute feedback information (Keltner, 1989). When trust develops among group members, a bond exists to help each group member perform as effectively for the team as he or she can. When individuals are drawn this tightly into a group, their interdependence is extremely high. By investing in one another through observation and feedback, interdependence is strengthened.

Why Groups Need Feedback

Groups that meet over a period of time require a great deal of time, energy, and other resources. Generally, group members are interested in performing well, making effective decisions, and creating positive relationships. Feedback can help group members understand how their groups work and how to make them work better (Schultz, 1999). That is, feedback helps the team or group learn about itself. Some groups that integrate performance feedback into their activities think of the group as a place of continuous improvement. However, "unless a team has data about how it is doing . . . there is no way it can learn. And unless a team learns, there is no way it can improve" (Hackman, 2002, p. 103).

Of course, by paying attention to how others react to them, group members are getting some feedback from other group members. Unfortunately, without an agreed-upon system for generating feedback, group members are likely to receive

Many of us are biased about our responsibility to groups. If the group succeeds, we tend to believe that the group's success should be attributed to us personally. If the group fails, we blame the group and avoid taking responsibility for its failure. We are more effective group members and a greater asset to our groups when we recognize this type of attribution bias.

biased feedback. Typically, you are more likely to give detailed feedback when the information is negative or the team or group has suffered a loss, and to give general feedback when the information is positive or the team or group is glowing after a success (Nadler, 1979). Feedback can also be biased by another tendency.

When asked how you contributed to a group's success, most of you would reply that you were personally responsible. But when asked how you contributed to a group's failure, you would probably avoid taking that responsibility. This attributional bias is common in group members. Virtually without exception, members claim personal responsibility when their group is successful and deny personal responsibility when their group fails (Forsyth & Kelley, 1994). This type of self-serving bias may cloud your judgment, keeping you from recognizing your true impact on the group. Another factor figures in here as well. Some people are optimists—they expect things to generally go well. Conversely, some are pessimists—they expect things to generally turn out poorly. Personality traits like these can also cloud your judgment of your impact on group interaction. Feedback —or information that evaluates or judges your communication performance—is one type of tool or intervention that can help you overcome this bias and improve your abilities as group members. Feedback also improves the functioning of the team. In successful teams, everyone is accountable all of the time (Larson & LaFasto, 1989). Thus each team requires some system of checks and balances —both at a team level and at an individual group member level. If you are still wondering whether a group really needs feedback about how well its members are communicating, consider this: Nearly 75 percent of all group problems are linked to interpersonal problems and poor communication (Di Salvo et al., 1989).

Initiating a feedback system in a group provides several benefits. First, group members who believe that their input to the group will be evaluated are less likely to become social loafers—those members who hide behind the efforts of other group members. Groups that include regular evaluation of group members automatically decrease the likelihood of social loafing. The evaluation process and potential feedback about individual performance usually motivate potential social loafers to take on other, more productive roles in the group.

Second, when feedback is regularly provided in a group, member identification with the group is enhanced. Members of effective and successful groups are committed to their continuing success. They want to know how they are performing and how they can increase their communication effectiveness in the group. As a result, their identification with the group is enhanced, and they become more committed to the group, creating stronger interdependence among group members.

Third, at the group level, group members who receive positive feedback about their group's performance and their interactions are more likely to be satisfied with group member relationships, believe that their group is more prestigious, be more cohesive, and believe that group members are competent at their task or activity (Anderson, Martin, & Riddle, 2001; Limon & Boster, 2003). Receiving positive feedback sets off a spiral, causing group members to enhance their beliefs about the group. As a result, group members are willing to mobilize and coordinate their skills, the amount of effort they are willing to put into the task, and their

Group Goal, Interdependence, and Group Identity

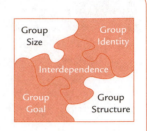

How group members give and receive feedback can help the group achieve its goals or weaken relationships among group members. Feedback, even about relational issues, should always be grounded in the group's goal or task. Reflect on your last group meeting. What feedback might have helped the group? specific group members? you? If you had the opportunity, how would you have constructed and delivered feedback to help the group become more effective? Would it have been difficult or easy to persuade everyone to participate in both giving and receiving feedback? How do you think giving and receiving feedback affects group members' interdependence and identity? What fears do you have in giving and receiving feedback? What about the fears of other group members?

persistence when faced with challenges (Bandura, 1986). Groups wanting to be successful need feedback to identify their strengths so they can capitalize on them. And groups wanting to turn failure into success need feedback to identify their weaknesses so they can make improvements. "Group Goal, Interdependence, and Group Identity" can help you explore the feedback process.

Levels and Types of Feedback

To be effective, feedback must be specific. Feedback differs in two characteristics: (a) the level, or to whom feedback is generated or what feedback is about, and (b) the type, or the intent or function of the feedback.

Levels of Feedback

Feedback can occur on many levels. Feedback may focus on how the group is working with procedures, how an individual is handling a specific group role in working with others, how one member sits silently saying nothing, how the group is dealing with a conflict, or how the organization is using the information the group provides.

Task and Procedural Feedback   Feedback at the task or procedural level usually involves issues of effectiveness and appropriateness. Issues of quantity and quality of group output are the focus of **task feedback**: Did the team win? Did the group raise enough money? To what extent did the group's presentation satisfy the judges? Thus, task feedback focuses on the outcome of the group's activity. **Procedural feedback** provides information on the processes the group used to arrive at its outcome. Is the brainstorming procedure effective for the group? Did group members plan sufficiently? Questions like these focus group members' attention on the task dimension of their activity. Groups need this level of feedback, especially after trying a new group procedure or passing a major milestone in the group's development.

Relational Feedback Feedback that provides information about the group climate or environmental or interaction dynamics within a relationship in the group is **relational feedback**. This feedback focuses group members' attention on how well they are working together rather than on the procedures used to accomplish their tasks. Questions that focus on the relational dimension of the group include Did the group manage conflict effectively? Were the leadership needs of the group adequately fulfilled? Did working on the task enhance cohesiveness among group members?

Individual Feedback Feedback that focuses on specific group members is **individual feedback.** This feedback may address the knowledge, skills, or attitudes a group member demonstrates or displays. A good place to start is with seven characteristics that affect an individual's ability to be an effective group member (Larson & LaFasto, 1989).

The first is intellectual ability. Can the person secure relevant information and relate and compare data from different sources? A group member who is analytical or creative is especially helpful to his or her group. The second factor is results orientation. The group member who can demonstrate the ability to work toward outcomes and complete activities helps further the progress of the team. The third factor—interpersonal skills—encompasses a group member's ability to relate to the feelings and needs of other group members. The fourth factor is the ability to plan and organize. The individual who is able both to schedule personal time and to work within the schedules of others contributes to the accomplishment of group goals. Typically, group members must handle several activities at once and have the ability to meet competing deadlines. The fifth factor is the individual's ability to demonstrate a team orientation. Can the person work collaboratively with others on complex issues? If so, the individual is revealing a commitment to the team on which others can depend. The sixth factor is maturity. The group member is considered mature when he or she acts responsibly when dealing with difficult people or situations. The final factor is presence or image. The person's willingness to present a friendly impression reflects positively on him or her and on the team. The characteristics of an ideal group member described in Chapter 5 apply here.

Feedback can cover any or all of these issues. But, in general, group members are going to respond to three main issues: (a) Do you demonstrate the essential skills and abilities needed by the team? (b) Do you demonstrate a strong desire to contribute to the group's activities? and (c) Are you capable of collaborating effectively with other team members? Remember that while you are being evaluated on these dimensions you are evaluating other team members as well.

Group Feedback At this level, feedback focuses on how well the group is performing. Have team members developed adequate skills for working together?

MASTERING GROUP SKILLS

Topics for Group Feedback

Although each group is different and unique, most groups will benefit if you and other group members reflect on the following questions. How would you answer these questions for one of your current groups? Would other group members provide similar responses?

Goals of the Group

1. Are members committed to the goals of the group?
2. Are members' personal goals in alignment with the group's goals?

Roles in the Group

1. Are roles and responsibilities within the group clear to all?
2. Who in the group is providing leadership?
3. Is the group responding well to this leadership?
4. Are other necessary roles covered by someone in the group?

Procedures and Processes

1. Are group members communicating effectively together?
2. Are decision-making procedures used appropriately?
3. Is conflict managed?
4. Does the group spend its time together effectively?

General

1. What are the strengths and weaknesses of the group?
2. Is someone or something outside the group hindering it?

Use these questions to guide a feedback session at the end of a meeting. Your answers could uncover issues that need to be addressed or resolved for your group to succeed. Even if no difficulties are uncovered, the group will benefit from reviewing its direction.

Does the role structure or communication network of the group support the group's task and activities? Has the team developed norms for communicating that help it accomplish its goals? Are there adequate and appropriate levels of group cohesiveness and group member satisfaction? Are the group's leadership functions being fulfilled effectively? Did the group develop a communication network that is conducive to its task? What decision-making procedures are group members effectively using? How well is the group managing conflict when it occurs?

Feedback at this level can have a dramatic impact on members' attraction to the group, as well as their feelings of involvement and self-esteem. Certainly, feedback to the group about its performance on its task increases group members' motivations to improve their performance. The more interdependently group members work together, the greater the impact of group feedback concerning the task (Nadler, 1979). "Topics for Group Feedback" will give you some ideas for using feedback in your groups.

Over time, it is important that a group receive both task feedback—feedback about the technical competencies or functional task activities of the team—and **teamwork feedback**—feedback about the group's interactions and members' relationships, cooperation, communication, and coordination (McIntyre & Salas, 1995). Using both task and teamwork feedback, a group can actually improve its development over time.

Types of Feedback

There are three types of feedback—descriptive, evaluative, and prescriptive—each of which has a different intent or function, and carries different inferences.

Descriptive Feedback Feedback that merely identifies or describes how a group member communicates is **descriptive feedback.** You may describe someone's communicator style, or you may note that someone's verbal communication and nonverbal communication suggest different meanings. For example, you say to Amber after a meeting, "You asked me to comment on how you communicated with others in the group. From my perspective, you were very dominant; you talked a lot and seemed very active in the group. I also felt that you argued each point introduced. Someone once told me that I was contentious when I did that. And you were precise. You said exactly what was on your mind."

Evaluative Feedback Feedback that goes beyond mere description and provides an evaluation or assessment of the person who communicates is **evaluative feedback**. For instance, after describing Amber's communicator style as dominant, contentious, and precise, you follow up by saying that this style causes other group members to avoid talking with her. Amber asks what you mean by that. You let her know that members with a more submissive style find Amber's style overwhelming, making it difficult for them to feel equal to her in the group.

Not only did you describe Amber's style, you evaluated her style as negatively affecting group member interaction. Too much negative evaluative feedback decreases motivation and elicits defensive coping attributions, such as attributing the feedback to others. At the extreme, it can destroy group members' pride in their group. In these cases, group members are likely to spend additional time rationalizing their failures (for example, finding a way to see a loss as a win) (Nadler, 1979). To be constructive, evaluative feedback that identifies group member deficiencies is best given in groups with a supportive communication climate in which trust has developed among members.

In contrast, favorable feedback generates motivation and increases feelings of attraction among group members (Nadler, 1979). Let's go back to Amber. After your feedback, Amber has toned down her dominant style and has quit arguing minor points. You say, "Great job today, Amber. I thought today's meeting went much better. That's due to you, of course." Naturally, we assume that positive evaluative feedback will have positive effects on a group. But can a group receive too much favorable feedback? Yes. A group inundated by positive remarks, particularly in the absence of negative evaluations, will start to distrust the feedback as information and perceive it as insincere.

Prescriptive Feedback   Feedback that provides group members with advice about how they should act or communicate is **prescriptive feedback**. For instance, after a group meeting which you believe was ineffective, you ask a group member you trust, "Got any advice?" Brian responds that he too was upset by how the meeting developed. "We've got to get the agenda to everyone sooner so they can prepare for the meeting. Could you remind Sara to do that? She trusts you, and you and she work together on other committees. If you'll do that, I'll talk with people informally after we get the agenda to remind them to get the information we need *before* the meeting." In this instance, Brian's feedback is prescriptive for you, the group, and himself. Try "Giving Specific Feedback" to develop your feedback skills.

Observing the Group

A powerful way to demonstrate the effectiveness of group process or group member relationships is to audiotape or videotape a segment of a meeting. Listening to or viewing the tape and then discussing it can motivate group members to improve their performance (Walter, 1975). Many sports teams do this after every game—win or lose—to enable the team to review its mistakes and to see in what situations the players performed effectively.

Before you suggest taping your group, let's explore the effects taping can have on groups. Some group members may be hesitant for their performance to be captured on tape and so become less talkative in the taped meeting. Conversely, some members may use the taping as an opportunity to show off by clowning around, making jokes, or talking more than usual. Usually, such behaviors diminish as the meeting progresses if other members avoid drawing attention to the taping process. Once the camera or tape player is set up, check to make sure it is working correctly and then leave it alone until the end of the meeting or until a group member asks that the recording device be turned off. If a group member makes this request, it should be honored without discussion or explanation.

A tape of your group's interaction provides a record of what you did (or did not) say, as well as how you said it. Hearing how you communicated in the group can help you determine which of your communication skills need improvement. Taping a group's interaction also helps the group as a whole determine how well its members work together. Taped interactions are undeniable testaments to who

SKILL BUILDER

Giving Specific Feedback

Learning to give effective feedback takes practice. Listed here are examples of feedback statements taken from transcripts of group meetings. The examples show both the intent of the feedback and the actual feedback given. After considering the level and type of feedback, evaluate the feedback given. If you think it is lacking in any way or is likely to be ineffective, rewrite the feedback to be more effective.

Level and Type of Feedback	Feedback Given	Your Feedback Suggestion
Individual, positive	"Connor helped us focus on the real arguments when he asked each of us to describe why we felt the way we did."	
Group, positive	"We did a great job, guys."	
Group, negative	"I think we all could do a better job of managing our tempers."	
Evaluative, relational	"Mark, next time, why don't you just bring a gun and shoot Darius? You were mad at him the entire meeting."	
Descriptive, group, task/procedural	"We made four decisions, each with a different decision-making strategy."	
Negative, group, relational, prescriptive	"We have to get along better."	

talked and who did not, to whose ideas were listened to and whose were not, and to what decision procedures worked and what ones did not. Groups, like individuals, can fall into patterns of communication. Periodically, you need to do an assessment of both.

When the group is ready to listen to or view the taped proceedings, it is best to focus on one aspect of the group's communication. For example, you could suggest that your group count the number of times talking turns were interrupted or assess the degree to which group members satisfied the five critical decision-making functions described in Chapter 7.

An analysis of taped proceedings will be more effective if you avoid focusing on specific group members. For example, it is better to analyze how the group maximized use of its leadership than to focus only on the leader's communicator style. In the former case, group members could listen to or view the tape to assess which leadership roles were distributed among group members and whether the group successfully avoided a pattern in which the leader talks after every member contributes. These are issues for which the entire group is responsible.

If you captured the group's interaction on video or DVD, you can also identify the structure of the group's communication network by drawing an **interaction diagram** of who talks to whom. First, draw a diagram to represent where group members are sitting. The first time a group member speaks, draw an arrow to the person to whom the message is directed. If the message is directed to the group as a whole, the arrow points away from the group (for ease in seeing the network). For each subsequent message, place a hatch mark across the arrow.

At the end of the interaction, the diagram will represent both the frequency and flow of messages sent to individual group members and to the group. An example of an interaction diagram is displayed in Figure 12.1. Before each tournament this baseball team meets for a strategy session. In just a few minutes of interaction, it is easy to see how the flow of communication is developing in the team. As expected, the coach and the team leader, who also plays first base, send the most messages to the group and specific group members. Notice also how a subgroup has developed among the right, left, and center fielders, and among the pitcher, catcher, and first base player. This isn't unusual, given that this is a meeting to develop game strategy. Also notice that the coach speaks most frequently to team members who sit across from him. This is not unusual either. The second base player and right fielder sitting immediately next to the coach are out of his line of sight. Finally, notice the second base player. He is the most isolated of team members. Remember, though, that the coach, first base player, center fielder, shortstop, and catcher are sending messages to the group as a whole. While no one is sending messages directly to the second base player, he is receiving the messages that are communicated the group as a whole.

Recall the description of communication networks in Chapter 3. Analyzing the diagram will help you to determine if the group has a centralized or decentralized network. This will reveal the degree of interdependence among members or their subgroups, as well as disparity in the frequency of member contributions or the pattern of group messages. Recall also that who talks to whom is just one type of communication network. An interaction diagram does not capture the quality of members' interactions. Thus, you must analyze the diagram relative to what the group was trying to accomplish in its interactions.

Although the focus of this chapter is on giving feedback to a group in which you participate, observing other groups and creating interaction diagrams of their meetings will make you more aware of how messages are exchanged in group settings. City councils and other governmental groups (such as planning commissions) hold public meetings anyone can attend. In some communities, these meetings are also broadcast on local cable channels. Listening and observing other group meetings can help you identify and recognize patterns of group conversation that, if you were participating, may go unnoticed. Although it's unlikely you'll have the opportunity to provide feedback to these groups, considering what you would give as feedback will strengthen your skills in giving feedback in your groups.

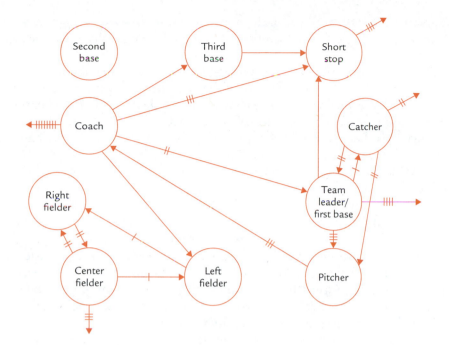

Figure 12.1 Example of an Interaction Diagram

Starting a Group Feedback System

It can be difficult to initiate a feedback system in groups. Often, this will be group members' first experiences with feedback and observation techniques. Here is one way of developing a feedback system that increases incrementally over time until a fully developed system is operating in the group. First, recognize that groups and members do not want to hear only negative feedback—feedback focused on what is *not* working. If a group hears only negative feedback, eventually its ability to function is seriously damaged (Smith & Berg, 1987). Groups and members are more likely to accept negative feedback when positive feedback is also included.

Observation and Feedback Process

For groups that have not used feedback systems before, start by introducing and explaining the concept of feedback at the end of one meeting. Individuals are often hesitant to disclose what they think or feel to others. To ease the group into the feedback process, ask each group member to write down three things that went well in the group session and three things that did not work so well. Focus their efforts on the task and procedural or the group level of feedback—how well the group worked together, how conflicts about which procedure to use kept the group from making a decision, how extensively group members shared the leadership function, or how well the group was able to work through its agenda. The idea here is to get group members started thinking critically about the group's process.

Starting with yourself, ask group members to alternate reading first a positive and then a negative comment until all of the comments are before the group. You may want to ask someone to write these down on a chalkboard or flip chart. Even if every group member chooses the obvious positives and negatives, the concept of feedback has been introduced in the group. Now, with the positives and negatives before the group, ask group members to select one positive that they will remember and use at the next meeting, and one negative that they can work on together at the next meeting. Before adjourning, ask each member to write down specifically what he or she will do to help the group overcome the negative the group selected. With this procedure, you call attention to the feedback process and stimulate members' thinking about how well the group is operating.

At the end of the next meeting, ask group members to repeat the process just described and to also write down three things they did that contributed to the group's success and three things that they could improve on to help the group. Then repeat the round robin disclosure of the group-level task or procedural feedback, both positives and negatives. Again select a positive and a negative for the group to work on at its next meeting. If you feel the group has developed a supportive communication climate and that trust has developed among members, you can practice more personal self-disclosure. Again starting with yourself, reveal one thing you believe you could improve on to help the group. For example, suppose you reveal that you found yourself talking merely to fill the silences between other members' comments. Now state what you intend to do about it: "So, at the next meeting, I'll try to limit my talking to times when I have something important to say that contributes to the conversation. If you think that I'm talking simply to be talking, would one of you remind me? Thanks." Now you have modeled for other group members a process of revealing a personal issue you would like to work on, your idea for improvement, and your commitment to bettering your communication within the group. When you are finished, ask another group member to continue this process.

If your group decides to use interaction diagrams or tapes to provide feedback, be sure to set aside time for the group to collect data and to hear the feedback reports. Groups that do this regularly are often more satisfied with their group experiences. Not only do group members have an opportunity to contribute to the group's decisions and actions, they have an opportunity to actively and positively influence the group's process. Do not be surprised if your group needs two or three sessions to feel comfortable with the feedback and observation process. To help create acceptance for using feedback, also set aside a few minutes to discuss the effectiveness of the feedback tools used. Perhaps the feedback is not accepted because group members are uncomfortable or do not understand how an interaction diagram can help them.

There is one final consideration in designing and implementing your group's feedback system. When relational problems—conflicts among members, leadership struggles—arise, there is a tendency to focus on the people involved in the conflict or leadership struggle. Doing so would prompt you to give relational feedback at the individual level. Before doing so, however, consider if and potentially how group structures—such as norms, communication networks, and role assignments—are contributing to the creation of relational problems. Also consider if the group's context (for example, who the group reports to) could be a source of relational issues. Oftentimes, helping the group restructure itself will eliminate or minimize these issues (Hackman, 2002).

Advice for Giving Feedback

The feedback process is not a blaming process. Rather, it should be used as an awareness strategy, a learning tool, and a goal-setting strategy. Many groups use feedback to help them determine and set goals. In this case, feedback is a motivational tool. Task groups frequently use feedback in this way. Feedback can also be used to help members become more aware of their group interaction performance. When group members have higher awareness, they pay more attention to their communication and its effects on others in the group. If you have been a member of any type of self-help or therapy group, you are familiar with this use of feedback.

For example, the leader of a stop-smoking support group notices that Noah frequently refers to his mother when talking about how he feels: "Noah, I noticed that you again said your mother made you feel that way when you were talking about your feelings of inadequacy. Can you restate how you feel without relying on your mom?" Noah responds, "I'll try. I just feel inadequate about being able to quit smoking. I need someone else to help me. I guess I'm just used to relying on her. Sorry, I wasn't supposed to say that." In this case, the leader's comment about Noah relying on his mother creates an awareness for Noah. It is unlikely that he even realized the extent to which she pops up in his comments.

Feedback can also help group members learn new skills. For example, after your softball team comes in from the field, your coach tells you, the catcher, "You have to have your glove up to catch the ball." Next time your team is in the field, you are sure to keep your eyes on the ball and to get your glove up before it is thrown by the pitcher.

In giving feedback, be sure to use specific examples from the group's interaction. This will focus group members' attention on what needs to be improved or what needs to be repeated. Also, use concrete words. Words like "great," "poor," or "okay" are vague and ambiguous, and using them in your feedback is not likely to help group members very much. More concrete words and phrases like "better than last meeting," "disruptive," and "we are maintaining the same level of effectiveness we achieved at the last meeting" are more meaningful and helpful to others. Finally, when giving feedback, be sure to explain the reasons behind your statements, especially when delivering evaluative or prescriptive feedback. Simply telling a group that it needs to improve how members share the leadership role does not provide enough detail for the group to understand how

Some groups cannot afford miscommunication. Using feedback can help group members communicate effectively and avoid communication failure.

sharing the leadership role was ineffective or how to better utilize members in that role.

When groups use feedback, disagreement should be welcomed and expected. It is not likely that every group member will agree with every one of your observations or views. One reason for integrating feedback into group interaction is to raise critical issues with the group. If you raise issues but do not give group members the opportunity to explore them, you have wasted your energy and the group's time. If other group members are silent after you give feedback, invite their questions and comments. At minimum, ask others if they agree with your view. If they do not or are expressing their disagreement nonverbally, ask questions to solicit their reactions. Statements like "Some of you may disagree with my assessment. If you feel differently, I'd like to hear what you think" may open the floor for discussion of the feedback.

Do not rely on one person as the observer of the group or the person responsible for giving feedback to the group. The feedback process should be jointly owned and operated by all group members. At some meetings, the observation process may be in the hands of one group member in the role of observer. Pass this responsibility around. Feedback can only become a regular part of the group's interaction when the group as a whole is involved in the process. Not only should all group members take responsibility for observing and giving feedback, but they all should understand that everyone is expected to participate in the discussion after feedback is given.

At its best, the feedback process should allow the group to discuss *undiscussable* issues—issues that are relevant to the group's task but that are perceived to have negative or political ramifications if discussed openly in the group (Schwarz, 1994). What issues are undiscussable? In groups, typical undiscussable issues include poor member performance (especially when it is the leader), lack of trust, and personality conflicts. Too frequently, group members deal with these issues by not talking about them or by discussing them with people outside the group. One way to overcome the problem of discussing the undiscussable is to acknowledge to the group that the issue may be considered undiscussable (Schwarz, 1994). "I realize what I'm about to say may be difficult for us to deal with" is an excellent way of raising an undiscussable issue.

What should a feedback system do for your group (SYMLOG Consulting Group, 1986)? Using feedback regularly, group members should be able to discover and correct misperceptions that cause communication failures. Group members should also discover that some aspects of their communication can be improved. And, as group members learn to express their dissatisfactions honestly and tactfully, they will actually come to like one another more. This happens because feedback provides opportunities to develop a greater understanding of why people communicate or behave the way they do. In addition, after using feedback systematically, group members should be able to express their appreciation for and satisfaction with the things they like about their group. This reinforces their ability to work together as a team. Also, using feedback allows group members to develop a clearer picture of their behavior and their communication expectations for one another. And, after using feedback, group members should be able to make decisions more effectively and efficiently. Finally, feedback systems help raise group members' awareness about how groups actually operate.

Summary

An additional responsibility group members have toward the group is to monitor their own and others' performance in the group. By giving feedback, members provide others in the group with information about the actions of individuals and the performance of the group. Feedback serves as an error detection device to help a group identify and begin to solve its interaction problems.

Verbal feedback can be based on observations of the group and accompanied by the use of interaction diagrams or audio- and videotapes of the group. Groups need feedback to overcome common evaluation biases and to help members communicate and perform more effectively. Benefits of initiating feedback in groups include discouraging social loafing, increasing group member identification, and increasing group efficacy.

The style in which feedback is delivered is important. The ability to be direct, frank, and helpful will enable others to accept and use the feedback you provide. And being open-minded, supportive, and positive encourages others to listen to you.

Feedback is identified by its level—task and procedural, relational, individual, or group. Task and procedural feedback focuses on quality and quantity issues and procedures or processes the group uses to complete a group activity. Relational feedback focuses on issues of group climate or environment. Individual feedback focuses on a specific group member. Group feedback focuses on how well the group is developing and maintaining communication processes. There are also three types of feedback—descriptive, evaluative, and prescriptive. Each has a different intent and carries different inferences.

Interaction diagrams provide feedback about who talks to whom and how much. Capturing the group's interaction on audio- or videotape provides powerful feedback. These techniques are strong reminders of what you did or did not say, as well as how you said it.

Groups should design their own feedback systems based on their needs and their comfort level with the different techniques. A group should use only one or a few techniques at a time. A good way to initiate a feedback system is to start slowly and gradually add additional types and levels of feedback as the group becomes comfortable with the process. Regardless of which type of feedback is used, a group should set aside time to hear the feedback reports. Doing so increases group member satisfaction.

Remember that feedback is not a blaming process. Rather, feedback should be used as a goal-setting strategy, an awareness strategy, and a learning tool. Feedback is more effective if specific examples from the group's interaction are given. Use concrete rather than vague words in describing members' interactions. When groups use feedback, disagreement should be welcome because not everyone will agree with all of your views or perceptions. If a group member must assume the role of formal observer, be sure to rotate this responsibility among everyone. At its best, everyone contributes to the feedback process. Feedback also allows a group to discuss *undiscussable* issues. Used effectively, feedback systems raise group members' awareness of their individual contributions to a group and of the overall performance of the group.

Discussion Questions and Exercises

1. Watch a television situation comedy or drama. Identify the main characters and their roles and responsibilities. If you were to design a feedback system for this group, what would you recommend?

2. Many of us are dissatisfied with the communication in our task groups. Knowing that your colleagues are likely be resistant to suggestions for implementing a feedback system, what arguments can you offer (and how might you deliver them) to convince them that a feedback system will be an important step in the group's development?

3. Talk with friends and relatives about their work, social, and community groups. To what extent do these groups integrate feedback into their communication?

Putting It All Together

In any group situation, group members simultaneously manage building relationships with other members, problem solving, making decisions, managing conflict, and designating and responding to leadership for the group. In the text, each of these group processes was explored separately to allow us to examine them in detail. But in group interaction, these processes converge. One statement by a single group member can provide information about several of these task and relational processes. A sequence of conversation can reveal a group's orientation to decision making despite group members not talking about it directly.

Two cases, developed from actual groups, are presented here to encourage you to watch the group conversation unfold, and to examine messages for information about these task and relational processes. The *Technology Team* case presents the group meeting of six business leaders as they discuss ideas for a business plan to stimulate economic growth in their region. Although members of the team have met at civic and community functions, they have not worked together before. Thus, working across organizational boundaries to develop a business plan as part of a civic project forces members to create relationships quickly to accomplish the task they were given. The *Alumni Group* presents the interactions of a group of State University alumni, each of whom now live in another city. Many universities establish alumni groups in major cities throughout the country in an effort to help alumni retain university affiliation. Additionally, alumni chapters recruit potential students and provide leadership in the support and promotion of the university. As with most alumni groups, university affiliation is their commonality. Members of this chapter graduated from State University across a 20-year time span.

Technology Team

To help guide the city's economic development, the chamber of commerce sponsored team meetings around five areas for economic development—biosciences, technology, riverside entertainment, entrepreneurship, and capital formation. After extensive study by a consulting group, nearly 100 community, civic, and business leaders in the region were invited to participate in the five teams, with the goal of producing business strategies for economic development. Individuals were identified for their expertise and known for willingness to work collaboratively across organizational boundaries. Thus, the chamber organizers believed that those invited could interact effectively and create innovative ideas. Each group had 90 days in which to meet and complete their business plan. Based upon the consultant's recommendation, Paul and Cathy were asked to cochair the technology team. Originally, the team had 11 members, but three dropped out after the first meeting citing scheduling conflicts, and two members couldn't attend today's meeting. Let's drop in on the technology team at its second meeting.

The group members are as follows:

- April, Vice President of Strategy and Development, ExcelTel
- Darryl, Senior Account Executive, Marketing Strategies
- Ed, Vice President of Technology Development, Incite
- Emily, Dean of Students, City Tech College
- Gene, VP of Internal Communications, HyperStrategies
- Paul, CIO, Classic Data Imaging

PAUL: April? Can you call the meeting together?

APRIL: Sure, Paul. Okay folks, let's get down to business. We are supposed to have only one more meeting after this one and we don't have our business plan completed yet.

PAUL: Okay, I've got the draft of the business plan, but I'm not sure that each of you has seen it.

DARRYL: Did you send it out over email? I'm not sure I got mine.

GENE: I got mine. (He returns to reading messages on his PDA).

ED: I didn't get one either . . . well, maybe my secretary has it. But I don't.

PAUL: Not a problem. I have extra copies. April? Will you pass them around (as he hands her the copies).

While the copies are passed around, group members get up to get lunch that is served as a buffet at one end of the meeting room. It take the group about 8 minutes to get lunch and return their seats. Everyone but Paul gets lunch.

PAUL: You can see what we have here—it's sketchy, but based on the pilot project Classic conducted up north. Everyone's interested in health issues. But, frankly, employers care more about health care than health. Health care is costing employers a tremendous amount of money. Essentially, no one system is set up to deal with health care. Right now that's parsed out based on employer and health care insurer. Public health departments are also interested in tracking health care information because they believe that will give them an edge on preventive treatments and epidemics. What do you think, Ed?

ED: No doubt some type of database would be helpful. But I don't want to be in it!

PAUL: (his voice reveals that he his stunned by Ed's remark) Okay, let's review the slides I brought to our last meeting.

An audible sigh from others in the room as Paul walks to the podium and brings up the PowerPoint presentation they saw at their first meeting. Gene gets up to take a phone call in the hall.

APRIL: (to the group) As cochairs of this team, I was excited when Paul introduced me to the idea of data integration, that's Paul's vernacular for making our region the hub of data capture and data processing to create a unique relational database . . . creating capabilities to integrate health care information across a number of platforms.

PAUL: Thanks, April. Okay, one more time: Each person uses technology in a variety of ways. I use my ATM and credit cards, I swipe my ID card when I go in and out of the gym and my office. I present yet another ID card when I go to the doctor or get prescriptions at the pharmacy. When I go to the emergency room, that's yet another database in which my medical information is entered. Each of these databases is separate; they are not linked together in any meaningful way.

EMILY: (as she enters the room, Gene follows her) Sorry I'm late. I just caught the tail end of that. Are you making your *pitch* again, Paul?

PAUL: Yes, I was just explaining about the relational database idea.

EMILY: Well, go on . . . (she waves her hand at him as if to give him the floor)

PAUL: So, if each of the data sources were connected we would be able to . . .

EMILY: (Interrupting him) Yes, we know . . . create a database with literally every piece of information known about your health and what health care you've had. Is that what you (to other members of the group) want?

ED: If I take myself out of the equation, then this sounds like a great idea. Linking a person's doctor visits with medical records could help our health departments do a better job of providing services. Just think of it! Had we known this information, we could have created a priority list of who should get the limited supply of flu shots and contacted them— instead of having people wait in line to be told that the supply ran out. My mom waited in line for over 3 hours. But when I think about my information in the database, that's another story.

PAUL: Oh, come on Ed. This is the wave of the future. You're in more databases than you know now. People are making marketing decisions based upon the loyalty card you're using at the grocery store. Why not let people use data to make decisions that matter for your health?

ED: Yeah, I use a loyalty card at the grocery story. But I'm not an idiot. I didn't give them my name and address. I don't want people tracking what I buy and when I buy it. All they know is some person has a particular buying pattern. They don't know it's me. Besides, I thought you said earlier that employers were more concerned about how much our health care is costing them. Are you pitching this from a perspective that advantages employers or advantages employees?

APRIL: (matter-of-factly) I think Paul's trying to convince us of the benefits of a relational database with our health information.

ED: Sure he is—because his company would benefit from it. And, yes, there would be benefits, but what about the downside of people knowing my personal health information.

DARRYL: But they know it already (exasperatedly).

ED: Yes, but each database is separate—they're not linked together. And, right now, I'm in control of who has that information. If Paul has his way, our team is going to recommend that all databases with any health information—from our doctors, hospitals, health insurers, employers, pharmacies—will be linked together. I just don't like it.

EMILY: We know the spiel, Paul. You just haven't convinced us. We can see the business applications, we can see the public health implications, and . . . but you can't see the potential negative effect on people's lives. And you haven't explained how having the relational database will reduce health care costs.

GENE: Or the ethics of it.

PAUL: The ethics? What could be more ethical than notifying you of a clinical trial for a disease you have?

GENE: That's my point, Paul! I should be the one making my health care decisions. Not someone else!

The group becomes silent, as if waiting for the air to clear.

APRIL: (With an apprehensive voice) I just want to remind everyone that we are supposed to be creating a business plan for one to three ideas that we can take forward to the strategic planning board. Is everyone okay if we make this our first idea?

EMILY: First idea? It's our only idea so far. No, let me correct that. It's the *only* idea Paul has let us discuss.

DARRYL: Sorry, Paul. I can't support this yet. Ed's right. This has great business applications but when you look at it on a personal level—it's terrifying.

PAUL: Come on, Darryl. You're company would be the first to sign up to use it.

DARRYL: Certainly there's a good deal of information that would be helpful to us. For example, to know how many people visit the doctor's office or emergency room for the flu. Or to know how many people are taking prescription medicine. . . . We could target our marketing to those folks to get them to switch to one of the over-the-counter products of one of our pharma clients. Sure. But how can we use the information in the relational database and not attach people's identities to it? You haven't explained that yet either.

EMILY: And he can't. Or won't (said under her breath).

APRIL: Okay, folks, my job is to keep the team moving ahead. Is there another idea for discussion . . . or, Paul, do you want to keep the floor?

PAUL: Sure, thanks, April. Okay, now back to the relational database. It's easy. Our programmers can parcel out information. As long as everyone has a unique identifier, then their names never need to be attached to the data. We could spot health trends by region, even neighborhood. Think of the public health ramifications.

DARRYL: That unique identification number? That's our Social Security number and we can see how easily that's been abused. Most organizations now create their own ID numbers for employees.

PAUL: That's my point. Besides your Social Security number, everyone should have one other unique identifier. In reality, everything should be consolidated under one number.

DARRYL: But, Paul, then someone who puts the relational database together has to know the connection between my identity and the identifier.

PAUL: No, no, no (downplaying Darryl's concern). We can create security around the whole thing.

EMILY: Paul, you're missing Darryl's point. For there to be a connection between an identity and a number, SOMEONE has to know both pieces of information. Our federal government knows who has which Social Security number. How could someone not know the connection for this database?

ED: I'm skeptical too. Why would people want a private company to hold that type of information?

PAUL: Because the federal government doesn't want to get into the business of all-encompassing relational databases.

ED: Then maybe there's a reason they don't. We've just gone through this HIPAA [Health Insurance Portability and Accountability Act] thing. How many releases did you sign this year?

PAUL: That's not the same.

ED: You're right. What you're proposing is worse.

APRIL: Okay, we're only got about 45 minutes left in this meeting. I need to report on our progress.

EMILY: I'm going to make a proposal. Paul, why don't you go ahead and develop this idea and let the rest of us focus on the other ideas. We have to have three. Is that right, April?

APRIL: Yes, three. Well, one to three. The strategic planning board didn't specify beyond that. I can ask if you want me to.

Paul leaves the room to answer his cell phone.

EMILY: Well, let's make it three. Ed, Darryl, Gene . . . do you have other ideas we can take forward?

GENE: Thanks for asking, Emily. The way I see it . . . we could be the heroes of this economic development project or the fools. Paul's idea is intriguing, but not fleshed out. And we don't have the right people at the table to tell us about the pitfalls.

EMILY: Yes, I can see that we need legal counsel, minimally, and probably someone from public health.

GENE: And the CEOs of several of the hospitals.

ED: Yeah, Gene, you're on to something. It's not the tech part of this that's problematic. Actually, that might be quite simple. It's the social implications that are troubling. Who has access to the data? To what information? For what purposes? Minimally, I'd have to know those answers before I would agree to be a part of this relational database Paul is trying to sell us on.

GENE: And how are we going to sell people on it? Not the organizations, the advantages to them are obvious. But people in the community. How will they respond to this idea?

EMILY: We're missing a lot of information. How can we divide up this task and get information before our next meeting?

Paul walks back into the meeting, displaying a shocked face that the group is having a discussion in his absence. The group quickly becomes silent.

APRIL: (Hesitantly) Paul, the group has a different perspective on the project. I think . . . I think you should listen to what they have to say.

Discussion Questions

1. Who is leading this group? What evidence do you have for your selection? What style of leadership is that person or persons displaying?

2. What factors are influencing the group's discussion and deliberation?

3. How would you assess the communication competence of each group member?

4. What is the climate of the group?

5. Have any norms developed in the group?

6. What conflicts are group members aware of? How are they managing these conflicts?

7. What conflicts might develop in the future?

8. What decision-making procedure would benefit the group?

9. What is the communication network among group members? Are there subgroups?

10. What suggestions would you make to the cochairs for managing future meetings?

11. What feedback would you give this group? **Who should give the feedback?**

12. What is the most important issue facing the group at this point? Relationship building, problem solving, decision making, managing

conflict, designating a leader, or responding to leadership? How would you put these group processes in order of importance for the group?

Alumni Group

State University alumni living in Central City have a formed an official alumni chapter. The group meets every weekend State University plays football or basket-ball, usually at a member's home, to watch the game. Outside of these two sport seasons, the group is not very active. Occasionally, the president of the Central City State University Alumni Group will host a barbeque, but this isn't an official alumni group event and not all members are invited. To cope with the dwindling participation, the president believes that the group needs more activities—more reasons to come together and share the State University spirit.

Terry decides that one way to increase participation and, perhaps, recruit more members would be to host a high school student planning to attend State University. Terry plans to have university recruiters identify a scholarship-deserving student who lives in Central City and has been accepted to State University. With the permission of the student's parents, Terry wants to the alumni group to hold fundraising activities to provide financial support for this student. He believes this is a great idea because students are accepted in early February and activities to help the student could be started while the group is engaged in basketball season and then give the group a reason to meet throughout the summer. Part of the reason for low participation and few new members, Terry determines, is that alumni not interested in sports aren't motivated to join the Central City chapter. Moreover, by focusing solely on sports, the alumni group is not living up to the chapter mission of helping promote the university by recruiting and providing financial support for students and the university.

Before the next alumni meeting, Terry talks with State University's alumni association and gets initial approval for his idea. The alumni advisor warns him, however, that the group must be willing to take on enough fundraisers to provide substantial support for the student. The group must be willing to raise at least $5,000. Terry introduces the idea at the group's first fall meeting.

The group members

- Terry, president of the alumni chapter for the last 4 years, and host of today's social event
- Alicia, member for more than 15 years, but generally comes to only one or two events a year
- Mark, a member for 5 years and classmate of Sam
- Sam, a member for 5 years, and its most vocal supporter
- Rami, recently moved to Central City; has only talked with Terry over the phone before today's event
- Cliff, a member for 3 years

TERRY: Thanks for coming. It's going to be a great game.

ALICIA: Thanks for having me. Here's my contribution (as she hands him a pot of chili).

TERRY: Great . . . can I talk with you for a few minutes in the kitchen?

ALICIA: Sure, let me get my coat off and I'll follow you in there.

Terry and Alicia move into the kitchen where three other alumni group members are fixing snacks. Six other alumni are in Terry's game room watching the pre-game activities.

TERRY: Alicia, you know Sam and Mark, right? And this is Rami.

ALICIA: Hi, everybody. I haven't seen you two (she nods in Sam and Mark's direction) since last spring. Rami, when did you graduate from State?

RAMI: Last year. I'm new to the city and thought this would be a good way to make friends.

TERRY: You're absolutely right my friend. State University alums are alums *and* friends.

Rami displays surprise at Terry's attempt at familiarity.

ALICIA: So, Terry, what did you want to talk about?

TERRY: (to the group in the kitchen) Well, I'd like for the chapter to do more than just get together for sporting events. I'd like to run an idea by you. What if we had fundraisers so we could give some financial support to a State student?

SAM: How much money are we talking about?

TERRY: Five thousand.

MARK: That's quite a bit for a group this small. What do we have? Twenty members at most?

TERRY: Well, yes, but I also thought that if we did different activities throughout the year we could also grow our membership.

SAM: Grow our membership? I like our group. Do we really want newcomers?

Rami looks down to avoid eye contact with Sam.

ALICIA: (Clears her throat.) Well, some new folks might be good for us. I don't often come to meetings because I've got other things to do on the weekend. I guess I came today mostly out of loyalty because it's the first game of the season. Actually, I could participate more when school's not in session. It's hard to find a babysitter on school weekends.

MARK: Why $5,000?

TERRY: I talked with an alumni advisor. He suggested that $5,000 was the minimum amount to provide a scholarship for a student. And we can award it to someone from Central City. The alumni association will help us identify a student from here who's already been accepted at State.

SAM: So, the kid is going to come to our meetings?

TERRY: Not necessarily. But part of our charter is to recruit students and provide financial support for the university.

ALICIA: I like this idea. You might get more women and people with families to participate if there was something other than football or basketball.

SAM: Man, the game is starting!

Terry, Sam, Mark, and Alicia move into the game room to watch the game with the others. Rami trails them. At halftime, Terry restarts the conversation.

TERRY: So, as I was telling the others, I'd like us to consider other activities so we can meet throughout the year.

MARK: (Now seemingly behind the idea) What would you guys think about doing other activities besides meeting on football and basketball weekends?

ALICIA: I, for one, would approve. When I do come, I'm usually the only woman here.

TERRY: It would be good for us to meet for other reasons. I'm suggesting that we hold fundraisers so we can provide financial support for a student going to State.

MARK: Yeah, he said we could recruit a student from Central City.

TERRY: No, not recruit . . . well, I suppose we could do that as well. But, actually, State will help us identify someone from here that has already been accepted.

CLIFF: You mean hold raffles, car washes, poker parties. . . .

TERRY: Whoa, Cliff. I meant that we could get together and seek donations from area businesses.

ALICIA: Why would area businesses want to support a university in another state?

TERRY: (realizing his blunder) Well, the student would be from here. . . .

The group becomes quiet as it is obvious that Rami has moved toward the front so he is closer to the television. He is intently focused on the halftime activities, and lets out a low "whoa!" when the drum major does a backbend to touch his hat to the ground behind him.

RAMI: The new guy is pretty good.

ALICIA: Rami, you seem to know what you're talking about.

RAMI: (mildly) Well . . . yes . . . I was in the band.

CLIFF: At State?

RAMI: (quietly) Yes.

CLIFF: What instrument did you play?

RAMI: I didn't. I was the drum major.

ALICIA: Ohmygosh! Rami, you were the drum major at State?

RAMI: Yes.

MARK: When?

RAMI: Last year. I was in the drum major squad my first two years and then the assistant drum major. Last year I was the drum major.

ALICIA: I can't believe. We watched you last year.

RAMI: Thank you, Alicia. It was an honor.

MARK: Rami, we could use you as a centerpiece of a fundraiser. That backbend thing is world famous. People would want to meet you.

RAMI: Thank you. But I'm just here to make friends. I would be glad to contribute money to a scholarship.

TERRY: Why didn't you say you were the drum major?

RAMI: I *was* the drum major. It doesn't matter now.

The group is now energized with its new member. People crowd around Rami asking him about the band's floating script formations and marching in the Rose Bowl and the presidential inaugural parades.

SAM: Okay. Okay. Sssssh everyone. The game's back on.

Terry waits until the group is settled again in the front of the television and then motions Mark, Alicia, Rami, and Cliff back into the kitchen.

TERRY: What do you think? Should we pursue the scholarship idea?

CLIFF: I'm interested . . . but some members (motioning back to the group watching the game) are only interested in the social events.

ALICIA: Well, fundraisers could be social.

CLIFF: No, I mean they're only interested in the social events that have to do with the team playing.

ALICIA: Oh.

TERRY: Well, everyone doesn't participate in these get-togethers. But I bet we could attract members who used to come but dropped out, as well as new members with other activities . . . and raising scholarship funds would actually achieve some objective.

MARK: Don't say that too loud. The group in the other room might rush you! And Sam would lead them.

TERRY: Very funny. I mean it.

RAMI: The five of us could be a steering committee and propose ideas to the group.

ALICIA: That's a good idea, Rami.

RAMI: I benefited from a band scholarship while at State. Without it, I wouldn't have been able to go full-time.

CLIFF: I'm in. But I do want to raise this concern. If we get too far away from social events, the group will dissolve.

MARK: I agree, but I don't see why fundraising activities can't also be social . . . and fun.

TERRY: Can we meet next week, say Friday after work to really start talking about this?

SAM: (From the other room) Hey, guys! What are you doing in there? We just scored another touchdown!

TERRY: We're coming. We're coming (as the group in the kitchen returns to be with the others).

Discussion Questions

1. Who is leading this group? What evidence do you have for your selection? What style of leadership is that person or persons displaying?

2. What factors are influencing the group's discussion and deliberation?

3. How would you assess the communication competence of each group member?

4. What is the climate of the group?

5. What evidence is there that norms have developed in the group?

6. What conflicts are group members aware of? How are they managing these conflicts?

7. What conflicts might develop in the future?

8. What decision-making procedure would benefit a group like this?

9. What is the communication network among group members? If there are subgroups, what are the relationships among the subgroups?

10. What suggestions would you make to Terry when he holds other social events for the alumni group at his home?

11. What suggestions would you make to the subgroup when it meets to discuss the fundraising ideas?

12. Is feedback appropriate for this group? If so, who should give it?

13. What is the most important issue facing the group at this point? Relationship building, problem solving, decision making, managing conflict, designating a leader, or responding to leadership? How would you put these group processes in order of importance for the group?

14. How is this group balancing its task and relational dimensions?

Appendix
Creating and Delivering
Team Presentations

You've been assigned a team presentation. Now what do you do? Whether you are a first-time or experienced presenter, presenting as a group creates some new challenges! This appendix is divided into three sections focusing on developing, preparing for, and making the presentation, respectively.

Developing Your Presentation

Thinking About Your Presentation

- As a group, outline or map your presentation. Decide who will be responsible for each part and for each transition. Even though individual members might specialize in various parts of the presentation, every group member is responsible for all of the material in the presentation.
- Consider the unique talents of your team members.
- All team members should have a part in the presentation.
- Consider your audience in developing the presentation material.
- Watch the local news for examples of how to make transitions between parts of the presentation.
- If you have been given 25 minutes for the presentation, plan on filling 20 of it. Presentations seldom start on time—perhaps because latecomers are accommodated, the previous class let out late, or a few announcements are made. It's better to finish early and have time for questions than to shove 25 minutes worth of material into 20 minutes or to run overtime.
- Ask yourself, What is the purpose of the presentation? to persuade? inspire? inform? teach? instruct? entertain?
- Develop your material with three specific main points you want the audience to learn from your presentation. Outline or map these points before you begin, deliver the three points, and summarize these points.
- Organize your points in one of these ways: (a) from simple to complex, (b) in chronological order, (c) from general to specific, or (d) from problem to solution.

Preparing for the Presentation

Setting Up the Room

- Ask your instructor if you can rearrange the room for your presentation. Changing how the room is set up creates interest and signals that something different is about to happen. If you do so, it should be done before any class members arrive.
- Try some of these shapes: a U-shape, angled tables or chairs, amphitheatre style, a circle with a large opening. Or turn all of the chairs in a different direction, making another wall the temporary *front* of the classroom.
- Don't use the lectern just because one is there. If you're not going to use it, remove it. A lectern can create an unnecessary barrier between you and your audience.

Using Visual Aids

- Make a commitment to using visual aids in your presentation. They add value to your presentation and increase your effectiveness.
- Use visual aids to serve as your notes, help maintain audience interest, underscore your points, and keep you focused.
- For every visual aid you use, ask whether it is worth it and what objective it serves. You and your group members are the presentation. The visual aids are just helpers.
- Don't use too many visual aids—no more than one per minute.
- Don't turn the lights out and show slides or overheads. This will only put your audience to sleep!
- Use visuals as reminders to yourself, but don't read them word for word—the audience can do that!
- If you have a list of concepts on an overhead, reveal each item as you talk about it. Otherwise, your audience will read the list while you are reporting on the first item. Revealing concepts item by item also helps you control your thinking and your rate of speaking.
- Simplify. Use the simplest visual aid that gets your point across—easily and clearly.
- Think horizontally; people are used to viewing television.
- Use color; it makes a greater impact.
- Include no more than four colors per visual.
- Use dark print on a light background or light print on a dark background.
- Maintain the same background color throughout your presentation.
- Don't use red for text. Use it to highlight with bullets, arrows, and so on.

- Avoid red/green contrasts; some people are color-blind.
- In planning a color scheme, use darker colors on the bottom, medium colors in the middle, and lighter colors on top.
- Use short titles.
- Use plenty of white space. Don't crowd the slide or chart.
- Use graphics, charts, pictures, audio, or video to help communicate complex ideas.
- Use pie charts to show the distribution of a whole into its component parts (for example, budgets or times).
- Use bar charts to represent quantity by the length or height of the bar. Use color-coding to help audience members interpret the bars (for example, red for this year and yellow for last year).
- Make sure the visual aids use a consistent form, color scheme, and type style so the result is a *group* presentation.
- Have all group members proofread all visual aids regardless of who designed or made them.
- Rehearse with the visual aids.

Preparing and Using Flip Charts

- Recognize that flip charts are one of the cheapest and most effective presentation aids (they can't break down; they allow the lights to be at their brightest). They can be prepared ahead of time or used spontaneously during the presentation.
- Don't use a flip chart if there are more than 30 audience members—not all members will be able to see it!
- Leave a blank page at the beginning of your flip chart pad.
- Staple a blank sheet behind each flip chart page you are going to use. This way writing won't bleed through, and it makes the pages easier to turn.
- Don't think you have to be an artist to use a flip chart. Well-spaced, large letters and simple figures and diagrams work well on flip charts.
- Use very light blue lines—which you can see but the audience can't—to help you keep your lettering straight and all the same height (2-inch height is recommended).
- As a rule of thumb, include no more than six lines per flip chart. Begin each item with a bullet so audience members can tell where to stop and start.
- Use two flip charts. One can be prepared ahead of time, and the other can be used spontaneously during the presentation.
- Place flip charts to the side of the presentation space. The presenter is more important than the flip chart.

Using PowerPoint Presentations

- Ensure that your disk, CD, or memory stick works with the computer you will be using.
- Ensure that the version of PowerPoint in which you created the presentation is the version installed on the computer. Not all versions are compatible.
- Have a *welcome* slide with the title of your presentation up when the audience comes in.
- The last slide should be a prompt for questions or provide contact information for the speakers.
- Consider having someone other than the speaker responsible for slide transitions (unless a wireless mouse is available). That way, the speaker is not trapped behind equipment.
- Incorporate charts, graphics, pictures, animation, and video to help make your point. Don't, however, let these features overshadow what you have to say.
- If your presentation is more textual than graphic, try using circles, squares, or triangles to group text together for more impact.
- For text, use the 6×6 rule: no more than six words per line, and no more than six lines per slide.
- Use uppercase and lowercase text.
- Put a paper copy of each slide on the floor. If you can read it while standing up, the type is probably large enough. If not, the type is too small.
- As you show a new slide, allow a second or two for the visual impact to sink in. Then give the explanation.

Creating Overhead Transparencies

- Use PowerPoint or another graphics program to make your overheads.
- If you want to write on your overheads during the presentation, be sure to use pens made especially for this (otherwise, what you've written is permanent!).
- Find a color printer to print your transparencies in color. Or use colored transparencies (if so, make sure to use only black printing) in a printer or in a copier.
- Print out a set of your overheads on plain paper for proofreading *before* putting your expensive transparencies into the printer or copier!
- To help make transparency handling easier, put each transparency in its own clear page protector. No need to remove the transparency from the page protector—the light will shine through just fine.

- Have your transparencies in order. Don't shuffle them during the presentation.
- Have a transparency on the overhead projector *before* you turn it on. Audience members should never see a lighted, blank screen.
- Leave the projector on while you're switching transparencies.
- Turn the projector off immediately after your last transparency, and step in front of the machine.
- If you won't be using the overhead projector for a few minutes, turn it off!
- Use teamwork in handling transparencies. You shouldn't have to ask a group member for the next overhead. Build those signals into your presentation.
- Make a group decision about how transparencies will be handled: from the right or from the left? Everyone should use the same system so transparencies do not get mixed up or out of order.
- Practice with an overhead projector. This is the best time to find the correct light level so that audience members can see the transparency and you!

Using Video

- Use no more than 2–3 minutes of video at a time.
- Know how to work the pause and stop buttons.
- Test the video out on others before you show it to your audience. Is it as funny or moving or dramatic as you think?
- Check the volume before the presentation.
- Queue up your video beforehand.
- If possible, bring both VHS and DVD copies.

Using Handouts

- Check for accuracy (grammar, punctuation, spelling).
- Don't reproduce your visual aids and distribute them at the beginning of the presentation. You'll be sure to lose your audience!
- If you must use a handout because of complexity or detail, distribute it when you come to that part of the presentation.
- Make sure the handout matches the visual aid you use in the presentation.
- If you want audience members to have a complete set of handouts, tell them they'll be available after your presentation, and hand them out as they go out the door.

Using Numbers and Statistics

- Round numbers off so the audience can remember them. Which would you remember better: nearly $5 million or $4,789,187?

- Use the most recent statistics you can find. Don't present 1990 figures in 2005. What were you doing in 1990?

Preparing Your Notes

- Put your notes on 5 × 7 note cards. They are easy to hold, and they don't make noise.

- Alternatively, try putting your notes on the four sides of an empty manila file folder. You can keep your handouts or overheads in it before and after the presentation.

Working as a Team

- Act like a team. A group presentation isn't a series of individual presentations.

- Agree on who will handle questions from the audience. Generally, those who presented the material should respond to the question.

- Identify who will do which parts.

- Work out transitions between sections. Use the next speaker's name in handing off—for example, "That covers decision-making groups. Now Ray will cover families as groups."

- Assign one member to keep track of the time during the presentation. Have preplanned cues for signaling information about time.

- Focus on the audience. Make the presentation to the audience, not your group.

- When you're not speaking, look at the person who is speaking.

- Be sure to tell the audience the agenda for your presentation. When multiple people speak, the audience needs a road map.

- Rehearse as a team.

Rehearsing Your Presentation

- Do not play it by ear. Your audience deserves a rehearsed presentation.

- Recognize that writing out the presentation is not the same as rehearsing it.

- Keep in mind that rehearsals tend to run shorter than the actual presentation. A 20-minute rehearsal usually means a 25- to 30-minute presentation.

- Rehearse using all of the visual aids and equipment you plan to include in the presentation. There is no substitute for a dress rehearsal.
- Have all members do their parts as planned. Filling in for someone at rehearsal increases the likelihood that you'll fill in for him or her at the presentation. Again, there is no substitute for a dress rehearsal.
- Review all visual aids for spelling, grammar, and punctuation.
- Check the voice levels of all presenters. Ask a couple of friends (but not anyone who will be part of the audience) to help you by playing the role of audience members during your rehearsals. They can give you valuable feedback.
- If you can, rehearse in the room you'll give your presentation in.
- Talk about what you'll wear for the presentation. You won't look like a group if four of you show up in dress clothes and one of you is in jeans. Clothing should be coordinated, but it doesn't have to match.
- Know that the best rehearsal is a video rehearsal. Get a friend to tape your presentation, or set up a camera with a wide-angle shot. Video is the most powerful tool for identifying flaws. If you don't have access to video, at least record the rehearsal on audiotape. You'll be amazed at what you'll hear.

Delivering the Presentation

Introduction

- Introduce all members of the group.
- Be sure to tell audience members why your topic is important. Give them at least three reasons they should pay attention to what you have to say.
- Capture the audience's attention by answering the question "What's in it for me?"

Communicating Verbally

- Don't start with humor or a joke.
- Don't apologize or make excuses for anything or anyone.
- Use specific language—for example, "We can increase membership by 60 percent" rather than "We can increase membership a lot."
- Use vivid language, paint word pictures, and use metaphors.
- Use action words.
- Use short, simple words.
- Eliminate clichés or overused phrases.
- Think of your presentation as a conversation with audience members.

- Anchor new information in something familiar to the audience.
- Use transitions:

"That brings us to our next point."

"Now that we've discussed X, let's talk about Y."

"So far we've covered decision making and leadership. Now let's take a look at conflict."

"In addition to consensus building, we need to address conflict."

"To begin, let's take a look at . . ."

"The next important factor is . . ."

"That's the first reason to be flexible as a leader. The next reason is . . ."

"Finally, let's consider . . ."

"In conclusion, . . ."

"To summarize . . ."

"We'd like to leave you with this thought."

Communicating Nonverbally

- Move around when you talk.
- Use hand movements and arm gestures.
- Vary the quality of your voice. It's easy to do this if you avoid the straight presentation of information. It's easier to be expressive when you use analogies, tell stories, give demonstrations, and ask questions.
- Make eye contact with your audience.
- Manage your nonverbal adaptors.
- If you're using visual aids, turn and look at the aid to get the point securely in your mind. Then turn to the audience and address the point to them. Keep looking at the audience until you are finished and are ready to address the next point on the visual aid.

Handling the Question-and-Answer Session

- While you're developing the presentation, make a list of questions you believe audience members will ask. Prepare an answer for each one.
- Be aware that you're likely to be met with silence if you ask, "Are there any questions?" Rather, ask, "Are there any questions about how leaders should be flexible?" or "Are there any questions about the twelve-step approach?"
- If you ask the audience a question, pause for a moment to give members time to think of one.

- If there are no questions, continue by saying "One question we had when we started our research was . . ." or "One of the most frequent questions asked about gun control is. . . ."

- When an audience member asks you a question, in your response restate the question so all audience members can hear it. Many times others in the audience haven't heard the question, which means you're responding to something that doesn't make any sense to them.

- Assuming the Q & A session happens at the end of the presentation, after the last question thank the audience for the questions and then summarize and close out the presentation.

Handling Interruptions from the Audience

- If you are interrupted by a question that will be answered later as part of your planned presentation, say, "Dale, I'm coming to that in about 2 minutes" or "The answer is yes, and I'll explain it fully in just a few minutes."

- If you are interrupted by a question that will not be part of your planned presentation, say, "Dale, that's a good question. I'd like to answer it at the end of the presentation."

- If you are interrupted by a question or comment that you prefer not to answer publicly, say, "Dale, that's interesting" (or "I hadn't thought of that"). "Let's talk about it after the presentation."

Suggested Reading

DiResta, D. (1998). *Knockout presentations: How to deliver your message with power, punch, and pizzazz.* Worcester, MA: Chandler House Press.

Peoples, D. A. (1992). *Presentations plus* (2nd ed.). New York: Wiley.

Spencer, B. H., & Angus, K. B. (1998). Demonstrating knowledge: The use of presentations in the college classroom. *Journal of Adolescent & Adult Literacy, 41,* 658–666.

Worley, R., & Dyrud, M. (Eds.). (2004). Presentation and the PowerPoint problem. *Business Communication Quarterly, 67,* 78–94.

Worley, R., & Dyrud, M. (Eds.). (2004). Presentation and the PowerPoint problem—Part II. *Business Communication Quarterly, 67,* 214–231.

Glossary

abstract A type of word that paints a broad generalization.

acceptance level Criterion for evaluating a decision; the decision must be not only technically correct but usable by others.

accommodating A win-lose conflict management strategy exemplified by trying to satisfy the other's concerns.

active listening A style of listening and feedback in which a receiver paraphrases what the speaker has said and asks questions to confirm what was said.

affection The need to establish psychologically close relationships with others.

affective conflict A type of conflict based on social or relational issues.

affiliative constraints A constraint to decision making based on the relationships among members of the group; fearing that relationships will deteriorate, some group members will exert undue influence on other group members.

agenda A list of activities or topics to be considered at a group meeting; should also include starting and stopping times, the location of the meeting, the attendees, and the overall goal of the meeting, as well as the specific goal of each agenda item and any preparations that group members should make.

animated A dimension of communicator style exemplified by expressive nonverbal behaviors and easy-to-read emotional states.

appropriateness A criterion of communication competence that is achieved when communication does not violate behavioral expectations, weaken relationships among communicators, or threaten any member's self-esteem.

area of freedom The degree of authority or responsibility a group has in completing its tasks or activities.

argument The task-related skill of presenting reasons for the position group members support or reject.

artifacts Objects used to convey nonverbal messages.

attentive A dimension of communicator style exemplified by letting others know they are being listened to; empathic.

avoiding conflict management strategy A nonconfrontive strategy for managing conflict, based on verbal, physical, or psychological withdrawal.

bona fide group perspective A theoretical frame that illuminates the relationship of the group to its context or environment by recognizing a group's permeable and fluid boundaries and the time and space characteristics of its interactions.

brainstorming A group procedure designed to help groups generate creative ideas.

centralized communication network Communication network that imposes restrictions on who can talk to whom and for which one or two group members control those restrictions.

chronemics The use of time; conveys nonverbal messages.

climate building The relational skill of helping group members become comfortable with one another and feel valued in decision making.

coalition formation Phenomenon that occurs when one member takes sides with another against yet another member of the group; creates an imbalance of power; can only occur with at least three group members.

code of conduct A group document that describes behaviors appropriate for the group.

coercive power A type of power resulting from the expectation that one group member can be punished by another.

cognitive conflict A type of conflict involving disagreement over interpretations or analyses of information or data; also known as *judgment conflict*.

cognitive constraints Constraints on decision making based on difficulties or inadequacies in group members' abilities to process information; occur when information or time is limited, or when the decision is more than group members can comfortably or normally handle.

coherence Attribute of group interaction when members' utterances are connected in an orderly and meaningful way.

cohesiveness The degree to which members desire to remain in the group.

collaboration A conflict management strategy based on parties sharing a superordinate goal of solving the problem even though their initial ideas for how to solve it differ.

collective efficacy A group member's belief that his or her group can be effective; developed by sharing ideas about group tasks and activities with other group members.

collectivistic A type of culture in which group work or teamwork is valued over individual accomplishment.

communication apprehension The fear or anxiety associated with either actual or anticipated communication with other people.

communication climate The atmosphere that results from group members' use of verbal and nonverbal communication and listening skills; can be defensive or supportive.

communication competence The ability and willingness to participate responsibly in a communication transaction exemplified by maximizing shared meaning with other group members and communicating with both appropriateness and effectiveness.

communication competency approach to leadership A model for leadership based on three principles: (1) Leadership is action that helps a group overcome barriers or obstacles, (2) leadership occurs through interaction, and (3) there is a set of skills or competencies that individuals use to exercise leadership in groups.

communication network The interaction pattern or flow of messages between and among group members; creates structure for the group based on patterns of who talks to whom.

communication overload Communication that is too extensive or complex and that comes from too many sources; causes stress and confusion among group members.

communication underload Communication that is infrequent and simple; causes group members to feel disconnected from the group.

communicator style The impression one leaves with others after communicating; includes the following dimensions: dominant, dramatic, animated, relaxed, attentive, open, friendly, contentious, and precise.

competing A distributive conflict management strategy exemplified by forcing; emphasizes one party winning at the other party's expense.

competitive conflict Polarizations; one side winning with the other side losing.

compromising A conflict management style; an intermediate strategy between cooperativeness and assertiveness; compromising may settle the problem but will also offer incomplete satisfaction for both parties.

concrete A word that is specific and clear.

conflict Situation in which at least two interdependent parties capable of invoking sanctions on each other oppose each other; based on real or perceived power; occurs because parties have mutually desired but mutually unobtainable objectives.

conflict aftermath The feelings that group members have developed as a result of a conflict episode; the legacy of the conflict interaction.

conflict management The relational skill of keeping group members focused on task-related ideas rather than personal differences.

connectivity The degree to which several groups share overlapping tasks or goals.

consensus A decision procedure in which each group member agrees with the decision or in which group members' individual positions are close enough that they can support the group's decision.

contentious A dimension of communicator style exemplified by argumentativeness and the desire to debate points.

control The need to establish and share power and control with others.

controlling behavior A dimension of defensive communication climate in which the sender assumes to know what is best for others.

cooperative conflict A type of disagreement that actually helps move the group along with its task or activities.

critical advisor A role in a group exemplified by suggesting disadvantages to alternatives posed, revealing hidden assumptions, and questioning the validity or reliability of information used as evidence; helps the group see errors in its logic and thinking; devil's advocate; constructively criticizes ideas brought before the group.

cultural distance The degree to which group members differ on dimensions of language, social status, religion, politics, economic conditions, and basic assumptions about reality.

decentralized communication network Communication network that allows each group member to talk to every other group member.

decision-making tasks The most common of group activities; the objective of the group's interaction is to reach conclusions through the sharing of information and the use of group members' collective reasoning.

defensive climate A communication climate based on negative or threatening group interaction.

delegating leadership style The best style for groups whose members are both willing and able to assume responsibility for group tasks.

dependence A relationship created with or accepted from other group members that puts the individual in a subordinate position.

description A dimension of a supportive communication climate that occurs when a group member responds to the idea instead of evaluating the group member who offered the idea.

descriptive feedback Feedback that identifies or describes how a group member communicates.

distributive conflict management strategy A win-lose conflict management strategy exemplified by competitiveness or accommodation; yields an outcome that satisfies one party at the expense of the other.

dominant A dimension of communicator style exemplified by taking charge and controlling interaction; confident, forceful, active, and self-assured.

dramatic A dimension of communicator style exemplified by some individuals talking more often and more loudly than other group members; uses exaggeration, emphasis, joking, story telling.

dyadic interaction Interaction between two people (a dyad); interpersonal interaction.

effectiveness A criterion of communication competence that is achieved when the goal of the interaction is satisfied.

egocentric constraints Constraints to decision making based on a group member's high need for control over the group or its activities, or on a group member's personal or hidden agenda.

embeddedness The degree to which the group is central to its larger organizational structure.

emergent leadership A type of leadership in which a group member is not appointed or elected to the leadership role; rather, leadership develops over time as a result of the group's interaction.

empathy A dimension of supportive communication climate that expresses genuine concern for other group members; conveys respect for and reassurance of the receiver.

equality A dimension of supportive communication climate in which trust and respect for all group members are expressed.

ethnocentric A culturally based bias allowing a person to judge events and people as good or correct when they are similar to events and people in his or her own culture.

evaluation A dimension of a defensive communication climate in which a group member uses language to criticize other group members.

evaluative feedback Feedback that goes beyond mere description to provide an evaluation or assessment of how a person communicates.

expert power A type of influence based on what a group member knows or can do.

false consensus A belief among group members that they all agree when they do not; agreeing to a decision only in order to be done with the task.

faultlines Demographic characteristics or other attributes salient for a particular group and its task; members are likely to communicate with similar others, which can divide a group into subgroups.

feedback (1) The process of asking questions, restating the message, or agreeing or disagreeing with a message sent by another group member; (2) information about individual group members' actual performance or the actions of a group.

formal roles Roles expected in most groups; easily labeled (leader or chair, vice-chair, secretary or recorder, program planner).

friendly A dimension of communicator style; positive recognition of others through behavior that encourages and validates; affectionate, sociable, and tactful.

functional coherence Attribute of group interaction when members' interactions help them accomplish its purpose or task in an orderly and meaningful way.

group Three or more members who identify themselves as a group and who can identify the interdependent activity or goal of the group.

group charter A group document that describes the goals or mission of the group.

group goal An agreed-upon task or activity that the group is to complete or accomplish.

group identity The result when members identify themselves with other group members and the group goal.

grouping People identified as a group when they have little or no expectation that interaction will occur with one another.

group maintenance roles Informal group roles that help define a group's relationships and develop a group's climate.

group potency Group members' collective belief that their group can be effective; based on beliefs about task capabilities of the group and group member relationships.

group roles Interactive positions within a group; the micro components of a group's structure.

group size The number of members in the group; the minimum number of members is three; the maximum number depends primarily on the complexity of the task or activity.

group structure The patterns of behavior that group members come to rely on; develops with or emerges from group rules and norms.

groupthink A type of faulty decision making based on the tendency of highly cohesive groups to adopt faulty solutions because members failed to critically examine and analyze options while under pressure from the external environment.

haptics The use of touch; conveys nonverbal messages.

heterogeneous group A group whose members represent distinct and different demographic characteristics.

homogeneous group A group whose members are similar with regard to their demographic characteristics.

idea generation The task-related skill of generating an adequate number of ideas for the group to deliberate before making a decision.

inclusion The need to establish and maintain satisfactory relations with others.

individual feedback Information that focuses on specific group members and their knowledge, skills, and attitudes.

individualistic A type of culture that values individual recognition more than group or team recognition.

individual roles Informal roles that are typically counterproductive for the group by focusing attention away from the group and its goal.

inference drawing The task-related skill of using analysis and reasoning to develop claims that go beyond the available information.

informal roles Roles that emerge naturally through group member interaction.

information bias Information used in decision making that is biased toward one alternative the group is discussing or that favors some group members over others.

informational power Persuasion or influence based on what information or knowledge a group member possesses, or presents as arguments to group.

in-group A type of influence based on group members' identification with other group members.

integrative conflict management strategy A win-win conflict management strategy based on problem solving or collaboration; produces an outcome with which all parties can agree.

interaction diagram A diagram identifying which group members talk to other group members and how frequently.

interdependence Phenomenon whereby both group and individual outcomes are influenced by what other individuals in the group do; group members must rely upon and cooperate with one another to complete the group activity.

intrinsic interest A task characteristic; the motivating potential of the task; based on group members' motivation to perform well and their attraction to the group, task, and other members.

kinesics The use of facial expressions, eye contact, hand gestures, or body posture; conveys nonverbal messages.

law of inherent conflict The premise that no matter the issue or group, there will be significant conflict stemming from different perceptions of relative factors.

leader A formal role; a group member who plans for and facilitates meetings, encourages and motivates group members, and acts as a group's link to its external environment.

leadership (1) As a process, how a person uses positive influence to direct and coordinate the activities of group members toward goal accomplishment; (2) as a property, the set of qualities or characteristics attributed to the person who holds the primary influential role; (3) the relational skill of counteracting cognitive, affiliative, and egocentric constraints present in decision making.

legitimate power A type of power based on the inherent influence associated with a position or role in the group.

majority influence The influence of the largest subgroup that uses social pressure to influence decision outcomes.

minutes A record of what the group did or accomplished at a meeting; should reflect who attended the meeting, what content was discussed, what was decided, who agreed to take on what responsibilities, and what the group plans to do next; usually taken by the group's secretary.

neutrality A dimension of defensive communication climate expressed when a group member reacts in a detached or unemotional way; a lack of warmth or caring for other members, making them feel as if they are not important.

nominal group technique (NGT) A decision-making procedure in which the group temporarily suspends interaction to take advantage of independent thinking and reflection before coming together as a group to discuss the ideas generated.

nonverbal communication Meaning derived from the way words are said or the use of behaviors to complement or substitute for verbal messages; occurs in many forms—vocalics, kinesics, proxemics, haptics, chronemics, and artifacts.

norm An expectation about behavior; an informal rule adopted by a group to regulate group members' behaviors.

normative conflict A type of conflict that occurs when one party has expectations about and evaluates another party's behavior.

open A dimension of communicator style; frank, approachable, and willing to disclose information about oneself.

out-group A group against which the in-group distinguishes itself.

pace The tempo or rate activity of group interaction.

participating leadership style The best style for groups whose members are able but unwilling to take responsibility for group tasks.

PERT Program evaluation and review technique; a decision technique that helps group members order the activities that must be completed to implement a decision.

planning The procedural skill of helping group members identify what needs to be done in what sequence to move from discussion to decision making.

population familiarity A task characteristic; the degree of member familiarity with the task and other group members.

power The influence of one person over another; the ability to get things done or to find needed resources; power bases are reward, coercion, legitimacy, expertise, information, and referent.

precise A dimension of communicator style exemplified by a concern for accurate and clear communication of ideas.

prescriptive feedback Information that provides group members with advice about how they should act or communicate.

problem orientation A dimension of a supportive communication climate that strives for answers and solutions to benefit all group members and to satisfy the group's objective.

problem recognition and framing The task-related skill of recognizing and agreeing upon the nature of the problem that requires a decision.

procedural conflict A type of conflict that occurs when procedures or group process are not discussed beforehand or when the group encounters a situation for which there is no precedent; conflicts about how the group should proceed.

procedural feedback Information about how effective specific procedures are for a group.

process enactment The procedural skill of addressing unforeseen circumstances in decision making.

provisionalism A dimension of a supportive communication climate that is committed to solving the group's problems by hearing all of the ideas; encourages the experimentation and exploration of ideas in the group.

proxemics The use of space; conveys nonverbal messages.

ranking A decision procedure in which members assign a numerical value to each available position; rankings are then ordered.

readiness The ability and willingness to perform group activities.

referent power A type of influence given by a group member to another member based on a desire to build a relationship with him or her.

relational communication Affective and expressive verbal and nonverbal messages that create the social reality of a group; a message with the purpose of creating connections and social influence.

relational competencies Skills individuals use to help manage relationships among group members and the overall communication climate.

relational dimension Group interaction that provides social and emotional support, as well as a mechanism for developing and maintaining role identities within a group.

relational feedback Information about the group climate or the environmental or interaction dynamics within group member relationships.

relaxed A dimension of communicator style exemplified by little anxiety; calm, collected, and confident.

reward power A type of positive influence; relationally oriented and based on such things as attention, friendship, or favors, or materially oriented and based on tangible influence such as gifts or money.

satisfaction The degree to which a group member feels fulfilled or gratified based upon experiences in the group.

secretary or recorder A formal role; a group member who takes notes to capture what happened in the group's interaction.

selective listening A frame for listening to others based on an unique perspective or specialized knowledge, which can make it difficult to understand other group members who have different perspectives or set of knowledge.

selling leadership style The best style for groups whose members are willing to take responsibility for group tasks but lack the skills or abilities to complete the tasks; requires high leader involvement.

Situational Leadership® model A model that describes leadership based on (1) the amount of task direction a leader gives, (2) the amount of relational support a leader provides, and (3) the readiness level of group members in performing their tasks.

social complexity A task characteristic; the degree to which group members are ego-involved; group members agree on how to proceed and on what should be accomplished.

socialization The reciprocal process of social influence and change between new and established group members.

social loafers Group members who do not perform to their maximum level of potential contribution; the group context allows them to contribute minimally but still reap the same benefits as other group members.

social loafing The idea that individual efforts decrease as the size of the group increases; a detachment from the group that occurs when group members feel as if they are not needed to produce the group's outcome or as if their individual efforts are not recognized by other members.

solution multiplicity A task characteristic; the number of alternatives available for solving the problem.

spontaneity A dimension of a supportive communication climate exemplified by a group member who is open and honest with other group members; creates immediacy with other group members.

standard agenda A decision-making procedure with a strict linear process for groups to follow in considering decision alternatives.

strategy A dimension of a defensive communication climate in which the sender manipulates others by placing him- or herself above the group or its task.

substantive conflict A type of conflict rooted in issues or ideas, or in some aspect of the group's task.

superiority A dimension of a defensive communication climate exemplified when a group member continually reinforces his or her strength or position over others.

superordinate goal A task or goal so difficult, time-consuming, and burdensome that it is beyond the capacity of one person.

supportive climate A communication climate based on positive group interaction.

synergy The result when the performance of a group goes beyond the capabilities of group members as individuals; communication among group members allows synergy to occur.

task communication Verbal and nonverbal messages instrumental to accomplishing group tasks and activities or perform group objectives; a message with the purpose of directing activities of a group.

task competencies Skills individuals use to help manage group tasks.

task difficulty A task characteristic; the degree to which a task requires significant effort, knowledge, or skill.

task dimension A group's interaction that focuses on its task, activity, or goal.

task feedback Information about the technical competencies or the functional task activities of a team.

task roles Informal roles that help the group move forward with its task or goal.

teamwork feedback Information about the group's interactions and members' relationships, cooperation, communication, and coordination.

telling leadership style The best style for groups whose members are both unable and unwilling to take responsibility for group tasks.

time flexibility Flexibility given to group members in dealing with time deadlines or pressures.

topical coherence Attribute of group interaction when members' interactions are focused on one topic.

transformational leader A type of leadership based on the premise that the leader sets an example for group members to follow; uses rhetorical skills to build a vision that members can identify with and use as a guiding force toward goal completion.

trust A group member's positive expectation of another group member; reliance on another group member in a risky situation.

vocal activity The amount of time a member talks in a group.

vocalics A form of nonverbal communication; meaning is derived from how the voice is used; includes inflection, tone, accent, rate, pitch, volume, number of vocal interrupters, and quality of voice.

voting A decision procedure in which group members cast a written or verbal ballot in support of or against a specific proposal; generally, a majority or two-thirds vote is needed to support a proposition.

References

Adato, A. (1975). Leave-taking: A study of commonsense knowledge of social structure. *Anthropological Quarterly, 48,* 255–271.

Adler, N. (1986). *International dimensions of organization behavior.* Boston: Kent.

Alper, S., Tjosvold, D., & Law, K. S. (2000). Conflict management, efficacy, and performance in organizational teams. *Personnel Psychology, 53,* 625–642.

Anderson, C. M., & Martin, M. M. (1995). The effects of communication motives, interaction involvement, and loneliness on satisfaction: A model of small groups. *Small Group Research, 26,* 118–137.

Anderson, C. M., & Martin, M. M. (2002). Communication motives (state vs. trait?) and task group outcomes. *Communication Research Reports, 19,* 269–282.

Anderson, C. M., Martin, M. M., & Riddle, B. L. (2001). Small group relational satisfaction scale: Development, reliability, and validity. *Communication Studies, 52,* 220–233.

Anderson, C. M., Riddle, B. L., & Martin, M. M. (1999). Socialization processes in groups. In L. R. Frey, D. S. Gouran, & M. S. Poole (Eds.), *The handbook of group communication theory & research* (pp. 139–163). Thousand Oaks, CA: Sage.

Anderson, S. D., & Wanberg, K. W. (1991). A convergent model of emergent leadership in groups. *Small Group Research, 22,* 380–397.

Applbaum, R. L., & Anatol, K. (1971). PERT: A tool for communication research planning. *Journal of Communication, 21,* 368–380.

Argyle, M., & Kendon, A. (1967). The experimental analysis of social performance. In L. Berkowitz (Ed.), *Advances in experimental social psychology* (vol. 3, pp. 55–98). New York: Academic Press.

Arrow, H., & McGrath, J. E. (1993). Membership matters: How member change and continuity affect small group structure, process, and performance. *Small Group Research, 24,* 334–361.

Arrow, H., McGrath, J. E., & Berdahl, J. L. (2000). *Small groups as complex systems: Formation, coordination, development, and adaptation.* Thousand Oaks, CA: Sage.

Arrow, H., Poole, M. S., Henry, K. B., Wheelan, S., & Moreland, R. (2004). Time, change, and development: The temporal perspective on groups. *Small Group Research, 35,* 73–105.

Avolio, B. J., Waldman, D. A., & Einstein, W. O. (1988). Transformational leadership in a management game simulation. *Group & Organization Studies, 13,* 59–80.

Avruch, K., & Black, P. W. (1993). Conflict resolution in intercultural settings: Problems and prospects. In D. J. D. Sandole & H. van der Merwe (Eds.), *Conflict resolution theory and practice: Integration and application* (pp. 131–145). New York: Manchester University Press.

Baird, J. E., Jr. (1976). Some nonverbal elements of leadership emergence. *Southern Speech Communication Journal, 42,* 352–361.

Baker, D. C. (1990). A qualitative and quantitative analysis of verbal style and the elimination of potential leaders in small groups. *Communication Quarterly, 38,* 13–26.

Baker, D. F. (2001). The development of collective efficacy in small task groups. *Small Group Research, 32,* 451–474.

Bales, R. F. (1950). *Interaction process analysis: A method for the study of small groups.* Cambridge, MA: Addison-Wesley.

Bales, R. F. (1953). The equilibrium problem in small groups, In T. Parson, E. A. Shils, & R. F. Bales (Eds.), *Working papers in the theory of action* (pp. 111–161). Glencoe, IL: Free Press.

Bales, R. F., & Cohen, S. P. (1979). *SYMLOG: A system for the multiple level observation of groups.* New York: Free Press.

Ballard, D. I., & Seibold, D. R. (2000). Time orientation and temporal variation across work groups: Implications for group and organizational communication. *Western Journal of Communication, 64,* 218–242.

Ballard, D. I., & Seibold, D. R. (2004). Communication-related organizational structures and work group temporal experiences: The effects of coordination method, technology type, and feedback cycle on members' construals and enactments of time. *Communication Monographs, 71,* 1–27.

Bandura, A. (1986). *Social foundations of thought and action: A social cognitive theory.* Englewood Cliffs, NJ: Prentice-Hall.

Bantz, C. R. (1993). Cultural diversity and group cross-cultural team research. *Journal of Applied Communication Research, 21,* 1–20.

Barge, J. K. (1994). *Leadership: Communication skills for organizations and groups.* New York: St. Martin's.

Barge, J. K. (1996). Leadership skills and the dialectics of leadership in group decision making. In R. Y. Hirokawa & M. S. Poole (Eds.), *Communication and group decision making* (2nd ed., pp. 301–342). Thousand Oaks, CA: Sage.

Barge, J. K. (2002). Enlarging the meaning of group deliberation. In L. R. Frey (Ed.), *New directions in group communication* (pp. 159–177). Thousand Oaks, CA: Sage.

Barge, J. K., & Hirokawa, R. Y. (1989). Toward a communication competency model of group leadership. *Small Group Behavior, 20,* 167–189.

Barge, J. K., & Keyton, J. (1994). Contextualizing power and social influence in groups. In L. R. Frey (Ed.), *Group communication in context: Studies of natural groups* (pp. 85–105). Hillsdale, NJ: Erlbaum.

Barker, V. E., Abrams, J. R., Tiyaamornwong, V., Seibold, D. R., Duggan, A., Park, H. S., & Sebastian, M. (2000). New contexts for relational communication in groups. *Small Group Research, 31,* 470–503.

Barsade, S. G. (2002). The ripple effect: Emotional contagion and its influence on group behavior. *Administrative Science Quarterly, 47,* 644–676.

Bartel, C. A., & Saavedra, R. (2000). The collective construction of work group moods. *Administrative Science Quarterly, 45,* 197–231.

Bass, B. M. (1981). *Stogdill's handbook of leadership: A survey of theory and research.* New York: Free Press.

Bass, B. M. (1985). *Leadership and performance beyond expectations.* New York: Free Press.

Bass, B. M. (1990). From transactional to transformational leadership: Learning to share the vision. *Organizational Dynamics, 18*(3), 19–31.

Baxter, L. A. (1982). Conflict management: An episodic approach. *Small Group Behavior, 13,* 23–42.

Bayazit, M., & Mannix, E. A. (2003). Should I stay or should I go? Predicting team members' intent to remain in the team. *Small Group Research, 34,* 290–321.

Bechler, C., & Johnson, S. C. (1995). Leadership and listening: A study of member perceptions. *Small Group Research, 26,* 77–85.

Bednar, D. A. (1981). Relationships between communicator style and managerial performance in complex organizations: A field study. *Journal of Business Communication, 19,* 51–76.

Bell, M. A. (1983). A research note: The relationship of conflict and linguistic diversity in small groups. *Central States Speech Journal, 34,* 128–133.

Bell, B. S., & Kozlowski, S. W. (2002). A typology of virtual teams. *Group & Organization Management, 27,* 14–49.

Benne, K., & Sheats, P. (1948). Functional roles of group members. *Journal of Social Issues, 4,* 41–49.

Bettenhausen, K. L. (1991). Five years of groups research: What we have learned and what needs to be addressed. *Journal of Management, 17,* 345–381.

Bettenhausen, K., & Murnighan, J. K. (1985). The emergence of norms in competitive decision-making groups. *Administrative Science Quarterly, 30,* 350–372.

Biddle, B. J. (1979). *Role theory: Expectations, identities, and behaviors.* New York: Academic Press.

Bonito, J. A. (2001). An information-processing approach to participation in small groups. *Communication Research, 28,* 275–303.

Bonito, J. A. (2002). The analysis of participation in small groups: Methodological and conceptual issues related to interdependence. *Small Group Research, 33,* 412–438.

Bonito, J. A. (2004). Shared cognition and participation in small groups: Similarity of member prototypes. *Communication Research, 31,* 704–830.

Bonito, J. A., & Hollingshead, A. B. (1997). Participation in small groups. In B. R. Burleson (Ed.), *Communication yearbook 20* (pp. 227–261). Thousand Oaks, CA: Sage.

Bormann, E. G., & Bormann, N. C. (1988). *Effective small group communication.* Edina, MN: Burgess.

Bormann, E. G., Pratt, J., & Putnam, L. (1978). Power, authority, and sex: Male response to female leadership. *Communication Monographs, 45,* 119–155.

Bradley, P. H. (1978). Power, status, and upward communication in small decision-making groups. *Communication Monographs, 45,* 33–43.

Brewer, M. B. (1995). Managing diversity: The role of social identities. In S. E. Jackson & M. N. Ruderman (Eds.), *Diversity in work teams: Research paradigms for a changing workplace* (pp. 47–68). Washington, DC: American Psychological Association.

Broome, B. J., & Fulbright, L. (1995). A multistage influence model of barriers to group problem solving: A participant-generated agenda for small group research. *Small Group Research, 26,* 25–55.

Brown, T. M., & Miller, C. E. (2000). Communication networks in task-performing groups: Effects of task complexity, time pressure, and interpersonal dominance. *Small Group Research, 31,* 131–157.

Burgoon, J. K. (1977). Unwillingness to communicate as a predictor of small group discussion behaviors and evaluation. *Central States Speech Journal, 28,* 122–133.

Burgoon, J. K. (1980). Nonverbal communication research in the 1970s: An overview. In D. Nimmo (Ed.), *Communication yearbook 4* (pp. 179–197). New Brunswick, NJ: Transaction.

Burgoon, J. K. (1985). Nonverbal signals. In M. L. Knapp & G. R. Miller (Eds.), *Handbook of interpersonal communication* (pp. 349–353). Beverly Hills: Sage.

Burkhalter, S., Gastil, J., & Kelshaw, T. (2002). A conceptual definition and theoretical model of public deliberation in small face-to-face groups. *Communication Theory, 12,* 398–422.

Canary, D. J., & Spitzberg, B. H. (1989). A model of the perceived competence of conflict strategies. *Human Communication Research, 15,* 630–649.

Cannon-Bowers, J. A., Tannenbaum, S. I., Salas, E., & Volpe, C. E. (1995). Defining competencies and establishing team training requirements. In R. A. Guzzo & E. Salas (Eds.), *Team effectiveness and decision making in organizations* (pp. 333–380). San Francisco: Jossey-Bass.

Carron, A. V., Brawley, L. R., Bray, S. R., Eys, M. A., Dorsch, K. D., Estabrooks, P. A., et al., (2004). Using consensus as a criterion for groupness: Implications for the cohesion-group success relationship. *Small Group Research, 35,* 466–491.

Cartwright, D. (1968). The nature of group cohesiveness. In D. Cartwright & A. Zander (Eds.), *Group dynamics: Research and theory* (3rd ed., pp. 91–109). New York: Harper & Row.

Cathcart, R., & Cathcart, D. (1996). Group lifetimes: Japanese and American versions. In R. S. Cathcart, L. A. Samovar, & L. D. Henman (Eds.), *Small group communication: Theory & practice* (7th ed., pp. 345–355). Madison: Brown & Benchmark.

Cawyer, C. S., & Smith-Dupre, A. (1995). Communicating social support: Identifying supportive episodes in an HIV/AIDS support group. *Communication Quarterly*, *43*, 243–258.

Chemers, M. M. (1993). An integrative theory of leadership. In M. M. Chemers & R. Ayman (Eds.), *Leadership theory and research: Perspectives and directions* (pp. 293–319). San Diego: Academic Press.

Chemers, M. M., & Murphy, S. E. (1995). Leadership and diversity in groups and organizations. In M. M. Chemers, S. Oskamp, & M. A. Costanzo (Eds.), *Diversity in organizations: New perspectives for a changing workplace* (pp. 157–188). Thousand Oaks, CA: Sage.

Cline, R. J. W. (1994). Groupthink and the Watergate cover-up: The illusion of unanimity. In L. R. Frey (Ed.), *Group communication in context: Studies of natural groups* (pp. 199–223). Hillsdale, NJ: Erlbaum.

Cline, R. J. (1999). Communication in social support groups. In L. R. Frey, D. S. Gouran, & M. S. Poole (Eds.), *The handbook of group communication theory and research* (pp. 516–538). Thousand Oaks, CA: Sage.

Cohen, S. G. (1990). Hilltop Hospital top management group. In J. R. Hackman (Ed.), *Groups that work (and those that don't): Creating conditions for effective teamwork* (pp. 56–77). San Francisco: Jossey-Bass.

Cohen, S. G., & Bailey, D. E. (1997). What makes teams work: Group effectiveness research from the shop floor to the executive suite. *Journal of Management*, *23*, 239–290.

Comer, D. R. (1995). A model of social loafing in real work groups. *Human Relations*, *48*, 647–667.

Courtright, J. A. (1978). A laboratory investigation of groupthink. *Communication Monographs*, *45*, 229–246.

Cox, T., Jr. (1995). The complexity of diversity: Challenges and directions for future research. In S. E. Jackson & M. N. Ruderman (Eds.), *Diversity in work teams: Research paradigms for a changing workplace* (pp. 235–253). Washington, DC: American Psychological Association.

Cox, T. H., Lobel, S. A., & McLeod, P. L. (1991). Effects of ethnic group cultural differences on cooperative and competitive behavior on a group task. *Academy of Management Journal*, *34*, 827–847.

Craig, R. T., & Tracy, K. (1983). Introduction. In R. T. Craig & K. Tracy (Eds.), *Conversational coherence* (pp. 10–22). Beverly Hills, CA: Sage.

Cronshaw, S. F., & Ellis, R. J. (1991). A process investigation of self-monitoring and leader emergence. *Small Group Research*, *22*, 403–420.

Cruz, M. G., Henningsen, D. D., & Smith, B. A. (1999). The impact of directive leadership on group information sampling, decisions, and perceptions of the leader. *Communication Research*, *26*, 349–369.

Daly, J. A., McCroskey, J. C., & Richmond, V. P. (1977). Relationships between vocal activity and perception of communicators in small group interaction. *Western Journal of Speech Communication*, *41*, 175–187.

De Dreu, C. K., & Van Vianen, A. E. (2001). Managing relationship conflict and the effectiveness of organizational teams. *Journal of Organizational Behavior*, *22*, 300–328.

Delbecq, A. L., Van de Ven, A. H., & Gustafson, D. H. (1975). *Group techniques for program planning: A guide to nominal group and delphi processes.* Glenview, IL: Scott, Foresman.

DeStephen, R. S., & Hirokawa, R. Y. (1988). Small group consensus: Stability of group support of the decision, task process, and group relationships. *Small Group Behavior*, *19*, 227–239.

Deutsch, M. (1969). Conflicts: Productive and destructive. *Journal of Social Issues*, *25*, 7–41.

Di Salvo, V. S., Nikkel, E., & Monroe, C. (1989). Theory and practice: A field investigation and identification of group members' perceptions of problems facing natural work groups. *Small Group Behavior*, *20*, 551–567.

Dominick, P. G., Reilly, R. R., & McGourty, J. W. (1997). The effects of peer feedback on team member behavior. *Group & Organization Management*, *22*, 508–520.

Dukerich, J. M., Nichols, M., Elm, D., and Vollrath, D. (1990). Moral reasoning in groups: Leaders make a difference. *Human Relations*, *43*, 473–493.

Dyce, J., & O'Connor, B. P. (1992). Personality complementarity as a determinant of group cohesion in bar bands. *Small Group Research*, *23*, 185–198.

Eadie, W. F. (1982). Defensive communication revisited: A critical examination of Gibb's theory. *The Southern Speech Communication Journal*, *47*, 163–177.

Eagly, A. H., & Johnson, B. T. (1990). Gender and leadership style: A meta-analysis. *Psychological Bulletin*, *108*, 233–256.

Eagly, A. H., & Karau, S. J. (1991). Gender and the emergence of leaders: A meta-analysis. *Journal of Personality and Social Psychology*, *60*, 685–710.

Eagly, A. H., Karau, S. J., & Makhijani, M. G. (1995). Gender and the effectiveness of leaders: A meta-analysis. *Psychological Bulletin*, *117*, 125–145.

Ellingson, L. L. (2003). Interdisciplinary health care teamwork in the clinic backstage. *Journal of Applied Communication Research*, *31*, 93–117.

Ellis, D. G. (1979). Relational control in two group systems. *Communication Monographs*, *46*, 153–166.

Ellis, R. J., & Cronshaw, S. F. (1992). Self-monitoring and leader emergence: A test of moderator effects. *Small Group Research*, *23*, 113–129.

Farmer, S. M., & Roth, J. (1998). Conflict-handling behavior in work groups: Effects of group structure, decision processes, and time. *Small Group Research*, *29*, 669–713.

Festinger, L., Schachter, S., & Back, K. (1968). Operation of group standards. In D. Cartwright & A. Zander (Eds.), *Group dynamics: Research and theory* (3rd ed., pp. 152–164). New York: Harper & Row.

Firestien, R. L. (1990). Effects of creative problem solving training on communication behavior in small groups. *Small Group Research*, *21*, 507–521.

Fisher, B. A. (1971). Communication research and the task-oriented group. *Journal of Communication*, *21*, 136–149.

Flippen, A. R. (1999). Understanding groupthink from a self-regulatory perspective. *Small Group Research*, *30*, 139–165.

Forsyth, D. R., & Kelley, K. N. (1994). Attribution in groups: Estimations of personal contributions to collective endeavors. *Small Group Research*, *25*, 367–383.

Fourre, J. P. (1968). *Critical path scheduling: A practical appraisal of PERT.* New York: American Management Association.

Franz, T. M., & Larson, J. R., Jr. (2002). The impact of experts on information sharing during group discussion. *Small Group Research*, *33*, 383–411.

Fraser, K. L., & Russell, G. M. (2000). The role of the group in acquiring self-defense skills: Results of a qualitative study. *Small Group Research*, *31*, 397–423.

French, J. R. P., & Raven, B. (1968). The bases of social power. In D. Cartwright & A. Zander (Eds.), *Group dynamics: Research and theory* (pp. 259–269). New York: Harper & Row.

Frey, L., & Sunwolf. (2005). The symbolic-interpretive perspective of group life. In M. S. Poole & A. B. Hollingshead (Eds.), *Theories of small groups: Interdisciplinary perspectives* (pp. 185–239). Thousand Oaks, CA: Sage.

Galanes, G. J. (2003). In their own words: An exploratory study of bona fide group leaders. *Small Group Research*, *34*, 741–770.

Gallupe, R. B., Dennis, A. R., Cooper, W. H., Valacich, J. S., Bastianutti, L., & Nunamaker, J. (1992). Electronic brainstorming and group size. *Academy of Management Journal*, *35*, 350–369.

Gardner, W. L., & Avolio, B. J. (1998). The charismatic relationship: A dramaturgical perspective. *Academy of Management Review*, *23*, 32–58.

Gastil, J. (1993). Identifying obstacles to small group democracy. *Small Group Research*, *24*, 5–27.

Gersick, C. J. G., & Hackman, J. R. (1990). Habitual routines in task-performing groups. *Organizational Behavior and Human Decision Processes, 47*, 65–97.

Gibb, J. R. (1961). Defensive communication. *Journal of Communication, 11*, 141–148.

Gibson, C. B., & Zellmer-Bruhn, M. E. (2001). Metaphors and meaning: An intercultural analysis of the concept of teamwork. *Administrative Science Quarterly, 46*, 274–303.

Golembiewski, R. T. (1962). *Making decisions in groups*. Glenview, IL: Scott, Foresman.

Goodman, P. S. (1986). Impact of task and technology on group performance. In P. S. Goodman (Ed.), *Designing effective work groups* (pp. 120–167). San Francisco: Jossey-Bass.

Goodstein, L. D., Nolan, T. M., & Pfeiffer, J. W. (1992). *Applied strategic planning: A comprehensive guide*. San Diego: Pfeiffer.

Gouran, D. S. (1988). Group decision making: An approach to integrative research. In C. H. Tardy (Ed.), *A handbook for the study of human communication: Methods and instruments for observing, measuring, and assessing communication processes* (pp. 247–267). Norwood, NJ: Ablex.

Gouran, D. S. (1990). Evaluating group outcomes. In G. M. Phillips (Ed.), *Teaching how to work in groups* (pp. 175–195). Norwood, NJ: Ablex.

Gouran, D. S. (2003). Communication skills for group decision making. In J. O. Greene & B. R. Burleson (Eds.), *Handbook of communication and social interaction skills* (pp. 835–870). Mahwah, NJ: Erlbaum.

Gouran, D. S., & Hirokawa, R. Y. (1983). The role of communication in decision making groups: A functional perspective. In M. S. Mander (Ed.), *Communications in transition* (pp. 168–185). New York: Praeger.

Gouran, D. S., & Hirokawa, R. Y. (1996). Functional theory and communication in decision-making and problem-solving groups. In R. Y. Hirokawa & M. S. Poole (Eds.), *Communication and group decision making* (pp. 55–80). Thousand Oaks, CA: Sage.

Gouran, D. S., Hirokawa, R. Y., Julian, K. M., & Leatham, G. B. (1993). The evolution and current status of the functional perspective on communication in decision-making and problem-solving groups. In S. A. Deetz (Ed.), *Communication yearbook 16* (pp. 573–600). Newbury Park, CA: Sage.

Gouran, D. S., Hirokawa, R. Y., & Martz, A. E. (1986). A critical analysis of factors related to decisional processes involved in the *Challenger* disaster. *Central States Speech Journal, 37*, 119–135.

Graham, C. R. (2003). A model of norm development for computer-mediated teamwork. *Small Group Research, 34*, 322–352.

Graham, E. E., Papa, M. J., & McPherson, M. B. (1997). An applied test of the functional communication perspective of small group decision-making. *Southern Communication Journal, 62*, 269–279.

Green, S. G., & Taber, T. D. (1980). The effects of three social decision schemes on decision group process. *Organizational Behavior and Human Performance, 25*, 97–106.

Green, T. B. (1975). An empirical analysis of nominal and interacting groups. *Academy of Management Journal, 18*, 63–73.

Greene, C. N. (1989). Cohesion and productivity in work groups. *Small Group Behavior, 20*, 70–86.

Gribas, J., & Downs, C. W. (2002). Metaphoric manifestations of talking "team" with team novices. *Communication Studies, 53*, 112–128.

Gudykunst, W. B., & Hall, B. J. (1994). Strategies for effective communication and adaptation in intergroup contexts. In J. A. Daly & J. M. Wiemann (Eds.), *Strategic interpersonal communication* (pp. 225–271). Hillsdale, NJ: Erlbaum.

Guetzkow, H., & Gyr, J. (1954). An analysis of conflict in decision-making groups. *Human Relations, 7*, 367–382.

Gully, S. M., Devine, D. J., & Whitney, D. J. (1995). A meta-analysis of cohesion and performance: Effects of level of analysis and task interdependence. *Small Group Research, 26*, 497–520.

Guzzo, R. A., Yost, P. R., Campbell, R. J., & Shea, G. P. (1993). Potency in groups: Articulation a construct. *British Journal of Social Psychology, 32*, 87–106.

Hackman, J. R. (Ed.). (1990). *Groups that work (and those that don't): Creating conditions for effective teamwork.* San Francisco: Jossey-Bass.

Hackman, J. R. (2002). *Leading teams: Setting the stage for great performances.* Boston: Harvard Business School Press.

Halone, K. K., & Pecchioni, L. L. (2001). Relational listening: A grounded theoretical model. *Communication Reports, 14*, 59–71.

Hansford, B. C., & Diehl, B. J. (1988). Verbal comments, ideas, feedback, and self-assessment during small-group discussions. *Small Group Behavior, 19*, 485–494.

Hare, A. P. (1982). *Creativity in small groups.* Beverly Hills: Sage.

Hare, A. P. (1994). Types of roles in small groups: A bit of history and a current perspective. *Small Group Research, 25*, 433–448.

Hargrove, R. (1998). *Mastering the art of creative collaboration.* New York: BusinessWeek Books.

Harrison, D. A., Price, K. H., & Bell, M. P. (1998). Beyond relational demography: Time and the effects of surface- and deep-level diversity on work group cohesion. *Academy of Management Journal, 41*, 96–107.

Hawes, L. C., & Smith, D. H. (1973). A critique of assumptions underlying the study of communication in conflict. *Quarterly Journal of Speech, 59*, 423–435.

Hawkins, K. W. (1995). Effects of gender and communication content on leadership emergence in small task-oriented groups. *Small Group Research, 26*, 234–249.

Hawkins, K. W., & Fillion, B. P. (1999). Perceived communication skill needs for work groups. *Communication Research Reports, 16*, 167–174.

Hawkins, K. W., & Stewart, R. A. (1991). Effects of communication apprehension on perceptions of leadership and intragroup attraction in small task-oriented groups. *Southern Communication Journal, 57*, 1–10.

Heath, R. G., & Sias, P. M. (1999). Communicating spirit in a collaborative alliance. *Journal of Applied Communication Research, 27*, 356–376.

Henningsen, D. D., & Henningsen, M. L. (2003). Examining social influence in information-sharing contexts. *Small Group Research, 34*, 391–412.

Henningsen, D. D., & Henningsen, M. L. (2004). The effect of individual difference variables on information sharing in decision-making groups. *Human Communication Research, 30*, 540–555.

Henry, K. B., Arrow, H., & Carini, B. (1999). A tripartite model of group identification: Theory and measurement. *Small Group Research, 30*, 558–581.

Herold, D. M. (1978). Improving the performance effectiveness of groups through a task-contingency selection of intervention strategies. *Academy of Management Review, 3*, 315–325.

Hersey, P., & Blanchard, K. H. (1974, February). So you want to know your leadership style? *Training and Development Journal, 28*, 22–37.

Hersey, P., Blanchard, K. H., & Johnson, D. E. (2000). *Management of organizational behavior: Leading human resources* (8th ed.). Upper Saddle River, NJ: Prentice-Hall.

Heston, J. K. (1974). Effects of personal space invasion and anomia on anxiety, nonperson orientation and source credibility. *Central States Speech Journal, 25*, 19–27.

Hirokawa, R. Y. (1982). Group communication and problem-solving effectiveness I: A critical review of inconsistent findings. *Communication Quarterly, 30*, 134–141.

Hirokawa, R. Y. (1983a). Group communication and problem-solving effectiveness: An investigation of group phases. *Human Communication Research, 9*, 291–305.

Hirokawa, R. Y. (1983b). Group communication and problem-solving effectiveness II: An exploratory investigation of procedural functions. *Western Journal of Speech Communication, 47*, 59–74.

Hirokawa, R. Y. (1988). Group communication and decision-making performance: A continued test of the functional perspective. *Human Communication Research, 14*, 487–515.

Hirokawa, R. Y., Erbert, L., & Hurst, A. (1996). Communication and group decision-making effectiveness. In R. Y. Hirokawa & M. S. Poole (Eds.), *Communication and group decision making* (pp. 269–300). Thousand Oaks, CA: Sage.

Hirokawa, R. Y., & Johnson, D. D. (1989). Toward a general theory of group decision making: Development of an integrated model. *Small Group Behavior, 20,* 500–523.

Hirokawa, R. Y., & Keyton, J. (1995). Perceived facilitators and inhibitors of effectiveness in organizational work teams. *Management Communication Quarterly, 8,* 424–446.

Hirokawa, R. Y., & Pace, R. (1983). A descriptive analysis of the possible communication-based reasons for effective and ineffective group decision making. *Communication Monographs, 50,* 363–379.

Hirokawa, R. Y., & Salazar, A. J. (1999). Task-group communication and decision-making performance. In L. R. Frey, D. S. Gouran, & M. S. Poole (Eds.), *The handbook of group communication theory & research* (pp. 167–191). Thousand Oaks, CA: Sage.

Hirokawa, R. Y., & Scheerhorn, D. R. (1986). Communication in faulty group decision-making. In R. Y. Hirokawa & M. S. Poole (Eds.), *Communication and group decision-making* (pp. 63–80). Beverly Hills: Sage.

Hoffman, L. R., & Kleinman, G. B. (1994). Individual and group in problem solving: The valence model redressed. *Human Communication Research, 21,* 36–59.

Hofstede, G. (1984). *Culture's consequences: International differences in work-related values* (abridged ed.). Newbury Park, CA: Sage.

Hofstede, G. (1991). *Culture and organization: Software of the mind.* London: McGraw-Hill.

Hollander, E. P. (1978). *Leadership dynamics: A practical guide to effective relationships.* New York: Macmillan.

Hollander, E. P. (1985). Leadership and power. In G. Lindzey & E. Aronson (Eds.), *The handbook of social psychology* (3, vol. II, pp. 485–537). New York: Random House.

Hollingshead, A. B. (1996). The rank-order effect in group decision making. *Organizational Behavior and Human Decision Processes, 68,* 181–193.

Homans, G. C. (1950). *The human group.* New York: Harcourt, Brace.

Jacobs, T. O. (1970). *Leadership and exchange in formal organizations.* Alexandria, VA: Human Resources Research Organization.

Janis, I. L. (1982). *Groupthink: Psychological studies of policy decisions and fiascoes* (2nd ed.). Boston: Houghton Mifflin.

Janis, I. L. (1989). *Crucial decisions: Leadership in policy making and crisis management.* New York: Free Press.

Jarboe, S. (1996). Procedures for enhancing group decision making. In R. Y. Hirokawa & M. S. Poole (Eds.), *Communication and group decision making* (pp. 345–383). Thousand Oaks, CA: Sage.

Jarboe, S. (1999). Group communication and creativity processes. In L. R. Frey, D. S. Gouran, & M. S. Poole (Eds.), *The handbook of group communication theory & research* (pp. 335–368). Thousand Oaks, CA: Sage.

Jarboe, S. C., & Witteman, H. R. (1996). Intragroup conflict management in task-oriented groups: The influence of problem sources and problem analyses. *Small Group Research, 27,* 316–338.

Jehn, K. A. (1997). A qualitative analysis of conflict types and dimensions in organizational groups. *Administrative Science Quarterly, 42,* 530–557.

Jehn, K. A., & Mannix, E. A. (2001). The dynamic nature of conflict: A longitudinal study of intragroup conflict and group performance. *Academy of Management Journal, 44,* 238–251.

Johannesen, R. L. (1983). *Ethics in human communication* (2nd ed.). Prospect Heights, IL: Waveland.

Johansen, R., Sibbet, D., Benson, S., Martin, A., Mittman, R., & Saffo, P. (1991). *Leading business teams: How teams can use technology and group process tools to enhance performance.* Reading, MA: Addison-Wesley.

Johnson, B. M. (1975). Images of the enemy in intergroup conflict. *Central States Speech Journal*, *26*, 84–92.

Johnson, V. (1991, June). Group decision making: When trying to persuade others, knowledge is power. *Successful Meetings*, *40*, 76–77.

Jones, T. S. (2000). Emotional communication in conflict: Essence and impact. In W. Eadie & P. Nelson (Eds.), *The language of conflict and resolution* (pp. 81–104). Thousand Oaks, CA: Sage.

Jordan, M. H., Field, H. S., & Armenakis, A. A. (2002). The relationship of group process variables and team performance: A team-level analysis in a field setting. *Small Group Research*, *33*, 121–150.

Jurma, W. E. (1979). Effects of leader structuring style and task-orientation characteristics of group members. *Communication Monographs*, *46*, 282–295.

Kameda, T. (1996). Procedural influence in consensus formation: Evaluating group decision making from a social choice perspective. In E. H. Witte & J. H. Davis (Eds.), *Understanding group behavior: Consensual action by small groups* (pp. 137–161). Mahwah, NJ: Erlbaum.

Katz, N., Lazer, D., Arrow, H., & Contractor, N. (2005). The network perspective on small groups: Theory and research. In M. S. Poole & A. B. Hollingshead (Eds.), *Theories of small groups: Interdisciplinary perspectives* (pp. 277–312). Thousand Oaks, CA: Sage.

Katzenbach, J. R., & Smith, D. K. (1993). *The wisdom of teams: Creating the high-performance organization.* New York: HarperBusiness.

Keltner, J. (1989). Facilitation: Catalyst for group problem solving. *Management Communication Quarterly*, *3*, 8–32.

Ketrow, S. M. (1991). Communication role specializations and perceptions of leadership. *Small Group Research*, *22*, 492–514.

Ketrow, S. M. (1999). Nonverbal aspects of group communication. In L. R. Frey, D. S. Gourna, & M. S. Poole (Eds.), *The handbook of group communication theory and research* (pp. 251–287). Thousand Oaks: CA: Sage.

Keyton, J. (1991). Evaluating individual group member satisfaction as a situational variable. *Small Group Research*, *22*, 200–219.

Keyton, J. (1992). Challenging interpersonal compatibility in groups. *Kansas Speech Journal*, *52*, 1–18.

Keyton, J. (1993). Group termination: Completing the study of group development. *Small Group Research*, *24*, 84–100.

Keyton, J. (1999a). Analyzing interaction patterns in dysfunctional teams. *Small Group Research*, *30*, 491–518.

Keyton, J. (1999b). Relational communication in groups. In L. R. Frey, D. S. Gouran, & M. S. Poole (Eds.), *The handbook of group communication theory & research* (pp. 192–222). Thousand Oaks, CA: Sage.

Keyton, J., & Frey, L. R. (2002). The state of traits: Predisposition and group communication. In L. R. Frey (Ed.), *New directions in group communication* (pp. 99–120). Thousand Oaks, CA: Sage.

Keyton, J., & Stallworth, V. (2003). On the verge of collaboration: Interaction processes versus group outcomes. In L. R. Frey (Ed.), *Group communication in context: Studies of bona fide groups* (pp. 235–260). Mahwah, NJ: Erlbaum.

Kiesler, S., & Cummings, J. N. (2002). What do we know about proximity and distance in work groups? A legacy of research. In P. Hinds & S. Kiesler (Eds.), *Distributed work* (pp. 57–80). Cambridge, MA: MIT Press.

Kirchmeyer, C. (1993). Multicultural task groups: An account of the low contribution level of minorities. *Small Group Research*, *24*, 127–148.

Kirchmeyer, C., & Cohen, A. (1992). Multicultural groups: Their performance and reactions with constructive conflict. *Group & Organization Management*, *17*, 153–170.

Knutson, T. J., & Kowitz, A. C. (1977). Effects of information type and level of orientation on consensus-achievement in substantive and affective small group conflict. *Central States Speech Journal, 28*, 54–63.

Kochman, T. (1981). *Black and white styles in conflict.* Chicago: University of Chicago Press.

Kramer, M. W., Kuo, C. L., & Dailey, J. C. (1997). The impact of brainstorming techniques on subsequent group processes: Beyond generating ideas. *Small Group Research, 28*, 218–242.

Kramer, M. W. (2002). Communication in a community theater group: Managing multiple group roles. *Communication studies, 53*, 151–170.

Kramer, T. J., Fleming, G. P., & Mannis, S. M. (2001). Improving face-to-face brainstorming through modeling and facilitation. *Small Group Research, 32*, 533–557.

Kraus, R. M., & Morsella, E. (2000). Communication and conflict. In M. Deutsch & P. T. Coleman (Eds.), *The handbook of conflict resolution: Theory and practice* (pp. 131–143). San Francisco: Jossey-Bass.

Kuhn, T., & Poole, M. S. (2000). Do conflict management styles affect group decision making? Evidence from a longitudinal field study. *Human Communication Research, 26*, 558–590.

Lammers, J. C., & Krikorian, D. H. (1997). Theoretical extension and operationalization of the bona fide group construct with an application to surgical teams. *Journal of Applied Communication Research, 25*, 17–38.

Larkey, L. K. (1996a). The development and validation of the workforce diversity questionnaire: An instrument to assess interactions in diverse workgroups. *Management Communication Quarterly, 9*, 296–337.

Larkey, L. K. (1996b). Toward a theory of communicative interactions in culturally diverse workgroups. *Academy of Management Review, 21*, 463–491.

Larson, C. E., & LaFasto, F. M. J. (1989). *TeamWork: What must go right/what can go wrong.* Newbury Park, CA: Sage.

Lau, D., & Murnighan, J. K. (1998). Demographic diversity and faultlines: The compositional dynamics of organizational groups. *Academy of Management Review, 23*, 325–340.

Leathers, D. G. (1979). The impact of multichannel message inconsistency on verbal and nonverbal decoding behaviors. *Communication Monographs, 46*, 88–100.

Lester, S. W., Meglino, B. M., & Korsgaard, M. A. (2002). The antecedents and consequences of group potency: A longitudinal investigation of newly formed work groups. *Academy of Management Journal, 45*, 352–358.

Lewicki, R. J., McAllister, D. J., & Bies, D. J. (1998). Trust and distrust: New relationships and realities. *Academy of Management Review, 23*, 438–458.

Li, J., Karakowsky, L., & Siegel, J. P. (1999). The effects of proportional representation on intragroup behavior in mixed-race decision-making groups. *Small Group Research, 30*, 259–279.

Limon, M. S., & Boster, F. J. (2003). The effects of performance feedback on group members' perceptions of prestige, task competencies, group belonging, and loafing. *Communication Research Reports, 20*, 13–23.

Littlejohn, S. W., & Jabusch, D. M. (1982). Communication competence: Model and application. *Journal of Applied Communication Research, 10*, 29–37.

Lovaglia, M., Mannix, E. A., Samuelson, C. D., Sell, J., & Wilson, R. K. (2005). Conflict, power, and status in groups. In M. S. Poole & A. B. Hollingshead (Eds.), *Theories of small groups: Interdisciplinary perspectives* (pp. 139–184). Thousand Oaks, CA: Sage.

Mabry, E. A. (1989a). Developmental aspects of nonverbal behavior in small group settings. *Small Group Behavior, 20*, 190–202.

May, L. (1987). *The morality of groups: Collective responsibility, group-based harm, and corporate rights.* Notre Dame, IN: University of Notre Dame Press.

Mayer, M. E. (1998). Behaviors leading to more effective decisions in small groups embedded in organizations. *Communication Reports, 11*, 123–132.

McCanne, L. P. F. (1977). Dimensions of participant goals, expectations, and perceptions in small group experiences. *Journal of Applied Behavioral Science, 13*, 533–540.

McCroskey, J. C. (1977). Oral communication apprehension: A summary of recent theory and research. *Human Communication Research, 4,* 78–96.

McCroskey, J. C., & Richmond, V. P. (1976). The effects of communication apprehension on the perceptions of peers. *Journal of the Western Speech Communication Association, 40,* 14–21.

McCroskey, J. C., & Richmond, V. P. (1987). Willingness to communicate. In J. C. McCroskey & J. A. Daly (Eds.), *Personality and interpersonal communication* (pp. 129–156). Newbury Park, CA: Sage.

McCroskey, J. C., & Richmond, V. P. (1992). Communication apprehension and small group communication. In R. S. Cathcart & L. A. Samovar (Eds.), *Small group communication: A reader* (6th ed., pp. 361–374). Dubuque, IA: Brown.

McGinn, D. (2000, October 16). Mired in meetings. *Newsweek,* pp. 52, 54.

McGrath, J. E. (1984). *Groups: Interaction and performance.* Englewood Cliffs, NJ: Prentice-Hall.

McGrath, J. E., Berdahl, J. L., & Arrow, H. (1995). Traits, expectations, culture, and clout: The dynamics of diversity in work groups. In S. E. Jackson & M. N. Ruderman (Eds.), *Diversity in work teams: Research paradigms for a changing workplace* (pp. 17–45). Washington, DC: American Psychological Association.

McGrew, J. F., Bilotta, J. G., & Deeney, J. M. (1999). Software team formation and decay: Extending the standard model for small groups. *Small Group Research, 30,* 209–234.

McKinney, B. C. (1982). The effects of reticence on group interaction. *Communication Quarterly, 30,* 124–128.

McKinney, B. C., Kelly, L., & Duran, R. L. (1997). The relationship between conflict message styles and dimensions of communication competence. *Communication Reports, 10,* 185–196.

Meier, C. (2003). Doing "groupness" in a spatially distributed work group: The case of video-conferences at Technics. In L. R. Frey (Ed.), *Group communication in context: Studies of bona fide groups* (pp. 367–397). Mahwah, NJ: Erlbaum.

Meyers, R. A., & Brashers, D. E. (1999). Influence processes in group interaction. In L. R. Frey, D. S. Gouran, & M. S. Poole (Eds.), *The handbook of group communication theory & research* (pp. 288–312). Thousand Oaks, CA: Sage.

Meyers, R. A., & Brashers, D. E. (2003). Rethinking traditional approaches to argument in groups. In L. R. Frey (Ed.), *New directions in group communication* (pp. 141–158). Thousand Oaks, CA: Sage.

Meyers, R. A., Brashers, D. E., & Hanner, J. (2000). Majority-minority influences: Identifying argumentative patterns and predicting argument-outcome links. *Journal of Communication, 50*(4), 3–30.

Milliken, F. J., & Martins, L. L. (1996). Searching for common threads: Understanding the multiple effects of diversity in organizational groups. *Academy of Management Review, 21,* 402–433.

Molleman, E., Nauta, A., & Jehn, K. A. (2004). Person-job fit applied to teamwork: A multilevel approach. *Small Group Research, 35,* 515–539.

Montgomery, B. M., & Norton, R. W. (1981). Sex differences and similarities in communicator style. *Communication Monographs, 48,* 121–132.

Moosbruker, J. (1988). Developing a productivity team: Making groups at work. In W. B. Reddy & K. Jamison (Eds.), *Team building: Blueprints for productivity and satisfaction* (pp. 88–97). San Diego: NTL Institute for Applied Behavioral Science and University Associates.

Mudrack, P. E., & Farrell, G. M. (1995). An examination of functional role behavior and its consequences for individuals in group settings. *Small Group Research, 26,* 542–571.

Mullen, B., Anthony, T., Salas, E., & Driskell, J. E. (1994). Group cohesiveness and quality of decision making: An integration of tests of the groupthink hypothesis. *Small Group Research, 25,* 189–204.

Mullen, B., Johnson, C., & Salas, E. (1991). Productivity loss in brainstorming groups: A meta-analytical integration. *Basic and Applied Social Psychology, 12,* 3–23.

Munduate, L., Ganaza, J., Peiro, J. M., & Euwema, M. (1999). Patterns of styles in conflict management and effectiveness. *International Journal of Conflict Management, 10,* 5–24.

Myrsiades, L. (2000). Meeting sabotage: Met and conquered. *Journal of Management Development, 19,* 879–884.

Nadler, D. A. (1979). The effects of feedback on task group behavior: A review of the experimental research. *Organizational Behavior and Human Performance, 23,* 309–338.

Neck, C. P., & Moorhead, G. (1995). Groupthink remodeled: The importance of leadership, time pressure, and methodical decision-making procedures. *Human Relations, 48,* 537–557.

Nicotera, A. M. (1994). The use of multiple approaches to conflict: A study of sequences. *Human Communication Research, 20,* 592–621.

Nord, W. R., & Tucker, S. (1987). *Implementing routine and radical innovations.* Lexington, MA: Heath.

Northcraft, G. B., Polzer, J. T., Neale, M. A., & Kramer, R. M. (1995). In S. E. Jackson & M. N. Ruderman (Eds.), *Diversity in work teams: Research paradigms for a changing workplace* (pp. 69–96). Washington, DC: American Psychological Association.

Norton, R. (1983). *Communicator style: Theory, applications, and measures.* Beverly Hills: Sage.

Norton, R. W. (1978). Foundation of a communicator style construct. *Human Communication Research, 4,* 99–112.

Nye, J. L. (2002). The eye of the follower: Information processing effects on attributions regarding leaders of small groups. *Small Group Research, 33,* 337–360.

Oetzel, J. G. (1995). Intercultural small groups: An effective decision-making theory. In R. L. Wiseman (Ed.), *Intercultural communication theories* (pp. 247–270). Newbury Park, CA: Sage.

Oetzel, J. G. (1998a). The effects of self-construals and ethnicity on self-reported conflict styles. *Communication Reports, 11,* 133–144.

Oetzel, J. G. (1998b). Explaining individual communication processes in homogeneous and heterogeneous groups through individualism-collectivism and self-construal. *Human Communication Research, 25,* 202–224.

Oetzel, J. G. (2002). The effects of culture and cultural diversity on communication in work groups. In L. R. Frey (Ed.), *New directions in group communication* (pp. 121–137). Thousand Oaks, CA: Sage.

Oetzel, J. G., Burtis, T. B., Sanchez, M. I., & Perez, F. G. (2001). Investigating the role of communication in culturally diverse work groups: A review and synthesis. In W. B. Gudykunst (Ed.), *Communication yearbook* 25 (pp. 237–269). Mahwah, NJ: Erlbaum.

Orlitzky, M., & Hirokawa, R. Y. (2001). To err is human, to correct for it divine: A meta-analysis of research testing the functional theory of group decision-making effectiveness. *Small Group Research, 32,* 313–341.

Osborn, A. F. (1963). *Applied imagination* (3rd ed.). New York: Scribner.

Pace, R. C. (1990). Personalized and depersonalized conflict in small group discussions: An examination of differentiation. *Small Group Research, 21,* 79–96.

Pavitt, C. (1993). What (little) we know about formal group discussion procedures: A review of relevant research. *Small Group Research, 24,* 217–235.

Pavitt, C. (1999). Theorizing about the group communication-leadership relationship: Input-process-output and functional models. In L. R. Frey, D. S. Gouran, & M. S. Poole (Eds.), *The handbook of group communication theory & research* (pp. 313–334). Thousand Oaks, CA: Sage.

Pavitt, C., & Johnson, K. K. (1999). An examination of the coherence of group discussion. *Communication Research, 26,* 303–321.

Pavitt, C., & Sackaroff, P. (1990). Implicit theories of leadership and judgments of leadership among group members. *Small Group Research, 21,* 374–392.

Pelled, L. H., Eisenhardt, K. M., & Xin, K. R. (1999). Exploring the black box: An analysis of work group diversity, conflict, and performance. *Administrative Science Quarterly, 44,* 1–28.

Pescosolido, A. T. (2003). Group efficacy and group effectiveness: The effects of group efficacy over time on group performance and development. *Small Group Research, 34,* 20–42.

Phillips, G. M. (1965). "PERT" as a logical adjunct to the discussion process. *Journal of Communication, 15,* 89–99.

Pondy, L. R. (1967). Organizational conflict: Concepts and models. *Administrative Science Quarterly, 12,* 296–320.

Poole, M. S. (1983). Decision development in small groups, III: A multiple sequence model of group decision development. *Communication Monographs, 50,* 321–341.

Poole, M. S. (1991). Procedures for managing meetings: Social and technological innovation. In R. A. Swanson & B. O. Knapp (Eds.), *Innovative meeting management* (pp. 53–110). Austin: 3M Meeting Management Institute.

Prapavessis, H., & Carron, A. V. (1997). Cohesion and work output. *Small Group Research, 28,* 294–301.

Propp, K. M. (1999). Collective information process in groups. In L. R. Frey, D. S. Gouran, & M. S. Poole (Eds.), *The handbook of group communication theory and research* (pp. 225–250). Thousand Oaks, CA: Sage.

Putnam, L. L., & Stohl, C. (1996). Bona fide groups: An alternative perspective for communication and small group decision making. In R. Y. Hirokawa & M. S. Poole (Eds.), *Communication and group decision making* (2nd ed., pp. 147–178). Thousand Oaks, CA: Sage.

Putnam, L. L., & Wilson, C. E. (1983). Communicative strategies in organizational conflicts: Reliability and validity of a measurement scale. In M. Burgoon (Ed.), *Communication yearbook 6* (pp. 629–652). Beverly Hills: Sage.

Randel, A. E. (2002). Identity salience: A moderator of the relationship between group gender composition and work group conflict. *Journal of Organizational Behavior, 23,* 749–766.

Raven, B. H. (1993). The bases of power: Origins and recent developments. *Journal of Social Issues, 49,* 227–251.

Ridgeway, C. L. (2001). Gender, status, and leadership. *Journal of Social Issues, 57,* 637–655.

Rimal, R. N., & Real, K. (2003). Understanding the influence of perceived norms on behaviors. *Communication Theory, 13,* 184–203.

Rodriguez, R. A. (1998). Challenging demographic reductionism: A pilot study investigating diversity in group composition. *Small Group Research, 29,* 744–759.

Rose, S. R. (1989). Members leaving groups: Theoretical and practical considerations. *Small Group Behavior, 20,* 524–535.

Rosenthal, S. B., & Buchholz, R. A. (1995). Leadership: Toward new philosophical foundations. *Business & Professional Ethics Journal, 14,* 25–41.

Rozell, E. J., & Gundersen, D. E. (2003). The effects of leader impression management on group perceptions of cohesion, consensus, and communication. *Small Group Research, 34,* 197–222.

Ruback, R. B., Dabbs, J. M., & Hopper, C. H. (1984). The process of brainstorming: An analysis with individual and group vocal parameters. *Journal of Personality and Social Psychology, 47,* 558–567.

Salazar, A. J. (1995). Understanding the synergistic effects of communication in small groups: Making the most out of group member abilities. *Small Group Research, 26,* 169–199.

Salazar, A. J., Hirokawa, R. Y., Propp, K. M., Julian, K. M., & Leatham, G. B. (1994). In search of true causes: Examination of the effect of group potential and group interaction on decision performance. *Human Communication Research, 20,* 529–559.

Sargent, L. D., & Sue-Chan, C. (2001). Does diversity affect group efficacy? The intervening role of cohesion and task interdependence. *Small Group Research, 32,* 426–450.

Scheerhorn, D., Geist, P., & Teboul, J. C. B. (1994). Beyond decision making in decision-making groups: Implications for the study of group communication. In L. R. Frey (Ed.), *Group communication in context: Studies of natural groups* (pp. 247–262). Hillsdale, NJ: Erlbaum.

Schullery, N. M., & Gibson, M. K. (2001). Working in groups: Identification and treatment of students' perceived weakness. *Business Communication Quarterly, 64,* 9–30.

Schullery, N. M. & Schullery, S. E. (2002). Relationship between group skills, temperament, and argumentativeness. *Communication Research Reports, 19,* 246–258.

Schultz, B. (1986). Communicative correlates of perceived leaders in the small group. *Small Group Behavior, 17,* 51–65.

Schultz, B. (1999). Improving group communication performance: An overview of diagnosis and intervention. In L. R. Frey, D. S. Gouran, & M. S. Poole (Eds.), *The handbook of group communication theory and research* (pp. 371–394). Thousand Oaks, CA: Sage.

Schultz, B., Ketrow, S. M., & Urban, D. M. (1995). Improving decision quality in the small group: The role of the reminder. *Small Group Research, 26,* 521–541.

Schutz, W. C. (1961). On group composition. *Journal of Abnormal and Social Psychology, 62,* 275–281.

Schutz, W. C. (1966). *The interpersonal underworld.* Palo Alto, CA: Science & Behavior Books.

Schwarz, R. M. (1994). *The skilled facilitator: Practical wisdom for developing effective groups.* San Francisco: Jossey-Bass.

Schweiger, D. M., & Leana, C. R. (1986). Participation in decision making. In E. A. Locke (Ed.), *Generalizing from laboratory to field settings: Research findings from industrial-organizational psychology, organizational behavior, and human resource management* (pp. 147–166). Lexington, MA: Lexington Books.

Schweiger, D. M., & Sandberg, W. R. (1989). The utilization of individual capabilities in group approaches to strategic decision-making. *Strategic Management Journal, 10,* 31–43.

Schweiger, D. M., Sandberg, W. R., & Ragan, J. W. (1986). Group approaches for improving strategic decision making: A comparative analysis of dialectical inquiry, devil's advocacy, and consensus. *Academy of Management Journal, 29,* 51–71.

Scott, C. R. (1999). Communication technology and group communication. In L. R. Frey, D. S. Gouran, & M. S. Poole (Eds.), *The handbook of group communication theory and research* (pp. 432–472). Thousand Oaks, CA: Sage.

Sharf, B. F. (1978). A rhetorical analysis of leadership emergence in small groups. *Communication Monographs, 45,* 156–172.

Shaw, M. E. (1973). Scaling group tasks: A method for dimensional analysis. *JSAS Catalog of Selected Documents in Psychology, 3,* 8.

Shaw, M. E. (1981). *Group dynamics: The psychology of small group behavior.* New York: McGraw-Hill.

Shea, G. P., & Guzzo, R. A. (1987). Groups as human resources. In K. M. Rowland & G. R. Ferris (Eds.), *Research in personnel and human resources management* (pp. 323–356). Greenwich, CT: JAI.

Shonk, J. H. (1992). *Team-based organizations: Developing a successful team environment.* Homewood, IL: Business One Irwin.

Sibbet, D. (1981). *Workbook/guide to group graphics.* San Francisco: Sibbet.

Sillars, A. L., & Wilmot, W. W. (1994). Communication strategies in conflict and mediation. In J. A. Daly & J. M. Wiemann (Eds.), *Strategic interpersonal communication* (pp. 163–190). Hillsdale, NJ: Erlbaum.

Sillince, J. A. A. (2000). Rhetorical power, accountability and conflict in committees: An argumentation approach. *Journal of Management Studies, 37,* 1125–1156.

Smith, K. K., & Berg, D. N. (1987). *Paradoxes of group life.* San Francisco: Jossey-Bass.

Sniezek, J. A. (1992). Groups under uncertainty: An examination of confidence in group decision making. *Organizational Behavior and Human Decision Processes, 52,* 124–155.

Spink, K. S., & Carron, A. V. (1994). Group cohesion effects in exercise classes. *Small Group Research, 25,* 26–42.

Spitzberg, B. H., & Cupach, W. R. (1984). *Interpersonal communication competence.* Beverly Hills: Sage.

Spitzberg, B. H., & Cupach, W. R. (1989). *Handbook of interpersonal competence research.* New York: Springer-Verlag.

Stevens, M. J., & Campion, M. A. (1994). The knowledge, skill, and ability requirements for teamwork: Implications for human resource management. *Journal of Management*, *20*, 503–530.

Stogdill, R. M. (1974). *Handbook of leadership*. New York: Free Press.

Stohl, C., & Putnam, L. L. (2003). Communication in bona fide groups: A retrospective and prospective account. In L. R. Frey (Ed.), *Group communication in context: Studies of bona fide groups* (pp. 399–414). Mahwah, NJ: Erlbaum.

Stohl, C., & Schell, S. E. (1991). A communication-based model of a small-group dysfunction. *Management Communication Quarterly*, *5*, 90–110.

Street, M. C. (1997). Groupthink: An examination of theoretical issues, implications, and future research suggestions. *Small Group Research*, *28*, 72–93.

Street, M. C., Robertson, C., & Geiger, S. W. (1997). Ethical decision making: The effects of escalating commitment. *Journal of Business Ethics*, *16*, 1153–1161.

Strijbos, J., Martens, R. L., Jochems, W. M., & Broers, N. J. (2004). The effect of functional roles on group efficiency: Using multilevel modeling and content analysis to investigate computer-supported collaboration in small groups, *Small Group Research*, *35*, 195–229.

Sunwolf, & Seibold, D. R. (1998). Jurors' intuitive rules for deliberation: A structurational approach to communication in jury decision making. *Communication Monograph*, *65*, 282–301.

Sunwolf, & Seibold, D. R. (1999). The impact of formal procedures on group processes, members, and task outcomes. In L. R. Frey, D. S. Gouran, & M. S. Poole (Eds.), *The handbook of group communication theory and research* (pp. 395–431). Thousand Oaks, CA: Sage.

SYMLOG Consulting Group. (1986). *The Bales report to your group*. San Diego: Author.

Thibaut, J. W., & Kelley, H. H. (1959). *The social psychology of groups*. New York: Wiley.

Thomas, K. W. (1977). Toward multi-dimensional values in teaching: The examples of conflict behaviors. *Academy of Management Review*, *2*, 484–490.

Thomas, K. W. (1992). Conflict and negotiation processes in organizations. In M. D. Dunnette & L. M. Hough (Eds.), *Handbook of industrial and organizational psychology* (pp. 651–717). Palo Alto, CA: Consulting Psychologists Press.

Thomas, R. R., Jr. (1995). A diversity framework. In M. M. Chemers, S. Oskamp, & M. A. Costanzo (Eds.), *Diversity in organizations: New perspectives for a changing workplace* (pp. 245–263). Thousand Oaks, CA: Sage.

Tracy, K. (1982). On getting the point: Distinguishing "issues" and "events," an aspect of conversational coherence. In M. Burgoon (Ed.), *Communication yearbook 5* (pp. 279–301). New Brunswick, NJ: Transaction Books.

Triandis, H. C. (1995a). A theoretical framework for the study of diversity. In M. M. Chemers, S. Oskamp, & M. A. Costanzo (Eds.), *Diversity in organizations: New perspectives for a changing workplace* (pp. 11–36). Thousand Oaks, CA: Sage.

Triandis, H. C. (1995b). The importance of contexts in studies of diversity. In S. E. Jackson & M. N. Ruderman (Eds.), *Diversity in work teams: Research paradigms for a changing workplace* (pp. 225–233). Washington, DC: American Psychological Association.

Tropman, J. E. (2003). *Making meeting work: Achieving high quality group decisions* (2nd ed.). Thousand Oaks, CA: Sage.

Tuckman, B. W., & Jensen, M. A. C. (1977). Stages of small-group development revisited. *Group & Organization Studies*, *2*, 419–427.

Van de Ven, A. H., & Delbecq, A. L. (1971). Nominal versus interacting group processes for committee decision-making effectiveness. *Academy of Management Journal*, *14*, 203–212.

Van de Ven, A. H., & Delbecq, A. L. (1974). The effectiveness of nominal, delphi, and interacting group decision-making processes. *Academy of Management Journal*, *17*, 605–621.

Vecchio, R. P., & Boatwright, K. J. (2002). Preferences for idealized styles of supervision. *Leadership Quarterly*, *13*, 327–342.

Waldeck, J. H., Shepard, C. A., Teitelbaum, J., Farrar, W. J., & Seibold, D. R. (2002). New directions for functional, symbolic convergence, structuration, and bona fide group perspectives of group communication. In L. R. Frey (Ed.), *New directions in group communication* (pp. 3–23). Thousand Oaks, CA: Sage.

Wall, V. D., Jr., & Galanes, G. J. (1986). The SYMLOG dimensions and small group conflict. *Central States Speech Journal, 37,* 61–78.

Wall, V. D., Jr., Galanes, G. J., & Love, S. B. (1987). Small, task-oriented groups: Conflict, conflict management, satisfaction, and decision quality. *Small Group Behavior, 18,* 31–55.

Wall, V. D., & Nolan, L. L. (1986). Perceptions of inequity, satisfaction, and conflict in task-oriented groups. *Human Relations, 39,* 1033–1052.

Walter, G. A. (1975). Effects of videotape feedback and modeling on the behaviors of task group members. *Human Relations, 28,* 121–138.

Walther, J. B. (2002). Time effects in computer-mediated groups: Past, present, and future. In P. Hinds & S. Kiesler (Eds.), *Distributed work* (pp. 235–257). Cambridge, MA: MIT Press.

Warfield, J. N. (1993). Complexity and cognitive equilibrium: Experimental results and their implications. In D. J. D. Sandole & H. van der Merwe (Eds.), *Conflict resolution theory and practice: Integration and application* (pp. 65–77). New York: Manchester University Press.

Watkins, C. E. (1974). An analytic model of conflict. *Speech Monographs, 41,* 1–5.

Watson, E. W., Kumar, K., & Michaelsen, L. K. (1993). Cultural diversity's impact on interaction process and performance: Comparing homogeneous and diverse task groups. *Academy of Management Journal, 36,* 590–602.

Watson, K. W. (1996). Listener preferences: The paradox of small-group interactions. In R. S. Cathcart, L. A. Samovar, & L. D. Henman (Eds.), *Small group communication: Theory & practice* (7th ed., pp. 268–282). Madison: Brown & Benchmark.

Watson, W. E., Johnson, L., & Merritt, D. (1998). Team orientation, self-orientation, and diversity in task groups: Their connection to team performance over time. *Group & Organization Management, 23,* 161–188.

Weitzel, A., & Geist, P. (1998). Parliamentary procedure in a community group: Communication and vigilant decision making. *Communication Monographs, 65,* 244–259.

Wellins, R. S., Byham, W. C., & Wilson, J. M. (1991). *Empowered teams: Creating self-directed work groups that improve quality, productivity, and participation.* San Francisco: Jossey-Bass.

Wellman, B. (1988). Structural analysis: From method and metaphor to theory and substance. In B. Wellman & S. Berkowitz (Eds.), *Social structures: A network approach* (pp. 19–61). Cambridge, UK: Cambridge University Press.

Whatule, L. J. (2000). Communication as an aid to resocialization: A case study of a men's anger group. *Small Group Research, 31,* 424–446.

Wheelan, S. A. (1994). *Group processes: A developmental perspective.* Boston: Allyn & Bacon.

Wheelan, S. A., Davidson, B., & Tilin, F. (2003). Group development across time: Reality or illusion? *Small Group Research, 34,* 223–245.

Wheelan, S. A., & McKeage, R. L. (1993). Developmental patterns in small and large groups. *Small Group Research, 24,* 60–83.

Wheelan, S. A., & Williams, T. (2003). Mapping dynamic interaction patterns in work groups. *Small Group Research, 34,* 443–467.

Witteman, H. (1991). Group member satisfaction: A conflict-related account. *Small Group Research, 22,* 24–58.

Wittenbaum, G. M. (2000). The bias toward discussing shared information. *Communication Research, 27,* 379–401.

Wong, C. L., Tjosvold, D., & Lee, F. (1992). Managing conflict in a diverse work force: A Chinese perspective in North America. *Small Group Research, 23,* 302–321.

Zimmermann, S. (1994). Social cognition and evaluations of health care team communication effectiveness. *Western Journal of Communication, 58,* 116–141.

Credits

Author Index

Subject Index